Politics

An Introduction

Politics

An Introduction

George A. MacLean
Duncan R. Wood

OXFORD

UNIVERSITY PRESS

OXFORD
UNIVERSITY PRESS

8 Sampson Mews, Suite 204, Don Mills, Ontario M3C 0H5
www.oupcanada.com

Oxford University Press is a department of the University of Oxford.
It furthers the University's objective of excellence in research, scholarship,
and education by publishing worldwide in

Oxford   New York

Auckland   Cape Town   Dar es Salaam   Hong Kong   Karachi
Kuala Lumpur   Madrid   Melbourne   Mexico City   Nairobi
New Delhi   Shanghai   Taipei   Toronto

With offices in

Argentina   Austria   Brazil   Chile   Czech Republic   France   Greece
Guatemala   Hungary   Italy   Japan   Poland   Portugal   Singapore
South Korea   Switzerland   Thailand   Turkey   Ukraine   Vietnam

Oxford is a trade mark of Oxford University Press
in the UK and in certain other countries

Published in Canada
by Oxford University Press

Library and Archives Canada Cataloguing in Publication

MacLean, George A. (George Andrew), 1967–
Politics : an introduction / George MacLean, Duncan Wood. – 1st ed.

Previously published under title: Introduction to politics.
Includes bibliographical references.

ISBN 978-0-19-543162-9

1. Political science—Textbooks.   I. Wood, Duncan R. (Duncan Robert), 1968–   II. Title.

JA66.M25 2010   320   C2010-900191-5

Cover Images: Student Demonstration, Vasiliki Varvaki/iStockphoto; Ambassador Bridge, Joe
Iera/iStockphoto.com; UN building, Alandj/iStockphoto; It's time for elections, Vladimir Cetinski/
iStockphoto; Canada coast guard at the American border, Seb Agudelo/Alamy; Old banknotes and
coins, Imagebroker/Alamy; and Hands up, Xavi Arnau/iStockphoto

Oxford University Press is committed to our environment. This book is printed on Forest Stewardship
Council certified paper, harvested from a responsibly managed forest, which contains a minimum of
10% post-consumer waste.

Mixed Sources
Product group from well-managed
forests, controlled sources and
recycled wood or fiber
www.fsc.org   Cert no. SW-COC-002985
©1996 Forest Stewardship Council

Printed and bound in the United States of America.

2 3 4 – 13 12 11 10

Brief Contents

Contents

Chapter 1

Studying Politics   3

Chapter 2

Finding a Common Vocabulary: Political Concepts   23

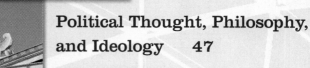

Chapter 3

Political Thought, Philosophy, and Ideology   47

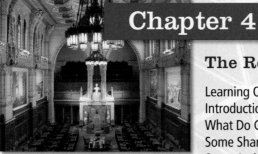

Chapter 4

The Role of Government   81

Chapter 5

Branches of Government   107

Chapter 6

Political Systems   133

Chapter 7

Political Participation: Elections and Parties   161

Chapter 8

Political Socialization and Culture   185

Chapter 9

Politics in Developed States   211

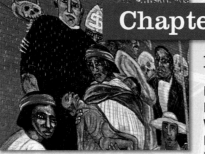

Chapter 10

Politics in Developing States   243

Chapter 11

International Politics and Foreign Policy   273

Chapter 12

International Security   305

Chapter 13

International Political Economy   327

Chapter 14

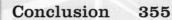

Conclusion   355

Preface

One of the most difficult tasks involved in introducing students to the study of politics is the choice of an appropriate textbook. Every instructor has his or her own preferences about the material, concepts, themes, and pedagogy contained in a first-year political studies text, so no book could possibly meet every requirement and partiality. The task of putting together an introductory text, then, is a delicate one. How might one assemble a coherent preparatory volume that addresses disparate views on what is to be presented, while at the same time posing some fresh and innovative ideas?

This book is an attempt to answer this very question. Fundamentally, its intent is to provide first-year post-secondary students with a comprehensive introduction to the study of politics. This text incorporates some essential questions of politics: Who has power in society, and why? How might groups participate in political activity? How can we distinguish among so many types of political systems? Why is conflict so prevalent in the world today? How is wealth distributed, and why does such inequity exist? In our design of this book, we considered a wide variety of ways these questions could be answered, theoretically, and through analysis. We decided that the best way to provide answers to these questions was to lead students through different approaches and topics. The 'answers', of course, will vary depending on your perspective and experience. This text presents a challenge to you: you may or may not have views on the nature of politics already, but by the time you're through this book and your course, you should have more questions than before, and perhaps you'll be thinking differently about what you assume you already know! If that's the case, then this book will have done its job. In any case, we'll return to this discussion in our conclusion.

Organization

This book is organized to introduce you to the study of politics in a comprehensive and constructive manner. **Chapter 1** presents the fundamental nature of politics and the field of political studies. We'll deal with some major approaches, concepts, and themes in the study of politics in this chapter, as well as how politics affects so many aspects of our daily lives. We'll also discuss the nature of citizenship, and what that means in the specific context of being Canadian. The substance of this chapter is essential for the rest of the text.

Chapters 2 and **3** examine in greater detail some of the major terms and areas of political thought in political studies. **Chapter 2** begins with an exploration of some important political concepts, including power, government, the state, legitimacy, and sovereignty. **Chapter 3** follows with an overview of political philosophy and the major schools of thought used in political studies, such as liberalism, socialism and communism, conservatism, environmentalism, feminism, nationalism, and fascism. It looks at both dominant and critical political ideologies, and the ideas that have driven the study of politics. This chapter also provides a survey of ideologies and political philosophy in Canada.

Chapters 4, 5, and **6** look at the importance of government. Beginning with **Chapter 4,** we examine the main forms of governments throughout history and today. The chapter deals with systems of government, the nature of government, objectives and activities of different governments, and points of view regarding the fundamental role that government ought to play. In this chapter we'll explain the distinctions among liberal democracies, authoritarian governments, and totalitarian systems. Government in Canada is given special attention here. **Chapter 5** covers primary structures and roles of government agencies and institutions. It looks deeper at the important levels of government activity, including the executive, legislative, judicial, and bureaucratic divisions. The two main types of government systems in the world today, parliamentary and presidential, are also compared and contrasted. Finally, **Chapter 6** considers the way that different political systems are organized in terms of their responsibilities and decision-making systems. Unitary, federal, confederal, and devolved political systems are all examined, with special attention to the history and development of power-sharing in Canada.

Chapters 7 and **8** are concerned with the roles played by individuals and groups in society. **Chapter 7** takes into account decision-making and electoral systems, campaign contributions, elections, and political parties. **Chapter 8** picks up the theme and looks at the social and political process of participation in political studies. Education, opinion polls, socialization, interest groups, media, and culture — all of these have an abundance of effects on how our political systems are run and the role we play in them. Together, these two chapters trace the formulation of ideas and information that influence citizens, and the way in which these ideas are played out on the political stage.

The next section of the book is dedicated to country case studies. This two-part examination of politics is undertaken in a comparative context, considering 'development' and 'underdevelopment' in the world today. We begin in **Chapter 9** with consideration of politics in many developed countries, including Canada, the United States, Japan, and European nations. These cases offer distinctive examples of how political and economic spheres influence governance. **Chapter 10** carries this discussion to the developing world, contemplating some of the significant approaches and perspectives regarding development in the so-called Third World, and in particular, how the development process is as varied as the countries involved. By way of example, the chapter surveys the development experience in Mexico and in China, presenting a diverse stance on the myriad of issues facing countries in the developing world.

The final section of the book takes on the study of politics on the world stage, using some of the primary concepts and themes discussed thus far in the book to a realm beyond the boundaries of national borders. **Chapter 11**, examines the state and sovereignty in a modern world, as well as the nature of the international system. This chapter scrutinizes some current themes and issues in global politics, including globalization, foreign policy-making, geography and population, diplomacy and law, nationalism, and different actors in the world today, including states, non-state actors, individuals, and multinational corporations. This chapter will also review the importance of foreign policy and diplomacy. **Chapter 12** is dedicated to the complicated issue of global insecurity: war, terrorism, peacekeeping, intervention, and conflict management. Here we will also look at Canada's changing role in Afghanistan.

Chapter 13 turns its attention to the important dynamic of 'international political economy' and its impact on domestic politics. This chapter illustrates the importance of international trade, production, and finance, as well as current themes such as world debt, leadership, and economic regionalism. Finally, **Chapter 14** is intended to provide some concluding thoughts. This chapter responds to the important question, Where do we go from here? Future studies, careers in political studies, and the way we can apply what we've learned are all given some thought in this concluding chapter.

Key Features

Pedagogical Features

Political studies, like any other academic discipline, has its own vocabulary and terminology. **Marginal definitions**, provided in each chapter, emphasize key terms and concepts, and a **full glossary** is included at the end of the book. Major themes and terms are also **highlighted** throughout the text. Every chapter contains both **self-assessment questions** and a list of suggested **further readings**. Links to important **websites** are also contained at the conclusion of each chapter. Throughout the chapters, **boxes** aid in the specifics of important themes and examples. **Images**, **tables**, **graphs**, and **figures** illustrate important points without interfering with the text itself. Finally, an **index** of all important terms, concepts, themes, events, and individuals is included at the end of the book.

Theoretical Framework

It is commonplace that most introductory textbooks begin with a survey of significant concepts (for example, the state, power, government, legitimacy, etc.), and a review of the philosophical tradition of political analysis (Plato's *Republic*, Aristotle's *Politics*, Hobbes' *Leviathan*, and so on). Taking a comparative theoretical approach (meaning that no specific theory is used as a core focus in the book), the text shows how the development of theory in political studies flavours the manner in which we must consider a contemporary and changing political climate, both domestic and international. The methodology of this text is not intended to be heavy-handed or overly theoretical; theory is central to the purpose of the book, but as an introductory volume, the text's principal goal is to demonstrate to students the sensitive and changing nature of philosophical thought in politics.

Features

Comprehensive Coverage

The text guides students through the basics of ideology and institutions of political studies before moving on to more complex discussions and sub-fields. Topic coverage spans the importance of government, political systems, political participation and culture, politics in developed and developing states, and international relations.

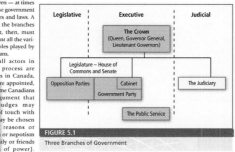

Institutions of Government

So far in this text we've established that anyone who is interested in politics needs to know something about government, and a bit about political ideas, too. We have already introduced government in Chapter 4, and we considered the vast array of government ideologies and roles played. But to answer questions like the ones posed above, we also need to know a little bit about the mechanics of government: the institutions, or 'branches' of government that work together in the interests of citizens (in theory, in any case). This will go a long way to stem that 'it's all so political' attitude we might otherwise fall back on.

Not all politicians have the same job. Some are part of the government: the party given enough electoral support to be the one to form 'government' and thus the power to make and enforce the laws and regulations of the land. The governing authority in a political system is made up of many different actors with varying levels of power. Some have far more responsibility in government and more latitude, or influence, in decisions and initiatives that governments take. A newly elected Member of Parliament (MP) in Canada, for example, won't have nearly the influence in real decision-making as one chosen to be part of cabinet. (We will return to the role of cabinet later in this chapter.)

And a cabinet minister will have substantially less 'latitude' than the prime minister. As in any other organization, there is a hierarchy in government.

Many politicians have relatively little real 'power' in setting a government's agenda; opposition party members, for instance, have minimal say in what governments set out to do. But even these opposition members have a crucial role to play in the performance of government. They cajole and question, criticize, and even — at times — work with the government to make policies and laws. A proper look at the branches of government, then, must take into account all the various political roles played by elected politicians.

But not all actors in the political process are elected. Judges in Canada, ... are appointed, ... me Canadians ... rgument that ... judges may ... f touch with ... nay be chosen ... reasons or ... n or nepotism ... ily or friends ... s of power).

Glossary sidebar:

Government
the institutions and people responsible for carrying out the affairs and administration of a political system

Member of Parliament
representative of voters in a parliamentary system

Cabinet
members of the executive level of government responsible for decision-making and administration of the bureaucracy

Cronyism
in politics, the practice of choosing or preferring friends or associates

Nepotism
in politics, the practice of choosing or preferring relatives

FIGURE 5.1
Three Branches of Government

Legislative	Executive	Judicial
	The Crown (Queen, Governor General, Lieutenant Governors)	
	Legislature – House of Commons and Senate	
Opposition Parties	Cabinet	The Judiciary
	Government Party	
	The Public Service	

4.6

Are Governors General Just Ceremonial?

There are times when the Governor General takes decisions that are quite significant. In 1926 Governor General Lord Byng refused Prime Minister Mackenzie King's request to dissolve Parliament (usually a ritual performed without question) and invited the opposition to form a government. That government, led by Arthur Meighen, failed to gain the support of Parliament, and Mackenzie King won the next election. The 'King–Byng' affair was quite controversial because, even though Byng acted within his constitutional rights, he was criticized for getting involved in electoral politics. Sometimes Governors General have no choice but to make decisions that have real political implications. In 2008, Governor General Michaëlle Jean decided to allow Parliament to prorogue (which suspends a period between sessions of Parliament, usually done when a government's agenda is completed and Parliament goes into recess). In this case, Prime Minister Stephen Harper requested this in order to avoid a vote of non-confidence by the other parties in the House of Commons, which would have permitted a coalition of the other parties to form a new government, or would lead to another election.

Governors General are often considered simply ceremonial, but at times their duties can have a serious impact on Canadian politics.

This was a controversial situation, because the Governor General, who is not elected, took a decision that significantly affected the Canadian Parliament, and allowed the Conservatives to stay in power.

Canadian Press

Dynamic Full-Colour Format

Colour-coded features help students navigate content, and an eye-catching design engages readers with the material.

name. Think of the importance of trade unions, for example, since the nineteenth century in redefining labour relations and winning important victories for workers' rights, or of women's organizations that have struggled for over a century to win the vote, civil rights, and gender equality in the workplace.

8.4
Civil Society and Globalization

Many civil society organizations have been criticized for their undemocratic and unrepresentative nature.

In recent years, one of the most vocal, high-profile, and best-organized civil society movements has been the anti-globalization movement. Now a regular feature at all major international summit meetings between government ministers or heads of government, the movement had its origins in 1988 with demonstrations against the International Monetary Fund (IMF) and World Bank at their annual meeting in Berlin, Germany. From that time, the anti-globalization movement has grown in size and activity, incorporating protests, hunger strikes, and email and Internet campaigns. Although the movement in fact incorporates a large number of different groups and organizations, in recent years an umbrella organization known as the Peoples' Global Action network has been used to bring together diverse causes.

Canadian and International Examples

Boxes throughout the text provide detailed snapshots of current examples, key debates, and influential figures from Canada and around the world.

Currency

Up-to-the-minute coverage of pressing political issues shows students the ever-changing nature of the political landscape.

However, there is another dimension to the use of state 'power' as it pertains to conflict management and resolution. States often use their powers of influence, gained through respect and authority in the international system, to avoid conflict or avert it from taking place. Often powerful states will send representatives to negotiate with other states, sometimes in cases where the powerful state has no immediate relationship, as a means of obtaining settlement. In addition, states sometimes use the threat of their power to persuade other states from taking actions that may be deemed detrimental to the international system.

Canadians might find it difficult to legitimize the use of war as a means of policy. Some would reason that warfare should be an obsolete policy, since far better courses of action are available to governments. But, for better or worse (and largely worse), war is still with us, and we must still strive to understand it.

There is great debate about whether humans are more 'war-like' today than in the past. Comparisons of historical studies of war and contemporary instances of war are controversial for a number of reasons. First of all, our written account of war today is far more detailed and accurate than in the past. Also, there are many more states in the world today, and as a consequence, we should expect the number of conflicts to rise, since the number of actors is larger than in the past. And, different interpretations of 'war' have existed throughout the ages: religious wars, civil wars, ethnic wars, guerrilla wars, world wars, for example.

Despite these difficulties, many analysts have attempted to number conflicts in the past as compared to the number that exists today. Although the totals in different studies tend to vary, it's generally accepted that the past 3200 years have seen more than three thousand violent conflicts.[2] Many research studies, from

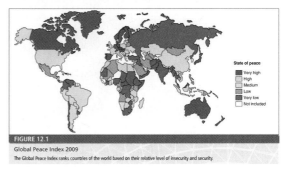

FIGURE 12.1

Global Peace Index 2009

The Global Peace Index ranks countries of the world based on their relative level of insecurity and security.

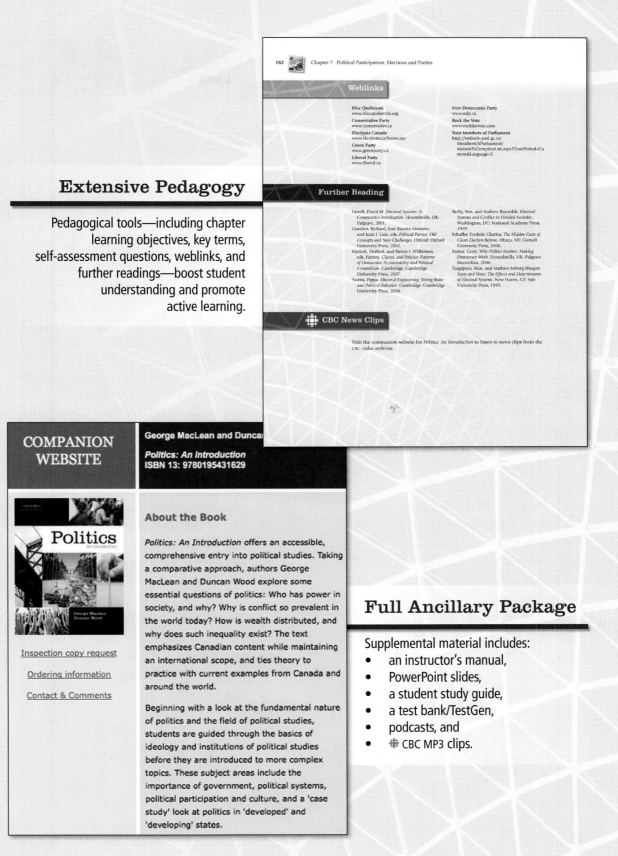

Extensive Pedagogy

Pedagogical tools—including chapter learning objectives, key terms, self-assessment questions, weblinks, and further readings—boost student understanding and promote active learning.

182   Chapter 7 Political Participation: Elections and Parties

Weblinks

Bloc Québécois
www.blocquebecois.org
Conservative Party
www.conservative.ca
Elections Canada
www.elections.ca/home.asp
Green Party
www.greenparty.ca
Liberal Party
www.liberal.ca

New Democratic Party
www.ndp.ca
Rock the Vote
www.rockthevote.com
Your Members of Parliament
http://webinfo.parl.gc.ca/
MembersOfParliament/
MainMPsCompleteList.aspx?TimePeriod=Current&Language=E

Further Reading

Farrell, David M. *Electoral Systems: A Comparative Introduction.* Houndmills, UK: Palgrave, 2001.
Gunther, Richard, José Ramon Montero, and Juan J. Linz, eds. *Political Parties: Old Concepts and New Challenges.* Oxford: Oxford University Press, 2002.
Kitschelt, Herbert, and Steven I. Wilkinson, eds. *Patron, Clients, and Policies: Patterns of Democratic Accountability and Political Competition.* Cambridge: Cambridge University Press, 2007.
Norris, Pippa. *Electoral Engineering: Voting Rules and Political Behavior.* Cambridge: Cambridge University Press, 2004.

Reilly, Ben, and Andrew Reynolds. *Electoral Systems and Conflict in Divided Societies.* Washington, DC: National Academy Press, 1999.
Schaffer, Frederic Charles. *The Hidden Costs of Clean Election Reform.* Ithaca, NY: Cornell University Press, 2008.
Stoker, Gerry. *Why Politics Matters: Making Democracy Work.* Houndmills, UK: Palgrave Macmillan, 2006.
Taagapera, Rein, and Mathew Soberg Shugart. *Seats and Votes: The Effects and Determinants of Electoral Systems.* New Haven, CT: Yale University Press, 1989.

CBC News Clips

Visit the companion website for *Politics: An Introduction* to listen to news clips from the CBC radio archives.

COMPANION WEBSITE

George MacLean and Duncan

Politics: An Introduction
ISBN 13: 9780195431629

Inspection copy request

Ordering information

Contact & Comments

About the Book

Politics: An Introduction offers an accessible, comprehensive entry into political studies. Taking a comparative approach, authors George MacLean and Duncan Wood explore some essential questions of politics: Who has power in society, and why? Why is conflict so prevalent in the world today? How is wealth distributed, and why does such inequality exist? The text emphasizes Canadian content while maintaining an international scope, and ties theory to practice with current examples from Canada and around the world.

Beginning with a look at the fundamental nature of politics and the field of political studies, students are guided through the basics of ideology and institutions of political studies before they are introduced to more complex topics. These subject areas include the importance of government, political systems, political participation and culture, and a 'case study' look at politics in 'developed' and 'developing' states.

Full Ancillary Package

Supplemental material includes:
- an instructor's manual,
- PowerPoint slides,
- a student study guide,
- a test bank/TestGen,
- podcasts, and
- CBC MP3 clips.

List of Boxes

Acknowledgements

Like any book project, this text is the product of a large number of people who contributed in various ways to its development. In the very early stages, sales and editorial representative Alan Mulder and acquisitions editor Katherine Skene were largely responsible for urging the co-authors to move ahead with a prospectus for a new introductory textbook in political studies. We are grateful to them for their vision and support.

A number of developmental editors were involved with the production of this book, but Kathryn West deserves special recognition for her unflagging support. It was a pleasure to work with such a dedicated and talented editor.

This book also has benefitted from the many useful comments and criticisms made by several colleagues who took on the task of reviewing it at its many stages. To these reviewers we are indebted for your time and your suggestions, which have contributed to this final work.

Some of our associates and research assistants were fundamental for the completion of parts of this book. At the Instituto Tecnológico Autónomo de México, we would like to thank Ana Victoria Borja for her extremely important help on this project.

We have discovered that writing a book such as this one takes more than simple authoring. It is the result of efforts both small and large by numerous people, some close friends and associates, and some colleagues we have not met. The final product is our own, however, and we alone take responsibility for any errors that it may contain.

George MacLean and Duncan Wood
August 2009

The authors and publisher would like to thank the following reviewers, along with those reviewers who wish to remain anonymous, whose thoughtful comments and suggestions have helped to shape this text:

John Soroski, Grant MacEwan College
John von Heyking, University of Lethbridge
Neil Hibbert, University of Saskatchewan

Politics
An Introduction

1 Studying Politics

After reading this chapter, you will be able to:

❋ understand the various approaches used in political studies

❋ realize how politics affects our daily lives

❋ consider the coexisting pressures of division and connection in a changing world

❋ examine politics at the international and the domestic levels

❋ consider what it means to be a citizen in Canada.

Introduction

Welcome to this textbook, and to the study of politics. We hope that this book not only broadens your understanding of the field, but also stirs some interest in the political world that surrounds you. Although this may be your first formal introduction to political studies, you will probably find that you already think about the subject matter more than you realize. Politics is one of those areas in life that we cannot avoid — even if we try our best to steer clear of it, we are affected by it in some way. The good news is that the more we get involved and become aware of the complexities of politics, the more we see how important our role is in our political world.

People are often cynical about politics. Perhaps they are convinced that their elected officials will never live up to their promises, or that their own role in the political process is so insignificant that their contribution will never be felt. In reality, though, our input is much greater than we think, and our involvement is crucial to the process. After all, if we cut ourselves off from the process entirely, how would we ever hold those elected officials to their promises? Healthy skepticism is a good thing — it keeps us informed and focused on improving our system. But cynicism without reflection really won't get us anywhere. It's better to be involved, and even critical, than to simply dismiss the entire process.

This book takes a critical look at politics. It questions our assumptions about politics, the approaches we take to study it, and how effective it is. Such study, we believe, is part of a healthy examination. But we don't stoop to cynicism. Rather, we view political studies as optimistic, a field where we try to build on success and correct failures, with the ultimate goal of creating a better political world that represents the many interests within it.

In this opening chapter, we will try to answer what may be the most important question you have going into the course: Why study **political studies**? It is a basic question, but one that affects everything we will touch on in the textbook. As well, this chapter will briefly introduce the chapters that follow; however, nothing here is the final word. (Of course, nothing else in this book is the final word, either; politics is nothing if it's not about constant debate!) Each point outlined in the chapter's learning objectives will be dealt with in greater detail in other parts of the book, too, but this first chapter will serve as a general introduction.

Political studies
formal study of politics within and among nations

Why Study Politics?

Political studies is just one of several disciplines presented to you as you begin your post-secondary studies. So, why choose it? What can this course, and this text, tell you about your daily life and the world around you?

Since you are reading this text and taking this course, it is already clear that the field of political studies must hold some interest for you. And it should: studying politics helps us understand more of our immediate surroundings, from what we see on the evening news to our direct involvement in the political process, where decisions are made that affect the well-being of ourselves and families, as well as the wider community.

1.1

Career Paths for Political Studies Graduates

You likely won't be surprised to learn that there are no postings for 'political scientists' in the help wanted ads in most newspapers. Then again, this is the case for most university fields. Political studies, like most other disciplines in the social sciences and humanities, does not train its students for specific careers; precisely because there are so many different directions that graduates may take it would be impossible to identify a specific training area. Political studies students become good writers and develop skills at public presentation, research, and problem solving. Political studies students learn to be critical and analytical thinkers. Critical thinkers are not just debaters or fault-finders. Rather, critical thought is a response to arguments, positions, evidence, experience, and observations with considered opinions about a proper course of action. Analytical thinkers take complex ideas and issues and break them apart to get at more deep-seated questions, such as why events take place, how situations can be improved, and how it is we come to know what we do.

Political studies is not a 'trade', so it would be wrong to expect to find a political science 'job' after your studies are done. However, the opportunities for students of politics are as wide as one's imagination. Some pursue graduate education at the master's and doctoral level to carry out research and teaching in political science. Others use their political studies degrees to follow additional professional accreditation, such as law school, journalism, or commerce. Politics can be useful for many different political careers, including positions in public service, public administration, and policymaking, or as government liaison workers, or even politicians!

"FRANK, ONLY YOU COULD READ A POLITICAL BIAS INTO THE WEATHER CHANNEL."

It's possible to find 'politics' in just about anything!

© Dave Carpenter/CartoonStock.com

Conflict resolution
process in domestic or international affairs where antagonism (either existing or potential) is sought to be reconciled through the use of mediation and negotiation

Conflict
differences in preferred outcomes among social groups

Socialization
process whereby individuals act in a social manner; creation of social and political authority and rules to regulate behaviour so as to permit operation of social units

Studying political studies helps us understand how events and decisions that seem far removed from our lives actually affect us in ways that we have not even thought about. Consider, for instance, these questions: What do people want out of life? What do countries try to provide for their citizens? How do we as individuals — and countries in the world arena — deal with others in our systems? What you do in life, and your circumstances, invariably affect your view of the political world.

Political studies helps us better understand how we organize ourselves in a social environment. It also teaches us how some individuals and groups benefit from society, while others do not. Since politics is an essential part of our daily lives, it is important that we try to understand how humans organize themselves into communities, and the effects these communities have on society as a whole. After all, politics allows for our collective survival, because with no formal organizing structure we would be left to fend for ourselves as individuals pitted against everyone else.

So, though debate and conflict over power and authority are inevitable in human communities, so too are attempts to resolve differences. Although politics is about **conflict resolution**, as well as **conflict**, humans are by nature competitive creatures who rely — for better or worse — on their political communities to ensure their personal survival.

What Is Politics?

To say that modern political life creates conditions of equality and fairness for all would give too much credit to individuals and their commitment to others. Indeed, politics in contemporary life is often marked by discord and controversy, rather than by equality for all. This has been the case since individuals first began organizing themselves into political units. Nevertheless, one of the fundamental goals of politics is fairness in society. However elusive this goal may be, politics has always involved controversy as well as co-operation, debate as well as accord.

In the seventeenth century, the English philosopher Thomas Hobbes argued that without society and the political authority that accompanied it, humans would suffer in what he termed a 'state of nature', or a situation marked by an 'everyone for themselves' frame of mind. Life would be, in Hobbes's view, 'solitary, poor, nasty, brutish, and short'.[1] He suggested that shaping human society — the process of **socialization** — is essential for the security of life itself. Politics, then, is a response to the natural tendency among human beings to come together and create larger organized groups. An integral part of that tendency is to seek a way to allocate the benefits and responsibilities that accompany the creation of a social unit. Politics and the sharing of benefits is also essential for the preservation of life itself.

One way to see how the 'political' exists in society is to consider how important decisions that affect a political community are made. Individual citizens who vote in an election or who attend townhall meetings on rezoning a neighbourhood or the future of local school board policies, for example, are part of a broader process that leads to **decision-making** by political authorities. Indeed, it is significant even if citizens do not take part because this can be viewed as tacit agreement with the status quo.

These actions, of course, are just one part of the decision-making process, which results in policies, laws, rules, and regulations that guide and shape society. This process is critical to the survival of a political community because it provides a framework that enables all members of the society to decide what acceptable conduct is.

In the title of his book *Politics: Who Gets What, When, How*, Harold Lasswell neatly described the fundamental question of politics.[2] In fact, many have come to define political studies in terms of the title of his book, because it alludes to the notion of power in the political sphere and, more to the point, who holds it. Lasswell's book examines how the essential **public goods** that result from political life are allocated to members of society. In every civilization (historical or present), political power has been used to gain control over wealth and resources — the public goods of a state.

Understanding public goods is essential for the study of politics. Public goods are the various benefits that are made available to citizens of a political organization, including, but not limited to, social welfare, economic efficiency, security from external attack, public safety, and political freedoms and opportunity. In short, they represent what is made available by government to the people, and provided for all. Not surprisingly, the type of government that holds authority will in many ways dictate the relative access to these public goods. For instance, political freedom is more widespread in **liberal democracies** than in **authoritarian** regimes.

It is useful to consider political life as a competition for scarce resources. Whether they are immediate and tangible goods such as money, food, or minerals, or more intangible goods such as power and influence, these resources are available to a political community. However, they are limited and (in most political systems) the method of distributing them results in inevitable divisions between (and within) different social strata in society: rich and poor, powerful and weak. Politics also leads to competition for other non-material objectives. For instance, not everyone shares the same values or recognition; some will have more of a participatory role in their political system and see their particular values upheld over others, while others may feel marginalized.

Although resources are limited and competition for them is great, the role of political authority is to allocate them to members of society. Allocation takes place through a system of decision-making and choice. Political actors, faced with the need to provide their citizens with public goods (or to protect those goods), consider the best avenues through which their political and economic system can generate and distribute public goods. Numerous specific goals are available to actors in a political system; decisions, therefore, are an indispensable component of political life. As members of society, we often spend our time concentrating on the

Decision-making
mechanism or pattern of relations involving different levels of government where determinations and judgments regarding the governance of political system are made (sometimes referred to as the 'black box')

Public goods
resources that are present in a political system where use by one individual should not affect use by others

Liberal democracy
political system based on freedom and individual liberty, and on the principle that governance requires the assent of all citizens through participation in the electoral process, articulation of views, and direct or indirect representation in governing institutions

Authoritarianism
political system requiring absolute obedience to a constituted authority

outcomes of decisions at the expense of understanding the process that actually led to the outcome. But, in order to truly understand the full extent of the determining factors that lead to such outcomes, we must analyze the process of decision-making.

Once decisions have been made, they are restricted or enforced by the rule of law. While relationships and choice in society may be considered natural consequences of human interaction, specialized agencies such as government are not; they are the product of human invention. Specialized agencies such as bureaucracies and Armed Forces are necessary to provide a means of regulating and maintaining society. So, in their own way, governments make decisions that govern societal relationships.

Politics is often considered in a pejorative way. We often hear of how things reflect 'politics as usual' or the 'politics of the situation' to describe events that have a negative impact on individuals and groups. But while politics has its negative aspects, political studies — the study of political life — is also much more than that. Political studies looks at competition, conflict resolution, allocating resources and justice, the exercise of power, choice, and a means of understanding. Political studies is a deliberately complex subject, and it has to be, given the wide array of issues to which it must attend.

Approaches Used in the Study of Politics

Political studies is basically an investigation of political events: What took place? How did it happen? Why did it unfold the way it did? Who benefited from the event and who did not? How did the event change the distribution of power within society?

In short, the study of politics is about the description and explanation of events, as well as a consideration of how things ought to be. In this way, political studies seeks to contribute to a better environment for citizens and political units. Political studies is a systematic examination of events in society. As a discipline, there is no consensus on how this should be accomplished, resulting in a rather fragmented field of study. But, as argued later in this chapter, this creates a vibrant and challenging discipline, with several important subfields of interest.

Political studies has a rich history, stemming back to the roots of the early philosophies of Aristotle and Plato. Aristotle, in fact, thought that politics was inherently human: 'That man is more of a political animal than bees or any other gregarious animals is evident,' [3] he wrote. He meant that while other creatures on earth may live in groups, only humans possess '*logos*', which means both 'language' and 'reason' in Greek. Therefore, humans can consider both 'just' and 'unjust' actions, and ultimately strive to make our political systems serve us better. We are, then, political animals by nature.

The actual creation in universities of departments of politics, political studies, or political science was a much more recent development, one that reflected a need to understand these aspects of our social lives. Political studies is one discipline in the **social sciences**; others include sociology, psychology, anthropology, social geography, and linguistics. Each of these disciplines has its own areas of interest,

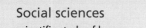

Social sciences
scientific study of human society and social relationships

and its own theories, concepts, and frameworks. Furthermore, each of these disciplines informs us about important aspects of our lives as social beings. Political studies is concerned with the governance of social units, the allocation of power and responsibility, and the relationship among political actors in society.

The study of politics was originally pursued in university departments of 'government', primarily in the United States and Great Britain. By the late nineteenth century, 'political studies' departments and faculties began to appear, driven by the convergence of interests of those studying government and economics. Not surprisingly, as this relatively new discipline developed and matured during the twentieth century, several competing approaches (or frameworks of analysis) were developed and fostered by political scientists.

The destruction caused by World War II led political scientists to consider ways that politics could contribute to the cause of peace. Throughout this book, we'll consider the massive effect this war had on politics. This photo shows the devastation in Saint-Lô, Normandy, in France during the Allied advance.

As in many fields, there are different names for the study of politics. The term 'political science', as we will see later, reflects the emphasis on social science methodologies that were popularized in the post–World War II era.

Many of the social sciences applied approaches and methods commonly used in the natural sciences to make the study of politics more rigorous. Although these approaches are still widely used in the study of politics (and it is considered a social science), different names have been used to describe the field: for example, political studies, political science, government, civics, politics. For our purposes, we have chosen *political studies* because it accurately reflects a broad perspective of the discipline.

Every discipline has its competing approaches and methods. Political studies is no different. Politics can be studied from the vantage point of political institutions, or human sociability, or ideologies. These methods — and several others, too — suggest ways to view the world, as well as the specific field of analysis that attempts to appreciate and comprehend politics in a way that is both meaningful and useful.

There are numerous approaches to the study of politics. The most common and perhaps the oldest method is called the **analytical approach**. This perspective views political studies as an **empirical** discipline, rather than a science. This approach views politics as a comprehensive field, rather than one that can be broken down into parts. However, the analytical approach, which is also sometimes called the **traditional approach**, makes it difficult to see political studies as a discipline because it argues that it is impossible to separate facts from values;

Analytical approach
perspective that views politics as an empirical discipline (one that can be observed), rather than a science; politics cannot be broken down into parts, but must be seen comprehensively

Empirical
analysis based not on concepts and theory, but rather what can be observed or experimented on

Traditional approach
method in politics drawing heavily on fields of law, philosophy, and history that relies on subjective evaluation of the observer; also called the analytical approach

1.2

Names of Politics Departments in Canada

Although university and college departments across the country may use different official names, they all teach similar courses and conduct research in the same fields. Here is a list of major departments across Canada, according to their nomenclature:

Political Science

Acadia
Alberta
Athabasca
British Columbia
Brock
Calgary
Cape Breton
Carleton
Concordia
Dalhousie
Guelph
Huron (Western)
King's (Western)
Lakehead
Laurentian
Laval
Lethbridge
McGill
McMaster
Memorial
Moncton
Montreal
Mount Allison
New Brunswick (Fredericton)
Northern British Columbia
Québec à Montréal
Regina
St. Francis Xavier
St. Mary's
St. Thomas
Simon Fraser
Toronto
Victoria
Waterloo
Western Ontario
Wilfrid Laurier
Windsor
York

Political Studies

Bishop's
Manitoba
Ottawa
Prince Edward Island
Queen's
Saskatchewan

Political and Canadian Studies

Mount St. Vincent

Politics

New Brunswick (Saint John)
Trent
Winnipeg

Politics and Economics

Royal Military College

Politics and Public Administration

Ryerson

Behaviouralism
perspective that concentrates on the 'tangible' aspects of political life, rather than values; objective was to establish a discipline that was 'scientific' and objective

human values and convictions, then, are just another 'part' of political life that cannot be fragmented from the field. The implication here is that any observer of political activity will have his or her own view and bias, which will implicate and affect their analysis. It is impossible to observe events in an objective manner, so political studies can never be a scientific discipline.

The analytical approach had its challengers, however. In an effort to make the field more precise, the **behaviouralists** emerged in the 1950s and 1960s, particularly in American political studies departments. They focused on the 'tangible' aspects of political life, rather than the value-laden perspective of the analytical approach. The objective of the behaviouralists was to establish a discipline that was 'scientific' and objective: political 'science.' Human behaviour, the behaviouralists argued, was at the heart of all political activity, so humans should be the centre of research. Behaviouralists concentrated on the scientific method, using variables, theories, axioms, and hypotheses in their research.

Behaviouralism after World War II

Sputnik 1 became the first human object in orbit in 1957. It transmitted data to earth while circling it for three months before burning up on re-entry.

The Soviet Union's successful launch of Sputnik 1 not only heated up the space race with the United States, but also inadvertently changed the study of politics.

The space race caused governments and universities to put more money into science than in the past, leaving fields like political studies to question their future. In fact, the term 'political science' came under some scrutiny for its lack of a scientific basis. The behaviouralist approach to politics emerged at this time, promising an objective method of predicting and explaining behaviour. It utilized the scientific method of observing, testing, and measuring events in an effort to establish hypotheses and conclusions about political events. Criticisms of political science and behaviouralism continued, however, as it became increasingly clear how difficult it is to 'quantify' (to measure ranges of actions) human behaviour. The approach fell into some disrepute, leading many to abandon the goals of prediction and universal assessment. The methods used in behaviouralism, however, remained in several streams of political science research: testing, hypothesis, conceptual development, comparison, and falsification. Humans act in variable and sometimes infinite ways, so the 'science' in political science will never be like the natural sciences. But the methods shared among the fields continue to be useful.

Post-behaviouralism
approach that attempted to reconcile the problems encountered by behaviouralism by allowing for values and ideology in its analysis

Structural-functionalism
approach that focuses on the role of political structures and their functions in society

Systems theory
approach that views politics as a system of interaction, binding political structures such as government to individual action; argues that politics is a dynamic process of information flows and responses that encompasses political institutions, groups, and individuals

Political economy
approach that views political and economic spheres as harmonious and mutually dependent perceptions of the world; relationship between people, government, and the economy

The behaviouralist 'school', however, was criticized for its attention to the scientific method. Many political scientists argued that in its attempt to be truly 'scientific', political studies had come to neglect the fact that values were an intrinsic element of political life, because the very focus of the behaviouralist approach — the human being — was so steeped in values, opinions, beliefs, and views of the world. A new approach, **post-behaviouralism**, came as a reaction to the negative aspects of behaviouralism. Post-behaviouralists tried to reconcile the problems encountered by behaviouralism by allowing for values and ideology in their analysis.

Nevertheless, there were still others who continued to disagree with the scientific method of both the behaviouralists and the post-behaviouralists, and at the same time rejected the analytical approach as too broad. The **structural-functionalists**, for one, concentrated on the role of political structures and their functions in society. What, for example, is the effect and role of the legislature? How does the bureaucracy affect politics? Is the judiciary an important actor in a particular system? Structural-functionalists represent a group within a larger classification of researchers called systems theorists. These analysts view politics as a system of interaction, binding political structures such as government to individual action. **Systems theory** argues that politics is a dynamic process of information flows and responses that encompasses political institutions, groups, and individuals. Systems theorists try to understand this process of decision and reaction among various types of political actors.

For **political economists**, another group of political scientists, the major drawback to all these approaches is that they do not focus on the relationship between power and wealth, or politics and economics. According to political economy, an approach that views 'interests' as paramount, political studies is the relationship between people, government, and the economy. How those interests are identified and pursued shows the fundamental power and influence in a political system, particularly because those interests tend to be focused on resources that are quite scarce; this brings us back to what Lasswell had to say about 'who gets what, when, and how' in politics. Governments affect many of the economic particulars of our lives, and of those around us, so political economists explore the role that governments have in both the political and economic spheres of the environment around us.

Chapters 2 and 3 in this book will delve into political concepts, philosophies, and approaches in much greater detail. But, simply put, political studies is concerned with five pervasive and related questions:

1. *What* is the political issue at hand?
2. *Who* is involved?
3. *How* did the events unfold?
4. *Why* did the events take place?
5. *How* was society affected by these events?

These are some fairly basic questions, but as you can now see, there are various approaches used by political scientists to try to answer them. A change in government, for example, might be explained in terms of different parties, and approaches or ideologies, institutional transformation, individual personalities, or the result of the political system itself. Even though this book will introduce you to a wide variety of approaches, it too has a central methodology or approach.

To try to deal with these basic questions, then, there are three main forms of analysis in this book. First, this text explores how politics is integral to modern life. Political decisions and events have a direct implication on our livelihoods and relationships in our communities. After all, a primary motivating factor for grouping together is to improve and preserve the conditions of what might be termed 'the good life' — security, prosperity, and fairness.

Second, this book takes a **comparative approach**. Though it is directed towards a Canadian audience, its focus is not exclusively 'Canadian', or even North American. Instead, we use examples and case studies taken from around the world, from Latin America to Europe, to Africa, and Asia. This gives us a cross-examination of different political systems and viewpoints. The book places these examples in the context of the Canadian experience. In short, if we want to understand our own political environment, we must look at other examples, too.

Third, the methodology of this text involves attention to several levels of political life. Various **levels of analysis** include the individual, groups, the state, and the international system. This focus on several levels shows the comparative nature of the textbook, and gives you, the student, a better-rounded introduction to the complex and ever-changing field of political studies.

Political Studies and Our Daily Lives

Politics surrounds us. When we think about it, politics really is part of our daily lives, since it involves organizing ideas, influence, or power and wealth over others. Regularly we hear of the 'politics' of the family, of organized religion, of business, of sport, or of the entertainment industry. Indeed, all aspects of our common experiences seem to be influenced in some form by politics or political conflict, even for those who think they do not know anything about politics. The 'political' nature of the family unit, or religion, business, sport, or entertainment has to do with the way that these elements of our society are organized, who controls them, and how we may all benefit from, or perhaps miss out on, their collective gains.

Even though we may not be aware of it, then, politics affects almost every part of our daily lives, from health and social care, to laws that regulate our behaviour, to the provision of goods and services made available to us. We often do not consider the political aspect of our daily lives unless we are faced with a situation that brings us directly into the political process, such as voting in elections, filling out annual tax forms, or taking part in political protests. Yet politics envelops us, and influences our activities within society in a very direct manner. And if politics so surrounds us, then so too should the study of it.

Division and Connection in a Changing World

It often has been remarked that the only constant force in political matters is change itself. Certainly, in our era this is true. The new millennium has been marked by extraordinary changes in our political environment, both at home and abroad: these

Comparative approach
method of political analysis that compares different systems of political authority, based on system type, time period, or form of leadership

Levels of analysis
approach to political studies that suggests that accurate analysis must be inclusive of international, domestic, and individual arenas of interaction

1.4

Involvement: Apathy to Action

Successive generations have been criticized for their lack of interest in political affairs. Usually, their critics are from the generation preceding them, and often based on a false nostalgia for the way things used to be. Reality suggests otherwise, however. To label an entire generation as 'apathetic' is both simplistic and unfair. Indeed, any generation has its share of those who get involved, and those who care not to. On the other hand, it is fair to say that political involvement today is different than it was in the past, specifically prior to the 1960s. During the 1960s, a unique change took place for a specific generation. As the baby boomers (those born between 1946 and 1964) became young adults, they reacted viscerally and harshly to the expectation that they would emulate their parents and their parents' parents. In short, their coming of age in the postwar period instilled in them a need to change the way we see politics. Deference to authority, an aggressive military stance, societal norms such as marriage and jobs at a certain age — these expectations were questioned, even rejected, as that generation matured and became involved in peace movements, social justice, and global order.

Clearly, a quick scan of the world situation today reveals that the 1960s didn't change everything. But much did change — in movements for civil rights and women's rights, government transparency, and a greater expectation that politics should serve the people, rather than the other way around. Today's younger generation is no less involved, from volunteer work to active engagement in the political process. The sheer quantity of information available to us now makes the 1960s demand for immediate change seem unachievable or even naïve, but we should remember that any change takes time, and that meaningful change probably requires action by groups of individuals who seek it. If we aspire to real progress, then all of us must commit ourselves to political action rather than succumb to apathy.

Globalization
the intensification of economic, political, social, and cultural relations across borders

Ethnic and religious conflict
war or opposition among different racial, linguistic, or religious groups

Protectionism
tendency of countries to safeguard their own economic sectors or industries using tariffs, quotas, or other forms of trade and investment legislation

include shifting global security threats, new political forces at home and abroad, greater understanding of the nature of shared challenges like those facing the global environment and poverty, and a greater degree of interconnectivity. These changes have presented new challenges as well as opportunities as we begin to understand the nature of this new milieu of domestic and international political affairs.

Political change is so interesting because both connection *and* division influence it. Increasingly, individuals, groups, and states are intricately connected to one another through political, economic, strategic, and cultural links. The **globalization** of the current era, where information about other systems and cultures is readily available to us, from media sources, our educational system, and the Internet, affects both the way we get information and the way we use it.

Yet at the same time, growing divisions are indicative of a complex and competitive environment for political and economic relations. **Ethnic and religious conflict**, the growing gap between rich and poor, economic **protectionism**, and political isolationism, for example, all reflect aspects of modern political life that are divisive and contrary. Often these problems are deeply rooted in efforts by political leaders to provide goods and services to their citizens. In fact, the forces of connection and division are intensely entwined: rising interaction among certain political players often leads to calls to reduce involvement in the affairs of others.

Division and connection illustrate a basic paradox in political life today: we may think we're more linked with others in the world, but often our 'understanding' leads to greater confusion and enmity. After all, just knowing someone doesn't mean we will get along with them, and being exposed to new ideas won't necessarily mean we will accept them. As the Chinese Taoist text *Tao Te Ching* reminds us, '[T]he more you know, the less you understand.' [4] Now, this isn't to suggest that we should just give up and not try to expand our knowledge of the world; it's simply a reminder that exposure does not ensure wisdom, understanding, or peace. In fact, looking at the world today, one is struck by the number of groups that seek to create their own nation-states — a goal that is inherently about division — in an era of unprecedented information and access to others. In short, division and connection are coexistent forces, and they remind us of the need to look outward while at the same time looking in.

Domestic and International Politics

Politics doesn't limit itself to borders, and political studies is not restricted to the study of our own nation-states. A truly comprehensive view of the world of political studies takes into account the domestic and the international: looking out and looking in. One of the important lessons we learn in political studies is that the borders that exist among states don't necessarily divide them; countries can be intricately connected to one another in ways that seem to transcend nationality and national frontiers. In fact, it might be argued that certain parts of Canada are more connected to their southern neighbour, the United States, than they are to each other. The fields of political studies, then, recognize the inherent relationship that exists between domestic and international subject areas.

Domestic politics is a subfield of political studies that concerns itself with the politics, governance, and political administration of national governments and individual countries. Depending where you take your classes in political studies, the options available to you regarding domestic politics can take you far from your home country. In Canada, most departments of political studies have a concentration on Canadian politics; that's not surprising, given the need to understand our own system. While it might be surprising to find courses in Canadian universities on the politics of, say, Cambodia, Switzerland, or Niger, it's not entirely beyond possibility. Furthermore, although these and other countries may not have full courses prescribed to them in Canadian universities, they likely are dealt with in courses that deal with Asian politics, or European or African politics. But were we to look at university course offerings in Phnom Penh, Bern, or Niamey, their countries would undoubtedly be the focus. (Whether Canada would be listed among courses in those institutions is another question!)

The point here is that where you are will reflect highly on the areas that you are expected to study. We may be in Canada, but we are expected to know a little bit about European politics, a lot about American politics, and some more about other places, too. Domestic politics restrains our focus to the country in question — its governing institutions, laws, economy, and relations with the outside world.

International politics
relations of a political nature that exist at the international level

That outside world is the realm of **international politics**. Often called international relations or world politics, this subfield of political studies takes a wider view of politics. Political relations among and between countries are as much an influence on our domestic frame of reference as what takes place 'at home'. International politics is concerned with the social, environmental, economic, military, and cultural relations across the globe, whether they are across one border between two countries, within a geopolitical region, or widely dispersed around the globe. Specifically, this subfield examines the political aspects of these relations.

Although most of the material in this text could be used for those interested in either domestic or international politics, there aren't any artificial lines drawn to distinguish the subfields. Some sections of the text deal with government institutions and decision-making; others deal with international security and economics. But as we move through the subject matter, we will come to see the natural relationship that exists between national and international politics.

Citizens and Canada

When did the United Empire Loyalists come to Canada? Which four provinces first formed the Confederation? Which province is the only officially bilingual one?

Citizenship
status granted to citizens that comes with responsibilities and duties as well as rights

Don't despair if you can't answer these questions off the top of your head; most of us can't. But these are the types of questions that new Canadians have to answer before they are granted **citizenship**. It's true: new immigrants to Canada must successfully pass a quiz on topics related to Canadian history, politics, economics, geography, and the privileges of citizenship. Although a passing 'grade' is just 12 correct out of 20, the questions aren't easy. Many citizens by birth would likely have trouble successfully completing the test.

1.5

Citizenship Quiz

Questions on the Canadian Citizenship Test change frequently. Here is a sample list of questions provided by the Public Library in Richmond, BC, based on multiple choice questions found in *A Look at Canada 2007*. Try the test! Even if some of the questions may be out of date by the time you read this, you should get a good sense of what new immigrants to Canada face. Answers are at the end of this chapter in Box 1.6.

1. When is Canada Day and what does it celebrate?
   a. June 15th of each year to celebrate the anniversary of Confederation.
   b. August 8th of each year to celebrate the joining of British Columbia to Confederation.
   c. We celebrate the anniversary of Confederation on July 1st of each year.
   d. May 21st of each year to remember Queen Victoria.

1.5 Continued...

2. When did the Canadian Charter of Rights and Freedoms become part of the Canadian Constitution?
   a. 1867.
   b. 1905.
   c. 1982.
   d. 1878.

3. Give an example of how you can show responsibility by participating in your community.
   a. Mind your own business.
   b. Have a party.
   c. Keep your property tidy.
   d. Join a community group.

4. What will you promise when you take the Oath of Citizenship?
   a. Pledge allegiance to the Queen, observe the laws of Canada and fulfill the duties of a Canadian.
   b. Pledge to be faithful to the Queen.
   c. Promise to observe the laws of Canada.
   d. Fulfill duties as a Canadian citizen.

5. What are the territories of Northern Canada and their capital cities?
   a. Alaska (Juneau) and Yukon Territory (Whitehorse).
   b. Northwest Territories (Yellowknife) and Alaska (Juneau).
   c. Northwest Territories (Yellowknife).
   d. Yukon Territory (Whitehorse), Northwest Territories (Yellowknife), and Nunavut (Iqaluit).

6. Which region covers more than one-third of Canada?
   a. Central Canada.
   b. Prairies.
   c. Atlantic Canada.
   d. Northern Canada.

7. One-third of all Canadians live in which province?
   a. Quebec.
   b. Ontario.
   c. Northwest Territories.
   d. Manitoba.

8. What is a major river in Quebec?
   a. Fraser River.
   b. St. Lawrence River.
   c. Niagara.
   d. Hudson Bay.

9. What are the three parts of Parliament?
   a. The queen, Governor General, and prime minister.
   b. The House of Commons, the Legislative Assembly, and the Senate.

1.5 Continued...

c. The queen, the Legislative Assembly, and the Senate.
d. The queen, the House of Commons, and the Senate.

10. What are the three levels of government in Canada?
    a. Federal, Provincial/Territorial, Municipal or Local.
    b. Federal, Provincial, and City.
    c. Federal, Territorial, and Provincial.
    d. Federal, State, and Local.

What does citizenship actually mean? Are there things that are specific to Canadian citizenship? These aren't questions that we would commonly think about, since they seem to be just part of being 'Canadian'. Yet being Canadian means not being something — or someone — else. Aside from dual citizens, Canadians aren't Americans, British, or French. Generally, citizenship is specific, however, and people are entwined with their birth nation or country of adoption.

Citizenship denotes membership in a political system, complete with the rights and responsibilities of that membership. Usually citizenship is related to nationality, or the national identity to which we assign ourselves; of course, some people relate themselves to a 'nation' without being a citizen of a country. Scots, Hausa-Fulani, or Cree, for instance, may all be Canadian but still maintain their distinctive nationalities. Later in this text we'll return to the issue of nationality and nationalism. In any case, citizenship brings with it the protection of the state as well as a legal relationship with a country.

Not everyone can lay claim to this relationship. There are certain conditions — such as being born in Canada or writing a citizenship test — that people must fulfill before they may call themselves 'citizens'. (Of course, birth is a much easier passage to citizenship.) Once people obtain citizenship, however, they can receive a wide array of benefits. In Canada, for instance, this means a number of rights and freedoms (including legal rights, equality rights, mobility rights, Aboriginal peoples' rights, freedom of thought, freedom of speech, freedom of religion, and the right to peaceful assembly). With rights come responsibilities, and for Canadians that means, for example, to respect others' rights and freedoms, to obey the law, and to preserve Canada's heritage and environment. In short, citizenship is not a blank slate — it's a relationship between the state and the citizen to work together to protect and develop Canada.

In addition to the new Canadians by birth, approximately 250,000 people become Canadian citizens in any given year. This number changes, based on the priorities and preferences expressed by the federal government; however, it's a substantial number — about three-quarters of 1 per cent of Canada's total population. Immigration is not a minor affair in Canada. Time spent in any major city (or even town) shows the pluralistic and **multicultural** nature of Canadian society. The benefits of such an expansive society are numerous, but with them come challenges as well. Canadian society has been described as a 'mosaic', an image only truly recognized with all its pieces in place. Others, like York University political

Multiculturalism
where several racial, cultural, or ethnic identities coexist peacefully in one nation

scientist Kenneth McRoberts, have called Canada 'multinational', marked most notably by its French and First Nations 'internal nations'.[5]

Clearly, you feel the importance to understand more about your citizenship. Even if you aren't Canadian by birth or immigration, you are taking this course in Canada at a Canadian university or college. The nature of the course material means that we will spend a considerable amount of time examining what it means to be a citizen of Canada. Yet as this chapter earlier suggested, knowing what it means to be Canadian — or a citizen of any other country, for that matter — means knowing a bit about the rest of the world, too. This is one of the goals of this text: to integrate our introduction to political studies so that we reflect our national as well as our international perspective.

And, if you wanted to check your citizenship suitability, the correct answers to the questions at the beginning of this section were (in order): 1775 to 1783; Ontario, Quebec, New Brunswick, and Nova Scotia; New Brunswick.

Conclusion

This chapter has introduced you to the study of political studies, acquainting you with the broad nature of political inquiry, our relationship to the political 'world', and our undeniable connection with the global framework of political relations. Political studies is about decisions and choice. It is about process, how decisions are made and to whose benefit. And it is also as much about the resolution of conflict as it is about conflict itself.

The following chapters will explore some of the themes introduced here. Chapter 2 will provide an account of the major concepts in political studies. Some of them have been introduced here, but Chapter 2 will provide more context and detail. Related closely to Chapter 2, Chapter 3 explores the main political philosophies and ideologies that form the basis of modern political studies. Chapter 4 introduces the role that government plays in our lives, including its different forms, schools of thought, and shared activities at all levels. Chapter 5 builds on the previous chapter, breaking government down into its specific parts and institutions. Chapter 6 examines the variety of political systems that exist in the world today. Chapters 7 and 8 consider the ways that we participate in our political system, from election votes to the impact of global media. Chapters 9 and 10 explore the distinctions between the 'developed' and 'developing' worlds, including some case studies of important examples from around the world. Chapters 11, 12, and 13 look at the international nature of political studies, including foreign policy, international relations, security and strategic studies, and the international political economy. Finally, Chapter 14 provides a conclusion to the course and the text.

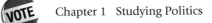

1.6

Citizenship Quiz Answers

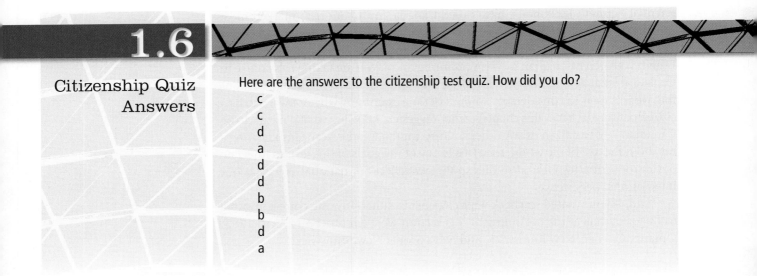

Here are the answers to the citizenship test quiz. How did you do?

c
c
d
a
d
d
b
b
d
a

Self-Assessment Questions

1. Why, and in what way, is politics such a central component of society? Can we become truly 'apolitical'?
2. Without government, would life truly be 'solitary, poor, nasty, brutish, and short'?
3. How does political studies fit with the other social sciences?
4. Why are Canadians so cynical about politics?
5. Should citizenship be open to all, or should there be limits?
6. Are we more divided or connected in a globalized world?

Weblinks

Canadian Political Science Association
www.cpsa-acsp.ca

Careers for Political Scientists
www.cpsa-acsp.ca/guides.shtml

Canadian Citizenship Test Home Page
www.cic.gc.ca/english/citizenship/cit-test.asp

Further Reading

Almond, Gabriel A. *A Discipline Divided: Schools and Sects in Political Science*. Newbury Park, CA: Sage Publications, 1990.

Aristotle. *Politics*. Trans. T.A. Sinclair. Harmondsworth, UK: Penguin Books, 1986.

Easton, David. *The Political System*. 2nd ed. Chicago: University of Chicago Press, 1981.

Hobbes, Thomas. *Leviathan, Or, the Matter, Forme and Power of a Commonwealth Ecclesiasticall and Civil*. Ed. Michael Oakeshott. New York: Collier Books, 1962 (first pub. 1651).

Laozi. *Tao Te Ching*. Harmondsworth, UK: Penguin Books, 1963, 1976.

Lasswell, Harold. *Politics: Who Gets What, When, How*. New York: Meridian Books, 1958.

Seymour, Michel, ed. *The Fate of the Nation-State*. Montreal and Kingston: McGill-Queen's University Press, 2004.

CBC News Clips

Visit the companion website for *Politics: An Introduction* to listen to news clips from the CBC radio archives.

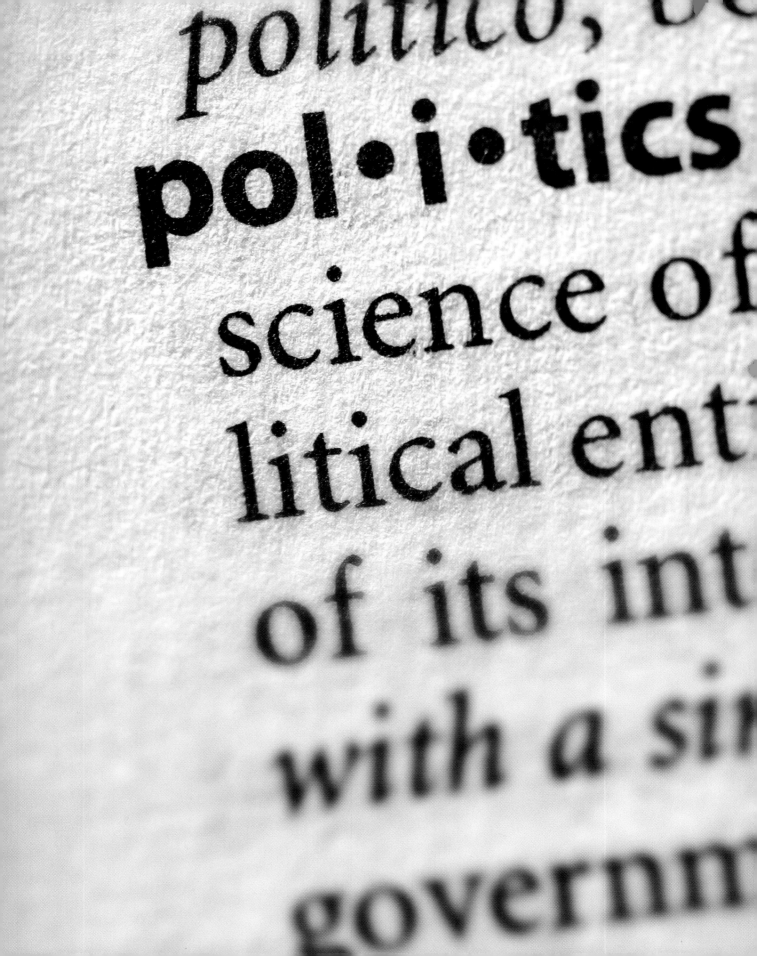

2 Finding a Common Vocabulary: Political Concepts

LEARNING
OBJECTIVES

After reading this chapter, you will be able to:

❋ define and explain concepts relating to political organization

❋ define and explain concepts relating to political action

❋ define and explain concepts relating to political values

❋ give examples of the significance and real-world applicability of these concepts.

Introduction: The Importance of a Common Language

Just as it is important to define and demarcate the field of political studies, it is vital that we establish a common language as students of political studies so that we can avoid unnecessary misunderstandings and make our dialogue more effective and efficient. Having a common language also helps to form a shared identity among scholars in the field, and it gives students the ability to prove themselves 'academically literate'.

Of course, almost every field of study has its own particular vocabulary, and political studies is no different. Aside from distinguishing the discipline from others, a specialized vocabulary is important because it allows us to create a 'mental picture' of some of the more significant ideas that are utilized in political analysis.

Concepts, then, are general notions or abstract ideas that are encapsulated in a specialized vocabulary.[1] The fact that this language is specialized is crucial, for we often devise distinctive interpretations of terms in political studies that we might otherwise understand in a different sense. For instance, as explained later in this chapter, the manner in which we consider the concept of nation in politics and the way we think about the term in everyday life are somewhat different.[2] Just as importantly, the ability to distinguish one kind of right (say, human) from another (civil) becomes important in both theory *and* practice. What is crucial is that a word, once we settle on it, is commonly used to refer to the same aspect of our experience, even if we apply it in a more conscious manner in the study of politics. Therefore, understanding these concepts, as applied in political studies, is a most important first step.

Concept
general idea emerging from events or instances

This is not to argue that all concepts are universally regarded or agreed upon. In fact, unlike the so-called hard sciences, such as physics and chemistry, there are no uncontested 'laws' or theories in political studies. There is no corresponding political theory to that of, say, the theory of relativity, or gravity, which are accepted as fundamental in the hard sciences. On the other hand, politics, like many of the social sciences, is marked by an ongoing debate about the utility of certain theories and concepts, as well as their interpretation.[3] However, despite the fact that many concepts in politics are 'essentially contested', that is, there is substantial disagreement on their specific meaning, many of our important concepts can be defined in a manner that allows us to use them in a fairly recognized manner.

This chapter will introduce you to key concepts used in the field and explain their significance in both theory and practice. Using specific examples (often contained in the boxes within the text), you will see the relevance of these concepts in the real world. We will cover concepts related to both the organization and practice of politics, as well as the ideas and values that lie behind both. It is important that you discuss these concepts with your colleagues and professors, and we expect you will run into differences of opinion over definitions and the priority to be given to certain concepts, especially those relating to political values.

Political Organization

In many ways, politics concerns the organization of life and relationships in a society, and for this reason, the way we define and think about the organizational aspects of politics is vital.[4] In this section we will examine some of the key terms and concepts relating to political organization.

As a form of social interaction, politics encompasses the way human beings govern themselves. But governance may only take place with the existence of certain specialized agencies. Governing also requires a polity, which is the form or process of organized government. It can mean a state, or it can refer more generally to a collection of individuals in a community that have a political relationship with one another. This form of political grouping is commonly called a 'body politic', and is a group of individuals tied together in a political connection.

There are a number of ways that we classify the body politic. Groups of people form political relationships with each other for many reasons, creating different types and forms of identity. In some cases, this identity is geographical. Here, the political relationship is rather self-evident, as groups of people that share a common territory will often create political units as a means of protecting that territory, or of regulating behaviour within the territory. Over time, the affiliations and relationships among people living in that territory will become based on more than just feelings towards land, or where they live. Values, belief systems, attitudes, and images of one's world are deeply shaped by the socialization people receive in their political communities, creating a system where 'identity' may be based on a multitude of reasons and rationales.[5] How we conceptualize political communities, and the labels we place on them, are essential elements for our political analysis.

Order
condition in which both units and interaction within a political system are marked by regularity and stability with the imposition of accepted and enforced rules, structures, and practices

System
a group of individual entities or actors that interact with each other to form an integrated whole

Organizations
structured relations existing within a political community that are established to distribute both the responsibilities and the privileges that arise from formal association with others

Institutions
groupings that have developed and are to attend to particular needs for society

Order is essentially the condition in which both actors and interaction within a political system are marked by regularity and stability with the imposition of accepted and enforced rules, structures, and practices.[6] Indeed, one of the basic preconditions for civilization is order, so as to provide a degree of customary activities and predictability within society. Though it is necessary for the continuance of governance and stability, order is often difficult to establish without sacrificing other desired conditions. Order is not only a condition, but also, as we will see later in this chapter, a value to which many individuals and groups in society may aspire.

A political order, then, is the collection of rules, laws, norms, customs, and conventions that delimit and hold together a society. Different kinds of political order include democracy, monarchy, and tyranny. Closely linked to the idea of a political order, in the language of political science, a **system** is a connected and organized body that represents a coherent whole. A political system, for example, is a conglomerate of numerous political structures that work together to drive the political aspects of social interaction. Since the parts of the coherent whole are so interrelated, change in one part usually means a change in all, such as the way in which changes in party leadership affect the politics of a whole political system in a state. Equally, an alteration in the rules concerning voting will have a far-reaching impact, not just on political parties and elections, but also on the balance of political power in the country. At the global level, the international political system embodies the individual units — the states — as well as the functional non-state actors (such as non-governmental organizations and multinational corporations) that comprise and affect the world arena. When there is a change in the distribution of power in the international system (such as the rapid and dramatic rise of China in recent years), it has an impact on all the actors involved.

Within any particular system, the term **organizations** refers to structured relations existing within a political community that are established to distribute both the responsibilities and the privileges that arise from formal association with others.[7] Organizations may range from political parties and interest groups, to private groups that allocate resources on a different level. It is important to recognize that these organizations can be local, national, or international, public or private, and can be based on economic, political, knowledge, cultural, ethnic, racial, or religious ties.

Directly related to organizations are **institutions**, which are groupings that have developed and are mandated to attend to particular needs for society.[8] Not just simply a grouping of individuals as in organizations, institutions have strict definitions regarding their structure and functions, and set out distinct roles for members of the institutions. Institutions, then, may or may not be organizations; similarly, not all organizations are necessarily institutions. Institutions may exist at the international level, or at the level of the national state. An example of an institution at the international level is the United Nations; at the national level, courts and political assemblies such as parliaments are also institutions. Institutions, and their strengths and weaknesses, have become one of the most important areas of political analysis in our discipline. Institutions are held to be strong when they are autonomous, transparent, accountable, and durable. Strong institutions are generally perceived to be an essential element of building a stable political and economic system in a country. Weak institutions, on the other hand, are often cited as a contributing factor to political instability, corruption, under-development, and undemocratic practices.

2.1

Institutions and Development

The successful political and economic development of a state is dependent on the construction and maintenance of strong institutions within. These institutions include the organs of government (executive, legislative, and judicial branches and bureaucracy), the institutions related to public security (policing and the courts), economic management (central bank, monopolies commission, stock markets, banking system), and information flows and transparency (a free media, access to government records). In almost all developing countries, some, many, or all of these institutions suffer from weaknesses, and strengthening them is seen as a necessary precursor to advancing development.

It is important to recognize that institutions can be public or private, formal or informal, and are not limited exclusively to organizations, but instead incorporate rules and conventions. In the case of Latin America, for example, scholars such as Guillermo O'Donnell and Douglass North have argued that the weaknesses of institutions, such as electoral commissions, the rule of law, and organs guaranteeing accountability, have played a role in underdeveloping the countries of the region. Of course, the most important institution that we deal with in political studies is the **state**.[9] The state is the collection of public institutions that governs a country's political and, to a greater or lesser extent, economic life. The state is distinguished from the government of a country by its more permanent nature: whereas governments will change, the state and its institutions remain more or less constant. This means that, although the party of government in, say, Canada, may change from Liberal to Conservative, the institutions of the state do not change.

States are highly specialized entities. As we will see later in the chapter on international relations, states are the only actors that exercise what is known as sovereignty. This means the absolute control and power over a defined geographical area. The Canadian state, therefore, exercises sovereign control over the geographical territory known as Canada, and within those borders, no other entity, not even the United Nations, can legally tell the Canadian state what it must or must not do. Max Weber famously noted that sovereign states maintain a monopoly over the legitimate use of violence in their territories, a facet that gives them enormous power and authority.

In our everyday lives we use the terms 'the state' and 'the **nation**', as inter-changeable ways of referring to our territorial community, or our country. But these terms actually have quite different meanings. Whereas states are legalistic entities with sovereign authority over defined people, resources, and territory, a nation is a group of persons who share an identity that is based on, but not limited to, shared ethnic, religious, cultural, or linguistic qualities. Interestingly,

State
a recognized political unit, considered to be sovereign, with a defined territory and people and a central government responsible for administration

Nation
a group of persons who share an identity that is based on, but not limited to, shared ethnic, religious, cultural, or linguistic qualities

these persons are part of a largely unacquainted group, since it is virtually impossible to 'know' everyone who shares your sense of identity. Therefore, nations are not, strictly speaking, states. However, nation-states refer to those sovereign states that are constructed along a shared national identity; true nation-states, therefore, are actually quite rare. Nonetheless, though these three terms refer to very distinctive relationships, they are sometimes used interchangeably in political discourse, such as references to Canada as a 'nation,' the member 'states' of the UN, or 'nation-states' in the international system.[10] It is important to be aware of the different meanings of these terms and to the contested nature of their usage.

2.2

The Concept of Nation and Sovereignty in Canada

Although this book tries to give you a clear definition of the terms we use in political studies, in the real world meanings can be blurred, contested, and often the cause of protracted political conflict. In Canada we use the term 'nation' to refer to the Canadian nation, meaning the people of Canada. But the word 'nation' is also used in Quebec to refer to the Quebec people, as a nation within the Canadian nation. For many years this has caused confusion and dispute within political circles and has exacerbated Quebecois calls for an altered relationship with the rest of Canada.

The issue was finally addressed at the federal level in November 2007 when the House of Commons passed a motion stating, 'That this House recognizes that the Québécois form a nation within a united Canada.' The Conservative government motion came after the Bloc Québécois introduced a motion stating that the Quebecois formed a nation without any reference to Canada. Prime Minister Stephen Harper explained afterwards that the term 'nation' was used in a socio-cultural rather than a legal sense. In other words, the acknowledgement of Quebec as a nation does not imply independence or any sort of sovereignty outside of Canada. This is a debate that is far from over in Canadian politics.

Sovereignty
recognition by other political authorities that a government is legitimate and rightful for a political community

There is another very important concept connected to the state that we must not forget. States are considered to be the highest authority in the system, and as such maintain sovereign control over their territory. **Sovereignty**, then, is the capability and legal status that allows a state to be in absolute control of its territory. Sovereignty is an attribute that is held by states and by no other actor in the world. The concept includes both internal and external dimensions: internally, for the state to be sovereign, it must exert control over its territory and people; externally, it must be recognized by other states in the international system as being the sovereign power.

Above the state, we find the international system. This term refers to the organization of states among themselves and the interactions they undertake. At this level, all states share the same legal status; in this sense they are equal. Nonetheless they are differentiated from one another by their size, their internal structures, their natural resources, their ideologies, their wealth, and their capabilities. Thus we can distinguish between the rich (developed) and the poor (developing) states, between capitalist and communist states, or between democratic and authoritarian states. But in the international system they will organize themselves into alliances and groupings according to their interests and preferences. They will interact with each other through diplomacy, trade, investment, cultural exchanges, and war. The international system may be said to be more or less stable depending on the frequency of armed conflict and the sustainability of economic growth it experiences.

Political Action

Many of the most important concepts in political analysis have to do with relationships of control. This is because so much of political life centres on the way in which power is distributed, whether it is among persons and groups in society, or among all the states in the international system. What differentiates these concepts from those dealing with the relational and more active nature of power is the way power is sought and maintained.

Power is often referred to as the principal concept in political studies because it attends to both the dynamic and static nature of political life.[11] That is to say, power may be pursued or maintained in an active manner (dynamic) through, for instance, the waging of war, or creation of economic trade zones; power may also be thought of as a measurement of politics (static), since we may examine comparatively actors in political life based on their access and control of power resources, such as natural attributes (oil and arable land, for instance), or **influence** (diplomatic expertise and respect). Power is an operative concept, in that it represents one's ability to do or act in a manner they would like. Furthermore, it allows us the opportunity to create a sort of hierarchy of actors and interests in political systems, since the exercise of power involves the limiting or impairing of the recipient's choice in some respect: to exercise power over someone involves controlling, to a lesser or greater extent, their freedom of action.

It is important for us to distinguish between different forms and manifestations of power. The kind of power wielded by the military is clearly very different from that exercised by big corporations. Even when we are talking about the same actor, there will be different power resources available. In a famous treatment of governmental power, Steven Lukes argued that there are 'three faces' of power that can be identified: decision-making power, non–decision-making power, and ideological power. The first concerns the most obvious and well-known form of governmental power, the kind seen through policy-making, legislation, and its implementation. The second form is the ability to set the agenda for discussion and debate, determining what issues receive priority in the policy process. The third form of power, according to Lukes, is the ability to influence people and mould the way they think.[12]

Just from Lukes's brief treatment of power, we can see how diverse and complex the term can be. Power can be derived from military, economic, ideological,

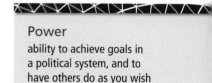

Power
ability to achieve goals in a political system, and to have others do as you wish them to

2.3

The Abuse of Power

We often read in the press and hear talk in the media of the 'abuse of power'. Whether it refers to corruption to gain access to limited resources, to the use of political influence to escape from prosecution, or perhaps to change the rules of government in such a way as to benefit the political elites, the abuse of power has a long history. Montesquieu argued in *The Spirit of the Laws* that the separation of powers, dividing the executive from the legislative from the judicial branch of government, was the only certain defence against the abuse of power stemming from the concentration of control in the hands of a small group of actors. But even with the separation of powers we can see how those in positions of power abuse their privileged status. There are countless examples of political appointees who received their post in exchange for supporting the governing party or making significant financial contributions to electoral campaigns.

knowledge-based, social, and patronage sources. Power can be exercised by a wide range of political, economic, religious, and social actors. But if we want to define power at its most basic level, we can say that it is the ability of an actor to achieve the goals that he or she sets for themselves. In international relations, Susan Strange usefully distinguished between *relational power* (that is, the ability of actor A to get actor B to do something that actor B would not otherwise do) from *structural power* (the ability to change and modify the political, social, and legal environment within which other actors have to operate).

We must also distinguish between *hard power* and *soft power*.[13] Hard power refers to the ability to provide incentives and punishments (carrots and sticks) to others in order to achieve the desired outcomes, whereas soft power relies on less tangible factors such as ideology, ideas, culture, and media. In international relations this distinction has become especially important when referring to the power resources of middle powers (neither the most powerful nor the weakest countries in the system) such as Canada, which find their hard power resources (such as military or economic power) limited but enjoy prestige and high standing in the eyes of other states due to their status as ethical states that behave as good international citizens through their contributions to peacekeeping, human rights, and multilateral institutions.

Whether at the level of the individual, the group, the state, or at the level of the international system, the pursuit of power is a fundamental facet of politics. It is also considered to be a rational form of behaviour, as it enables the aforementioned actors to achieve the political, economic, and social goals they set for themselves.

Influence is closely related to the concept of power, since it refers to the effect that one person, or group of persons, has on another.[14] Like power, influence is also an operative concept because it represents the capability of actors to persuade others to do their will. Power and influence are often referred to in tandem by virtue of their logical connection: influence is most often used to procure power,

Influence
the ability to change behaviour in others without exerting direct power over them

and power is often an essential requirement for influence. Influence and persuasion are more difficult to quantify than most forms of power, but this does not mean that they are less important. Think of how important influence can or has been in your own life: the influence of other individuals, groups, or even ideas can change behaviour. In politics, influence matters because of the way that it can serve as a substitute or complement to power. It also gives us pause to remember that seemingly 'weak' actors in the system can still play a role and are worth studying as their ideas, knowledge, or culture may help to decide outcomes.

2.4

The Cult of Personality

Mary Evans Picture Library/Alexander Meledin

Joseph Stalin cemented his control over the Soviet state by using a propaganda machine to build up his cult of personality.

In many authoritarian or totalitarian regimes (for a full explanation of these terms see Chapter 4), legitimacy in the domestic political arena is increased by using propaganda and the mass media to develop a cult that venerates and worships the personality of the leader. In countries as diverse as Argentina, Zimbabwe, Italy, North Korea, Cambodia, and China, governments have encouraged the building up of myths surrounding the personality of political leaders. Joseph Stalin, for example, as leader of the Soviet Union from 1924 to 1953, used all means available to him to establish himself as an unchallengeable authority in the Soviet political system. His happiness and well-being were equated with those of the country as a whole, and he was credited with being the father of the nation, an unusually talented strategist and ultimately infallible.

Stalin's example has been echoed in more recent times by North Korea's leader Kim Jong-Il. Known to his people as the 'Dear Leader', Kim Jong-Il is credited not only with being the supreme leader of the nation, but also as the source of all happiness and good things.

Authority
the power or right to force obedience

Authority is essential in understanding the use of power in a political system. Authority basically refers to the 'right' of a group of persons to exercise procedures that are required to regulate the community.[15] Authority involves the granting of rights and responsibilities from the public to particular individuals and groups that undertake to govern the political unit. Because it is impossible for every member of a political system to govern themselves directly, individuals and groups are chosen to represent the interests of the broader community in order to administer the activities and affairs of the system. Max Weber's classic typology of authority identified three different forms: traditional, rational-legal, and charismatic. *Traditional authority* refers to the authority of actors whose legitimacy derives from the fact that their power is passed down from one generation to the next, either within a family or within a larger social group. *Rational-legal authority* is most common in modern states and societies and derives from the existence of and respect for a set of accepted laws, norms, and rules. Lastly, Weber points to *charismatic authority*, where the recognition of the right to rule derives from specific qualities of the person concerned. In some cases, a mixture of two or maybe even all three of these different types of authority may be present in a leader.[16]

Leadership
group of individuals that lead society

Leadership is a concept that plays an important everyday role in politics.[17] Despite the existence of well-formed, solid institutions, and though a political system may be highly democratic, strong or weak leadership on the part of individuals or groups may determine the capacity of the system and society to advance, resolve pressing problems, and overcome political stalemate. Leadership may, or may not, be associated with power. Influence often plays a crucial role in deciding leadership, and this is one of the factors that help to make leadership a quality and concept that is difficult to quantify.

Legitimacy
what is lawful, appropriate, proper, and conforms to the standards of a political system

Legitimacy is integral to the notion of authority.[18] Legitimacy refers to the belief of a political community that those who are in authority are there for justifiable and worthy reasons. 'Certification' of a rightful mode of governance, then, is transferred from the constituency to political authorities through the granting of the 'right to rule'. For instance, in most democratic states, such as Canada, the legitimacy to rule is granted when individuals elect politicians to act on their behalf in the greater interest of the political unit. But, as we noted above, legitimacy can derive from other, less rational factors. For example, the legitimacy of the kings and queens of European states for many centuries derived from their bloodline or their family ties. Even today in Canada, we have a monarch who claims legitimate rule over the country because of her connection by birth to a line of monarchs in the British Isles before her. It is important to remember that legitimacy can be gained, but that it must be maintained and it can also be lost, and once lost it is very difficult to regain. In the modern world, political (as opposed to religious or moral) legitimacy depends upon a number of factors, including the capacity to deliver public goods and guarantee basic safety, freedoms, and standard of living to the majority in society. Any political authority that fails to do that will lose legitimacy and risks being turned out of office.

The link connecting power, authority, and legitimacy is an intriguing one, and has been a subject for theoretical and philosophical inquiry for centuries. For political authority must exercise power in order to establish its primacy and to

2.5

Charismatic Leadership

Former US president Bill Clinton is renowned for his charm and charisma and for using them to achieve political goals.

We have already discussed the phenomenon of the cult of personality in politics. Closely connected with that is the notion of charisma, and the highly particular way in which some leaders are able to gain the support of others and exercise influence by means of their personality. Identified by Weber as one of the three forms of authority, charismatic leadership is exhibited by those individuals who display extraordinary and exceptional qualities. Sometimes this has to do with intelligence; in other cases it concerns a more complex mix of physical attractiveness, wit, and achievement. An example is former US president Bill Clinton, widely recognized as one of the most charismatic leaders in United States history.

But there are other examples that are more puzzling. Adolf Hitler, for example, someone almost universally recognized as evil and responsible for some of the most heinous crimes against humanity, was also seen by the German people in the 1930s and 1940s as a very charismatic personality. His passion, his oratory, and his background as a proto-revolutionary gave him a standing with the masses in Germany that helped him to win and maintain power.

rule; but it must exercise that power in an acceptable way to maintain its legitimacy. If the authority loses legitimacy, then it risks losing power too, or must rule through coercion and imposition in an *authoritarian* fashion. We might therefore posit that political authority, to maintain its legitimacy, must focus not only on the exercise of power, but also on the legitimate exercise of power to maintain the support of the society it aims to rule.

Laws are rules that are customarily enacted in societies to prohibit or promote certain activities. Furthermore, laws are enforced with the imposition or threat of punishment by organized authorities in society. Laws are, simply put, a regulatory mechanism within political systems, but are not the only forms of routine activity. Norms, beliefs, customs, and ideas, for instance, also shape behaviour within political units, but none share with laws the punitive dimension — imprisonment, fines, and the like. Laws do not, however, only proscribe behaviour and prescribe punishments. They can also be used to provide incentives and encourage certain types of behaviour.

A special kind of law is known as **legislation**. Also known as *statutory law*, this is law that is passed by the *legislative branch of government*, or in Canada's case, by the Parliament. Legislation is one of the most obvious manifestations of governmental power and activity, and occupies much of the government's time and efforts. In Canada, legislation that is enacted by the legislative branch is known as an Act of Parliament. The executive branch of government, however, in order to be effective, must implement legislation, and this is where the government bureaucracy becomes crucially important.

Connected to, but different from, legislation is the concept of **policy**. Public authorities, private corporations or social groups, or even individuals can make policy. In this book we will be referring primarily to government policy, but in everyday discourse you will hear diverse actors talking about their 'policy'. A policy is simply a coordinated plan of action designed to achieve a predetermined set of goals. Its link to legislation is that governments will probably seek to enact legislation as part of their policy, but will use a whole range of other political actions as well, including special appointments, media campaigns, and even diplomacy. Policy, therefore, is an integral aspect of government activity, and in some ways we can judge governments by the direction, strength, and success of their policies.

There remains one fundamental set of concepts that in many ways drive and underlie the concepts described and explained above. Values are the ideas that we hold most dear in our political, social, and personal lives, and the hierarchy of these values in society will be crucial in explaining why one particular political reality dominates over other possibilities.

Values

As a method of establishing the relationship amongst members of a social unit, political analysis is very much concerned with the quality of life.[19] We know that we need one another to live and prosper, but we do not always find our current

Laws
rules imposed on society by the governing authority

Legislation
laws enacted by governing authority

Policy
laws or principle of performance adopted by a government

human situation entirely satisfactory. In response to the desire to achieve a better life, questions arise about how political authorities maintain and oversee the distribution of public benefits, as well as opportunities. The preference given to certain values over others, therefore, is a basic question of political studies.

One of the most commonly discussed values in politics is that of **equality**. However, though it is customary to refer to the 'equality' of humans, if we were to carefully study the differences among individuals, as well as the level of opportunities and benefits that are available to them, our notion of equality as 'parity' in a political system would be challenged. Put simply, in the real world, all persons have different qualities and strengths, and those features translate into different levels of benefits, based along distinctive areas of interest. We should be careful, then, to distinguish between different kinds of equality. *Political equality*, for instance, refers to the right to participate in the political activities of one's society and to be treated evenly by it. *Social equality*, on the other hand, indicates the equal status given to everyone's basic characteristics and needs as part of a larger social conglomerate. And *economic equality* refers to the approximate equivalent distribution of benefits accrued from the exchange of goods and services.[20] It is important to bear in mind that equality, in all these senses, designates an attempt to provide parity of opportunity to all these public goods. Furthermore, equality is directly related to freedom since individuals and groups must be allowed to seek out social benefits for true equality to exist.

The concept of equality has been fundamental to the development of political ideas in the Western world since the work of the modern political philosophers, such as Thomas Hobbes and John Locke. The ancient Greek theorists, such as Plato and Aristotle, refused to accept the equality of human individuals, seeing the differences between them as more important. This is, of course, just one definition of equality: that humans are equal in terms of their capacities, both physical and mental. Hobbes and Locke changed our understanding of the word, so that it came to be seen in terms of deserving equal consideration or treatment. This is political equality. The justifications for this kind of equality are varied. Hobbes claimed that no individual was so far superior to others in terms of capacities as to be invulnerable to them, or able to permanently subdue them. Locke, on the other hand, claimed that human equality stemmed from the fact that all humans were equal inheritors of the earth.

It is important to note here that Locke based his understanding of equality in the idea that human beings inherited the earth from God, and therefore our equal rights can be traced back to a fundamentally religious origin. For those people who do not believe in the existence of a divine supreme being, we need to come up with some other justification for our belief in human equality. Do we return to Hobbes's ideas that equality stems from the essential vulnerability of all humans? Or should we look instead to those philosophers such as John Rawls, who in his 1971 work *A Theory of Justice* argued that all rational humans would choose an initial preference for equality if they were unsure of the opportunities that would be extended to them in life?

By the second half of the twentieth century it had become a standard idea in Western political philosophy that individuals should be treated equally, regardless

Equality
'parity' in a political system

of their physical strength, wealth, race, or beliefs. This does not, of course, translate into equality of wealth, political influence, or opportunity. Though this may seem the logical conclusion to be reached from a starting position of equality, most philosophers have developed schemes of thought in which high degrees of economic and political inequality are justified. Locke, for example, allowed for an economic system of unequal appropriation despite his insistence on individuals' fundamental equality. Adam Smith relied on a premise of equality to justify the free market system, insisting that such economic relations would help to reinforce equality.

From the basic concept of equality we can see many important consequences for the real world of politics. Racial equality, of course, stresses the equal treatment of individuals from all racial backgrounds. Gender equality is a term that you may already have come across, which emphasizes the equal treatment of masculine and feminine genders. Though political philosophers in the past wrote of the equality of all humans, they generally referred to one-half of the human family, men. Since the suffragette movement of the early 1900s, and with the rise of *feminism* as a political and social movement in the 1960s demanding gender equality in terms of pay and opportunities, this irrational imbalance has been redressed in political philosophy. [21] The rise of feminism, as well as demands for equal treatment for racial minorities, show the continuing importance of the value of equality for both political theory and political practice.

Social order

recognized structure of power, responsibility, and liberty

Social order is one of the values in political philosophy that is both necessary to secure other values, but that also may contradict those values.[22] We can understand order as the absence of chaos and the presence of a recognized structure of power, responsibility, and liberty. Although to Canadian students of politics in the twenty-first century this value may be taken for granted, to many people in the world today, and certainly to the political philosophers of earlier times, it was one that was far from assured. Much political philosophy has been written at times of upheaval or turmoil in human society, and, while many welcomed that change, to others it threatened to replace established political, social, and economic structures with little more than chaotic anarchy. To Thomas Hobbes, this was the fundamental issue in political philosophy. He sought to establish the conditions by which human individuals would be protected from the ravages of civil war, which would render life 'solitary, poor, nasty, brutish, and short'. Only with order assured would there be the possibility of human progress in other areas such as industry, agriculture, or the arts. As will be seen in the examinations of political ideologies that follows in Chapter 3, order is a value of primary importance for the ideologies of *conservatism* and *fascism*.[23]

Security

freedom from danger or injury

Security may also be a primary value for individuals and groups in society, depending on the political, economic, and social climate.[24] Closely related to order, security is a value that we tend to take for granted when we have it, and only realize its importance when we lose it, or find it threatened. In the United States, in the period leading up to the terrorist attacks of 9/11, security was not an issue that gave the majority pause to think. After 9/11, however, security rose to the top of the political agenda, and was recognized by most people as a priority for government. In many countries of Latin America, including Brazil and Mexico,

Violence and Crime in Canada

Canada has a reputation for being a peaceful, safe country in which violence is not widespread and in which citizens feel secure. Comparisons are often drawn with the high levels of violence and crime in the United States, and Canadians are proud of their country's peaceful society. Nonetheless, it would be wrong to assume that Canada is without problems in this regard. Newspaper headlines constantly remind us of a growing problem of gun-related crime, particularly in cities, and of rising levels of violence, especially in more economically depressed areas. A ranking undertaken by *Maclean's* magazine in 2008, using statistics from 2006, showed that although Canada's murder rate was dramatically lower than that of the US, on other types of crime on a per capita basis certain Canadian cities matched or surpassed their US counterparts. Interestingly, on a per capita basis, the cities with the highest levels of crime in Canada were not Toronto or Montreal but rather Regina and Saskatoon. In fact, the top nine most dangerous cities were identified as from the Prairies and Western Canada. This can be partly explained by the multiple social issues and the very real economic problems facing the populations of these cities.

the question of personal security has dominated political debates in recent years as levels of violence and kidnapping have soared.

Progress is spurred by the belief that a better society is possible through the nurturing and development of a state of affairs in order to improve conditions and advantages.[25] The 'belief' aspect of progress is significant, then, because at the core here is the confidence that the destination of a better life is obtainable. Belief in progress is basically optimistic, suggesting that betterment comes through the passage of time, and is buffered by scientific knowledge, which allows us increased control over our destiny and more understanding of the human condition. Inherent in progress is a recognizably elevated outlook on the world. This is in the tradition of liberal humanism, which regards all reform and social movement as part of the effort to release humans from the oppressive nature of superstition, and seeks to create an environment of controlled improvement. We have to be careful, though, when we talk about progress. Others could view what may seem as a step forward to us with suspicion and fear. For example, in the nineteenth century, European cultures firmly believed that they were bringing progress and enlightenment to Africa through colonization; we can now appreciate the costs of that. In the contemporary world, the replacement of traditional social and cultural arrangements by more 'modern' systems, an integral part of the process of globalization, may be seen by us as progress, but it is not without its negative aspects. Although we would not necessarily want to live in those more traditional societies, the disappearance of those societies often means the loss of cultures, languages, and social diversity that may have direct costs for the individuals in those societies, and unforeseen costs for us all in the long run. What's more, the link between progress, technology, and controlling our destiny

Progress
advancement in society towards a better and improved state of affairs; an integral element of liberal political theory

has become all the more complicated in recent decades with the rise of genetic engineering and biotechnology, which adds to the debate about what kind of progress we want for humanity.

Justice is an issue that is intractable in political life, since the 'many' will always be governed by the 'few'. The result of this is concern about the possibility of abuse in the political system. A 'just' system, then, is one where activities are sought in the interest of the community as a whole, and not simply the limited interests of the political governors. Justice ought not to be only in the interest of those in political power; it embodies the exercise of legal authority in the interests of the political community — the pursuit of the equitable and legitimate aspirations of the ruled.

There are three senses of justice that require discussion here. First, the concept of justice is most commonly associated with legal affairs. We say that a legal outcome is just if we believe that fairness has prevailed, that all relevant evidence has been taken into consideration, and that the individuals or groups concerned have received what they deserve. A modern Western legal system is considered just if every individual receives equal treatment in the eyes of the law, regardless of race, wealth, religion, or social position. In that sense, legal justice is closely associated with the value of equality.

However, the second meaning of justice, in its political and social sense, is something quite different. It has its roots in the political philosophy of the ancient Greeks and concerns not the legal relationships within society, but rather the structure of society itself. When we talk of **social justice** in contemporary political discourse we refer to the same issue: Upon which principles do we structure our society?

The most famous discussion of justice in this sense was written by Plato, who lived from 427–347 BCE in ancient Athens. Although his ideas on the division of responsibilities and duties in society seem alien to modern Western readers, Plato nonetheless put forward a convincing case as to why his model should be seen as being just. His idea was that it was fitting or appropriate for each individual to carry out the role in society to which he was best suited by his nature. Later philosophers, while developing markedly different models of justice, have continued to structure these models based on their understandings of what human nature is. Some, such as Hobbes and Locke, have chosen the concept of fundamental human equality, while others, such as Marx, have built on their understanding of humans as creative beings to develop their own particular concepts of justice.

Lastly, we often hear talk of **economic justice**. In this sense justice refers to the economic system in place in a country, region, or indeed globally. Again, economic justice can take on various meanings, based either on efficiency, equality, or equity: that is, the hierarchy of values chosen by the political authorities concerned. An idea that is commonly associated with economic justice is the notion of redistribution, which is taking economic resources from certain groups in society and redistributing them to others. Most often this refers to redistributing wealth from the rich to the poor, but it is possible for the opposite to happen. In many developing countries over the past fifty years there has been an ongoing redistribution of wealth from society to the ruling classes, often through corruption and exploitation. Karl

Justice
state of affairs involving the maintenance of what is morally right and fair

Social justice
an equitable distribution of goods and values in society

Economic justice
the redistribution of economic resources from certain groups in society to others

Marx held that capitalism was responsible for a redistribution of wealth that led to the increasing impoverishment of the masses and growing wealth for the capitalist classes. Such debates about economic systems, and the idea of economic justice, has been one of the most important political issues of the second half of the twentieth century, both nationally and globally.

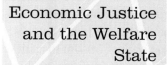

2.7

Economic Justice and the Welfare State

Popperfoto/Getty Images

Sir William Beveridge was the founder of the modern welfare state in Britain, arguing that it was necessary to fight the 'five giants': Want, Disease, Ignorance, Squalor, and Idleness.

The notion that a minimum standard of living should be provided for all citizens, regardless of their income, is well established in political theory. But it only became a reality in the second half of the twentieth century in most developed countries, and still has not been achieved in almost all developing states. Although examples of state-run pension plans occur throughout history, the origins of the modern welfare state are to be found in the 1942 Beveridge Report in the United Kingdom, in which Sir William Beveridge outlined the need for a comprehensive state program to address the terrible problems facing the poor in Britain in the 1940s. By providing adequate income, a national health service, a comprehensive education system, subsidized housing, and full employment, the state could overcome these problems. Beveridge's ideas resulted in the creation of the welfare state in the UK, a model that was copied in many other countries around the world.

Liberty
freedom from despotic control

Freedom
ability to act without constraint

Negative liberty
areas of activity in which governments do not interfere, where an individual is free to choose

Rights
socially acceptable, morally correct, just and fair privileges granted to members of a political community

Positive liberty
freedom to achieve one's full potential

Licence
unlimited freedom to do as one pleases

Duties
related to rights — responsibilities to protect rights

Liberty is one of the most important values in political studies and is often used interchangeably with the word **freedom**. In everyday usage we talk about the liberty to be able to do certain things, that is, in areas of action not prohibited by law. But liberty is a more complex concept in political studies. Isaiah Berlin identified two forms of liberty, one negative, and the other positive. It is important not to apply our preconceptions of what is positive and what is negative in this regard. Berlin talks of **negative liberty** as the kind of liberty central to the philosophies of Anglo-Saxon political thinkers, and indeed the kind of liberty that we most commonly refer to. The negative part of this term means the areas of activity in which governments *do not interfere*, where an individual is free to choose. An example of a negative liberty would be the liberty to choose one's lifestyle. It is obvious that this notion of liberty is closely associated with the idea of **rights**.

Positive liberty, on the other hand, is understood as the freedom to achieve one's full potential.[26] This is the kind of liberty included in the political philosophy of Jean-Jacques Rousseau. It involves being free from human desires and the destructive or divisive emotions that prevent human individuals and human society from reaching their true potential. This freedom from desires could take the form of developing beyond greed, racism, or laziness, or it could involve being provided with the economic means to be able to escape such feelings. This kind of liberty reserves a significant area of activity for the state, to restrain or re-educate, or to engage in programs of redistribution, so that individuals can be free from their own harmful impulses or have the economic means to be able to fulfill their potential.

The two forms of liberty explained above seem to be diametrically opposed: it would be impossible to maximize positive liberty while at the same time maximizing negative liberty. However, it is not difficult to find many examples of both the negative and positive forms in contemporary Western society. Many societies, for example, hold the freedom of expression (a negative liberty) as sacred, while at the same time promoting programs of positive discrimination (positive liberty) in the workplace. Governments defend the right to privacy while at the same time using progressive taxation systems to fund health care and welfare systems. In fact, economic redistribution and the welfare state are the clearest examples we have of positive liberty.

One last point needs to be made about liberty. The modern political philosophers such as Locke made a distinction between liberty and **licence**.[27] Liberty concerns personal freedom but it is not unlimited, whereas licence suggests unlimited freedom to do as one pleases. To exercise liberty an individual must not compromise the liberty or rights of others. Clearly, liberty carries with it responsibilities and, some have argued, **duties**.[28]

The concept of rights, as mentioned earlier in this chapter, is intimately linked to the concept of liberty. Moreover, it is a concept that is commonly used in everyday political, legal, social, and economic discourse.[29] We hear criminal suspects on television shows claiming that they 'know their rights' and that they have a 'right to a fair trial'. All adults over the age of 18 in Canada claim the 'right to vote'. United States citizens claim a 'right to free speech'. But what are rights? How do we know that they exist?

The first thing to point out is that rights can take different forms. There are civil rights as well as human rights. Civil rights are defined particularly, depending on the political and legal system concerned. Human rights, on the other hand, are considered to be universal, inalienable (that is, they cannot be given up or transferred), and are generally held to be the most precious and basic of human assets. Nonetheless, it would be difficult to say that any rights are absolute or predetermined. Rights are defined differently in different times and places. They are essentially creations of a particular political system and age. The universal right to be free from slavery, for example, is a relatively new invention, a right that took shape over the course of the nineteenth century and was finally enshrined in the United Nations Universal Declaration of Human Rights. The right to vote only became universal in Western political systems in the twentieth century; until the 1930s most countries continued to deny women the right to vote.

Thus, rights are intimately linked to politics. It was this realization that brought the nineteenth-century English philosopher Jeremy Bentham to claim that rights were 'nonsense on stilts', that is, a meaningless idea elevated so that it appears much more important than it really is. It would be difficult to publicly defend such a position today, but this shows that no matter how universal we consider rights to be, they are nonetheless temporal. It is only if we believe that rights are given by a deity or nature that they take on a universal and eternal character.

Something also must be said about the matter of duties. Philosophies that focus on individual rights have been criticized as being atomistic, based on selfishness and destructive of the idea of community. A focus on the individual, it has been said, ignores another more important aspect of human life, namely that we are social animals. One response to this criticism is that rights are but one side of a delicate balance in political life; along with the possession of rights goes the need for duties. It can be said that duties are the corollary of rights. Whenever an individual or group holds a right to a particular freedom or resource, there exists a concomitant duty on the part of someone else to provide or protect that right. But the relationship between rights and duties is more complex than this simple equation. It has been argued that possessing rights in society carries with it a duty to respect others' rights and also to contribute in some form, economic, cultural, or functional, to society as a whole. By stressing that individual duties are inextricably linked to individual rights, it is possible to maintain a healthy respect for the individual, as well as an emphasis on human community. Duties in the contemporary world range from paying taxes, to respecting the law, to the military draft in times of war.

As noted earlier in this chapter, many political philosophers have focused not on the importance of the individual, but rather on the social nature of human beings. To philosophers such as Plato and Rousseau, the individual was less than human when separated from a society and community. To such philosophers a political system should be so structured as to preserve, protect, and nourish the needs of the community ahead of those of the individual. To put it in Rousseau's terms, the general will must come before any particular or private will. We will learn more about these philosophers and their ideas in the next chapter.

Community
social, political, cultural, and economic ties that bind individuals to one another

Related to this is the concept of **community**.[30] First of all we must say that it is more than just a collection of individuals; the whole is more than just the sum of its parts. Community consists of the social, political, cultural, and economic ties that bind individuals to one another. To some extent tradition plays an important role, though community can be preserved, or even extended, by changing established practices. Community is a context, an environment in which human individuals develop their particular talents, capabilities, and perhaps most importantly, their identities. Without that environment, human beings cannot develop their true potential, or even their very humanity. In those philosophies that emphasize the value of community, the values of duties and positive liberty play a central role.

2.8

Community and the Individual

One of the most important political questions in today's world is the relationship between the individual and the community. As you will see in the chapter that follows, liberal approaches to politics hold the individual as sacred, and work towards expanding the area of individual freedom. This, of course, impacts directly on our conceptions of society and community. What responsibilities does the individual human being have to the society in which he or she lives? To what extent does that individual depend upon society and community for his or her well-being? What, ultimately, is the link between rights and duties?

As noted elsewhere in this chapter, many believe that humans cannot be separated from the societies in which they exist, that 'being human' depends upon the families, groups, and nations in which we live. Certainly it is difficult to imagine life without the company of others. But where does our responsibility to the group as a whole begin and end? Should we be willing to sacrifice personal freedoms so that the lives of others are improved? Or should personal freedoms be held as sacred?

Identity

In an earlier section of this chapter we talked about national and regional identities. But identity has become an increasingly important concept in political studies in recent years in many more ways than that. Ask yourself the question, What is my identity? and you will find that you have multiple dimensions to your identity: you may be a woman, daughter, sister, student, Liberal, Canadian, environmentalist, and feminist, or you may be a man, son, brother, father, Italian-Canadian, athlete, hockey fan, and vegan.

We can distinguish between individual identity and group identity. Individual identity is what marks each of us as unique or different, whereas group identity is what ties us to others. Cultural or ethnic identity, for example, is important because it gives us an identity as part of a broader social group.

In political studies, the concept of identity has taken on greater importance in recent years because minority groups have asserted their desire to be recognized as both different and worthy of recognition as a distinctive groups within society. Leaders in this trend have been groups who identify themselves based on race, ethnicity, sexual orientation, gender, or religion.

However, in recent years the debate over identity has become more complex. Clearly, our identity is made up in part by our interactions with society, but we also have the right and the ability to define ourselves in the terms we see fit. Because of this, how one person defines him- or herself as a liberal may be very different from how another 'liberal' individual sees him- or herself. The same could apply to many different identities. This gets us into the debate between essentialism and non-essentialism, that is, whether there are absolute, fundamental traits that define us (as men, women, Canadians, liberals, conservatives) or whether the reality is much more diverse.

Conclusion

The purpose of this chapter was to acquaint you with some of the most important terms and concepts in political studies and to demonstrate the significance and relevance of these seemingly abstract terms for the real world of politics. This serves to initiate you into the specialized language of political studies, and to create a common language among you as a group of students, allowing you to enter into more fruitful debates and discussions. These concepts will be essential tools for you throughout this course and your continuing research in political studies, but do not think that they are only of relevance in the university setting. On the contrary, these terms will appear to you continuously in the real world, in the press, on television, and above all in parliamentary debates and political disputes.

Self-Assessment Questions

1. What is the relationship between rights and duties in your daily life? How does this relationship apply in the world of politics?
2. Should voting be considered a right, a privilege, or a duty?
3. Should society give more emphasis to freedom, equality, security, or some other value? How should these various values be balanced?
4. Research a particular government policy and find out what pieces of legislation have come out of it.
5. What is the difference between the state and the nation?
6. Should the individual come before the community or vice versa?
7. What should be the limits of state power?
8. When does the legitimacy of the state come into question?

Weblinks

Amnesty International
www.amnesty.org

Crime Reduction Canada
www.crimereductioncanada.com

Democracy Online Game
www.positech.co.uk/democracy/democracy1.
html

Democracy Watch Canada
www.dwatch.ca

Human Rights Watch
www.hrw.org

Department of Justice Canada
www.justice.gc.ca/eng/index.html

Universal Declaration of Human Rights
www.un.org/en/documents/udhr

Further Reading

Berlin, Isaiah. *Four Essays on Liberty*. New York: Oxford University Press, 1990.

Gaus, Gerald F. *Political Concepts and Political Theories*. Boulder, CO: Westview Press, 2000.

Gunther, Richard, José Ramón Montero, and Juan J. Linz, eds. *Political Parties: Old Concepts and New Challenges*. Oxford: Oxford University Press, 2002.

Heywood, Andrew. *Political Ideas and Concepts: An Introduction*. New York: St. Martin's Press, 1994.

Huntington, Samuel P. *Political Order in Changing Societies*. New Haven, CT: Yale University Press, 1968.

Inglehart, Ronald. *Human Values and Social Change: Findings from the Values Surveys*. Leiden and Boston: Brill, 2003.

Kenny, Michael. *The Politics of Identity: Liberal Political Theory and the Dilemmas of Difference*. Cambridge: Polity Press, 2004.

Keohane, Robert O., and Joseph S. Nye. *Power and Interdependence: World Politics in Transition*. 2nd ed. Cambridge: HarperCollins, 1989.

Lukes, Steven. *Power: A Radical View*. 2nd ed. Houndmills, UK: Palgrave Macmillan, in association with the British Sociological Association, 2005.

Migdal, Joel S. *State in Society: Studying How States and Societies Transform and Constitute One Another*. Cambridge: Cambridge University Press, 2001.

Miller, David. *Liberty*. New York: Oxford University Press, 1991.

Mingst, Karen A. *Essentials of International Relations*. 3rd ed. New York: W.W. Norton, 2004.

Putnam, Robert. *Bowling Alone: The Collapse and Revival of American Community*. New York: Simon & Schuster, 2000.

Richter, Melvin. *The History of Political and Social Concepts: A Critical Introduction*. Oxford: Oxford University Press, 1995.

CBC News Clips

Visit the companion website for *Politics: An Introduction* to listen to news clips from the CBC radio archives.

3 Political Thought, Philosophy, and Ideology

LEARNING OBJECTIVES

After reading this chapter, you will be able to:

❊ understand the importance and place of political philosophy and ideology

❊ explain the relationship between theory and reality in political studies

❊ identify the differences between the major political ideologies

❊ understand the history of the development of political thought

❊ identify many of the most important political philosophers of the past two and a half millennia.

Introduction

In this chapter we will discuss the importance of abstract political thinking and why it matters for our understanding of political life and activity in the real world. In doing so, we will cover the most important philosophies, ideologies, and thinkers of the last two and half thousand years. Understandably this means that we cannot go into great details of these philosophical figures and their ideas, but this chapter will serve as an introduction to the sub-field of political philosophy and hopefully will inspire you to engage in further research. It is important to remember that the ideas and systems of thought described in the pages that follow have had a huge impact on the development of political activity throughout history, and many are still relevant for discussions in both policy and academic circles in the twenty-first century.

The chapter begins with a discussion of what political philosophies and **ideologies** are, so that the reader will be able to determine the significance of the ideas that follow. There then follows a survey of the most important ideologies that the student of political studies will encounter, focusing on both their political and economic aspects. Lastly, the chapter discusses the relevance of ideas, philosophies, and ideologies for the everyday business of politics. Throughout the chapter, boxes are dedicated to individual political philosophers and thinkers, to help you to get an idea of their lives, contributions, and impact.

Ideology
set or system of ideas that form the basis of a political or economic system and provide guidance and direction for political leadership

What Is Political Philosophy?

Before addressing this fundamental issue, we must ask one other question, namely, What is **philosophy**? The word itself comes from the ancient Greek word *φιλοσοφαί (philosophia)*, meaning love of knowledge. There was, of course, philosophy before there was political philosophy, and it concerned investigations into the nature, or essence, of life and its constituent elements. The early philosophers of the Western World, such as Heraclitus and Pythagoras, conducted theoretical investigations into the nature of Nature itself. In that sense they conducted an early form of natural science, but one that relied less on practical tests than on mental gymnastics, the forming of ideas and connections between ideas. Philosophy is thus a search for understanding.

Political philosophy can be said to follow a similar logic. It is an inquiry into the nature of politics, one that seeks understanding of things political. It is an endeavour to understand the nature of political life, not just at a given time or place, but across the spectrum of human experience. We must be careful here. Political philosophy is not so much a form of inquiry that attempts to understand the *mechanics* of politics and political systems as it is one that represents a creative process of analyzing what happens in the world of politics and attempts to construct modes of improving that world. In this way, political philosophy seeks to understand more than just the nature of politics. In addition, political philosophers attempt to explain the *significance* of political phenomena in order to improve our understanding of politics and to better design solutions for the problems that mark human life and society.

This implies, quite correctly, that there is a definite and inescapable link between political philosophy and the real world of politics. This link is two-dimensional. First, political philosophy must have some root in the realities of politics, social interaction, human nature, and ultimately Nature itself. If this link is somehow lost, the work of philosophers will be useless, for their ideas would be too far removed from the real world, and will probably be meaningless as well. Thomas Hobbes, for example, whose ideas are examined later in this chapter, related his political philosophy to his understanding of human nature, in both its physical and psychological meanings. He saw humans as selfish, aggressive, often violent individuals. Jean-Jacques Rousseau, on the other hand, held a very different conception of human nature, one that viewed humans as being essentially peaceful, sentient creatures; he therefore produced a body of theory that stands in stark contrast to Hobbes's work. What's more, political philosophies are shaped by the times in which they are created. Plato's concerns for a declining Athenian city-state, Hobbes's desire to see an end to the social and political chaos of the English civil war, and Marx's reaction to the horrors of capitalism in nineteenth-century England — each shaped their analysis of the nature of politics and of human society.

Yet political philosophy is much more than an exercise in studying political and social realities. It is linked to the real world in another, more creative and timeless fashion. For political philosophy not only tells us *what is*, but also *what ought to be*. This is not merely a **Utopian** enterprise that seeks to create a perfect world.[1] Rather, because of its basis in the perceived realities of human nature

Philosophy
study of questions about existence and knowledge, ethics, justice, and morality based on logical reasoning rather than empirical methods

Utopian
idealized place or system, an ideally perfect society; individual or approach aspiring to impractical perfection

and society, political philosophy seeks to define the political conditions that will create the best *possible* society. There are many examples of this kind of endeavour in the history of political philosophy, from Plato's *Republic* to John Rawls's *A Theory of Justice*. Each examines the basic conditions surrounding human life and seeks to correct the failings of the real world by designing specific political structures. An excellent example is the political and economic theory of Karl Marx. He based his ideas for the improvement of society directly on his analysis of the social, political, and economic conditions that have prevailed throughout history. In fact, it would be more accurate to say that his understanding of the relationship between economics and politics is one that determines the political and economic system that he proposes as a solution to the problems facing nineteenth-century capitalist society.[2]

The History of Political Thought

It is important that we recognize that the history of political philosophy is a long one, going back several thousand years. In this sense, political philosophy really can be seen as a debate across the ages, and across cultures and geographic space. This view reinforces the idea that political philosophy is really about timeless questions concerning political life. Whereas such political inquiry took place across the world — and the Chinese and Islamic branches of political philosophy are fascinating for their differences and similarities to the West — this chapter focuses mainly on the history of Western philosophy. That history begins with the classical philosophers of ancient Greece, philosophers such as Plato and Aristotle. Their work, and that of their fellow philosophers, investigating the nature of politics, political life, and good government, created the bases for future inquiry and set the tone for the kind of questioning that would mark Western political philosophy for the next two thousand years or more. Essentially, the Greeks asked simple questions about politics that have produced incredibly complex and diverse answers. Questions about justice, stability, and the relationship between individuals and the state have always featured strongly.

After the classical period, we move on to the medieval political philosophers. During this time, political inquiry in the Western world was driven by questions concerning the relationship between political life and Christianity. Best exemplified by the thought of Thomas Aquinas, medieval political philosophy placed the requirements of theology above the requirements of human needs. However, Aquinas made two major contributions. First, he introduced the medieval Christian world to the thought of Aristotle (that had for a long time been lost and preserved only in the Muslim world), and second, he sought to bring Christianity and politics into harmony. His 'scholastic' method, using deductive reasoning, was copied by political philosophers for centuries after.

Modern political philosophy can be said to begin with the work of the Renaissance thinkers, such as Niccolò Machiavelli, who applied a purely secular, non-religious approach to politics. By examining the nature and use of political power, Machiavelli opened the way for other thinkers, such as Thomas Hobbes,

3.1

Plato
(427–347 BCE)

Plato's ideas about the role of government and the good society are still debated today.

The city-state of ancient Athens was a highly developed society that generated great advances not only in the areas of the arts and sciences, but also in political and social thought. Plato, a teacher in the city's academy, was the first thinker to write down his thoughts on politics and philosophy in a comprehensive fashion. He wrote his most famous work, *The Republic*, in the form of a narrative between his teacher, Socrates, and other prominent Athenians. This means that we are unable to decide whether the ideas conveyed in this book are those of Plato or his master. Either way, *The Republic* exists as both a work of philosophy and a record of the debates about the political future of ancient Athens. However, as some have put it, *The Republic* is a 'city in speech' and serves as an ideal type that can be juxtaposed with reality. It is also a work of political philosophy that transcends the particular circumstances of time and place.

The Republic is a book about justice, but justice in its broadest, most philosophical sense of 'what is right'. Plato proposes social and political justice through a state organized according to individuals' capabilities and personalities. Those who are naturally equipped to be strong and courageous should engage in militaristic functions; those who excel at an art or craft should devote themselves to such activities. Most importantly, however, those individuals who are best equipped to be philosophical should become the rulers of the state, for they best understand the idea of justice. The image of Plato's *Republic* is of a rather repressive, controlling state, one that does not allow for much personal freedom, and is unappealing to contemporary students of politics. Yet it would be wrong to judge it by today's standards. Plato was attempting to find permanent solutions to the problem of political order, and his proposal is an ideal, probably unachievable, form of political organization. Yet in outlining such an ideal, Plato gives us the first offering in a debate about the just or good state that continues to the present day.

to examine the basis of power and its use to create a stable form of government. Following on from these thinkers came a number of philosophers who focused on the question of rights and liberty, and founded the liberal branch of political theory. The influence of thinkers such as John Locke and Jean-Jacques Rousseau is remarkable: their ideas are still quoted in political debates today.

The modern era extended up until the early twentieth century, and incorporated the ideas and philosophies of Adam Smith, John Stuart Mill, and Karl Marx. These thinkers show the variety and diversity of political philosophy in the modern period, defending and critiquing capitalism, arguing for liberty and tolerance, and proposing alternative modes of production and government.

In the twentieth century, the contemporary period of political philosophy began. Again we see huge diversity. The work of thinkers such as John Rawls and Robert Nozick reflected many of the classic questions of political philosophy concerning good government and the community, whereas the post-modern movement in political thought has focused on a more critical approach to philosophy, questioning the origins of our ideas and beliefs, and arguing for a more 'social constructivist' understanding of politics. **Social constructivism** argues that values and beliefs are the result of particular social relations, processes, and realities, and therefore it is difficult, if not impossible, to establish any objective concept of what is good or just. Constructivism as both a philosophical approach and way of understanding political life has acquired great importance in recent years in political studies.

Social constructivism
a sociological and political meta-theory that explains the interactions between individual agents, their social groupings, and their environment

How does political philosophy proceed, or, to put it another way, how is it done? Essentially, political philosophy concerns the asking of questions, and the proposing of answers to those questions. The questions are perennial. What is human nature? Should the community come before the individual? What is the extent of my liberty as an individual in human society? When is a government action legitimate? What would life be like in the absence of government? How can we justly divide the product of a society? The answers to these questions, however, are temporal and particular to each philosopher. The answer proposed by Rousseau, for example, to the question of what the importance of the individual is vis-à-vis the community, is very different from that put forward by Locke. The former emphasizes the political community as an organic body that takes precedence over the individual, while the latter focuses on the importance of individual liberty.

It has been quite accurately claimed that political philosophy constitutes a quest for the good life, the good society, and, of particular importance, for the *just* society. Social justice is an ever-recurring theme throughout the history of political philosophy, but its meaning and its form change from philosopher to philosopher. As can be seen from the studies that are included in this chapter, the Platonic or Socratic conception of justice is difficult to relate to the formulation of the same concept in Rousseau, just as Marx's conception of justice is wildly different from that of John Locke. This tells us that, to a large degree, these conceptions of justice depend upon the social, economic, and political conditions of their time, and thus can be seen as socially constructed.

Although the norms established by political philosophers depend upon their own societies, their own knowledge, and to a certain extent their own personal experiences, and although the idea of what is just varies from century to century, and from philosopher to philosopher, it remains the goal of political philosophy up to the present time. As noted above, political philosophy is not merely a descriptive exercise; rather it is an attempt to establish norms, that is, rules or ideals for political behaviour and political reality. It is intriguing to examine what different philosophers at different stages of history in very different societies have established as their preferred definition of the just society, and may well help us to put our own conceptions in the proper context. For philosophy is a universalist and timeless exercise, a dialogue across time that helps us to examine our own ideas and preconceptions in a broader context.

One reason for the (often wide) variations in the conception of the just society is that different philosophers have placed different emphases on different moral and political values. To some, such as Hobbes, the idea of social order is paramount. To others, such as Locke, the concept of **liberty**, formulated

Liberty
freedom from despotic control

3.2

Aristotle
(384–322 BC)

Aristotle was the intellectual inheritor of Plato's philosophy, yet his work is quite different. A student of Plato, Aristotle was concerned less with proposing an ideal state than with the practical application of philosophy to the problems of everyday politics. In this way we can say that Aristotle was a philosopher who believed in the politics of the possible. In addition, Aristotle can be seen as the founder of the study of politics in a scientific way, for a large part of his work is concerned with classifying and rating different political systems, trying to determine the best possible organization of the state.

However, though Aristotle's approach to political philosophy is very practical and scientific, it also seeks to establish a link between ethics and politics, to seek the 'good'. Aristotle's two most famous works, *The Nicomachean Ethics* and *The Politics*, examine the two areas separately, but there is little doubt that there is an inescapable link for him. Indeed, the only difference between ethics and politics for Aristotle is that ethics concerns what is right and good for the individual, whereas politics concerns what is right and good for the community. Aristotle had a clear idea that the needs of the community came before those of the individual, and for him the height of rational behaviour was public action, or participation in the running of the city-state. What is more, a good individual can only prosper in a good community, and therefore politics, for Aristotle, is fundamental to ethics, and vice versa. Although Aristotle favoured 'aristocracy' — a city-state ruled by a select group of men who dedicate themselves to the good life both for themselves and the city — he argued that in the real world it would face problems; he supported a system of mixed government, combining elements of aristocracy, monarchy, and democracy.

It is worthwhile pointing out that Aristotle explicitly recognized the importance of economics in the organization of political systems. A 'good' economic system must allow individuals to acquire wealth, for this is a natural inclination in humans; they seek wealth because it allows them, in turn, to acquire goods that satisfy their natural needs and desires.

Authority
the power or right to force obedience

as freedom from interference by **authority**, receives the most attention, though not to the neglect of equality. For Rousseau, liberty is again fundamental, yet he defines that liberty less as freedom from interference, and more as freedom from human passions and desires. For some philosophers, individualism and preserving individual liberties is central; for others, humans are incomprehensible apart from their social setting, and this understanding of humans as social animals guides them towards philosophies that emphasize the general over the particular or private good. It is important to note that most of the influential political philosophers over the centuries have recognized the importance of more than one value; what is key in determining the political systems they outline is the priority that each gives to a series of values. Is equality the most important value to be respected by society? Or should equality be accorded an inferior position to order in the hierarchy of values?

The differences between value hierarchies, and thus between political philosophies, have created a philosophical debate or discourse that stretches across not just geographical space, but time as well. Though it should not be thought that Hobbes was directly responding to Plato's ideas when he wrote *Leviathan*, he was joining in a dialogue about political ideas in which Plato too had participated. The existence of these contrasting and sometimes conflicting philosophies creates the possibility for comparison and indeed cross-fertilization of ideas for the student of political studies. It is this discourse that makes the study of political philosophies so challenging and at the same time rewarding: to view the collected wisdom of history's most eminent political thinkers and to evaluate their ideas on the basis of social and political conditions, both when these ideas were transcribed and in the present day. Just as importantly, it is this discourse that makes political philosophy a living, vital, and central part of political studies. The discourse that continues across the centuries ensures that politics is an ever-changing, always fascinating area of study, and you are encouraged to join in this intergenerational, inter-societal conversation.

Political realism
an approach to politics that emphasizes power and interests over ideas or social constructions

3.3

Niccolò Machiavelli (1469–1527)

From Aristotle, through St. Augustine and the Christian political philosophers, there had been a perennial commitment to combining ethics and morality with politics. With the work of Niccolò Machiavelli, we see a dramatic break in that tradition. Machiavelli, who was intimately involved in the politics of the Italian city-states of the late fifteenth and early sixteenth centuries, put forward a new political philosophy based on political expediency, where ethics and ideals played a secondary role to the pursuit of power and control. This philosophy came to be called **political realism**, and it has been one of the most important theoretical and analytical approaches in the study of politics ever since.

It should not, of course, be thought that politics had never before been based on these principles — we know that governments have behaved in such a way since the time of the ancient Greeks, and probably earlier. However, Machiavelli

3.3 Continued...

was the first philosopher to explicitly defend them as a basis for sound government. As with most philosophers, Machiavelli's work can be understood and interpreted on two levels: one, an attempt to find solutions to the most important political problems of his time (in this case the internal divisions of the Italian city-states), and two, a prescription for political action that would provide for sound government regardless of time and place.

Machiavelli argued that there should be a definite separation of ideals and morality from politics. Politics should instead be guided by an examination of human behaviour. If governors, or Princes as Machiavelli prefers, understand human nature and behaviour, they will better be able to formulate policies to rule effectively and consolidate their power. He proposed that it is better for a Prince to be feared than loved by his people, though this must be achieved without inspiring popular hatred of the government. Machiavelli's approach to the study of politics can be seen as the beginning of modern political philosophy, and his contribution was soon added to by Thomas Hobbes.

Ideology

What constitutes an ideology? Essentially it is a set of related, generally consistent, ideas and beliefs that provides a basis for political action. Ideologies contain both descriptive and normative elements: that is, they contain interpretations of the world, and statements of how it should be. They reflect particular hierarchies of **values**, and help to shape people's perceptions and images of reality. One ideology might reflect an emphasis on the value of order over liberty, while another might emphasize the value of efficiency over **justice**. It is by examining the hierarchies of values embodied in ideologies that we can identify the differences between them, and also understand the impact they have on the world of politics.

Political (and economic) ideologies bear some resemblance to religions: they are more or less coherent belief systems (based on assumptions and preconceptions), can be proved neither wrong nor right (yet often contain normative judgments and assumptions), and provide a basis for human action. Ideologies, however, generally focus on the material and physical aspects of life, rather than the spiritual. However, religious inquiry was commonly also a concern for the political thinkers of Greece, Rome, and medieval Europe, and still finds some representation in political thought in contemporary Anglo-Saxon political systems. Although the word 'ideology' and the adjective 'ideological' have a negative connotation in today's world, ideologies are a fundamental aspect of political life because they frame the debates that dominate political and economic systems and guide political action, which in turn helps determine both political and economic reality (see the section on the relevance of ideas later in this chapter). Most importantly, ideologies often drive political action and can bring conflict, progress, repression, or transformation. This is what really distinguishes an ideology from political theory: though its major ideas may come from a particular

Values
principles, standards; what an individual or community esteems as meaningful

Justice
state of affairs involving the maintenance of what is morally right and fair

IMAGES

reflections and impressions of reality; not reality

↓

ATTITUDES

implicit assumptions regarding images

↓

VALUES

standardized normative views of the world

↓

BELIEFS

certainties and faith in values

↓

IDEOLOGY

sets of beliefs that prompt actors to maintain a political system

FIGURE 3.1

What Makes Up Ideologies?

branch of political theory, it is a call for action in the real world, rather than merely an inquiry into the way things are.

Because ideologies are sometimes, but not always, based on the philosophy and thought of groups of thinkers, they can be said to follow *schools* of thought. Ideologies are by their nature divisive phenomena, in large part because different ideologies contain markedly different ideas, perceptions of reality, and prescriptions for the just or best political system. It is common, therefore, for ideological conflict to either cause, or at the very least *colour*, many political debates and disputes. Ideologies, however, are not necessarily mutually exclusive. An individual, group, political party, or indeed a society can be both liberal and nationalist, as was the case of the United States during the Cold War. Similarly, a political grouping can combine nationalist economic policies with a socialist political plan of action. Ideologies are flexible things, often compromised with ideas taken from other ideologies and schools of thought. Furthermore, there is surprising variation to be found within ideologies; within one school of thought and ideas there can be individuals who appear to be completely opposed. More importantly, ideologies change over time and both affect and are affected by political, economic, and social realities. They are evolutionary; understanding the evolution of ideologies will in turn help us to understand progressive as well as revolutionary change in political systems.

Having distinguished between ideology and political philosophy, what follows is a treatment of different categories of political thought. It is by no means exhaustive but it does give the student of politics an introduction to the most significant political belief systems of modern times. Readers should take care to cross-reference these philosophies with the descriptions given of important political philosophers to learn more about their origins and broader implications.

Liberal Thought

Progress

advancement in society towards a better and improved state of affairs; an integral element of liberal political theory

Underlying both political and economic forms of liberal thought is an assumption that progress is possible and likely in human affairs.[3] **Progress**, of course, can mean many things to different people, but for liberals it implies an improvement of the human condition, materially, intellectually, or in terms of freedom. Thus it would be tempting to say that liberal thought is an optimistic system of political thought, one that expects progress to come, and also provides a political and economic program that should bring progress. However, it rests on an essentially

3.4

Thomas Hobbes (1588–1679)

© Alan King engraving/Alamy

Hobbes's idea of the state was one of a supreme authority that could protect and control all members of society.

Whereas Machiavelli brought to the study of politics a determination to see things as they really are, Thomas Hobbes developed both a scientific approach that was unrivalled in his time and a body of philosophy that addressed the most basic of political questions, namely, how to avoid civil strife and the breakdown of society. His most important work, *Leviathan*, remains an essential text for contemporary students of political philosophy.

Hobbes's overriding concern in his writings was to establish the theoretical foundations for strong and enduring government. This concern arose from the fact that he lived during the English Civil War and he believed that event to have resulted from a crisis of authority in the English political system. He compared the chaos of this period to an imaginary period in history before the creation of governments. This he called the state of nature, and he insisted it would be wholly unsuitable for human life. In essence it is a state of war of all against all, where there is no room for industry, agriculture, or the arts. Hobbes himself described it as a state in which life is 'solitary, poor, nasty, brutish, and short', and every human was at the mercy of others. Hobbes held firmly to the idea of the essential equality of human beings, in that none was so strong or clever that another could not kill him or her. The only way out of this terrible situation is the creation of a government, led by a sovereign, which would have almost unlimited power over its subjects. According to Hobbes, this would be the only way that peace would endure.

Though Hobbes granted his sovereign extreme rights, he also gave the office duties towards its subjects. Firstly, the sovereign must provide peace, and a system of law and order to maintain that peace, if individuals are to give up the freedom they

3.4 Continued...

possess in the state of nature and subject themselves to an overarching power. It is important to note that for Hobbes, human beings are fundamentally rational in their behaviour. However, Hobbes goes further than this, for the sovereign does not only provide peace, but must also provide for the basic necessities of the people. Hobbes is quite specific that if the sovereign does not guarantee a basic standard of living, he will be unable to rule. Hobbes is quite practical about this — unless the office of the sovereign takes care of its subjects, they are sure to rebel and there will be a return to the state of war. Hobbes's legacy was to show the importance of order before freedom, as the prerequisite for all other goods in society.

negative perception of human nature, namely, that human beings are selfish and need laws and rights to live together in harmony. One last general point about liberal thought: it is a diverse, often divergent, philosophy containing many different strands. Because of this, it is quite possible for two liberals to be opposed over seemingly fundamental issues. In the past hundred years or so, some of the most vehement ideological and political debates have taken place within the school of liberalism. As always in such cases, when two groups within the same school find themselves opposed to each other, the charge of 'ideological heresy' becomes common and the conflict is intensified.

Liberal political thought finds its roots in the philosophy of John Locke (see Box 3.5) but has evolved since the seventeenth century into a diverse branch of philosophy incorporating the ideas of many political thinkers. It is founded on the notion that the individual is the basic unit of human society and must be held sacred. The human individual is believed to be a rational, self-interested creature, whose desires and interests are of paramount importance. Individuals are to be held responsible for their own actions and deserving of merit for their own achievements. Society itself takes its nature from the way in which it protects and nurtures the individuals within.

Because of this focus on the individual, the values of liberty and rights are central to liberal thought because they are the means of protecting the individual from both the state and other individuals. State laws should be directed towards maximizing the self-determination of each individual, the only limit being that such self-determination does not inhibit the self-determination of others.[4] Equality is also fundamental to liberalism, but only in the sense of equality of liberty and rights, not equality of wealth or social status. In this regard, equality also concerns equality of opportunity: the opportunity to exercise preferences, but not equality of outcomes. This is of particular importance with regard to economic liberalism.

Here, however, it is important to identify two strands of liberalism, strands that are directly connected with the two meanings of liberty. Lockean or classical liberalism, based on the political philosophy of John Locke, emphasizes the idea of negative liberty, which is the freedom from interference by others or by political authorities. This strand has developed in Anglo-Saxon societies and is very much concerned with political rights. The second strand, that of reform

Rights
socially acceptable, morally correct, just and fair privileges granted to members of a political community

Self-determination
ability to act in free choice without external compulsion

Negative liberty
areas of activity in which governments *do not interfere*, where an individual is free to choose

3.5

John Locke
(1632–1704)

Just as Hobbes viewed the experience of the English Civil War as a crisis of authority, John Locke saw the same event as stemming from a lack of legitimacy on the part of the English monarchy. This perspective coloured Locke's approach to political philosophy, and we have come to associate him with a school of thought that demands legitimacy from government. In Locke lie the roots of modern liberalism, and the concept of consent is central.

In his most famous work, *Two Treatises of Government*, Locke's understanding of the state of nature was markedly different from that of Hobbes. Locke saw it as being more peaceful, but still inconvenient and certainly unproductive. His idea of human equality was also different from that of Hobbes, for he held it to be equality of right, not mere equality of vulnerability. How did human beings come to leave this state of equality and create civil societies? Locke's answer lay in the notion of consent, and he argued that for a political system to be legitimate, the consent of the governed must have been obtained, and must be maintained.

Locke also used consent as a key concept in explaining economic systems. Locke argued that all humans were equal inheritors of the earth, and therefore deserved equal access to its fruits and riches. How, then, did we reach a system of unequal acquisition and such great inequalities of wealth? He proposed that the original condition of equality was fundamentally inefficient; as time went on, and populations expanded, it made more sense to combine individual landholdings so that more efficient agricultural methods and economies of scale might be employed. However, in order for people to legitimately transfer their equal rights to access to the land, Locke supposed that they gave their consent. Being rational individuals, the only way in which they would give their consent would be if their condition were equal to or better after the transfer than before. So for Locke, unequal acquisition is only legitimate if the poor are better off than they would be if the transfer of their equal right to the earth had never taken place. The protection of their property, the rule of law, and good government are the focus of Locke's emphasis on what we would call negative liberty.

liberalism, carries with it the idea of **positive liberty** and an expanded role for state action. This branch of liberal thought developed much more strongly in continental Europe and finds its roots in the philosophy of Jean-Jacques Rousseau.[5]

Because the individual is sacred in both strands of liberalism, the idea of consent plays a very important role. Government is only seen as being legitimate if it carries out its functions with the consent of the governed. If a government has the consent of those it rules, the actions it takes will not violate their individual rights. If a government lacks the consent of the people, however, the actions it takes will be imposed and the principle of individual self-determination will have been contradicted. This establishes the idea of the contract in liberalism; that an implicit deal exists between individuals in society, and between them and the government. If either side violates that contract, then rights and privileges can be revoked.

Positive liberty
freedom to achieve one's full potential

3.6

Jean-Jacques Rousseau (1712–78)

Rousseau remains one of the most eccentric, unique figures in the history of political philosophy, and his work is markedly different from that of the English philosophers of the seventeenth and eighteenth centuries. Though Rousseau, too, used the notion of the state of nature as a beginning for his philosophy, his understanding is different from that of both Hobbes and Locke. In *The Second Discourse* (also known as *The Discourse on Inequality*) he described the state of nature as a state of perfection where humankind lived in harmony and peace with itself and nature. What ended that paradise, according to Rousseau, was the institution of private property, which brought with it inequality, conflict, and all the evils now known to humans. For with property came power, and humans began to dominate and subjugate one another.

Rousseau's description of the corruption of humankind is chilling, and we are tempted to think that he advocates a return to the idyllic state that preceded civilization. However, Rousseau believed that such a return was impossible; instead he proposed a new political system that establishes a compact between government and subjects. He outlined this system in *The Social Contract*, a work that sought to establish the basis for legitimate government, that is, one that does not contradict the will of its subjects. To achieve such harmony, Rousseau invented the concept of the **general will**. When humans create a civil society and establish a sovereign to rule over them, they must also establish laws that reflect the general will, that is, the will of the community as a whole. This should not be misinterpreted as an extreme form of democracy. In fact, Rousseau meant for the general will to reflect not just the will of the people but also their true interests, that is, what is good for them.

This leaves the door open for authoritarianism in Rousseau's political thought. Should an individual's **particular will** not be in harmony with the general will, the government would have the right to try to reform that person's will so that it came into line with the general. The greatest evil for Rousseau was when either a government refused to follow the general will, or when particular wills came to dominate the general will. To prevent the latter from happening, Rousseau proposed that individuals be educated to overcome their selfish desires, to free themselves from their passions. This notion is now known as positive liberty, that is, the freedom from our baser instincts.

General will
the will of the community as a whole

Particular will
the will of the individual, as expressed by Rousseau

It would be an ideal (and perhaps disturbing) world, though, if there were unanimous consent for every government policy or course of action. Under liberal thought, governments act on principles of majority consent, in varying forms. This suggests that a minority of subjects in the political system will not be able to fully exercise their right to self-determination. How does liberalism deal with this problem? First, it can be argued that as long as everyone has had the chance to express his or her preferences, then, under the principle of equality of opportunity (not equality of outcomes), justice has been served. Secondly, liberalism carries with it a commitment to the principle of tolerance. In liberal systems minorities are respected and protected and even encouraged. John Stuart Mill, for example, argued that the existence of minorities and diversity in human society was something that benefited everyone in that society.

The need for self-determination, consent, and tolerance has linked modern liberalism closely with democracy, although it is important to remember that the classical liberals were far from being democrats, either in theory or practice. Liberals such as Locke distrusted democracy and remained highly elitist. It was only in the nineteenth century that liberalism and democracy became linked. The form of **democracy** is crucial; pure democracy will threaten the tyranny of the masses, and the stifling of minorities.[6] What is needed is a form of democratic government in which minorities are allowed to flourish. Democracy is important for modern liberals because it is the process by which each individual exercises the right to self-determination, gives or denies consent to government, and allows for the representation of minority views. In essence it is where the contract between government and society is made explicit.

The economic form of liberalism stems from the political and also relies on the value of liberty. What's more, there is a strong sense of crossover between liberal political and economic theories. John Locke used his political theory as a defence of unequal or capitalist acquisition. Adam Smith, on the other hand, argued that market relations between individuals would serve to reinforce notions of equality and liberty. Beginning with Smith, liberal economic thought has been committed to free markets, that is, market economies with minimal state intervention. Because of this adherence to market economy, the economic form of liberalism is often referred to as **capitalism**, a system that rewards competitiveness and efficiency.[7] The market mechanism is held to be the most efficient way of organizing an economic system and of maximizing individual, as well as societal, welfare. As with liberalism's political form, human individuals are represented as self-interested creatures who seek personal gain. In addition, humans are by their nature economic, and have a natural tendency towards trade and exchange. Because of this, markets are seen as occurring naturally wherever human communities exist.

Once again the individual is liberalism's basic and most important unit. Individual property rights are seen as one of the most basic, property being an extension of the self. Individuals are rational utility-maximizers, which means that they seek to maximize their preferences. They will continue to do so until the cost of pursuing those preferences outweighs the benefit to be had from them.

The existence of selfish individuals, acting rationally in their own interests, serves to benefit not just themselves, but society as a whole. This principle of the harmony of interests is well established in liberal theory. Bernard de Mandeville first explicitly made references to the principle in his 1705 work *The Fable of the Bees, or Private Vices, Publick Benefits*. He argued that humans acting in their own interests are like bees gathering nectar. Each bee does so because it enjoys nectar, yet it also benefits the hive in general by bringing nectar back for the production of honey. If the bees become committed to the virtues of honesty and selfless behaviour, the hive will simply cease to function. He matched this to human society, arguing that through selfish behaviour by individuals, civilization advances. Adam Smith adapted the principle and called it the **invisible hand**.[8] Under market economics, self-interested individuals will maximize efficiency and economic growth over time as they engage in competition against each other. This will benefit society as a whole, though it is important to realize that the benefits will not be distributed equally, nor is it guaranteed that all individuals will benefit at all.

In the social sphere, liberalism is marked by a tolerance for different lifestyles, ethnic and racial diversity, and equal treatment for all. This reflects the ideas of John

Democracy
political system based on the principle that governance requires the assent of all citizens through participation in the electoral process, articulation of views, and direct or indirect representation in governing institutions

Capitalism
economic system where production and distribution of goods relies on private capital and investment

Invisible hand
Adam Smith's notion that economic forces left on their own would lead to maximize efficiency and economic growth over time as they engage in competition against each other; benefits to society as a whole exist without political interference

Stuart Mill, who established the notion that diversity in society, the existence of eccentrics, and non-interference from others in private lives was not only desirable, but also beneficial for human society. In some countries, this liberal approach to social values is highly controversial, despite the existence of liberal economic and political systems. In these countries, such as the United States of America, although the political and economic spheres tend towards liberalism, conservatism is common in the social sphere. Equally, we can find people who are socially liberal, but economically believe that the state should play a more interventionist role.

Communism

political theory, based on writings of Marx and Engels, that espouses class conflict to form a system where all property is publicly owned and each citizen works to his or her own best ability and is compensated equitably

Socialism

The roots of socialism as a political and economic system of thought are not quite as long as those of liberalism; nonetheless they extend back to the early nineteenth century.[9] Socialism emerged in France and Britain in the 1820s as a term favoured by the political movements of the Owenites in Britain and the Saint-Simonians and Fourierists in France.[10] Although the term communism, which has close links to socialism, appeared earlier (in the late eighteenth century), it

3.7

Adam Smith (1723–90)

In the mid-eighteenth century, Scotland produced a series of important political and economic thinkers in a movement known as the Scottish Enlightenment. Adam Smith emerged as the most famous of these and it is his influence, perhaps more than any other philosopher of his period, that is still keenly felt in contemporary political economy at the beginning of the twenty-first century. Smith incorporated a distinct economic thought into the liberalism of Locke, and introduced the doctrine of the free market into political economy.

Like the political philosophers who came before him, Smith had his own political program — he was determined to provide an ideological opposition to the doctrine of economic nationalism and particularly mercantilism, which he saw as both inefficient and conflict causing. In *The Wealth of Nations*, Smith saw market relations as working to the benefit of all people, because everyone would benefit from more efficient modes of production. Smith introduced the concept of the invisible hand, a force inherent in economic liberalism that would ensure progress for all without any conscious direction from government.

Yet Smith wrote not only of the economic advantages of market-based economics, but also of their political consequences. He argued that economic relationships based on contracts and bargains required that individuals see each other as essentially equal. Indeed, he credited market relations with ending the oppression of feudalism.

Smith believed strongly in the liberation of the economy from government interference. Furthermore he argued for free competition between firms, the free movement of goods in and out of countries, the free movement of workers, and the free movement of capital. All of this would lead to progress, which Smith defined as rising real per capita income. Adam Smith fundamentally altered the way we look at economics, and it is in his work that all liberal economists find their ideological roots.

3.8

John Stuart Mill
(1806–73)

One of the most important liberal thinkers of the nineteenth century, John Stuart Mill strongly influenced modern economics, politics, and philosophy. Mill was the son of James Mill (1773–1836), who with Jeremy Bentham (1748–1832) had founded **Utilitarianism**. Utilitarianism is a philosophy that seeks to maximize the pleasure, or utility, of individuals in society. Mill took the precepts of utilitarianism and adapted them to what he saw as the main challenges of nineteenth century British society. Of particular importance for this chapter and this book, Mill saw himself as a political economist, and sought to combine the lessons of both politics and economics to produce a version of social science that could be applied to policy at the local and national levels. Mill argued that the lessons of political economy should be used to improve society and the lives of individuals. His thought was deeply influenced by his wife, Harriet Taylor, and it is seen as a more humanitarian doctrine than that of his father and Bentham. He was sympathetic to the ideals of socialism, and was one of the first male proponents of women's rights. Among his works, *On Liberty* (1859) is his best-known book, but Mill's *Principles of Political Economy* (1848) and *Utilitarianism* (1863) marked him as a great political philosopher and political economist.

One of Mill's central preoccupations was with individuality. This led him to advocate **toleration** of eccentricities and unusual behaviour and practices, as long as such things did not interfere with the freedom or well-being of others. He saw that democracy was in danger of suppressing individuality as the masses dominated minorities, and that conformity would bring about a mediocre society. This attitude towards the individual informed Mill's opinions on political economy. Though agreeing with many of the principles of socialism, he argued that the state should limit its role in the economy to the distribution, not the production, of goods.

is appropriate to view communism as one form of socialism.[11] The same is true of Marxism, the sub-set of socialism that has been dominant in its history.

Socialism has provided the most important philosophical, political, and economic challenge to liberalism over the past one hundred and fifty years, and its principles are generally opposed in both political and economic realms to the liberal tradition. Although the great socialist experiments in the Soviet Union and other parts of the world failed, socialism as a system of political thought has evolved and become an important mainstream perspective. Indeed, the sheer ideological diversity of socialism is impressive. Utopian socialism, revolutionary socialism, reformist state socialism, ethical socialism, pluralist socialism, and market socialism have all figured as important sub-sets of socialist thought. What follows is a description of the most important political and economic elements that can be said to constitute the heart of socialist thought.

Each branch of socialism shares with the others a concern for human community and society and order over concerns about the individual and his or her rights. This can be seen in the origins of the word 'socialism' itself. The Latin roots of the word suggest community and companionship between human individuals.

Utilitarianism
a branch of political thought that states that the worth of a particular action is determined by its contribution to overall utility, meaning the balance of happiness and unhappiness in society

Toleration
the acceptance or protection of individuals, groups, and types of behaviour that may be disapproved of by the majority in society

Humans can only be understood as part of society, for without that common tie individuals are less than human. Human nature for socialists is inseparable from society and social life. The emphasis on the group above the individual is seen clearly in Marxist analysis, which focuses on the role of social classes in human history. Humans are identified as belonging to one class or other, and their identity and interests are defined with reference to those classes. Having said this, socialist thought dictates that humans are rational and capable of self-development and progress, elements shared with liberalism.

Though some socialist philosophers can be seen to be critical of egalitarianism except as a final goal, socialism is fundamentally an egalitarian belief system, teaching that all human individuals, men and women regardless of race and creed, are deserving of equal treatment.[12] Socialism does not teach that all humans are equal in terms of their capabilities or faculties; rather it recognizes the many differences to be found among individuals. Nonetheless it argues that these differences are less important than the underlying similarities shared among them. This does not seem much different from liberalism, yet the consequences for socialist ideology are radically different. Essentially, as we will see in reference to the economic elements, it implies a doctrine of redistribution based upon the principle of 'from each according to their capabilities, to each according to their needs'. In this sense, socialism attempts to satisfy human needs, rather than merely providing the opportunity for individuals to do so themselves. Further, socialism is committed to equal access to health care and education so that equality extends beyond the purely economic domain.

Socialism is generally seen as defending the state and its role in human society and the economy. It must be remembered, however, that for many socialists, the state has been seen as the enemy, a system of repression that represents the interests of one class over others. Marx, in particular, argued that the state was controlled by the **bourgeois**, capitalist class, and would therefore need to be overthrown so that the working classes could claim the political and economic power that was rightly theirs.[13] Nonetheless, most socialists call for an expanded role for the state in fulfilling the economic, social, and political needs of the people, once the revolution has occurred and popular control of the political process has been established. The state should represent the will of the people, a will that is assumed to be egalitarian in nature.

The economic side of socialist thought has already been touched upon, in the sense that socialists generally hold to the principle of economic redistribution to fulfill the needs of all individuals in human society. This implies an expanded role for the state in the economy, and many socialists argue for a command economy, run in its entirety by the state. Those socialists who do not go quite this far still prefer the state to play an active role in the economy, one that works to even out the inequalities caused by capitalism. Public ownership of industry is a common theme, as is progressive taxation. The economy is to be harnessed by the socialist state, so that it adequately serves the needs of human society.

It is important to note that for socialists the economy and politics are inextricably linked. In fact, it is impossible to understand Marxist thought without understanding the link between economics and politics. Marxists argue that political

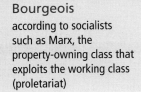

Bourgeois
according to socialists such as Marx, the property-owning class that exploits the working class (proletariat)

relations and processes stem from and are shaped by economic relations and processes.[14] Socialism is highly critical of capitalism as it is destructive of the very values socialists seek to promote, such as community and fellowship. Further, unequal or capitalist acquisition creates severe material inequalities in society, which the socialist state will then have to rectify.

It is also important to point out that Marx believed that human nature itself was inherently linked to labour and to production. Human beings, he argued, were best able to express themselves through creative means, by mixing their labour with raw materials through the means of production. Capitalism as it existed in the nineteenth century, Marx's argument goes, was harmful to the worker's nature because it involved the alienation, or separation, of them from their labour and its products. This concern brings Marx to insist upon equal access to the means of production for all humans, so that they may exercise their human nature. At the beginning of the twentieth century, socialism underwent a crisis from which two main streams emerged. The first, revolutionary socialism, was championed by Rosa Luxemburg and argued that the only way for capitalism to be overthrown was through violent revolution. The second variation was led by Eduard Bernstein, and looked to the possibility of reform rather than revolution. Bernstein's ideas, known as evolutionary socialism or reformism, were important because they led to the formation of political parties across Europe that represented the 'acceptable face' of socialism, and evolved into the social democratic movement. The SPD, or Social Democratic Party in Germany, the Labour Party in Britain, the New Democratic Party in Canada, and left-wing democratic parties across the world find their intellectual heritage in Bernstein's ideas. The creation of the modern welfare state, and the mixed economy whereby government and private business work alongside each other in the productive process, were made possible by the ideological framework of social democracy.[15]

Karl Marx (1818–83)

The horrific conditions in many factories in Victorian Britain inspired Karl Marx to launch his attack on capitalism.

3.9 Continued...

Karl Marx is probably the most important political philosopher of the nineteenth century, and his ideological legacy dramatically altered the course of history. Marx's system of thought was deeply affected by his own personal experiences. Living in London, he observed with horror the way in which nineteenth-century capitalist industry treated the working classes. The working conditions and pay levels of labourers in England (indeed across Europe) at that time were not only desperately low, but seemingly things were getting worse. These observations were confirmed by his friend and lifelong colleague and supporter, Friedrich Engels, who had been studying the living and working conditions of the working class in Manchester.

The approach to political thought proposed by Marx had two major dimensions. First, it was **materialist**, meaning that it took as its starting point understanding the physical and economic basis for society. For Marx, the system of production is the basis on which any social and political system is founded. By examining the distribution of economic power, and most importantly by determining which social groups control the means of production, Marx argued that one could then explain the nature and shape of the political system of a society.

The second key concept in Marxian thought is that it uses **dialectics**. This rather daunting word simply means that ideas and processes throughout history come up against each other, and from the clash of ideas, or of economic processes, a new reality is born. For Marx the whole of human history could be explained by materialism and dialectics. As economic change took place, so would social and political change.

Applying his own approach, Marx saw the history of humankind as the history of conflict between the social classes. As the economy changed from agricultural to capitalist, society was transformed from feudal to capitalistic, and the political order became dominated by the bourgeoisie, or middle classes, in the place of the aristocracy. This, however, was merely a forerunner to the eventual transformation of society that would take place when capitalism inevitably reached its own crises of overproduction and underconsumption. At this time the working classes would overthrow the bourgeoisie in a socialist revolution.

Though these predictions about capitalism have yet to come to fruition, it is Marx's analytical approach that makes his system of thought so important to the study of politics and political economy. The way in which Marxian thought studies the interaction of politics and economics is a fine example for modern students, no matter what is thought of Marxism as an ideology.

Materialist

in Marxism, understanding the physical and economic basis for society

Dialectics

in Marxism, where ideas and processes throughout history come up against each other, and from the clash of ideas, or of economic processes, a new reality is born

Nationalism

Nationalism arose as a political phenomenon in the late eighteenth century with the onset of the French Revolution and then the Napoleonic Wars. It spread throughout Europe during the nineteenth century and was harnessed by governments as a way to increase their political power. It featured as a central political movement in both world wars, and in the inter-war period. In the postwar period, nationalist approaches continued to be important during the Cold War and in the process of decolonization as new developing countries entered the international system and their governments tried to strengthen their control over society. In recent years nationalism has once again emerged as an important ideology in the world. It has featured as a central element in the outbreak of ethnic violence in areas of the world such as the Balkans. In Russia, Vladimir Putin's efforts to re-establish his country's dominion over neighbouring states have been heavily coloured with nationalistic rhetoric. The economic manifestations of nationalism have also been increasingly evident, as many countries have reacted negatively to the dramatic rise of China, and also as the financial crisis that began in 2008 took hold.

Nationalism has been one of the most powerful ideological tools employed by politicians throughout the years. It represents an appeal to human individuals to unite together with other members of their nation, to recognize the ties that at the same time bind them and set them apart from people of a different nationality, and to create, promote, or protect political institutions designed around the national identity. It is the political form of a fundamental impulse in human nature, the need to belong. By marking ourselves as part of a heritage common to those we see as similar to ourselves, which is at the same time different from the heritage held by other groups in human society, we create a distinction that is an extension of the human family or tribe.

What, though, is a **nation**? As we noted in Chapter 2, writers on nationalism have pointed to several features that must be common to a group of people for them to be called a nation:

- language;
- territory;
- traditions, culture, and history;
- race or ethnicity; and
- religion.

Though some nationalities do not hold the elements of race or religion in common, throughout history each has played an important part in forming nations and in marking them off from other social groupings.[16] In the sixteenth century, for example, Henry VIII used religion (the Anglican Church) to pull the English people together and unite them against both the Scots and the Catholic peoples of continental Europe. Race was a central element in Nazi nationalist ideology, which asserted the superiority of the Aryan people over all others.

But what is nationalism? Essentially, it is an ideology that not only seeks the separation of one nation from others, but also seeks to create and protect the political institutions and mechanisms needed to ensure the prosperity of that nation, its values, traditions, and culture.[17] Its most prominent form is seen in the demands of certain groups for independence or sovereignty. Such demands are frequently to be heard from Irish nationalists, Scottish nationalists, and Quebec nationalists, for instance. Because national self-determination is seen as being a supremely important goal, violence is not unusual in the political programs of nationalist movements. Yet the political form of nationalism is not only seen in social movements demanding independence. It is also apparent in the actions of governments that discriminate against and persecute what they consider to

Nation
a group of persons who share an identity that is based on, but not limited to, shared ethnic, religious, cultural, or linguistic qualities

be alien elements in their societies. Throughout history Jewish people have been used as a target for nationalist governments trying to unite their populations. In more recent memory, immigrants have become a target in many European and North American countries as an identifiably separate and, certain political parties claim, threatening element in society.

Nationalism signifies, once again, the superiority of the group over the individual. It has been commonly used to suppress individual rights and freedoms in order to boost the strength and solidify the identity of the nation. Throughout history nationalist forces have been responsible for much of the violence, persecution, and bigotry that have plagued human affairs. However, nationalism has also been a positive tool that has united sometimes disparate peoples and has led to the creation of political and economic institutions that have proved to be more efficient than those that preceded them. The rise of nationalism marked a significant phase in political development and contributed greatly to the political landscape that persists with us today.

There is clearly a very close link between nationalism and war. In the eighteenth, nineteenth, and twentieth centuries, nationalism was considered a useful ideological tool by governments in times of war, and war itself is a powerful driving force behind nationalist sentiment. Indeed, the identification of a foreign or even domestic enemy is a commonly employed argument for promoting nationalism.

Just as the focus of political nationalism is the creating and preserving of the institutions of statehood, economic nationalism takes as its goal the strengthening of the nation-state through economic means. Economic nationalism grants the state an expanded role in the economy, not just through economic policy, but also often through actual ownership of certain sectors. Economic nationalism can and does occur equally in democratic and authoritarian societies, though there are deep philosophical tensions in the case of the former.

Other Systems of Thought

Conservatism

When we say that someone is conservative we generally mean that they are cautious, in favour of established methods and lifestyles, and that they are resistant to change. As a political ideology and perspective, conservatism shares many of these features. It seeks to conserve the best of what has come before for future generations and is concerned with maintaining political and social traditions and customs, which are seen as being an integral part of human life. The origins of conservatism are to be found in the work of Edmund Burke, a British political writer and activist in the eighteenth century. He argued that the dramatic developments and turbulence of the French Revolution, far from improving peoples' lives, had in fact degraded the human condition and endangered social stability.[18] This attitude towards rapid change is a marked feature of conservatism to this day. It would be wrong, however, to say that conservatives are opposed to all change; rather, they are concerned with the pace of change and its extent.

Conservatives view society as being organic; just as importantly they see it as essential for human development. This is a crucial difference to liberalism. For conservatives the individual can only be understood in relation to the greater whole of society and his or her place in it. On the other hand, the smooth and effective functioning of society depends on individuals fulfilling their own individual functions. Due to this division of labour, society is not only organic, but also hierarchical in nature. Conservatives believe that some perform functions in society that are more important than others, and they should receive greater rewards and be more influential than others who perform less crucial functions. In addition, conservatives believe that history has defined certain groups in society to be more important than others and has suited them for that role. It is from this claim that the notion of social classes is legitimated in conservative thought.

As intimated earlier in this chapter, history plays a central role in conservative thought, not just in defining the shape of society but also the nature of its government and constitution. The state is seen as having evolved throughout history, not merely created from nothing, as the liberal contract theorists would argue. Traditions and customs play a key role in government, and for conservatives the constitution is not merely a collection of written statements, but also the conventions that have developed around them. This makes conservatism less legalistic, but at the same time more human and easier to relate to than a lot of liberal theory.

This element of evolution in the nature of government is mirrored by conservatives' changing views towards democracy. Early conservatives were highly skeptical of giving the choice of leadership over to the masses, but latter-day conservatives in Canada and the United States and Britain, for example, have become firm defenders of the principles of representative democracy. Nonetheless, there remains a strong sense of paternalism in conservative thought. What's more, leaders are not only there to exercise power, but also to protect the interests of those whom they lead, and such interests may be defined by the leaders, just as legitimately as those they govern. One of the key 'interests' that persists amongst conservatives is that of law and order, which for many is given preference over concepts such as equality and freedom.

Having said this, it would be wrong to paint a picture of conservatives as favouring the state over individual rights. Conservatives have, throughout history, been fervent defenders of rights and equality. John Adams, for example, who was the second president of the United States and generally considered to be the father of American conservatism, argued for republicanism, and although he believed firmly in the idea of social classes, he also argued for the inclusion of all men in the political process, regardless of their social status (although he did believe that owning property should be a prerequisite in this regard).

It is important to point out that there are significant variations in conservative doctrine across countries. One such difference is concern about the role of religion and morality in society. Since its origins, conservatism has been concerned with social ethics, norms, and morality because they are seen as being amongst the most important traditions that bind society together. However, in modern times, conservatives in Canada and the United Kingdom have been more willing to adopt a more liberal approach to such issues, whereas their ideological counterparts in the United States have been much more emphatic about the central role to be played by Christian morals in defining the 'good society'.

Feminism

The ideals of feminism began with a very simple maxim: 'equal rights for women'. This early feminist demand may seem unremarkable to many today, yet it was a truly revolutionary slogan in the late nineteenth and early twentieth centuries.[19] To understand this we only have to recognize the inordinately unequal treatment to which men and women were subjected. Throughout history women have been placed at the mercy of the male gender in almost every aspect of their lives and, with few exceptions, have led an existence that can be said to be at best highly restricted. Feminism is a system of thought that has grown from the mere recognition of this historical reality into a set of demands concerning the status of women in every aspect of human life. Like all philosophies, there is a great variance among thinkers and writers within the feminist school. As with all ideologies, there are moderates and extremists, and such labels shift over time.

The goal of equal treatment for women is, of course, a highly liberal one because liberalism calls for equal rights and freedoms for all human individuals regardless of gender. Yet none of the classical liberal philosophers sought to apply their principles to the matter of gender, and it was only J.S. Mill who chose to address the issue directly (in his work *The Subjection of Women*). Before this, however, Mary Wollstonecraft had launched an early philosophical defence of the rights of women in her 1792 work *A Vindication of the Rights of Women*. It was left to female political activists of the late 1800s and early 1900s to demand rights for women, which we now take for granted. In the mid- to late eighteenth century an American woman, Susan B. Anthony, became the most heralded feminist activist as she campaigned for the right to vote (suffrage). Though the struggle was not won in her lifetime, women eventually received the right to vote in 1920 in the United States, in England in 1920 (limited franchise, meaning that only women over the age of 30 and who rented or owned property could vote) and 1928 (full voting rights), and across Canada between 1916 (Manitoba, Saskatchewan, and Alberta) and 1940 (Quebec), with the other provinces granting rights in between. These gains, however, did not signal the end of the feminist struggle; rather they marked the beginning of a long fight to change the lives of women around the world. As the movement has developed, so has the ideology behind it, and feminism has changed from a simple claim for equality to a complex and varied grouping of political, social, and economic thought.

The two main thrusts of modern feminism are concerned with justice and gender roles. Feminism's concern with justice relates to the issue of equal treatment for women in the workplace and society. Issues such as equal pay, the 'glass ceiling' (whereby women are prevented from rising to senior managerial and executive positions), affirmative action, maternity leave (or parental leave as some feminists would advocate), and sexual harassment are some of the higher-profile and indeed most important issues for the feminist movement.

These are, however, only the most obvious of feminism's aims. Just as important are its concerns with the broader issue of gender, concerns that include roles

Suffrage
granting of the right to vote

in society, language, and even male-constructed patterns of thought. Gender is different from the word 'sex' because it refers not to the biological nature of a person (male or female) but rather to the socially constructed roles and images we have of men and women. Women's roles in society are about more than just the right to work, or to hold positions of influence. Feminism questions traditional roles for women as wife, mother, or caregiver. The institution of marriage has been questioned because of the subjection that many women over the ages have received as wives. In terms of the family, the issues of choice, timing and who should play the primary role as caregiver to children are very much up for debate in modern society and it is largely thanks to the work of feminists that this is so.

One of the highest profile issues of the feminist movement has been the area of reproduction, and in particular the right to abortion. The debate over abortion has remained a hotly contested one for many years in many countries, especially the United States, and, while there have been significant advances for those arguing for increased or total choice for women over their reproductive functions, it is far from being a decided issue. Neither should it be thought that all feminists agree on abortion rights; as with so many other issues and other ideologies, diversity of opinion marks contemporary feminism.

In the past twenty years a third wave of feminist thought and action has emerged. This takes issue with the basic, 'essentialist' idea from earlier waves of feminism that all women share a common nature or identity and with the dominance of middle-class, predominantly white female conceptions of what women want and need. The third wave argues that women should be encouraged to define their own identities, and to define their own conception of feminism. Authors and thinkers such as Jennifer Baumgardner and Amy Richards have emphasized this more pluralistic, diverse interpretation of feminist thought.

An interesting phenomenon to observe within feminism is the way in which seemingly radical issues have crossed over to become mainstream in their nature. The right to vote itself was considered a radical and revolutionary issue when it first emerged; the same could be said for women in Parliament, equal pay for women, or even the exclusionary nature of words such as 'chairman' or 'mankind'. In the area of political studies itself, gender analysis was long seen as a marginal and unusual sub-field; now it is viewed as an established, mainstream dimension of the discipline.

Environmentalism

The 'green movement' that arose in the 1980s in Europe and North America and forced changes in government policy on the environment marked the birth of a new approach oriented towards the protection of the earth's natural resources and the promotion of more simple lifestyles. Environmentalism is truly both a political and an economic ideology because it identifies modern economic systems as the scourge of nature. It also shares certain ideas in common with anarchism because it sees modern industrialism as a hierarchical system that restricts human freedom.[20]

The ideological roots of environmentalism are several, being found in romanticism, pacifism, socialism, and, as mentioned above, anarchism. The anti-nuclear movement of the 1970s and 1980s produced significant political momentum that, combined with the work of non-governmental organizations (NGOs) such as Greenpeace and Friends of the Earth, helped to change public opinion and raise consciousness about the problems facing the global and local environments.

Within environmentalism is a belief that the destruction of the biosphere, the finely balanced system that sustains life on this planet, is imminent unless radical changes are brought about. Science has played a key role in the ascendance of this ideological approach. As more and more scientific evidence concerning climate change, ozone depletion, and ground, air, and water pollution have emerged, alongside evidence of their harmful effects on human health, more and more people have become aware of the need for more environmentally friendly approaches to economic development. There is a current focus on re-educating public opinion so that people call for governmental change with regard to pollution and the use (and overuse) of non-renewable natural resources. The main targets for environmentalists are heavy industry and petroleum companies, and the ideology promotes alternative sources of energy (such as solar power, wind energy, or biofuels) and alternative lifestyles that consume less.

The economic implications of environmentalism are closely connected to this overall vision. It seeks to persuade individuals to seek natural rather than consumer pleasures, and to reduce the amount that people consume, in terms of goods and energy. This is a direct challenge to contemporary Western lifestyles and an indirect attack on the Western economic system. Environmentalism attacks this system more directly by focusing on sustainable development rather than economic growth. Sustainable development is a concept that embraces not only the provision of basic needs and the expansion of economic activity, but also health, individual freedoms, education, and human longevity, of this generation and those to come.

The successes of environmentalism at a practical level are many. Without the efforts of the movement we would not have seen new policies at the national level directed towards recycling and pollution control. At the international level, the notion of sustainable development has become a maxim for international aid agencies and development organizations. The reality of climate change has made almost everyone aware of the need for more ecologically sound policies and practices, and environmentalism has moved firmly into the mainstream.

Sustainable development
model of economic growth that seeks to use renewable resources so as not to destroy the environment in which human beings have to live

Fascism

'Fascist' is one of those words that have passed from politics into everyday use in English. We use the word to indicate that someone or something is dictatorial and intolerant. However, the true meaning of 'fascist' is to be found within the ideology of fascism and its close cousin, National Socialism. These ideologies, close enough to be examined as one, call to mind the atrocities of the Second World War and modern brown-shirted skinheads threatening racial violence, but must also be examined at the level of their underlying philosophical ideas.[21]

Fascism is fundamentally different from many mainstream ideologies in its perception of human psychology because it rejects the laws of human reason that are fundamental to liberalism and socialism. It sees human individuals as influenced more by myths and romanticism than by logic, and appeals to them in this way. One of the most important myths for fascism and national socialism is the myth of blood, race, or *volk*. Such nationalism is central for fascism because it promotes the group (in this case the folk or nation) over the individual, a fundamental element of fascist thought. The individual takes his or her identity only from within the nation and must direct all efforts towards helping that group. Property is privately held but must be used to strengthen the nation as a whole, not for personal gain. The *volk* is to be protected from all other nations or races, and racial superiority is commonly a part of national socialist political propaganda.

According to fascist thought, the nation should be organized within by the state, with a national leader (*Führer* in German) at its head. This leader is an unquestioned authority who determines the interests of the nation and directs not only state policy but also individual morality. The leader represents, indeed embodies, the will of the people and is seen as the only person capable of interpreting that will. The structure of the state is hierarchical, with a clear chain of command from the leader down. In practical terms this means extreme authoritarianism, and the willingness to use force, indeed violence, to ensure order and compliance.

Anarchism

The word 'anarchist' makes most people think of an individual, probably young, who is committed to the violent overthrow of government and society. The system of anarchism, however, is much more complex than and not nearly so extremist as the popular image suggests. Anarchism is really concerned near primacy of the individual, in which outside interference into the people's will, especially that of government and the state, is minimized. It is a form of libertarianism that stresses the sanctity of the human individual and seeks to promote the moral autonomy of the same.[22]

Anarchism has a long history that extends back to early Christian thought and beyond. The word itself (an-archy) simply means the opposite of hierarchy, and therefore absence of government. It is important to remember that anarchy is not the same thing as chaos or the absence of peace and order. Most anarchists believe firmly that human life would be more peaceful and human needs more completely taken care of in the absence of the state. It is important to note that anarchism as an approach seeks change not through politics but through society or through overthrow of government. Having said this, some anarchists have pointed out that revolution generally leads to the installation of a new government and thus a new authority structure to struggle against. Nonetheless, throughout the late nineteenth and the twentieth centuries the most obvious forms of anarchist activity have been to strike against the representatives of authority. Anarchism has at times been a potent ideological force that has inspired direct political action, often in the form of violent attacks upon the organs of government, but also in the form of peaceful protest and **propaganda**.[23]

Anarchist thought has a rather unique perspective on the economy and in particular on industrialism. It blames the process of industrialization for much of the oppression of the individual seen in modern society. This is because industrial organization requires a passive, compliant, and ordered populace from which it

Propaganda
spreading of information, true or otherwise, for the purpose of aiding a cause or to make an audience react in a certain way

takes its workers. Government and industry work alongside one another to suppress individual freedoms and impose a set order upon society. Further, anarchists argue for a simple lifestyle in which needs are taken care of, yet excess is not known. This marks anarchism as a deeply anti-consumerist ideology. It was Pierre-Joseph Proudhon, possibly the most famous anarchist writer, who stated, 'Property is theft', though not all anarchists go to such extremes.

Anarchist thinkers do not believe that economic and social organization will be absent in the world they envision. Rather, instead of governments forcing citizens to comply with rules and laws and modes of interaction, society would organize itself, with an emphasis on community management and the mutual solution of common problems. Michael Albert's ideas on providing alternatives to capitalist globalization, and his emphasis on community-based organization, are clear examples of this kind of thinking. Although some may criticize this kind of thinking for its essentially idealistic nature, a number of anarchist experiments around the world in small communities have been successful over time.

Political Islam

In the early twenty-first century in Canada, and indeed in many countries in the West, it has become important for us to understand a little about the ideas

---

3.10

John Rawls (1921–2002)

In the 1970s an American political scientist, John Rawls, took an idea from the political philosophy of Hobbes, Locke, and Rousseau, and started a debate that helped to shape political philosophy at the end of the twentieth century. In *A Theory of Justice*, Rawls took the concept of the 'state of nature', a heuristic tool used by many philosophers in the seventeenth and eighteenth centuries, and renamed it the 'original position'.

Instead of a mythical state in which humans are removed from society and subjected to the will of others and to the wilds of nature, Rawls formulated a hypothetical situation in which each individual is ignorant of everything about him- or herself, including the proclivity for risk-taking. By asking what the human individual in this situation would choose in creating a political and economic system, Rawls hoped to find the basis for a just society. Rawls's answer was that each individual would likely opt for a political and economic system that is democratic and that guarantees a minimum level of material welfare.

Shortly after Rawls published *A Theory of Justice*, Robert Nozick wrote, by way of response, the work *Anarchy, State, and Utopia*. In this rebuttal to Rawls, Nozick argued that rather than providing the ethical and philosophical basis for the welfare state, the original position (as formulated by Nozick) would promote the choice of libertarian society in which the role of the state is severely restricted, and the individual is held sacred. The debate between Rawls and Nozick became one of the most important debates of the twentieth century, and it brings to mind the contrast between the philosophies of Thomas Hobbes and John Locke.

and concepts behind Islamic political thought. As we mentioned earlier, Islamic philosophy has an even longer history than its European Christian counterpart. It was thanks to Islamic culture that the ideas of Aristotle were preserved, and then retaken into European thought by Thomas Aquinas. And Islamic political inquiry showed a level of sophistication and realism that was surprising when contrasted with contemporary thinkers in Europe.

Medieval Islamic thought in particular highlights the link between politics and Islam, but also between political philosophy and the realities of power. The strongest example of this can be found in the idea of the Khilafat or Caliphate, a government inspired by Islam that rules over its subjects using Islamic law. In fact, the Caliphate of Sunni Islam at its high point in the eighth century extended over an area from North Africa to the Middle East to Eastern Europe and Spain.

Also of importance is the concept of Ummah, which emphasizes the global community of Muslim peoples. It is a key idea in Islam that stresses not only internationalism, but also the superiority of Islam over other religions and cultures. Also central to early Islamic thought was the link between science and religion and the methodological search for the truth and the importance of studying nature.

The best known Islamic philosopher, one whose ideas are still cited today as relevant and insightful, was Ibn Khaldun. Writing in the fourteenth century, he was a scholar whose interests extended from history to economics to law to military strategy to astronomy; his work on the nature of the state and its rights and duties is surprisingly modern in its understanding of the way in which the state often abuses power. He wrote about concepts such as the importance of social or tribal cohesion and the role of religion in generating such unity, and he understood the historical tendency for empires to rapidly decay.

Modern Islamic political thought reflects some of these established tendencies but also has moved into a more radical phase. Sayyid Qutb (1906–66), in particular, wrote extensively on the immoral nature of American society and argued for a revival of traditional Islamic values. He proposed the use of Islamic law or **Sharia**, and the use of **Jihad** in both defensive and offensive ways against the West. Jihad has two main meanings: first, it can be used to describe a moral struggle or struggle for righteousness; second, it can be used in the sense with which we are more familiar today, that is, as a form of holy war.

The ideas of Qutb were inspirational and helped lead to the rise of **Islamic fundamentalism**. This was seen most dramatically in the Islamic revolution in Iran in 1979 and in the ongoing struggle of organizations such as al-Qaeda, the group behind the September 11, 2001 (and many other) terrorist attacks. The spread of these ideas across the globe is one of the most important factors having an impact on the political stability in the developing world, and on relations between Islam and the West.

We should not assume that all Islamic political thought can be tied to fundamentalism, jihad, or al-Qaeda. Contemporary political Islam should be seen today as a vibrant force with moderate elements that are opposed to the strict imposition of Sharia. However, many dominant trends in today's Islamic thought are more traditional and fundamentalist.

Caliphate
government inspired by Islam that rules over its subjects using Islamic law

Sharia law
sacred law of Islam

Jihad
two meanings: first, a moral struggle or struggle for righteousness; second, a form of holy war

Islamic fundamentalism
religious movements advocating a return to the 'fundamentals' of Islamic religious texts

The Relevance of Ideas

Throughout history the evolution of ideas has had a dramatic impact on the real world of politics and the economy. Most dramatically we can look to the ideas of Karl Marx as the basis for a transformation of political-economic systems at both national and international levels in the nineteenth and particularly in the twentieth centuries. In this case, a new way of understanding politics and economics inspired organized social unrest, new government approaches to social and economic programs, and ultimately revolution. But we could also mention the importance of nationalism and liberalism in motivating governments and groups within society to organize themselves and prepare for both conflict and competition.

The interaction between philosophy, on the one hand, and government policy on the other, was never more clear than in the adoption of Keynesian economic and social policies by Western governments in the 1940s and 1950s. By seeking to modify capitalism to smooth its highs and lows and thus reduce its negative effects on the population, Keynesian economic policy became the norm for most of the postwar period, and the consensus only broke down in the 1970s during a prolonged period of economic stagnation. At that time the ideological approach known as neo-liberalism appeared, and it in turn influenced government policies throughout the world. With the economic and financial crisis at the end of the first decade of the twenty-first century, a neo-Keynesian approach to economic policy-making seems likely to emerge.[24]

It is in such transitions that we see the other side of the interaction between political thinking and political practice. The movement of history and developments in the world of politics and the economy bring reform, revolution, and the creation of new ideas in the world of political and economic thought. Unless philosophical inquiry reflects the realities of the human world, it will remain separate and disconnected from it. Philosophy, remember, should help us to understand our political and economic systems before it shows us ways to change them. Marx's ideas were shaped by his experiences of the industrial revolution and the terrible working conditions of British manufacturing workers. He explained the causes for these conditions before arguing that revolution was the only way to improve the workers' lot.

Today we benefit from the normative discussions contained in classical and modern philosophy when we contemplate the relationship between the state and individuals and society, particularly in debates over rights. Think, for example, of current-day debates in the United States over the rights of undocumented migrants. Are they, as human beings, equally deserving of access to education, health care, and social security as American citizens, even though they entered the country illegally? How should we define citizenship itself? Luckily we have thousands of years of relevant arguments, debates, and ideas stored in the annals of political philosophy that serve us well here.

Political ideas and philosophy, then, are an essential, living, and evolving element of political studies. It is all too easy to dismiss the importance of ideas, to classify them as mere 'castles in the air'. Future trends in politics, at both national and international levels, will be shaped equally by developments in the practical

and theoretical worlds. It is our job as political scientists to both understand the major strands of political philosophy and their impact on debates in the real world, and also to participate in the intergenerational debate over their validity.

Conclusion

This chapter has looked at the central place occupied by ideas, philosophies, and ideologies in the world of politics. As you have seen, these ideas constitute a huge spectrum of thought that extends not just from left to right, as we have traditionally perceived politics, but also in many other directions and indeed dimensions. The debates and compromises that take place between ideological and philosophical positions remain one of the most vibrant and important areas of political studies.

The ideas put forward by the most important thinkers throughout history have become a basis for political debate, social movements, political change, and at times revolution. But just as importantly, though less dramatically, political thought has influenced the structures of governance, their shape and level of public inclusiveness. Ideological and philosophical perspectives underlie all such structures in the real world and it is to these that this book now turns.

Self-Assessment Questions

1. In what way is political philosophy a timeless exercise?
2. Which of the philosophers you have covered in this chapter speak most clearly to your personal political concerns?
3. Give examples of philosophical debates that spread across generations.
4. On what basis should we view all humans as equal?
5. How can Western liberal ideas and the tenets of political Islam be seen as compatible?

Weblinks

Feminist Theory Website
www.cddc.vt.edu/feminism

Greenpeace
www.greenpeace.org/international

Liberal International
www.liberal-international.org

Socialist Worker
socialistworker.org

UNIFEM and Gender Issues
www.unifem.org/gender_issues

Utilitarianism
www.utilitarianism.com

Further Reading

Alvarez, Sonia E., Evelina Dagnino, and Arturo Escobar, eds. *Cultures of Politics/Politics of Cultures: Re-visioning Latin American Social Movements.* Boulder, CO: Westview Press, 1998.

Balaam, David N., and Michael Veseth. *Introduction to International Political Economy.* Upper Saddle River, NJ: Prentice Hall, 2001.

Beramendi, Pablo, and Christopher J. Anderson. *Democracy, Inequality, and Representation: A Comparative Perspective.* New York: Russell Sage Foundation, 2008.

Cohn, Theodore H. *Global Political Economy: Theory and Practice.* New York: Pearson Longman, 2008.

Giddens, Anthony. *The Global Third Way Debate.* Cambridge: Polity Press, 2001.

Heywood, Andrew. *Political Ideas and Concepts: An Introduction.* New York: St. Martin's Press, 1994.

Kriesi, Hanspeter. 'The Organizational Structure of New Social Movements in a Political Context.' In *Comparative Perspectives on Social Movements: Political Opportunities, Mobilizing Structures, and Cultural Framings.* Ed. Doug McAdam et al. 3rd ed. Cambridge: Cambridge University Press, 1996.

McCaffrey, Stephen C. *Understanding International Law.* Newark: LexisNexis Group, 2006.

Migdal, Joel S. *State in Society: Studying How States and Societies Transform and Constitute One Another.* Cambridge: Cambridge University Press, 2001.

Norris, Pippa. *Electoral Engineering: Voting Rules and Political Behavior.* Cambridge: Cambridge University Press, 2004.

Olson, Mancur. *The Logic of Collective Action: Public Goods and the Theory of Groups.* Cambridge, MA: Harvard University Press, 1971.

Shklar, Judith N. *Political Thought and Political Thinkers.* Ed. Stanley Hoffmann. Chicago: University of Chicago Press, 1998.

CBC News Clips

Visit the companion website for *Politics: An Introduction* to listen to news clips from the CBC radio archives.

4 The Role of Government

LEARNING
OBJECTIVES

After reading this chapter, you will be able to:

❋ contrast various points of view regarding the role of government

❋ understand and distinguish among the primary forms of government systems

❋ recognize and apply the major compositions of government systems

❋ apply the form and composition of government to the Canadian case.

Introduction

This chapter will introduce you to the numerous forms of government that exist today, as well as to the ideologies and roles played in the relationship between government actors and citizens. You will find that the types of governments that operate in the international system today are affected by the ideologies outlined in Chapter 3 that shape the attitudes and belief systems of their societies. As well, we will spend a little time thinking about the distinctive form of government we have in Canada.

The different ways that we think about government are important in this context because our attitudes shape the role it plays in our society. Citizens in a liberal democracy such as Canada, for instance, will have a very different perspective about the tasks and responsibilities of government than those socialized in a more closed authoritarian system. In fact, Canadians probably have different perspectives about their government than citizens who live in ones closely related to our own; for example, our views about government are quite different from those of American citizens. We'll return to this comparison later in Chapter 5. Overall, a better understanding of the ideologies that underlie various governments helps us grasp the functions that institutions and branches of government have. We will also return to those different branches of government in Chapter 5.

This chapter begins with an overview of what governments do, regardless of their ideology. Here we will look briefly at different political systems — the political structures and key actors that shape government action. Not everyone agrees on what governments ought to do, of course, so we will spend some time looking at various schools of thought regarding the role of government. The focus then shifts to government composition, particularly the distinctions between federal and unitary systems. This is followed by an account of some of the major forms of government today, including totalitarian, authoritarian, and liberal democracies. Finally, before turning to the concluding notes, the chapter evaluates the unique role government plays in Canada, and its parliamentary system of government, which is the consequence of its distinctive history and links to the Westminster form of government established in the United Kingdom.

What Do Governments Do?

Depending on the type and needs of particular societies, governments can be structured in distinctive ways and look very different. Some emphasize the role of the legislature. Canada is an example — here, cabinet ministers and even the prime minister must also be Members of Parliament. Others, however, focus more on separating the powers of the legislature from those of the executive level of government. As we will see in the following chapter, American politics has always been based on this balance of power between its Congress and the presidency. Nevertheless, in all cases, government provides a means to regulate the activities that take place within society and to enforce the rules and regulations necessary to make social interaction work. Various theories have been offered to explain the tendency of humans to organize themselves and make rules for their community. Some have suggested that political communities are created in response to the fear that humans have of isolation. This reflects what Hobbes said about the 'state of nature' and its consequences.

That is to say, individual freedoms, though desirable in some respects, also bring about demands from people, and these demands often conflict with those of others. As well, individual freedoms can lead to the fear of being conquered by another. Political organization and the creation of political units result in a form of 'security in numbers' because individuals no longer fear isolation. Politics, after

4.1

Hobbes and the State of Nature

Thomas Hobbes (1588–1679) was an English philosopher who was a pioneer in Western ideas about government. In his most famous work, *Leviathan* (a 'leviathan' is a Biblical mythical monster), he described the unnatural tendency we have to form governments. Hobbes felt that the 'natural' state for humans was complete independence, with no overarching authority. The problem, however, was that this state would be unlivable, because everyone would do whatever it took to survive, leaving us in a situation where life would be, as he wrote, 'solitary, poor, nasty, brutish, and short'. Even the strongest among us would be vulnerable, because alliances of weaker actors could overcome the stronger. There would be no law, and no order. The only way out of this, Hobbes argued, was to create government to force obedience and provide security and order.

all, is about how we form political communities, rather than living in isolation, and there is always a delicate balance between freedoms and security. Most political systems, at least liberal democratic ones, seek ways to best achieve this balance. In addition, political communities produce accumulated benefits, such as access to greater wealth, justice, social guardianship, and the distribution of responsibilities.

In very basic terms, governments exist to accomplish two goals. The first is to provide the necessary security assurances for its citizenry: maintaining and protecting territorial integrity, national resources, and the population itself from outside attack or exploitation. The second goal, which can be realized only after securing the first, concerns the welfare goals of its citizens: providing adequate social conditions, opportunities, and benefits for its people. As you can see, there is a very important relationship between security and welfare. Security must be in place before welfare can be provided to citizens. But if citizens feel that their standard of living could be improved, or worse, that government has impeded their ability to gain or maintain access to the basics of life, they may rise up. Now, this could simply mean that people might challenge their government, say, by electing other politicians who claim they will provide benefits. It could be much worse, however; citizens could rebel against their government were they to feel that their standard of living was threatened by their rulers. Fundamentally, people must feel secure before welfare can be provided, but a contented citizenry is also a requirement for a secure and stable political system.

Government, then, is an agency to regulate behaviour in society. It represents a process through which the society is protected and sustained. But government is not just a process; it is also a set of administrative, legalistic, and political structures that actually carry out the process of governance. The judicial structure of government, for instance, is responsible for interpreting, applying, and upholding the laws of the land. Similarly, legislative structures establish a forum for interaction among political actors (usually elected officials). There may be — and usually are — many levels of structures within a political unit, as well as numerous significant political representatives (politicians) who all compete and work within government. We will consider these structures in greater detail in Chapter 5.

Not surprisingly, political analysts are particularly interested in both the process and the structure of political interaction. That is, they think about the way politics plays out, as well as the political arrangement or composition of government that is in place. Indeed, these two dynamics are central for political inquiry because they inform us about the primary actors in a political unit and the environment in which they act.

Process and structures in politics are important. Political scientists who study Canadian politics (often called 'Canadianists' to describe their main area of research) look at how politics functions in Canada, as well as the decisions and policies that are put in place. Think about the budget, for example. Every year the Canadian government must declare how it intends to spend taxpayers' money. Defence, social programs, new roads, and transfer payments to provinces (which we will examine later in this chapter) are all accounted for. The budget process, however, is about more than just dollars and cents. It involves a number of stages, starting with priority-setting in the cabinet and ruling political party, consultations with experts and other levels of government, financial accounting, right up to the presentation of the budget to Parliament, and votes in both houses (the House of Commons and the Senate). To understand the budget properly, we need to consider both the structures that guide it (cabinet, bills in Parliament, powers of the government and the two houses, for example) as well as the process of decision-making (how a government establishes priorities, who has authority, and how those decisions are made). Taken together, the process and structure of politics tell us much more about why and how decisions and policies are made.

Although society 'pre-existed' government as a natural and evolutionary phase of human interrelationships, government is essential to create a political unit. Even before 'states' as we know them today existed, there was always some type of political authority in place. Tribes, villages, city-states, even families, have some hierarchy. We may not call them all 'government,' but in many ways the same process occurs within them: in each of these units we have to think about security, economic welfare, decision-making, authority, and justice.

Governments and politics are tightly related because in order to move beyond a loose hierarchy towards something more established and permanent, people need to agree on how society will be run. Rules need to be in place, and some authority must enforce them. For instance, consider the differences between the game of football and the jungle chase between hunter and prey. Simply put, both are competitive environments, with the benefits of one (either a football team, or the hunter or prey) eliminating those of the other. After all, only one team can actually win a football game, and either the hunter or the prey will prevail in the jungle. Which environment, then, is closer to that of politics? The answer to this question lies in the *nature* of the competitive environment. Although there are similarities between the 'football and jungle' illustration, there is one very important distinction: the football game involves rules and referees. Imagine a football game with no referees

or linespeople: the rules could not be imposed, and disagreement and disorder would prevail. There are, of course, no 'referees' judging the conduct or outcome of the jungle hunt, and the participants are left to their own devices regarding the outcome.

In one sense, governments are rather like referees: they exist to create and pattern the basic rules of the system so that order may prevail, both domestically and internationally. However, not all governments have the same rules. The Canadian budget example mentioned earlier involves a different process and set of political structures than we would see in, say, the United States. It is also possible, of course,

We may argue with referees' calls, but the game would be bedlam without them.

for governments to break rules. We see this repeatedly throughout history: governments contravene or circumvent the rules that they themselves have agreed to protect. But in general we would like to think that governments enforce rules.

Because governments are given the right to exercise the legal use of force, they are able to enforce the rules and laws of a political unit. Yet to maintain this control and power, a government must have the support of its people. Although some governments may secure the 'support' of their people through fear (for example, through authoritarian rule that leaves no other options for people), they are most successful in gaining support by providing the basic requirements of government: meeting a political community's security and welfare goals.

Governments may be thought of as one of the 'outcomes' of politics because organizing social units inevitably leads to the creation of governing bodies. Governments are considered 'sovereign' bodies (discussed later in this chapter) in that they alone are given the legitimate authority to make and carry out rules and regulations on behalf of the community; they are, therefore, the highest authority in a political system. However, it is always important to remember that their authority and legitimacy derive from the people they govern, and these can be lost or taken away if they behave in such a way as to damage the interests of society or of major groups within it.

Some Shared Objectives of Government

The primary objective of every government is to provide for the independence, stability, and economic and social well-being of all its citizens. Some are far more effective at doing this, and others are obviously less concerned about their citizens. It is crucial to note the difference among government types here because some forms of government, such as authoritarian systems, consider the 'well-being' of their citizens in markedly different ways than what we are used to in a liberal democracy. This isn't that surprising, because authoritarian governments do not have to rely on the electoral support of their people.

Despite their differences, every country in the international system is first and foremost concerned with maintaining its national survival. This is part of the 'security' of the state that we discussed previously. The continued endurance of a state leads in part to the recognition by the rest of the international system of its legitimacy. Legitimacy is the lawful and proper right of a government to have authority within defined borders, over a distinctive population, and covering the resources available to the political unit. When other states recognize the legitimate authority and autonomy of a state, then that independent state may be considered sovereign, meaning that no other political body has authority over that state.

But sovereignty depends on both domestic legitimacy and external recognition. Part of sovereign recognition by other nations relies on the stability of the country. In turn, this stability lies in the ability of the governing authorities in the state to allow for the transfer, in an established manner, of political power to subsequent leaders. This 'preserves' the state, despite significant changes to

Legitimacy
what is lawful, appropriate, proper, and conforms to the standards of a political system

Sovereignty
recognition by other political authorities that a government is legitimate and rightful for a political community

The Problem with Sovereignty

Sovereignty refers to the ultimate right granted to government to rule over a country. Technically, sovereignty can also be granted to a group or even an individual, but in modern politics, we usually use the term to describe the supreme authority given to a government. Prior to the Peace of Westphalia in 1648 that ended the Thirty Years' War in Europe, sovereignty had various interpretations, depending on the type of political system in question. Sovereignty was even applied to individual rulers in some cases, meaning that sovereign authority literally moved with the individuals granted the powers. The Peace of Westphalia ended a lot of this confusion by connecting sovereign authority to governments, and introducing the idea of non-interference, which meant that other governments would not have the right to meddle in the affairs of others. Today, there are problems with sovereignty. First, there are no formal 'rules' for granting sovereignty. So, in deference to the People's Republic of China, for instance, we don't recognize the sovereignty of Taiwan, even though we happily trade with and travel to that country all the time. China considers Taiwan a breakaway part of the territory under its sovereign rule.

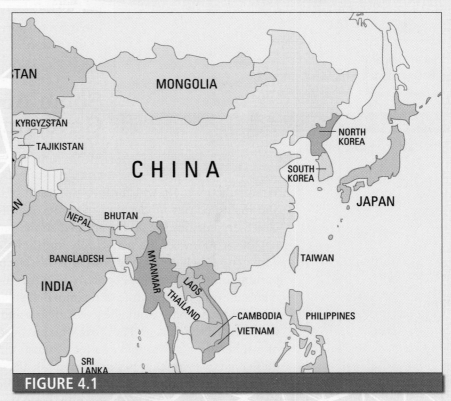

FIGURE 4.1

China (People's Republic of China) and Taiwan (Republic of China) both lay claim to the name 'China'.

It is up to individual countries, then, to decide whether to grant sovereignty to other governments; these countries have to live with the consequences of granting, or not granting, sovereign recognition. Another problem with sovereignty is the

4.2 Continued...

doctrine of non-interference. Does this mean, for example, that we have to ignore cases of genocide (when groups are deliberately being targeted, often by their own government)? As we will see later in this text, the concept of sovereignty has come under increasing pressure in the twenty-first century.

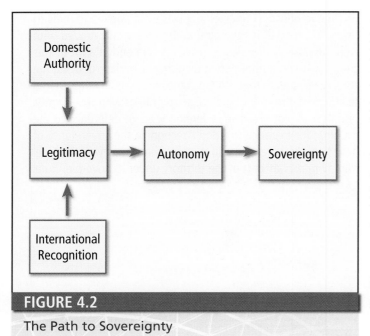

FIGURE 4.2

The Path to Sovereignty

its core. Aside from allowing for the transfer of power, governments must also maintain domestic peace through the maintenance of legal systems and policing. Furthermore, governments maintain their legitimacy, especially among their own people, by creating the conditions that lead to the betterment of the way of life in that country. Governments may improve the individual welfare of their citizens through access to education, social benefits, health care, attempts to eliminate poverty, advances in technology, and improving the infrastructure (roads, services, and the like) of the nation.

Some Activities of Government

At one time the role of government was fairly simple. Immediately following the Peace of Westphalia in 1648, which came as a result of the European Thirty Years' War and instituted our modern sovereign recognition of states, governments were largely responsible for, and concerned about, protecting themselves from external attack. Many see the perfect role for the state to be as minimal as possible. 'Minarchists' believe that the powers of the state ought to be limited to providing basic security for citizens. Popularized in the 1800s, the idea of a 'night watchman state' was one example of the minarchist ideology. In theory, the only role that these states have would be to ensure law and order. Other aspects of politics would be left to citizens. For those who see freedom in every aspect as the goal of a state, minarchism makes a lot of sense. Ultimately, however, the call for these night watchman states dissipated as citizens became more democratically involved, and groups within society became more organized. Labour unions, for instance, grew in strength and number in the 1800s as greater attention was paid to the plight of the worker. Minarchism could not provide the resources and welfare benefits groups demanded, and consequently greater emphasis was given to social democracy. Today, libertarians hold similar views about a greatly reduced role for government.

But even until the mid-twentieth century, governments were primarily affected by the need to preserve and maintain their own security. Since then, however, governments have grown much larger, and the emphasis on the welfare needs of citizens has occupied an increasingly important role in the latter half of the twentieth century. Deepening democratization is one reason that the role for the state has increased. As people became more engaged in their political systems, the call for greater distribution of public goods grew as well. Governments came to see the challenge posed by ideological newcomers such as communist parties. As we will see later in this book, governments adapted by taking on elements of socialist ideology in a new form of democratic socialism that stressed even more the importance of redistribution and equality. With this came the growth of the modern welfare state.

That is not to suggest that security from attack and war is not a great concern for governments; it still is. In Canada, for instance, the military and defence budget is about 9 per cent of the total yearly budget (not including debt and deficit financing).[1] Other countries spend much more. In the United States, for instance, defence accounts for 21 per cent of the whole budget.[2] What's more, the US budget is much larger than Canada's (more than 10 times, actually), but it is the percentage of spending on defence that highlights the importance of the issue. Nonetheless, population growth, economic challenges, competition for scarce international resources, the increased complexity of decision-making, the nature of bureaucracy, and rising (and decidedly different) demands of citizens have led to sustained growth in governments' size and power. A fundamental challenge to this growth in mandate and demands is the way in which governments may carry out these new and wider responsibilities. Citizens increasingly demand that governments give them increased services for the same amount of taxes paid, and in many countries, calls for reduced taxation are a perennial feature.

In broad terms, government activities fall under four main categories: economic management, government aid and subsidies, institutional and bureaucratic regulation, and program development and administration. Each of these functions is fundamental to the effective governing of society, and to the provision of public goods.

Economic management takes place when governments pass resources from one revenue source to other bodies without setting designated requirements as to their use. Think, for instance, of the diverse levels of economic strength in Canada, where whole sets of provinces are referred to as 'haves' or 'have-nots' based on their economy, relative to the other provinces. The problem that arises with such widespread and disparate levels of economic activity concerns the ability of governments to provide services at an equal level. If Canada were simply one province, the level of services, such as welfare, health care, education, and the like, would be based on the strength of one economy and — therefore — one source of tax revenue. However, with thirteen different economies (including the Northwest Territories, Nunavut, and Yukon), the ability to provide basic services in Prince Edward Island, for example, is quite different than in Ontario. The result is the policy of equalization payments, which redistributes revenue from wealthier provinces to the poorer ones in order to 'equalize' services available to all Canadians.

4.3

Equalization in Canada

Equalization payments are one way that the Canadian government ensures that government services are provided equally — or as equally as possible — to all citizens regardless of where they live. Simply put, a portion of revenue (taxes) collected by the federal government is divided among provinces and territories (the three territories are given funds through a separate program administered by the federal government called Territorial Formula Financing). The federal government assesses per capita revenue in each province based on taxes (personal, property, business, and consumption), as well as income from natural resources. That figure is compared to the national average per capita, and from that provinces are considered 'haves' or 'have-nots'. The have-nots receive equalization payments. These are also known as 'transfer payments' and are spent by the receiving provinces as they deem necessary. (Newfoundland 'have not' no more: www.cbc.ca/canada/newfoundland-labrador/story/2008/11/03/have-not.html.) Other federal payments include the Canada Social Transfer and Canada Health Transfer, which are meant to fund social and health programs in each province to ensure equal services across the country. Equalization has been around in one form or another since Confederation, but the plan was formalized in 1957 when Louis St Laurent was prime minister. Equalization payments today cost the Canadian government almost $12 billion per year (the total federal budget is about $240 billion per year).

Government aid and subsidies represent a more active form of intervention, where monies are provided to some individuals and groups, but usually with requirements regulating their use. An excellent recent example of this was in 2009 when the Governments of Ontario and Canada subsidized automobile manufacturers General Motors and Chrysler with over $10 billion to keep their Canadian plants open. Alternatively, governments may wish to encourage exploration of new resources, or research and development in a particular sector that holds the promise of future employment and revenue, such as oil exploration or the microchip industry. Regulation refers to the rules of conduct imposed by government on its individual and corporate citizens in their affairs. Although traditional areas of regulation include a nation's Criminal Code, governments may also use regulation as a policy instrument for a number of purposes. In fact, more so than any other role, the regulatory responsibilities of government have a significant effect on our daily lives. From regulating the macro economy (monetary policy and fiscal policy) and the micro economy (labour, industry, pricing, markets, subsidies, etc.) to social policy and political processes, and even morality (for instance, setting age admission regulations for films, or laws on alcohol consumption), governments perform important regulatory functions on an ongoing basis.

Program development and administration allows government to move beyond merely supervising how other people conduct their affairs, and creates opportunities for governments themselves to complete tasks on their own. For instance, a government may seek a free trade arrangement with another country, or increase social welfare. One example of how difficult this can be concerns health care in the United States. In the early 1990s, Hillary Clinton addressed the topic when her husband Bill Clinton was president. The proposals for universal health care that she suggested were eventually defeated, criticized for their cost and government involvement.[3] More recently, the Obama administration has returned to the thorny issue of providing universal health care for Americans. It is no less controversial this time around. Two more obvious examples include the government's role in its national defence and diplomacy, where government actually exercises a monopoly as the only actor with the right to carry out these tasks.

Schools of Thought Regarding the Role of Government

Opinion varies widely as to how governments can best advance the economic and social well-being of their citizens. Three separate approaches, or 'schools of thought', have been developed to help us understand economic benefits to the public: the liberal approach, socialism, and the welfare society.

The first of these perspectives, the liberal approach, is customarily associated with the writings of Adam Smith. Smith was the best-known proponent of **laissez-faire** (which means to 'let be'), and argued that government is an opponent of human liberty; therefore, he suggested, the role of government should be severely curtailed in the activities of the economy.[4] The laissez-faire approach holds that governments should not act as a regulatory agency within the economy, thereby allowing a 'free-market system'. In this system, citizens could strive for their own pursuits, allowing competition and self-interest to produce the conditions where every member of the community would work to his or her own best advantage to create a society where all benefited from the actions of every member. Working to each individual's personal maximum potential is referred to as 'comparative advantage', where individuals' sacrifices and deeds serve the interests of the larger society. This system of free markets and laissez-faire constitutes what we commonly think of as a 'capitalist' system.

The perspective of socialism argues the contrary. Socialist theorists argue that the possibility that every member will work to his or her own greatest potential in the interests of serving the common good is offset by the more probable reality that a few overly self-interested persons will do particularly well in a political-economic system, and the majority of the population will do poorly. Socialism holds that government, not individuals, ought to maintain ownership and control of the modes of production and instruments of the economy in order to regulate a system that will truly serve the interests of society at large. We can see here how socialism is in reality a criticism of capitalism: whereas capitalism suggests that individuals should be left free to decide how economic benefits will be distributed in the system, socialism presents the opposite argument. Rather than yielding to a competitive environment where social welfare relies on the community concerns of individuals, socialism assumes that individuals must suppress their own interests in order to serve the greater good of the community.

Laissez-faire
'to let be' — economic theory that suggests that a reduction in political control will benefit the economic system

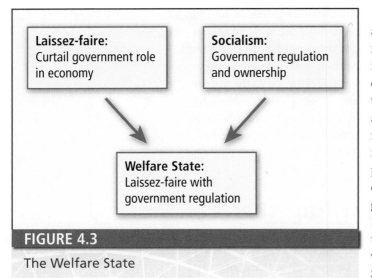

FIGURE 4.3

The Welfare State

The third and final approach is something of a mix of the two previous examples, and it best represents the type of political systems that exist in most advanced democracies today. The mixed-economy approach essentially allows for a system that is governed by a laissez-faire approach, but also permits governments to act authoritatively to restrict any abuses of the system. A 'welfare state' is created that provides the means for individual protection and quality of life, such as health care, employment insurance, pensions, and social programs for the elderly, children, and unemployed. But simultaneously, private interests, rather than the government, largely run the economy. The welfare state is exemplified in Canada, the United States, and Scandinavian states such as Sweden.

4.4

The Welfare State

The welfare state is a relatively new phenomenon in government but has roots that trace their way back through history. It assumes that government has a responsibility to provide the conditions for well-being and happiness to all its citizens. The ancient Greeks discussed this role for government in their discussions of justice and the proper relationship between government and the governed. Welfare state policies would include providing health care, employment benefits, care for the aged, and the infrastructure needed for citizens to achieve their highest potential. The welfare state has an interesting relationship with capitalism, which sees wealth and production as the responsibility of private interests. First, the benefits of capitalism brought greater opportunities for governments to provide welfare benefits, largely through more taxation revenue. Second, the welfare state became a way that capitalist economies in the twentieth century were able to blunt the socialist criticism that capitalism was fundamentally inequitable and biased against the poor. As more and more capitalist states adopted welfare state policies in the twentieth century, the role for government increased and the power of capitalism grew.

Libertarianism
ideology based on freedom of speech, action, and thought; the role of government should be limited

Other political perspectives are less 'economically' based. **Libertarianism** is reflective of the minarchist model we reviewed earlier in this chapter. Like minarchism, this perspective envisions a greatly reduced role for the state. Some go so far as to compare libertarians with anarchists, who feel that government should be eradicated entirely, but libertarians see a limited role for government, constitutionally bound and restricted. Citizens are seen as responsible to themselves. The authority of government is based on a sense of mutual agreement between governed and the governors, used mainly to protect citizens from harm or injustice caused by others. The individual freedoms of citizens, both political and economic, are to be ensured at all costs, and governments are never to wield the power of the law over its citizens without justification.

Totalitarianism holds a very different view of government. Unlike the minarchist tendencies of libertarianism, totalitarianism sees a complete immersion of government in society, influencing and affecting all aspects of social, economic, and political life. Freedoms are greatly restricted, opposition — in party or any other form — is usually denied, and ideological control is evident in the manner in which totalitarian governments monitor or manage almost every aspect of life. While libertarianism has not led to the formation of a government (though there are many libertarian movements in most countries, including Canada and the United States), totalitarianism has the dubious record of being behind many of the most dictatorial and treacherous governments of the modern age. Commonly associated with governments such as the current North Korean regime, recent historical examples include the Taliban rule in Afghanistan, the Soviet Union, East Germany, and fascist Italy; these political systems are dedicated to ensuring that every aspect within the state — schooling, production, social interaction, even religion and family — serve the political aspirations of the government. The role for government in these systems is truly 'total', leading to the name.

There are many other government 'types' that may or may not share similar frames of reference for the 'role' for government. **Monarchies** are those with supreme power in an individual, **theocracies** are ruled by religious leaders, **aristocracies** have hierarchical elites, **despots** have absolute power, and **juntas** are military governments, usually dictatorships. There are many other forms of government, and they may have very different ideas regarding the role of government, even if they share the same type.

Forms of Political Systems

In some respects this chapter provides a connection between the more detailed explanation of political ideologies in Chapter 3 and the overview in Chapter 5 of government institutions. It is important that we see the interaction among political structures themselves, as well as the environment in which they interact, in order to fully comprehend the implications of ideology and political thought for government. To get there, we must first take a closer look at the ideologies that frame political systems.

From a strictly functional perspective, just about anything any government does (or does not do, for that matter) stems from one of four main objectives:

1. Maintaining the political system: unless a system has a capacity for persisting over time it will disappear or be overtaken by a more powerful form of governance. System maintenance involves providing political and economic goods to the community at large with the broader goals of preserving the government. One example of this is the way that the Canadian government transfers funds to

Monarchy
form of government with monarch as head of state

Theocracy
political system ruled by religious leaders

Aristocracy
political system ruled by a hierarchical elite

Despot
political leader who rules with absolute power and authority

Junta
military government, usually a dictatorship

provinces and territories in order to ensure equality of services across the country. Though it may seem a little severe, it is nonetheless possible that the Canadian federation would break apart — or at least be challenged greatly from within and social cohesion would suffer greatly — were there to be serious differences in what citizens were able to enjoy in one part of the country or another.

2. Adapting the political system: governments must adapt to a variety of changes, including population, distribution of wealth, technological advances, and challenges from within (for example, revolution or terrorism) and without (for example, war). Some of these are radical; civil war, for instance, could lead to the breakdown of the government, or even the creation of a new political system. But most adaptation is more evolutionary, as governments respond to challenges such as an economic upheaval or a crisis in resource availability. In 2003, for example, the Canadian government committed over $150 million to a new broadband high-speed Internet initiative in Canada's North. In part this was an instance where the government was trying to rectify a fundamental inequality, access to the Internet in remote parts of the country, but it also shows how governments have to respond to developments that affect citizens in a very real manner.

3. Integrating interests and needs: a political system has to continuously work at making a whole out of parts. To do so, a system must have the political, cultural, and economic tools necessary. For instance, Canada has to contend with provincialism and regionalism and uses policies of power-sharing, promoting Canadian culture, and economic distribution to maintain its federal structure. Equalization is an example of this. Canada's government distributes funds throughout the country to ensure that interests in one part do not come at the expense of those in another. Canada has also embraced multiculturalism as an approach to ethnic diversity in the country, encouraging respect and peaceful coexistence between multiple ethnic groups.

4. Goal-setting: every political system must set its objectives. Individual governments do this all the time; for instance, in the case of Canada, the Speech from the Throne opens a new session of Parliament (or provincial legislatures, too). Governments use the speech to outline the direction and goals for the coming session, and also to remind citizens of their intentions. A properly functioning and integrated government will continually reference its objectives — for example, job creation, national security, or tax reduction — in statements and speeches in an effort to establish priorities and an agenda. The continued viability of a system is in large part contingent on the attainability of these goals.

It should be kept in mind that these four functions of political systems — maintenance, adaptation, integration, and setting goals — are mutually dependent.

That is, success in one role usually depends on success within another. And, despite widespread differences among political systems, each basically pursues these similar goals.

Political observers have long noted the distinctive ways that governments achieve their goals. The Greek philosopher Plato, in his book *The Republic*, first considered how the conduct of rulers and their institutions affect the relationship between state and society. Plato offered a typology (a method of classification and interpretation of concepts) of government, distinguishing among the different types of governance that existed during the Greek era.[5] Interestingly, most of those types are still exemplified in forms of government today or strongly resemble contemporary systems. Later, one of Plato's students, Aristotle, examined the 'natural' relationship that exists between the rulers and the ruled in his book *Politics*. He saw this relationship as a 'partnership'. This Platonic/Aristotelian model distinguished forms of governments, and classified them according to the manner and conduct of rule, and those charged with governing the political community. But in every case, a special responsibility lay with government in its partnership with the community.[6]

However, Plato did not think highly of democracy. He feared it would descend to mob rule, with no checks over authority and an inequitable distribution or allocation of public goods. Plato suggested that 'rule by the many' required a legal framework to manage the relationship between rulers and the ruled; he considered this essential so as to avoid the potentially adverse affects of majority rule (particularly the submission of minority interests to majority rule). Plato's answer was the 'polity', or constitutional democracy.

Constitutions are a part of a broader legal and statutory environment that serves to structure the activities permitted within a political unit. For most countries, the constitution represents the 'basic law' of the land. And for constitutional democracies, the 'constitution' is also at the core of a country's political system and traditions. Therefore, it represents the fundamental law of the political community and sets the limits for political interaction. As such, a constitution provides the political 'rules' for a society and prescribes the composition of a society's political institutions and their interaction with society.

4.5

Unwritten Constitutions

You would think that the basic law for any country would be written down somewhere in a single document. The US constitution, for instance, was actually written down in a single document. It can be seen today, at the National Archives in Washington, DC. Now, there have been several constitutional amendments to the original document — twenty-seven, in fact, with the most recent made in 1992. But some other countries do not have a written constitution. The United Kingdom, for example, does not have a 'written' constitution. But this can get confusing. One might conclude that an unwritten constitution has no enforcement value, since it is not compiled as a single document. Making matters more perplexing is the idea of 'codification', which means to collect jurisdictional laws in a legal

4.5 Continued...

code. However, in constitutional circles, a codified constitution is considered one passed into law as a single legal instrument. Most states, including Japan and the United States, have codified constitutions. Other countries, like Canada, have more than one constitutional document. The constitition of Canada is made up of the Constitution Act of 1982 and the Constitution Act of 1867. There are also unwritten constitutional elements in the Canadian constitution, and amendments as well. Yet these 'uncodified' constitutions (that is, not in a single source) are still binding, and in the Canadian case, they are 'written'. So, 'written' and 'unwritten' constitutions are not necessarily 'codified' or 'uncodified', respectively. In the UK, the constitition is 'unwritten' (it is made up of written judgments, treaties, and statutes, but also unwritten royal privileges, and prerogatives, and political conventions), and uncodified (not a single document), but is nonetheless legal.

Though we often consider constitutions — the basis of modern polities — to be the domain of democracies, it is important to note that many other types of political systems have adopted constitutions as a central institution for government rule and political relationships. The relationship between government and citizens in contemporary society is a complex one. In an age of mobility, transparency, and broad freedoms, there nonetheless needs to be a clear set of parameters regarding what is permissible in society. Sovereignty, then, is still essential. We grant sovereignty to governments not to limit the freedoms of individual citizens, but rather to provide a system within which those freedoms can best be secured. For a variety of reasons, then, it is fairly evident that we require a legalistic framework such as a constitution as a necessary component of a modern political system. First, constitutions set out in a formalized manner the principal institutions of government and their interrelationship. The constitution is the best place to start when you want to know what the legislature or executive branches of your government are supposed to do (we will deal with this in more detail in Chapter 5). Second, constitutions provide the framework within which ordinary laws are made. Criminal Codes and the laws of the land must be 'constitutional' in order to be effective. Third, a constitution may set out the relationship between government(s) and individual citizens, prescribing what a government can and cannot do to its citizenry. Constitutions will also usually outline which levels of government are supposed to provide what services and roles. Finally, constitutions are more than just legalistic documents. They also represent a symbol of the nation. Constitutions provide a portrayal of a country's character, its core ideology, and belief system. In the case of the United States, for example, the American constitutional goals, and indeed the intent of the nation, can be summarized in its preamble:

We the people of the United States, in order to form a more perfect union, establish justice, insure domestic tranquility, provide for the common defense, promote the general welfare, and secure the blessings of liberty to ourselves and our posterity.

In Canada, 'Peace, order and good government' — which is really a constitutional 'residual' power stipulating that powers not allocated explicitly in the Canadian constitution would go to the federal government — has come to represent a larger sense of purpose for Canadian society. It is often used by governments to typify Canada's interests at home and abroad.

Constitutions are often referred to as 'living documents' because they are amended or changed often. The American case is a good one — that constitution has been amended twenty-seven times. New understandings of constitutions, however, may appear without an amendment. Different legal interpretations over time may mandate new understandings. For instance, the courts constantly interpret and apply the constitution in legal determination, resulting in different meanings for the basic law of a country as determined in a particular time or place. The original drafters of the Canadian constitution would not likely have foreseen challenges to Canadian law on issues such as same-sex marriage or shopping on Sundays. This is the very reason why constitutions must be allowed to change: values and preferences change over time, and so do factors such as economic conditions or political relations.

The Canadian constitution is an excellent example of a living document. Like other constitutions, it sets out the basic law for the country, outlines the mechanism of government, and lists the rights of Canadian citizens. Most Canadians know that there were two major constitutional Acts that created our current constitution. The British North America Act of 1867 gave legislative authority to the new 'Dominion' of Canada, and all other constitutional powers were granted to Canada in 1982 when the British Parliament passed the Canada Act (1982). The first 'constitution of Canada,' however, was the Constitutional Act of 1791; this Act was preceded by the 1763 Royal Proclamation which set out the constitutional rules for the Province of Quebec (and this one was later replaced by the Quebec Act of 1774!). Real independence from the United Kingdom came with the Statute of Westminster in 1931, when Canada received legislative authority equal to the UK. In any case, the 1867 and 1982 Acts comprise the core of the Canadian constitution, and the 1982 Act also included the new Charter of Rights and Freedoms, which presented the individual and collective rights of citizens that would be constitutionally bound. The previous examples of constitutional challenges — same-sex rights, freedom of religion, and the like — are based on the rights provided in the Charter.

Liberal Democracy

Democracy owes its roots to several strains of political thought. However, its most influential foundation may be found in the tradition of liberalism. In fact, the two terms are often used interchangeably, though they ought not to be, given their strict definition. Democracy has become one of the most common terms in political analysis today to the point that it might be considered one of the most overused concepts available to political scientists and observers. Democracy has come to have as many implications and meanings as there are employers of the term.

Given the Platonic roots of democratic thinking, it is not surprising to learn that the term 'democracy' itself is taken from the Greek *demos*, meaning 'the people', and *kratos*, which means 'authority'. Far from the simple conclusions about 'mob' rule, democracy takes into account the need for checks and balances over political authority (in order to avoid the appropriation of interests by the few, for example), and also recognizes that many interests exist within a political community. In short, democracy recognizes that rule by all is simply impossible, but that pluralism — the idea that power in a political system is distributed among many different groups — is essential for security and equity.

The compromise between what the ancient Greeks saw as the potential failure for democracy (the 'tyranny' of the majority) and the need to allow for public participation came in the form of the 'polity', with a central role for constitutionalism and the rule of law. Essentially, this required even the majority to accept the rule of law, and limit its behaviour. The central components of liberal democracy include:

- Equality of political rights: where every member of the society may participate in activities of the political unit — voting, running for office, protesting, and the like. No particular political rights are held for a select group of people; for instance, though parliamentarians in Canada alone are permitted to vote in the House of Commons or Senate, (almost) everyone has the right to seek such offices (see Chapter 7).
- Political participation: this is related to the equality of political rights, distributing political responsibilities among the ruled, and the rulers. This may involve direct participation of individuals, such as in a referendum, or indirect participation, where political authority is transferred to individuals elected by the masses to represent their views. Interest groups, or pressure groups, are another example of how citizens become involved in the policy-making process through lobbying politicians.
- Majority rule: recognizes that all votes are held equally, so that the majority of votes should govern.
- Political freedom: entrenches the rights of citizens to participate freely in the political process, limited only by the laws of the community. Participation and representation can only be considered legitimate if individuals are encouraged and allowed to share in the political process in a free environment.

Liberal democracy in Canada is based fundamentally on classical liberal ideas. Individual rights, free economic markets, and the responsibility of government to its citizens are all hallmarks of traditional classical liberal democracy, but are also core elements of Canada's version. In many ways similar to liberal democracy in the United States — at least with regard to the above-listed points — Canada's version adopted an allegiance to a monarch rather than the republicanism inherent in American liberal democracy. The hereditary nature of monarchism has led some critics to suggest that Canadian liberal democracy is actually aristocratic or monarchical at the top, rather than democratic, but in reality the legal and actual role played by the monarch in Canada is largely symbolic and without real political effect.

In addition to the classical liberal aspects of Canadian liberal democracy, we must also consider the social elements of Canada's case. Social progressivism and internationalism, coupled with a redistributive state (see commentary elsewhere in this chapter regarding equalization, for instance), are representative of the 'other' half of Canada's liberal democracy. Same-sex marriage, minority rights, freedom from religious prosecution, and equality of the sexes are just a few of the examples we might use to describe the social liberal nature of Canada's liberal democracy. This is an important point because, while liberalism tends to be related most closely to politics and the economy, liberal democracy in Canada demonstrates an important social liberalism, too. We'll return to this in greater detail in Chapter 9.

Before spending a bit more time and attention to the peculiarities of Canadian government, we should address the main challengers to liberal democracy: authoritarianism and totalitarianism.

Authoritarianism

In our everyday lives, most of the states that we hear about are liberal democracies. In many ways, this is a function of where we live, our domestic political environment, and the culture in which we have been socialized. It is also a result of the interaction of our political community with others: generally, the lion's share of international activities undertaken by Canada are with other liberal democratic countries. But according to most studies, including those of non-aligned private institutes like Freedom House, most political systems in the world today are not liberal democracies. Most might best be described as **authoritarian** systems, requiring some degree of obedience to a constituted authority and a severe lack of freedoms.

In short, authoritarian systems are the antithesis of liberal democracies. At their root, authoritarian systems require their citizens to submit to the consent of the government institutions. Authoritarian states are coercive in that they may rely on the use — or threat — of force to gain acceptance of the ruled and to suppress dissent. Authoritarian 'regimes' (such concentrations of absolute power in government are often disparagingly referred to as regimes) are elite-driven, meaning they are governed by a powerful, often wealthy, minority, and all political (and often social, economic, and cultural) activities are strictly overseen by state authorities. Although authoritarian systems may use ideology as a tool of control, they are not ideologically bound; they may be left-wing, right-wing, religious, military, civilian, capitalist, or communist.

These forms of governments tend to be highly concentrated and insular, though not all are. Centralization, rather than decentralization, permits authoritarian states greater control and authority over individuals and groups.

Although authoritarian states are prone to control as much of the state and society as possible, there are often areas of private life that remain free. Citizens may, for example, hold views that differ from an authoritarian government, or

Authoritarianism
political system requiring absolute obedience to a constituted authority

even support challengers to the rulers. However, this is done at much greater risk than in liberal democracies, where opposition is fostered and considered a healthy part of a diverse political system. There is no guarantee that these limited rights may be upheld, and authoritarian states differ widely on the degree to which debate and resistance may be permitted.

Totalitarianism

Totalitarianism
authoritarian political system that not only controls most social interaction, but is also marked by a desire by the government to force its objectives and values on citizens in an unlimited manner

Often used as an equivalent of authoritarianism, **totalitarianism** is in fact a variant of authoritarian rule. But what distinguishes totalitarianism from authoritarianism is the emphasis on ideological control. That is, totalitarian political systems not only control most social interaction, but also are marked by a desire by the government to force its objectives and values on citizens in an unlimited manner.

Totalitarian regimes seek to dominate all aspects of society and to subordinate all citizens to the wishes of the elite rulers. Governance is best described as tyrannical (the harsh and arbitrary exercise of authority). Since there are usually no rules protecting citizens, majority participation is replaced by the interest of the dominant political authority, and the use of strength and fear is often used to maintain supremacy.

One aspect of totalitarian rule is its emphasis on ideologically redeveloping society from the top down, including fundamental belief systems and values. This results in the further consolidation of the power for totalitarian leaders. Those leaders tend to form an elite, as government control is concentrated in a few individuals, often involving a single leader with inordinate power. Despite all this, totalitarian regimes will often attempt to maintain the semblance of democratic institutions, such as holding elections, that are manoeuvred and manipulated to meet the requirements and wishes of the government. As previously mentioned, however, dissent is suppressed, often forcibly, so forming an alternative option to totalitarian rule is practically impossible.

Another example of maintaining democratic appearances is to establish a constitution. It was often said during the Cold War (1945–91) that the Soviet Union — a totalitarian state if ever there was one — had the most democratic constitution in the world. Rights and freedoms were ensured in Soviet basic law, but in real life this was nothing but words on paper. Totalitarian regimes will control information, too. The less information getting in from the outside world, the lower the probability that dissent will appear. Recently, during the Beijing Olympics, Chinese authorities were criticized for not permitting open access to information on websites about political protest in Tibet. State-controlled media in China stringently limits free access to outside voices of dissent.

A final tactic of totalitarian governments concerns their use of fear to achieve political goals. For example, citizens in Hungary during the Cold War lived in dread that the secret police (the ÁVH) would take them away to their headquarters on Andrássy Avenue where they might be tortured or executed. (The building is now a museum depicting those dark days under communist and fascist rule.) Children were encouraged to report teachers or even family members whom they suspected were plotting against the government. One can only imagine how terrible such a state would have been, particularly for those of us who were raised in a liberal and free political environment.

Liberal democracies, authoritarianism, and totalitarianism represent the three primary classifications of political systems. Although there are numerous variants of governments, such as **transitional governments**, where the move from authoritarianism to liberal democracy results in elements of both with a gradual change to democracy, these three forms represent the basis for most political communities. Right-wing or left-wing, secular or religious, elitist or pluralist, multicultural or ethnically restricted, all political systems roughly fit into one of these broad classifications.

The composition of government, on the other hand, is another way of arranging political systems. Once we understand the basic ideological underpinnings of a system, it is equally important to consider the manner in which political authority and decision-making is appropriated. We will examine that in greater detail in the following chapter.

Transitional government
political system in which the move from authoritarianism to liberal democracy results in elements of both, with a gradual change to democracy

Government and Canada

Like any other country, Canada shares characteristics with others, but also has its own unique features. It is an example of a liberal democracy, as we discussed earlier, something it shares with many of its closest allies, including the United States, Great Britain, France, and Germany. Canada's government is a constitutional monarchy, meaning that its constitution grants ultimate authority to its head of state, the British monarch. The prime minister is the head of government in Canada; it is the head of government who really controls the direction policy-making takes. Heads of state in Canada are more ceremonial. (Other countries, such as the United States, combine the powers of head of state and head of government.) The Governor General represents the monarchy in Canada, and each province has a Lieutenant Governor. The three territories — Yukon, Northwest Territories, and Nunavut — do not have a Lieutenant Governor, but rather a Commissioner, who represents the federal government in the territories rather than the monarch. (The territories do not have any independent jurisdictional powers, and their authority is derived from what the federal government grants them.) Although the Governor General has the highest level of political responsibility as far as the Canadian constitution allows (for instance, he or she must provide Royal Assent to federal statutes before they become law; Lieutenant Governors do the same for provincial laws), in the real world of Canadian politics, his or her role is largely symbolic or ceremonial.

Canada is also a parliamentary democracy, which means that its legislature — the federal parliament – has elected members. The House of Commons is made up of elected members based on constituencies in all provinces and territories. However, the other 'half' of Parliament, the Senate, is not an elected body. Here, the Governor General, on the advice of the prime minister, appoints members. So, in this respect, all of Parliament is not 'democratic', but the part that has the most responsibility — the House of Commons — is composed of

4.6

Are Governors General Just Ceremonial?

There are times when the Governor General takes decisions that are quite significant. In 1926 Governor General Lord Byng refused Prime Minister Mackenzie King's request to dissolve Parliament (usually a ritual performed without question) and invited the opposition to form a government. That government, led by Arthur Meighen, failed to gain the support of Parliament, and Mackenzie King won the next election. The 'King–Byng' affair was quite controversial because, even though Byng acted within his constitutional rights, he was criticized for getting involved in electoral politics. Sometimes Governors General have no choice but to make decisions that have real political implications. In 2008, Governor General Michaëlle Jean decided to allow Parliament to prorogue (which suspends a period between sessions of Parliament, usually done when a government's agenda is completed and Parliament goes into recess). In this case, Prime Minister Stephen Harper requested this in order to avoid a vote of non-confidence by the other parties in the House of Commons, which would have permitted a coalition of the other parties to form a new government, or would lead to another election.

Canadian Press

Governors General are often considered simply ceremonial, but at times their duties can have a serious impact on Canadian politics.

This was a controversial situation, because the Governor General, who is not elected, took a decision that significantly affected the Canadian Parliament, and allowed the Conservatives to stay in power.

elected representatives. The two houses — Senate and Commons— show the 'bicameral' nature of the Canadian Parliament. The provinces and territories have unicameral, or one-house, legislatures. The prime minister and cabinet ministers are also Members of Parliament. (The constitution does allow cabinet ministers to have a seat in Senate rather than the House of Commons. The prime minister rarely exercises this option, however.)

Further authority and powers are given to the provinces and territories (and then, of course, municipalities have their own powers, and First Nations communities also have independent authority). But in Canada, ultimately authority resides in the central government (Canada is not a 'federal' state in the strictest sense of the word, but is more of a 'quasi-federal' system; we discuss this elsewhere in this book). For instance, aside from the independent powers given to the federal government by the constitution, the Peace, Order and Good Government clause (discussed earlier in this chapter) assigns any 'residual' powers to the federal government.

With such a large country to govern (the second largest in the world after Russia), combined with its difficult geography and distinctly regional economic advantages (for instance, oil and gas, fisheries, and manufacturing), Canada has its distinctive challenges for managing the economy, providing equal services, and program development. Most of Canadian citizens, more than 90 per cent, actually, live within 160 kilometres of the US border. As we will consider later in Chapter 9, this means that the highly interdependent economic relationship between the two countries tends to frame much of the commerce that Canada is involved in. And, as Canada is a trading state out of necessity, the US market is more than just essential for the standard of living Canadians have come to expect.

Yet Canadians live all over the country, and the government is responsible for administering its programs everywhere. Equalization payments are made by the federal government to those provinces and territories that are unable to provide services at a level expected in other parts of the country due to the cost of the services, or the lack of revenue needed. Canada is a welfare state, meaning that it provides certain resources to citizens, such as health care, employment insurance, and old age benefits based on need. This is another example of the redistributive aspect of Canadian politics and economics, which we will return to from time to time in this text.

And Canada is also a regulatory state. The economy in Canada can be defined as capitalist, but one with a large degree of government involvement. Government regulates the macro economy, setting interest rates, taxes, and monetary policy, for instance; but it also has a large role in the micro economy, with important regulations for industry and maintenance of the economic infrastructure. It is a necessity that the Canadian government be so involved in the economy, given its sheer size (ninth largest in the world), and its heavy dependence on international economic relations for our standard of living.

At various points later in this text we will take a closer look at other aspects of Canada's government. In Chapter 5, for instance, we will examine the institutions and branches of the Canadian government, picking up on some of the points we have looked at here. Then, over the remaining chapters, we look more directly at Canadian federalism, elections, and interest groups, economic relations abroad, and foreign policy.

Conclusion

No two governments are the same. While certain characteristics may be shared, such as a type of economy or political system, every one has its specific aspects. In Chapters 9 and 10, for example, we look at some individual cases to see just how diverse countries in the world are today. But part of what we do as political scientists is to draw comparisons and distinctions among political systems. This 'comparative method' of analysis has been part of our field for as long as people have looked at their own governments and thought of ways to improve them.

We have looked at the three main categories of governments — liberal democratic, authoritarian, and totalitarian systems. We have examined the main goals of countries, to provide security and stability for citizens and, at least in liberal democracies, to protect freedoms and wealth. Governments manage economies, offer aid and subsidies in order to maintain a degree of equal distribution of goods and services, regulate the bureaucratic and administrative elements of the political system, and extend welfare benefits to the general public. With this in mind, we will turn our attention to the branches of government in the following chapter.

Self-Assessment Questions

1. Why, and how, is politics such a central component of society?
2. What is government, and why is it necessary?
3. How does government regulate social and economic relations within a political unit?
4. Should the level of government involvement in contemporary society be limited or expanded?
5. Should government reduce, or increase, its role in society?
6. Without government, would life truly be 'solitary, poor, nasty, brutish, and short'?

Weblinks

Westminster Parliament
www.parliament.uk

United States President's Office
www.whitehouse.gov

United States Government
www.usa.gov

Canadian Government
canada.gc.ca/home.html

Peace of Westphalia
www.historylearningsite.co.uk/peace_of_
westphalia.htm

Canadian Constitution
laws.justice.gc.ca/en/const/index.html

United States Constitution
www.archives.gov/exhibits/charters/
constitution.html

Hungary's House of Terror
www.terrorhaza.hu/en/museum/first_page.html

Further Reading

Acemoglu, Daron, and James A. Robinson. *Economic Origins of Dictatorship and Democracy: Economic and Political Origins.* Cambridge: Cambridge University Press, 2006.

Almond, Gabriel A. *A Discipline Divided: Schools and Sects in Political Science.* Newbury Park, CA: Sage Publications, 1990.

Brooks, Stephen. *Canadian Democracy: An Introduction.* 6th ed. Don Mills, ON: Oxford University Press, 2009.

Clarke, Paul A. B., and Joe Foweraker. *Encyclopedia of Democratic Thought.* London: Taylor & Francis, 2001.

Deakin, Nicholas, and Margery Garrett Spring Rice. *Origins of the Welfare State.* London: Routledge, 2000.

Easton, David. *The Political System: An Inquiry into the State of Political Science.* 2nd ed. Chicago: University of Chicago Press, 1981.

Hobbes, Thomas. *Leviathan, Or, the Matter, Forme and Power of a Commonwealth Ecclesiasticall and Civil.* Ed. Michael Oakeshott. New York: Collier Books, 1962 (first pub. 1651).

Howlett, Michael, Alex Netherton, and M. Ramesh. *The Political Economy of Canada: An Introduction.* Don Mills, ON: Oxford University Press, 1999.

Jackson, Robert. *Sovereignty: Evolution of an Idea.* Cambridge: Polity Press, 2007.

Laswell, Harold. *Politics: Who Gets What, When, How.* New York: Meridian Books, 1958.

Linz, Juan José. *Totalitarian and Authoritarian Regimes.* Boulder, CO: Lynne Rienner Publishers, 2000.

CBC News Clips

Visit the companion website for *Politics: An Introduction* to listen to news clips from the CBC radio archives.

5 Branches of Government

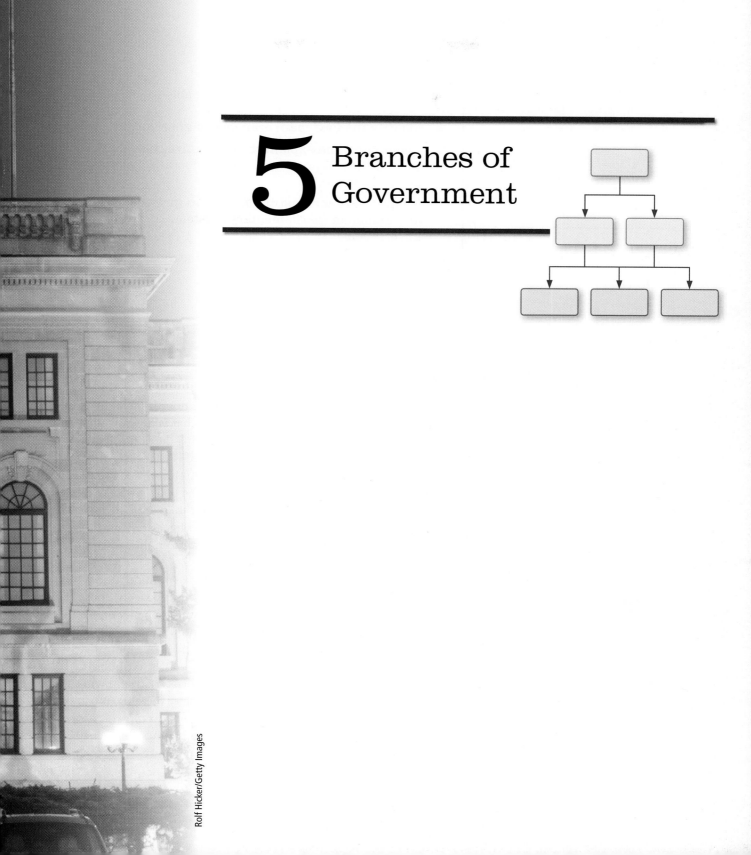

LEARNING
OBJECTIVES

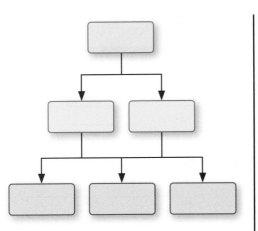

After reading this chapter, you will be able to:

✳ identify the four main branches of government

✳ understand and explain the distinctive roles that each of these branches play in democratic systems of government

✳ compare and contrast the American (presidential) and Canadian (parliamentary) systems of government

✳ apply the form and composition of government to the Canadian case.

Introduction

Do all politicians have the same role to play? What does it mean to be 'in cabinet'? Should judges be elected, too? And what is it, really, that bureaucrats do, aside from being criticized for making the political process unnecessarily complicated?

These are just a few of the many questions that we ask regarding our political structures and the people who work in them. Often we simply decide that the whole thing is too complicated — or frustrating — to figure out, and we throw up our hands and declare, 'It's all so political.' Well, it *is* political; that's the point!

But as we're discovering in this book, 'political' doesn't have to mean impenetrable. In fact, a little knowledge about our political system goes a long way towards a better understanding of just why things seem so complicated: they are complicated, and for a lot of very good reasons. A country like Canada, for instance, is a huge entity: politics, economics, culture, and all the other parts of our society. Governments are large organizations out of necessity, since there's so much involved in even the everyday activities of government, not to mention the more immediate and sometimes emergency measures political actors must occasionally take.

"You can't take the Ethics course-you're a Political Science major."

Though the common view may be that 'political' is separate from 'ethical,' the two are entwined.

Institutions of Government

So far in this text we've established that anyone who is interested in politics needs to know something about government, and a bit about political ideas, too. We have already introduced government in Chapter 4, and we considered the vast array of government ideologies and roles played. But to answer questions like the ones posed above, we also need to know a little bit about the mechanics of government: the institutions, or 'branches' of government that work together in the interests of citizens (in theory, in any case). This will go a long way to stem that 'it's all so political' attitude we might otherwise fall back on.

Not all politicians have the same job. Some are part of the government: the party given enough electoral support to be the one to form '**government**' and thus the power to make and enforce the laws and regulations of the land. The governing authority in a political system is made up of many different actors with varying levels of power. Some have far more responsibility in government and more latitude, or influence, in decisions and initiatives that governments take. A newly elected **Member of Parliament** (MP) in Canada, for example, won't have nearly the influence in real decision-making as one chosen to be part of **cabinet**. (We will return to the role of cabinet later in this chapter.)

And a cabinet minister will have substantially less 'latitude' than the prime minister. As in any other organization, there is a hierarchy in government.

Many politicians have relatively little real 'power' in setting a government's agenda; opposition party members, for instance, have minimal say in what governments set out to do. But even these opposition members have a crucial role to play in the performance of government. They cajole and question, criticize, and even — at times — work with the government to make policies and laws. A proper look at the branches of government, then, must take into account all the various political roles played by elected politicians.

But not all actors in the political process are elected. Judges in Canada, for example, are appointed, not elected. Some Canadians make the argument that appointed judges may become out of touch with citizens, or may be chosen for political reasons or even **cronyism** or **nepotism** (choosing family or friends for positions of power).

Government
the institutions and people responsible for carrying out the affairs and administration of a political system

Member of Parliament
representative of voters in a parliamentary system

Cabinet
members of the executive level of government responsible for decision-making and administration of the bureaucracy

Cronyism
in politics, the practice of choosing or preferring friends or associates

Nepotism
in politics, the practice of choosing or preferring relatives

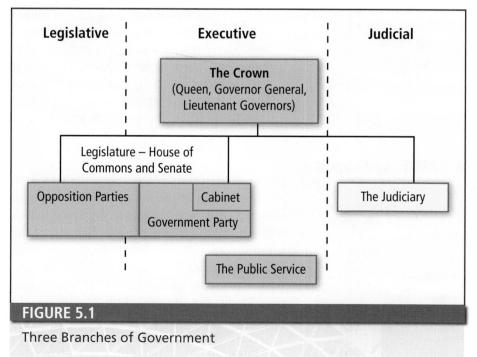

FIGURE 5.1

Three Branches of Government

5.1

Does a Cabinet Minister Have to Be Elected?

As Canadians steeped in the tradition of democratic governance, we might assume that all cabinet ministers are elected. After all, our fusion of powers means that these ministers must also be Members of Parliament. But not all Members of Parliament are elected: senators are appointed. And, at least technically, a cabinet minister doesn't have to be elected. But our political tradition requires them to have a seat in Parliament. So, a prime minister may name someone to cabinet before they are in Parliament (it would be assumed that they would then seek one), or choose a senator for a cabinet position. It's risky business — the prime minister may be criticized for overriding the principle of democratic representation — but it does happen. In 2006, Prime Minister Stephen Harper named Michael Fortier minister of public works and government. Fortier was a Quebec senator, and Harper had few Conservatives to call on from that province. He chose Fortier to establish regional balance in cabinet. And it's not just governments that do this from time to time. In 2007, former Ontario premier Bob Rae was named to Liberal leader Stéphane Dion's 'shadow cabinet' (the name given to a group of opposition members who concentrate on the actions of the government cabinet and voice an alternative to the government's policy) to be the opposition critic on foreign affairs. Until Rae was elected to the House of Commons, Bryon Wilfert, the associate foreign affairs critic, had to speak for Rae in the House. Coincidentally, Dion had experience in this regard. In 1996, then prime minister Jean Chrétien appointed Dion minister of intergovernmental affairs, even though Dion had no seat in either house. He later won a seat in 1997, but until then he was not able to speak or vote in the House of Commons.

And then there are all those political actors who aren't part of government. Those elected under the banner of a competing party may find themselves in a legislature, a congress, or a parliament, but not part of the governing authority of the political system. Rather, they are part of the **opposition**. This doesn't mean their job is unimportant. On the contrary, a vital part of democracies is the existence of a vocal opposition constantly keeping the elected government in check. Different roles, but all part of the democratic process.

Opposition
one or more parties that are not part of government but form a check on the ruling power of the elected party

Electorate
people in a political system with the right to vote in elections; enfranchised citizens

These critics of the Canadian system feel that those chosen by the people must oversee the job of the courts. But the opposing point of view is compelling, as well. Courts and judges are supposed to be independent and non-political. While it might be that a judge may reflect the desires of those making their appointment, it is usually the case that judges are chosen for their expertise and ability to provide balance on interpreting the law. Were they elected, we could similarly be suspicious of political interests coming into play; after all, they'd have to win the support of the **electorate**. How would they do this without showing some preferences?

As we'll see later in this chapter, and also in Chapter 9, judges in Canada are chosen on the basis of judicial independence, a concept that is integral to the notion of freedom of decision-making. But in some countries, such as the United States, some judges are elected, which is a nod to the other side of the debate that suggests they too should reflect the will of the people. In fact, both of these points of view can be seen as democratic, since democracy is about the involvement of the people, but also about the preservation of the independent will of the people. We'll look at this in greater detail later.

As far as the much-maligned **bureaucrats** go, their role in the political system is perhaps the most unpopular — and most misunderstood — among Canadians. Bureaucrats are indispensable for governments to carry out their agendas. Indeed, government is a vast mechanism, and the sheer number of its divisions and its numerous roles make the bureaucracy a necessity. Governments make legislation, oppositions criticize and look for changes, judges interpret and advise, and bureaucrats implement. That, as we will see later, is an oversimplification of the process; however, it's fair to say that, without the bureaucracy, governments would be completely ineffective.

This chapter, then, builds on the previous one, where we discussed various types of government, their activities, and their objectives. This chapter, and the one that follows it, will provide some more detail about branches and systems of government. This one will begin with an examination of the key political structures and actors that shape government action in liberal democratic systems. Three represent the common divisions of power in these systems (**executive**, **legislative**, and **judiciary**), and the other is the **bureaucracy**, the largest and in some ways most active (though perhaps also the most ignored) wing of government. The executive, legislative, judicial, and bureaucratic branches of government comprise the basic parts of the government machinery. Take away one, and a vital part of what we need government to do will disappear. Working together, they complement each other's roles in a joint effort to provide citizens with the wide range of services they expect.

Bureaucrats
those responsible for carrying out public policy; public employees

Executive
usually the top level of government, or the leader; maintains leadership of the entire political system, and often reflects the leadership and preoccupations of the dominant political party

Legislative
referring to the body of a political system with the responsibility to make laws, and known as the legislature

Judiciary
judicial (courts) level of governance

Bureaucracy
division of government responsible for carrying out public policy, and staffed by public employees

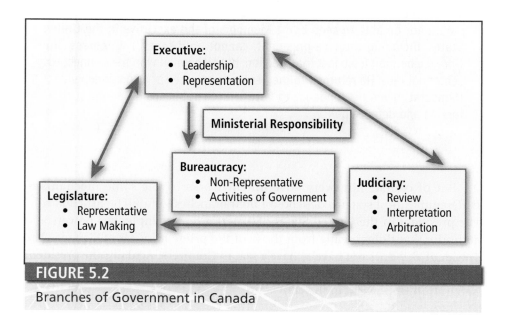

FIGURE 5.2

Branches of Government in Canada

5.2

VP or Senator? Joe Lieberman and the 2000 US Election

The 2000 election in the United States was controversial for many reasons — George W. Bush won the presidency by just 537 votes cast in Florida. But another story comes from that election. Joe Lieberman, who was running for the vice-presidency on the Al Gore ticket, was a senator from Connecticut.

Former vice-president Al Gore and senator Joe Lieberman appear before delegates at the 2000 Democratic Convention at the Staples Center in Los Angeles, CA.

He allowed his name to stand for re-election for senator, meaning that he was effectively running for two positions at the same time. Of course, he would not be able to keep both! Members of the executive in the United States, including the vice-president, cannot hold seats in Congress. The Gore–Lieberman team lost that election, but Lieberman won the Connecticut senatorial race. He returned to the Senate, where he sat as an 'independent Democrat' given his tendency to vote with Republicans on issues such as foreign and defence policy.

Congress
legislative chamber of government in the United States

Separation of powers
division of powers among several institutions in government (e.g., legislature, executive) to avoid concentration of authority

But of course, not every government works by the same mechanism. Different political systems depend on their branches to fulfill a particular role. The president of the United States of America, for example, has powers and authority that differ greatly from those of the prime minister of Canada. The president also does not have to have a seat in **Congress**. Actually, the president is not allowed to have a congressional seat; this is part of the concept of the 'separation of powers' in the US.[1]

The Canadian prime minister, on the other hand, must also have a seat in Parliament. This is part of the notion of the **fusion of powers**. Separation and fusion of powers both represent different ideas of how democracy should best be implemented. And while neither is necessarily better than the other, just try to convince a parliamentarian in Canada that they should adopt the American way, or vice versa! Different political systems build a **political culture** that, over time, becomes a central aspect of society.

The way these offices are chosen, the relationship they have with the other branches of government, and their ultimate jurisdiction over their respective countries could not be more unlike in many respects. Even in cases where the countries seem to share so much in common, as do Canada and the United States, a close examination of their political systems reveals such disparity that one might think they are based on completely different principles. Yet similarities also abound; these are, after all, offices found in democratic states, ones that share many values and objectives. Indeed, the United States and Canada provide a perfect case study for how governments are distinct. History, tradition, law, custom, and ideology have resulted in two quite different systems. We will take a close look at the presidential and parliamentary systems of government in this chapter to see how the application of government roles can evolve into unique examples. Later, in Chapter 9, we'll spend some time looking at the United States and Canada in a broader context.

The Executive

The executive branch in government is the 'top level' of administration and authority. Regardless of their various strains, all executives are responsible for carrying out the business of government and representing the country. In modern political systems there are basically three types of executives. Their differences are mostly based on the degree to which they are separated, or connected, with the legislative branch.

The first instance involves an executive that is part of the legislative body. The parliamentary system used in Great Britain and Canada is an example of this model. Here the executive is directly responsible to the legislature through such practices as the '**question period**,' where the government must answer to the queries and criticisms of members of parliament.

The second executive type is characteristic of the presidential system of government. In this model, the executive is formally separated from the legislature. The United States is the best example of this. Unlike the Canadian system, where executive members have seats in the legislature and carry out the formal activities of Parliament with their non-cabinet colleagues, the executive in the United States, the president and cabinet, are separated.

Finally, the third type of executive also involves a formal separation of powers between the legislature and the executive. However, behind this formal link lies the real power of the regime, usually centred in the party executive of the

Fusion of powers
political system where legislature and executive powers are combined, though specific powers may be granted to each level

Political culture
set of attitudes, beliefs, and values that underpin any political system

Question Period
time allotted in House of Commons for members of the house to ask questions of the prime minister or cabinet ministers

5.3

Question Period or Shouting Match?

Canadians who have clicked past parliamentary cable channels on their television dial will be familiar with the seeming rancour that occurs in the Canadian House of Commons. For the uninitiated — and indeed for many familiar with the system — question period seems to be more of a free-for-all than a formal role for the Parliament. ('Parliament' is based on the French word *parlement* or 'discussion', though one might wonder what type of discussion takes place with several people speaking loudly all at the same time across an open floor.) Question Period is nonetheless an essential part of Canada's political system, and it has a long history. The first one took place in 1867 just after Confederation, as an opportunity for the opposition members to hold the government to account. Today, Question Period typically is held in either the morning or the afternoon, and lasts 45 minutes. Questions may be asked of the prime minister or members of the cabinet, and are overseen by the Speaker of the House. The Speaker's job is to maintain decorum in the House, which has become all the more difficult with the advent of television coverage. Though it may seem a free-for-all, it is bound by many rules, including who may ask questions of whom, when, and for how long. Members must ask questions indirectly, speaking through the Speaker, hence the familiar refrain, 'Mr. (or Madam) Speaker', which precedes the question.

governing elites. The governing systems of the former communist states of Eastern Europe, and the current government in Cuba, illustrate this third model. It shows the basis of power in authoritarian systems, where elected politicians may exist, but elite members of political parties hold real power.

Executive bodies perform many different functions. Some are constitutionally laid out, and others are more a matter of practice. The executive performs different functions in society, in government, and in the party from which it has been selected. In most states the executive, particularly the leader, provides leadership for the whole political system. In Canada, for instance, that is the prime minister. The monarch, the queen or king, formally holds the position of head of state in Canada. The Governor General is the official representative of the monarchy in Canada (and lieutenants governor have this responsibility for the provinces). While these roles are largely symbolic, the prime minister is the head of government with more substantive political powers. In the United States, the president is both head of state and head of government.

The executive in many systems (including Canada's) provides partisan leadership to the party. The Canadian prime minister is also the leader of the party that forms a government.

Indeed, the prime minister is first selected to lead the party and, only as a result of electoral victory, becomes the prime minister. In those systems that link the executive to the legislature, the executive provides leadership within the legislature.

Perhaps most importantly, at least on a day-to-day basis, the executive provides leadership and supervision for the whole bureaucracy. In a legal–constitutional

5.4

When Parties Must Co-operate: Coalition Governments

Sometimes parliamentary government isn't so simple. While ordinarily governments are formed on the basis of a ruling party — the one that receives the most votes in a federal election — there are times when there is no single party in power. Coalition governments are formed when several parties (often two, maybe more) come together to create a unified executive branch. Usually, this is because there is no majority among the parties that received votes; however, minority governments are quite common too, when a party that receives the most votes forms a government. Though they are often difficult to manage, coalition governments offer an alternative to the uncertainty of minority governments, or the possibility of asking voters to return to the polls once again. Countries that have a tradition of many strong party options, such as Italy or Israel, offer examples of coalition governments. Other countries have only two major parties; the United States is an example where the two main parties receive most of the vote and one therefore is given a majority. In Canada, there has been a long tradition of third-party influence with the New Democratic Party. But more recently, there has been a growth in popular support for several different parties: the Liberals, Conservatives, NDP, the Bloc Québécois, and even the Greens. This has resulted in more talk of coalition governments in Canada because the prospects for majority scenarios seem less likely than in the past.

---

sense the bureaucracy has no independent life of its own. It is supposed to be the technical arm of the cabinet. In Canada this is well illustrated by the doctrine of **ministerial responsibility**.

Ministerial responsibility can be seen in all instances of the **Westminster parliamentary system**. Stemming from a tradition established in the United Kingdom, this means that ministers are responsible for actions of all agencies and civil servants under their jurisdiction. It is an important concept, because it means that ministers cannot simply call on the collective decision-making of cabinet or even a party **caucus**, but rather answer for the activities of their own individual ministries. It is also an important example of democratic principles: bureaucrats are not elected, remember, so the activities of the bureaucracy must be answerable somewhere. And that falls to the minister. Although it may be impossible for ministers to know every detail and activity of their ministry, they are nonetheless responsible for everything that happens within it.

In modern politics, two views have become quite widespread. The first is the idea that legislative bodies are simply 'rubber stamps' for executive decisions. This would suggest that the real authority in politics lies at the top, and the elected legislatures, which are ultimately directly responsible to the people, have far less influence. According to this view, principles of democracy, meaning governance by the elected representatives of the people, are replaced by executive rule with little (if any) accountability to the parliament. Perhaps to ameliorate this attitude, parliamentary ministerial responsibility — binding the executive to the legislature

Ministerial responsibility
principle in parliamentary systems that requires members of the political executive, both individually and as a group, to remain accountable to the legislature

Westminster system
British model of parliamentary representative government

Caucus
group of elected representatives, usually based on party membership, but which may also be grouped by race, gender, geographic representation, etc.

Legitimation

providing legitimacy, or legal force or status, to political decisions; in accordance with established or accepted patterns and standards

— is considered vital in the parliamentary tradition. Political scientists speak of **legitimation** in this context, referring to how political institutions 'legitimate' the actions of politicians through a formal and legalized process.[2]

The second view goes even further, arguing that it is the bureaucracy that in fact governs most political systems, increasing even further the distance between the people and decision-makers. After all, members of the bureaucracies are anonymous, frequently protected by their terms of office, and not subject to scrutiny by the electorate. We'll return to the bureaucracy presently, but it is important to recognize that bureaucracies are the administrative 'arm' of government; real decisions and direction come from government, which is held to inspection by others, such as the opposition as well as other groups in society.

The Legislature

Historically, legislative bodies developed as a means of reducing the absolute power of the monarch or absolute ruler. Even today, the US Congress or Canadian Parliament represent an institutional 'check' on the otherwise unbridled power of the executive. Legislatures present a voice for citizens in the form of representation, a formal law-making entity (keep in mind that governing parties cannot make laws on their own; they must seek and obtain the assent of the legislature, including opposition members), as well as a chamber for debate and discussion.

From a legal point of view there are three main types of legislatures. The first one operates within the doctrine of legislative 'sovereignty' or supremacy. Britain's Westminster parliamentary model is a primary example of this type of legislature. This doctrine rests on a number of principles. First, the legislative branch of

5.5

The Ultimate Power? The Right to Declare War

The US presidency is often referred to as the most powerful position in the world. There are many good arguments for this. But the president, like any other head of government, must work with the legislature. There are real independent powers of the presidency, such as appointments, clemency, some emergency powers, and certain foreign policy roles. But these are limited and the most important decisions — those involving the lives of US soldiers — are actually taken in Congress. Both houses of Congress must vote in a majority to declare war; the president cannot do so independently. In Canada, declaring war is a 'prerogative power', meaning that it is made by the sovereign — that is, the Governor General as the representative of the monarch. However, in practice, military action in Canada is decided by cabinet and debated in Parliament. Any declaration of war must receive approval by Parliament. Interestingly, Canada has only 'declared war' once, against Germany in 1939. It waited a week after the British declaration as a demonstration of its independence. In both examples, though with different processes, we see the importance of the legislature.

government is the highest authority. This means that a government (presidential or parliamentary) has to have the assent of the legislature before decisions can be carried out. In these systems, the legislature is beyond interference by either the courts or the executive. That's not to suggest that there will be no exchange of information and ideas among the levels; there always will be. But the legislature remains independent and ultimately autonomous.

In this model, legislatures have no limits to the extent of their jurisdiction, although there are reasonable limits to what legislatures will undertake. In practice (and in law) the absolute power of the legislature is limited by the principle of the rule of law, constitutional conventions, and other customs and practices entrenched in the legal and political culture of the country. But legislatures cannot establish rules or laws that would bind future legislatures; a law created today cannot be expected to last forever. Legislatures must always be permitted to re-examine laws for another time and place. Imagine, for instance, if the laws on suffrage that were created before women were permitted to vote were to last *in omne tempus* (forever). It would be ridiculous to think that we should live by a code implemented in the past, with no changes. Of course, some of those past laws are perfectly acceptable today. We just do not know which ones will fall out of favour in the future.

The second type of parliamentary institution operates in a constitutionally prescribed context. It usually divides governance between the legislative branch and the executive and is usually subject to judicial scrutiny through the process of judicial review. The US Congress is an example of this model, where certain powers are reserved for the presidency and others are granted to the Congress. Foreign trading relations, declaring war, creating militia, and establishing post offices are some of the many powers given to Congress in the US constitution.

The third category, of which Canada is a good example, is a 'mixed' system. In such systems the legislature is viewed as a supreme authority but subject to several limitations. Thus, the Canadian Parliament, for example, shares its supremacy with the provincial legislatures. And certain rights and roles are given to the provincial legislatures, rather than the federal Parliament. Education policy, for instance, is decided and implemented by the Canadian provinces. Further, as a result of the Constitution Act, 1982, the Charter of Rights and Freedoms has given the Canadian courts greater scope for judicial review. Consequently, the courts are often asked to rule on the '**constitutionality**' of certain issues.

Constitutionality
being in accordance with a constitution

5.6

Constitutionality and Same-Sex Marriage

Although it wasn't until 2005 that same-sex marriage became fully legal in Canada, the struggle to recognize these unions had been ongoing for some time. In 1999, Canada's Supreme Court ruled that same-sex couples were entitled to the same financial and legal benefits as other couples. This started a process of judicial review of marriage definitions and the extension of rights. Ultimately, the legalization of same-sex marriages came as a result of judicial review of the constitutionality of bans on them. Interestingly, although provinces and territories had bans on

5.6 Continued...

same-sex marriage, constitutional reviews of the laws revealed that the federal government only has the right to define marriage, and it had not, to that point, either included or excluded same-sex couples. The 'unconstitutional' positions of provinces and territories led the federal government to investigate the inclusion of same-sex marriages. A motion in the House of Commons by the Canadian Alliance (now the Conservative Party) to uphold a heterosexual interpretation of marriage was defeated, and led to the Liberal government's request of the Supreme Court to examine the constitutionality of same-sex marriages. That led to the 2005 legislation of the Paul Martin Liberals to expand the legal definition of marriage to include same-sex couples. The decision by the Canadian Parliament to change the laws to incorporate same-sex marriages is a good example of how social mores and prevailing attitudes change over time, demonstrating the importance of the ability of legislatures to be free to take different decisions over time.

Legislative Structures

Not all legislatures have the same powers, and not all legislatures look the same, either. In the Canadian Parliament, for instance, the legislature is divided into the lower House of Commons and the upper house, the Senate. These two houses are part of what is called a **bicameral** legislature. Many examples of legislatures use two chambers. The US federal government, as well as those in Mexico, Italy, the United Kingdom, Russia, India, and Brazil all have bicameral legislatures. In some systems both chambers are of roughly equal status (for instance, the United States). In these cases, powers are generally equal in both, though responsibilities may differ. In others, the second or Upper House is largely symbolic and frequently appointed or based on hereditary membership (for instance, the Senate in Canada and the House of Lords in the United Kingdom).

Bicameral
legislative or parliamentary body with two assemblies

Having two chambers provides greater oversight and checks over the activities of others. For instance, though the Canadian Senate is often criticized for having appointed members, it has an important function. It reviews legislation coming from the 'lower' house, the House of Commons, offering amendments or suggestions; this has been known historically in Canada as a 'sober second thought'. It may seem quaint to have such a role in modern government, but the Senate does present another opportunity for review of potential legislation.

There are also **unicameral** legislative bodies. These have a single house, and are usually found in smaller political systems, or those that have a very strong unitary form of government (see the following chapter for more details about unitary governments). Provinces and territories in Canada, for instance, are unicameral. Although bicameral systems are touted as having built-in oversight and checks, advocates of unicameralism see the second house as redundant.

Unicameral
legislative or parliamentary body with one assembly

National governments in Israel, Hungary, Finland, and Turkey, among others, all use a unicameral structure.

Legislative structures, unlike bureaucracies or courts, operate for an arranged period of time. However, sometimes the term of a legislature may be concluded before the expiry of the maximum period by a call for an election. In Canada, for instance, the maximum period for parliament to sit is five years. Furthermore, the manner in which legislative bodies operate (regardless of the type) is constrained by a multitude of written and customary rules that, to a considerable extent, dictate outcomes. Legislatures also operate with a variety of committees and legislative subgroups.

Legislative Functions

Although the word 'parliament' has its origins in the French verb *parler* ('to speak'), the lawmaking function is always mentioned as the first and foremost function of any legislative body. We discussed Question Period previously; that part of Parliament represents an important tradition, but the ultimate objective is to set out laws. Another function of legislatures is the control, scrutiny, and audit of the executive and bureaucracies. Legislatures do this in a number of ways. First, legislative proposals have to be introduced in Parliament. The Canadian cabinet may have an initiative it wishes to pursue, but it cannot be legal until Parliament passes it. Second, money is always a crucial matter. When governments propose initiatives that involve spending taxpayers' money, they must have the Parliament's authority for these financial expenditures. Government budgets, for instance, must be passed by the legislature.

5.7

Can Government 'Stop'? Lessons from the Clinton Era

Imagine a scenario where a government proposes a budget, and a hostile legislature refuses to pass it. What happens? In the Canadian case, this would result in a vote of non-confidence, and there would be an election. (This happens from time to time; in 1979, it brought the Joe Clark Progressive Conservative government down and resulted in the election of the Liberals under Pierre Trudeau.) In the United States, on the other hand, it could lead to stalemate. In 1995, the Clinton administration proposed a budget to Congress that the Republican-dominated legislature refused to pass. The Republicans, led by Speaker of the House of Representatives Newt Gingrich, thought that this would show the weakness of Bill Clinton's presidency, then in the middle of its first term. Clinton refused to budge, hedging his bets that the US public would support him. The impasse led to an effective 'shutdown' of the US government, as it no longer had a budget mandate to pay for its operations. Over $800 million in wages and salaries were held up, and the American people came to see this largely as a dispute between Gingrich and Clinton. Gingrich unadvisedly made comments that Clinton was not giving him proper respect. Former Republican House Leader Tom DeLay wrote in his book *No Retreat, No Surrender: One American's Fight* that Gingrich said he forced the shutdown because Clinton made him sit in the back of Air Force One on the return flight from the funeral of Israeli Prime Minister Yitzhak Rabin. Political and public support swung heavily to the Clinton side of the debate. The budget eventually passed, and Gingrich lost a great deal of political support from his own party and from the electorate. In the congressional election the following year, the Democrats gained seats at the expense of the Republicans, and won back control of the House.

And on the subject of money, the performance of government in the area of fiscal management as well as meeting policy objectives, and the activities of the executive and the civil service, are subject to parliamentary critique (see our discussion of Question Period, for instance).

Yet perhaps the greatest function legislatures perform is that of **representation**. Given the connection between politicians and their constituencies, they view themselves as representatives of, and are expected to represent, their constituencies. This is performed in several ways. First, political representatives bring the general policy expectations and evaluations of their constituents to the attention of the executive and the legislature. Second, they are expected to secure some benefits (such as jobs, government contracts, and industrial development) for their local constituency. Third, they assist individuals (or groups) that face bureaucratic 'red tape' or have grievances against the government. Fourth, through their representation, debates, and voting, legislatures ensure the accountability of the executive. Legislatures also are agents of political socialization, since we frequently become aware of certain issues as a result of parliamentary debate.

Representative democracy is at the heart of our political systems. Whether they are Parliaments, Congresses, or some other form of legislature, representative institutions such as these are created to serve the interests of citizens. Importantly, representation in democratic systems permits an orderly and fair mediation of differing opinions and interests among citizens; this is never perfect, however. Representative democratic institutions set out an alternative to dictatorship, monarchies, oligarchies, or any of the other systems of governing we have covered in this book.

The Judiciary

The rule of **law** in democracies is considered the bedrock of legitimacy. Citizens may be allowed to vote, but without recourse to law and the courts, their rights and liberties cannot be assured. The courts, legal codes, judges, and lawyers are all part of a fundamental aspect of modern democracies. And the judiciary — the name we give to the entire system — is an essential part of the separation of powers in any political system: the role of interpreting law must be kept separate from those who make the laws.

In a very broad sense the judiciary, or the courts, performs three main functions: it rules on the constitutionality of public and private acts; it interprets laws; and it adjudicates disputes.

In Canada, the powers of the judiciary are outlined in the constitution. The highest court in Canada is the Supreme Court. Judges (or 'justices') in this court, as well as superior, appellate (appeal courts), criminal, and provincial and territorial judges are appointed by the federal or provincial governments. Law in Canada is governed mostly by **common law**, which means that decisions are made on the basis of precedent, previous decisions, and case law, except for Quebec, which uses **civil law**, where legislative bodies at the municipal and provincial levels enact laws through statutes, ordinances, and regulations. Later we will look at these two types of law in the Canadian context.

Representation
the act of standing for the views of others; election of a representative to symbolize the collective view of all constituents

Representative democracy
political system in which voters elect others to act on their behalf

Laws
rules imposed on society by governing authority

Common law
legal system where decisions are made on the basis of precedent, case law, or previous decisions

Civil law
legal system where legislative bodies enact laws through statutes, ordinances, and regulations

Constitutionality Ruling

Various levels of government will often refer legislation or intended legislation to the courts for an opinion as to whether the legislation in question is within their jurisdiction. For example, before repatriating the Constitution, the Canadian federal government asked the Supreme Court to determine the legality of its intended action. As a result of the inclusion of the Charter of Rights and Freedoms in the Constitution, many pieces of existing legislation have been referred to the courts in order to determine their constitutionality.

Thus, in the Canadian context, courts rule whether a federal statute, provincial legislation, or a municipal bylaw is within the scope of the Canadian Constitution. In those jurisdictions that have constitutional bills of rights, courts also have to rule on the content of individual rights, both in terms of the right itself as well as the extent of the duties that we all have with respect to the rights of others. This is an important role for the judiciary, and can often have widespread effects for the country as a whole. Decisions of the Supreme Court of Canada, for example, are *stare decisis*, where legal precedents have to be followed by the courts, and in the case of the Supreme Court, means they are binding for all lower courts.

"I KNOW IT'S NOT CONSTITUTIONAL, BUT IT SURE WOULD BE FUN."

Fun or not, ruling on constitutionality is a vital role for the courts.

© Peter Hesse/CartoonStock.com

Judicial Legal Interpretation

Statutes, common law, and other legal instruments frequently are unclear or have internal contradictions. In some political systems, even without recourse to legal action, courts can be called upon to provide a binding interpretation. In other systems they intervene only in the event of a dispute. In this latter scenario, legal interpretation is often shared with a variety of other structures (mostly bureaucracies), although court interpretations usually have higher legal and cultural status. In one such case, the Supreme Court of Canada was asked to consider French language rights in Manitoba in 1984. At that time many different authorities had various opinions on the legality of laws enacted only in English. The Supreme Court ruled that the Manitoba Act of 1870, as well as the Canadian Constitution, required both languages to be used. Effectively, this meant that any laws not printed in French as well as English were not binding. However, the Court gave the province a five-year period to make necessary changes before the ruling came into effect.[3]

Judicial Dispute Adjudication

Conflict resolution through the courts is the most effective and most common means of dealing with disputes. Of course, there are governments that employ coercion or force to make citizens abide by laws, but in liberal democracies the courts are there to provide a means of adjudication. In order to perform that function adequately, courts must be perceived as independent. To this effect, many political systems grant judges a degree of independence and security of tenure unparalleled by any other structure.

The appointment of judges is the most vulnerable point in this area. If judges are elected (as is the case for certain courts in the United States), they may be perceived as owing favours to their supporters. If, on the other hand, they are appointed, they can be viewed as tools of the governments or as being rewarded for political support. Neither of these views is necessarily wrong, as good arguments can be made for both, but it does highlight the sensitivity of judicial objectivity: no matter how they ascend to their positions, judges must be seen as fair.

Adjudication, then, is a crucial role for the court system. The entire range of legal disputes, from property cases, to divorces, to criminal charges must have a form of adjudication that is seen as legitimate and effective.

The Bureaucracy

The bureaucracy is the most common part of government that most citizens deal with on a personal daily basis. Getting a driver's licence renewed, dealing with tax officials or customs and immigration officials at international borders, or ensuring that one's older relatives receive their pension will likely involve a level of bureaucracy. Thus, when people speak of dealing with the government, they are usually talking of some contact they have had with a public servant or bureaucrat. More often than not, these are seen as negative dealings, largely because we tend to recall the situations where things don't end up so favourably. But if we think about the ways in which we encounter 'government' we cannot help but conclude that bureaucracies are an essential and, yes, even effective part of government.

Nevertheless, Canadians are often frustrated by the seeming inflexibility and complexity of what they consider is a simple procedure. This so-called red tape is a result of the fact that every activity of public servants is directed towards carrying out some specific law of the land.

Hence, public servants assume a different kind of responsibility from most people offering services in society. While many people (such as clerks, farmers, labourers, or professionals) are in a position to use their discretion within the limits of their own or their company's policy without personal hazard of having to violate a law in order to meet their customers' needs, public servants seldom have the power to

© hammondovi/iStockphoto.com

The term 'red tape' originated with the English practice of binding official documents in red cloth. We now see it as a nuisance or unnecessary hindrance.

apply personal discretion. Further, bureaucrats also realize that it is they who will suffer the consequences of stretching the rules. This is because the bureaucracy is burdened by the weight of a monumental set of rules and regulations that they must apply but that they played little role in formulating. So, the next time you feel you are unnecessarily delayed at a border crossing, for instance, think about the myriad responsibilities those border officials have. And think, too, of what we expect of them: a safe and secure system that also operates efficiently. It's a tall order, and it is true that bureaucracies can be inefficient, and even corrupt, especially in countries where accountability and democracy may not be held in high regard.

There is another much smaller group of civil servants who are seldom seen or heard of but who wield enormous political power. These include the top public servants who are in frequent contact with political leaders. It is they who run the various government departments and have access to the political ministers responsible for the legislation affecting their areas. Although these individuals may have little 'latitude' in actual decision-making (they are, after all, unelected officials), they can have tremendous influence with those who do. Thanks to their expertise and past experience, senior government bureaucrats often will be called on by their political masters for assistance in directing policy. How information flows in government, and — importantly — how decisions are made about money, will mean significant influence by certain members of the civil service. In Canada, the Privy Council Office (PCO) works as a 'hub' of the civil service, providing a non-partisan link between the bureaucracy and the cabinet. The Clerk of the Privy Council is considered the 'top' civil servant in the Canadian government.

The size, structure, and operations of any governmental bureaucracy depend on the role that society gives to the state. In most Western democratic countries, the state has assumed responsibility for all sorts of social, medical, and educational programs. It has regulatory power over many spheres of economic activity, and this development has expanded the civil service to include experts in all the areas of government involvement. In Canada, for example, there are well over half a million people who work directly for the federal government, organized in departments, departmental corporations, agency corporations, proprietary corporations, and other agencies. Bureaucracies exist at all levels of government: federal, provincial/state, and municipal. We can see, then, that government is also a major player in society when it comes to labour.

One of the questions often raised about the public sector is whether or not our public servants, particularly at the senior level, have the right to participate actively in partisan politics. Should senior officials or any public official have the right to lobby or promote a party platform or candidate, or run in an election as a candidate? Since the public service is based on the merit system, it is necessary that those who carry out the policies of their political masters be neutral. While cabinets come and go and the political party in power switches according to the will of the voters, the public servants' responsibility is to ensure that government services continue, and they must serve with equal loyalty whomever the Canadian people decide should form the government. This is easier said than done, especially at the higher levels where public servants give advice on policy content and implementation. This problem of neutrality is increased when one government remains in office for an extended period of time, and public officials develop a personal relationship with politicians of one party.

The resilience of the civil service flows from its pivotal position in modern government. There may be at times a trade-off between the expertise we expect in bureaucracies, and the sometimes exaggerated influence they may have in decision-making. In modern governments, the civil service houses and organizes the expertise required by the modern state. Because government ministers are generalists, they must rely on bureaucrats if they are to understand and resolve the complex problems they face. Legislatures, and, in turn, political executives, must continue to delegate decision-making power to civil servants and bureaucratic agencies. Civil servants are required to give meaning and purpose, through rule-making, to the vaguely stated preferences of their political masters. In short, the civil service does much more than implement policy passively. Permanent bureaucratic structures create an institutional culture and knowledge base that can only help the administration of government over time. It makes policy, shapes the views of other politicians and citizens, and routinely enacts decisions that profoundly influence citizens.

Presidential and Parliamentary Systems

Presidential and parliamentary systems are the two most consequential types of political systems today. The foundations for these two systems are rooted in the history of Great Britain: the parliamentary system is representative of the Westminster model (the name given to the British parliamentary system), while the presidential system was produced as a result of revolt in the United States against the parliamentary system in the late eighteenth century. Although some totalitarian and authoritarian states have 'adopted' some features of these systems (usually in an effort to lend some degree of legitimacy to their regime), both the parliamentary and presidential configurations of government, or hybrid combinations of the two, exist in liberal democracies.

The main feature separating the two systems relates to the separation of powers, or the manner in which power is granted to the levels of government — usually the executive, legislature, and judiciary, but also at times the bureaucracy. The separation of powers is crucial here because it shows ways in which power is prevented from misuse by one wing of government.

For the architects of the American system of government in the late eighteenth century, there was concern that simply arbitrarily giving some people power would lead to corruption. Therefore, there needed to be some system of oversight. But while some were concerned that power might lead to corruption, another prevailing view was that the strength of the nation would be diminished if some degree of control and authority were not given to some levels of government. There were a number of mechanisms put in place to try to overcome these two concerns.

In the United States, the presidential system disallows anyone from holding office in more than one level of government, and each level is given a review of proceedings at the other levels. So, for instance, legislation passed in the US Congress (the lower House of Representatives and the upper Senate chamber) must be approved by the executive — the president. However, if the president were to veto (the constitutional right to reject) legislation, the matter might then be turned back to the Congress, where a two-thirds majority in both houses could overturn the veto. Similarly, the Congress has the right to reject bills proposed by the president, limit appointments, or even impeach the president. One can see, then, the emphasis in the American system is on what is termed **checks and balances**, or the ability by one level of government to limit the independent actions of another.

In contrast to the presidential system, the parliamentary system relies on a fusion of powers, bringing together the responsibilities and rights of different levels of authority within government. In particular, the fusion of powers unites the capacity of the executive and legislative levels of government. For example, unlike the presidential system, members of one level of government in a parliamentary system — say, a cabinet minister or prime minister — are required to be members of, or seeking office in, Parliament. We'll examine these and other differences later in the chapter.

Despite persistent questions regarding the relative benefits of one system over the other, the presidential and parliamentary systems represent the two dominant political systems in the world today. Often states adopt elements of one or both in an attempt to create what might be termed a composite or 'hybrid' system. One of the basic differences between the two systems is the emphasis on internal checks and balances within the presidential system, on the one hand, and the importance placed on representation (meaning the government is not limited by counterbalancing influences) in the parliamentary system, on the other.

Veto
refusal to endorse, or blocking of, a decision

Checks and balances
system of inspection and evaluation of different levels and branches of governments by others

Government in Canada

Because we live in a constitutional democracy, and because it is crucial to understand one's own political system in order to compare it with others, we should pause to consider the Canadian experience. We have touched on Canadian cases and examples throughout this chapter, but some further information is necessary. (We will also look at other aspects of Canadian politics in Chapter 9.)

Canada is a constitutional democracy, and its institutions are representative of the division of powers within a modern federal democracy. Historically, Canada's chief constitutional document has been the Constitution Act of 1867. It is a legalistic document containing over 140 sections that outline the general rules by which government is to be conducted in Canada. The 'preamble' of the Constitution Act states that Canada is to have 'a constitution similar to that of the United Kingdom'. Because the British constitution is not embodied in a single document but rather consists of a series of laws and practices, including all acts of Parliament and the gradual evolution of institutions and traditions, Canada has inherited the British system of parliamentary government and the tradition of common law (note, however, the prevalence of civil law in Quebec, which reflects its French roots).

The nature of the relationship between the executive and the legislative branches of government, and between the federal and provincial levels of government, has developed into a unique system of government with its own body of customs and traditions.

The Constitution Act, in addition to providing for the union of the colonies, had to encompass two contradictory constitutional principles: the evolutionary nature of British constitutionalism and the necessity of providing specific jurisdictional guidelines in order to guarantee the protection of certain rights demanded by the colonies entering Confederation. The issue here concerned how to apply an existing constitutional system based on hundreds of years of collected history and political tradition to a newly minted system with its own unique features.

Thus, in accord with British tradition, three major branches of government were established: the executive, legislative, and judiciary. In order to take into account the consideration of local government, the constitution created a federal system and determined the distribution of legislative powers between the federal and provincial legislatures. This latter distribution of powers and the Charter of Rights and Freedoms (1982) are perhaps the most important elements of the Canadian constitution and are certainly the most controversial. And structurally, the Canadian political system was based on a federal model.

Canadian Federalism

Federalism
form of governance that divides powers between the central government and regional governments; often, particular roles and capacities are given to the regional governments

Confederalism
political system of divided powers where added power is given to the non-central governments, and limited authority and power is conferred to the central government

Federalism describes a manner of dividing and allocating power among different political authorities such as provinces and the federal government. (We will return to a more detailed discussion of federalism in Chapter 6.) It is also the most adequate description of the political structure in Canada. At the outset, in 1867, the federal government was given what were considered the major powers, while the provinces were supposedly restricted in their authority to matters of local concern. Although we often hear of 'Canadian Confederation' in 1867, Canada really never was a **confederal** state. Confederation refers to the union of unitary actors, where certain powers are gathered and given to a central authority while the pre-existing actors retain a large degree of independence in internal and external affairs. Many powers reside in the central government in Ottawa, and others, such as education and health care, are administered by the provinces. Given the range of powers that have been decentralized to the provinces, some prefer to use the term 'quasi-federalism' to define Canada's structure.

The general division of powers between Ottawa and the provinces is set out in sections 91 and 92 of the Constitution Act. The Act gave the federal, or central, government the authority to 'make laws for the peace, order and good government of Canada in relation to all matters not coming within the classes of subjects by this act assigned exclusively to the legislatures of the Provinces'.[4] Here is where the commonly used phrase 'peace, order, and good government' originated. Although it may not have the same 'ring' as 'life, liberty, and the pursuit of happiness', which appears in the US Declaration of Independence, it has come to summarize a lot of Canadian political culture. However, from a constitutional perspective, it is a 'residual clause' used to show where power ought to reside when it is not clarified outright. In Canada, this residual power is given to the central government, demonstrating again the tendency towards federalism in Canadian politics.

As well, the Constitution Act included a list of specific powers intended not to detract from the general power, but to clarify those areas specifically within general jurisdiction. Among these comprehensive federal powers are: jurisdiction over the public debt, Crown land, the raising of money by any mode or system of taxation, and the regulation of trade and commerce. In addition, by virtue of the reservation and disallowance provisions of the Constitution Act, the federal government can unilaterally invalidate any provincial law within a year of its passage. Reservation and allowance were first included in the constitution to permit the monarch to override decisions of parliament. It has not been used since 1943, and would certainly be seen as an infringement on provincial affairs; indeed, many wish to have it removed. However, it was not removed in the Constitution Act of 1982.

The Constitution Act provides for no general power at the provincial level but specifies those areas exclusively within provincial jurisdiction. Among the most important areas are: control over property and civil rights, the power of direct taxation, and education — with certain qualifications. Section 95 of the Constitution Act gives the 'Dominion' (the outdated term for the federal government) and the provinces parallel jurisdiction over immigration and agriculture. A subsequent amendment has given the Canadian Parliament authority to enact laws in relation to old age pensions.[5]

Canadian Courts and the Constitution

One major aspect of change in Canadian federalism is the role for judicial interpretation of the Constitution. As has been discussed above, both the central and provincial governments have the authority to enact laws within their respective domains; in so doing, either level of government may seek to amend the constitution.

In Canada the judiciary is given the task of ensuring that legislation enacted at the provincial or federal level falls within the boundaries of the constitution. Following Confederation, the Judicial Committee of the British Privy Council (JCPC) was the final court of appeal for Canada. This lasted until 1949, when the Supreme Court of Canada became the final court of appeal. Although bound by previous decisions in deciding cases, judicial interpretation has played an important role in shaping the direction of Canadian federalism.

The Constitution Act of 1982 is the other 'half' of Canada's constitutional history. It signified full independence from Great Britain, created the Charter of Rights and Freedoms, included rights for Aboriginals, and established an amending formula for the constitution. There was some controversy in the '**patriation**' (sometimes called 'repatriation') of the constitution from Britain in that Quebec refused to support the Act. Quebec wanted to have a constitutional veto, and when this was not forthcoming, it decided not to support repatriation. To this day, Quebec is not a signatory to the constitution, which is nevertheless considered binding throughout Canada.

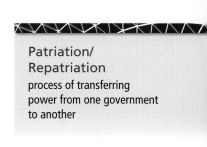
Patriation/ Repatriation
process of transferring power from one government to another

With the passage of the 1982 Constitution Act, the role of the judiciary changed immensely. Some critics of the new constitution claim that the Canadian Supreme Court will now resemble its American counterpart (but without the review and confirmation of appointments currently enjoyed by the US Senate), and that this is a further erosion of the role of Parliament in the Canadian political system. Before the Constitution Act of 1982, the judiciary was only called upon in order to decide which level or levels of government had jurisdiction within a disputed area. As a result of the inclusion of the Charter of Rights and Freedoms in the Constitution Act of 1982, the judiciary was given the authority to judge legislation outside the powers of both levels of government. In brief, with the repatriation of the Canadian constitution in 1982, the role of the judiciary in Canadian political life expanded markedly; further, the Charter of Rights and Freedoms has had broader implications for Canada's political system, as outlined in the section that follows.

The Charter of Rights and Freedoms and Individual Citizens

The inclusion of the Charter of Rights and Freedoms has added an element of profound respect for basic civil liberties and human rights to our Constitution.

In effect, the Charter has extended the scope of the constitution from the 'macro' level of the state and its institutions to the 'micro' level of individual rights. As a result of the Charter, there have been three significant ramifications for the political system. First, human rights issues have achieved a new importance in Canadian politics, which reflects the focus on individual rights in the Charter. Second, the courts have provided a new avenue of recourse for infringements on individual rights and freedoms. This is part of how the role of the courts has been extended since the repatriation of the constitution. And third, provincial human rights codes and legislation pertaining to the individual have moved into line with the federal Charter.

5.8

The Charter: Individual or Collective Rights?

The Canadian Charter of Rights and Freedoms is no doubt considered a major part of the **repatriation** of the Canadian constitution of 1982. Before the Charter, Canada had the 1960 Canadian Bill of Rights, but it had limited effect because it was not a constitutional document. The Charter changed that. At its core, the Charter ensures the rights of individuals, something which was criticized by those who sought more attention to the rights of communities and the collective. Some wanted to see it take on more of a 'social charter' role, including welfare-type goods, such as guarantees of housing, a minimum standard of living, and access to education. Given Canada's historical support for individual rights, such as its support for the United Nations Declaration of Human Rights, which concentrates on the person, it is not surprising that the Charter would take the individual as its focus.

Some experts have argued that the inclusion of a Charter of Rights and Freedoms in our constitution has amounted to nothing less than a revolutionary change in our system of government. Of note here is the new role for the courts, now given policy-making power much beyond what they have traditionally possessed. Others suggest that the Canadian judiciary has always had a fairly significant influence on policy, and the Charter will only slightly expand this power, particularly with respect to questions of social justice and minority-language rights. In any case, when the courts deem legislation unconstitutional because it violates the rights of individual citizens, the political consequences are immense: in some cases either or both levels of government may be denied the right to legislate. Therefore, it is possible that policy-making authority could be shifted from other branches of government to the judiciary, in particular the Supreme Court of Canada.

Canadian Law

As mentioned previously, there are two major legal systems in the world. The first has its roots in Roman law and is referred to as civil law. In a civil law country, the role of the legislature is emphasized over that of the courts. Statutes are assumed to constitute a complete, original statement of the social will of the community. Law, then, is derived from the actions of legislatures. The civil law system is found in continental European countries, especially those possessing a Roman heritage, as well as the province of Quebec. This legal system is characterized by an emphasis upon statutes and codes of law. Much of civil law may be traced back to the code prepared for the Roman Emperor Justinian and known as the Justinian Code (AD 533). One of the better-known examples of civil codes is in France, prepared for the Emperor Napoleon in 1804 and known as the Code Napoleon.

The other legal system was developed in England and is known as common law. Common law is defined in the authoritative *Black's Dictionary of Law* as the body of those principles and rules of action, relating to the government and security of persons and property, which derive their authority solely from usages and customs of immemorial antiquity, or from the judgments and decrees of the courts recognizing, affirming, and enforcing such usages and customs, and in this sense, particularly the ancient unwritten law of England.

Great Britain, Canada (except Quebec), the United States, Australia, New Zealand, and many of the former British colonies adhere to this model of law. In practice the two systems are no longer so distinct (or perhaps never were). Common law countries have endless statutory instruments and civil law countries rely on precedents to some extent.

Among some of the important principles inherent in the Canadian legal system are: higher law takes precedence over inferior law, regardless of its origins from courts or legislatures and the principle that later laws replace earlier ones. Above all, Canada, like every political system claiming legitimacy, recognizes the principle of the rule of law. This principle in its simplest form means that people are to be governed according to a known set of rules that affect all members of a polity and are arrived at in a constitutional manner.[6]

Conclusion

This chapter has introduced you to the forms and composition of different branches in contemporary government. We have seen that, in many ways, the ideological roots of political systems influence their type of government and the scope of its powers. The relative importance granted to the executive, the legislature, the courts, and bureaucracies differs depending on prevailing ideologies and political culture. In recent years we have seen the concentration of legislative and administrative power in both the executive and bureaucracy. In turn, the power of the legislative branch has decreased as policy-making has become more complex. Courts in turn have received new powers of interpretation under the Constitution Act, 1982. Understanding the individual roles these branches of government play, as well as their interrelationship, is essential.

The two political systems that influence us most are our own, and the American variant. In a comparative context we have analyzed the differences between the Canadian and American forms of government — parliamentary and presidential; together, they represent the primary models of government employed by most states today. And given where we live, this chapter has also introduced you to the fundamentals of Canadian government: its primary institutions, normative influences, and structure. The next chapter will take us a bit deeper into our study of different political systems. We will pick up on many of the themes we have introduced in this chapter, particularly with regard to the way that we divide power and authority among different actors.

Self-Assessment Questions

1. What are the four primary functions of any political system?
2. Why are constitutions so integral for liberal democracies?
3. Why is decentralization (or the lack of it) so important for the composition of political systems?
4. How has Canada developed a federal structure from an originally 'confederal' model?
5. What is meant by 'repatriation' of the constitution?
6. How has the Charter of Rights and Freedoms given new emphasis on the individual? How has it affected the role of the judiciary?
7. What is the difference between 'common' and 'civil' law?
8. In what way has the principle of the 'separation of powers' been applied by the presidential and parliamentary systems?
9. What are the four primary institutions in government? What are their individual responsibilities?
10. Why are bureaucrats unelected?

Weblinks

Parliament of Canada
www.parl.gc.ca

Prime Minister of Canada
www.pm.gc.ca/eng/default.asp

Governor General of Canada
www.gg.ca

Canada's Court System
www.justice.gc.ca/eng/dept-min/pub/ccs-ajc

Canada's Constitution
laws.justice.gc.ca/en/const/index.html

United States House of Representatives
www.house.gov

United States Senate
www.senate.gov

United States White House
www.whitehouse.gov

United States Courts
www.uscourts.gov

United States Constitution
www.archives.gov/exhibits/charters/
constitution.html

Further Reading

Bakvis, Herman, Gerald Baier, and Douglas M. Brown. *Contested Federalism: Certainty and Ambiguity in the Canadian Federation*. Don Mills, ON: Oxford University Press, 2009.

Black, Henry Campbell. *A Dictionary of Law*. 3rd ed. St. Paul, MN: West Publishing, 1933.

Brooks, Stephen. *Canadian Democracy: An Introduction*. 6th ed. Don Mills, ON: Oxford University Press, 2009.

Dawson, R. MacGregor, and W.F. Dawson. *Democratic Government in Canada*. 5th ed., rev. Norman Ward. Toronto: University of Toronto Press, 1997.

Dyck, Rand. *Canadian Politics: Critical Approaches*, 5th ed. Toronto: Nelson, 2008.

Genovese, Michael A. *The Power of the American Presidency: 1789–2000*, New York, NY: Oxford University Press, 2001.

Lowi, Theodore J., Benjamin Ginsberg, and Kenneth A. Shepsle. *American Government: Power and Purpose*. 9th ed. New York: W.W. Norton, 2006.

MacIvor, Heather. *Parameters of Power: Canada's Political Institutions*. Toronto: Nelson Education, 2006.

Welch, Susan, John Gruhl, Michael Steinman, John Comer, and Susan Rigdon. *American Government*. 10th ed. Florence, KY: Wadsworth, 2005.

CBC News Clips

Visit the companion website for *Politics: An Introduction* to listen to news clips from the CBC radio archives.

6 Political Systems

LEARNING OBJECTIVES

After reading this chapter, you will be able to:

❋ understand the differences among the unitary, federal, and confederal forms of government

❋ recognize the strengths and weaknesses of the unitary system of government

❋ recognize the strengths and weaknesses of the federal system of government

❋ see the diversity that exists in the real-world examples of both forms of government

❋ comprehend the nature of the Canadian system of federal government and the challenges it faces.

Introduction

As we have seen in earlier chapters, it is not accurate to think of the state as operating in the same way as a human individual. The state is split within, particularly between its executive, legislative, and judicial branches. In this chapter we will see how the geographical distribution of power, between the central government and the regions of a country, will impact upon the nature of its political system.

A quick glance at most maps of Canada will show you that, in political terms, the country does not exist as one continental-sized bloc. You will notice, of course, that Canada is divided up into different geopolitical units, known as provinces and territories. These units maintain a specific relationship with each other, on the one hand, and with the national or federal government in Ottawa on the other. Responsibilities, powers, and political and economic control are distributed between federal and provincial governments, and we see that at both levels representatives are chosen by the people in elections. In the United States of America we find a similar situation, with the individual states bearing the responsibility for a wide range of issues and holding considerable political control and influence.

Now look at a map of the United Kingdom. Even though there are similar geographical divisions that exist between counties in that country, it is quite clear that those units do not have nearly the same amount of power or control as Canada's provinces. In the UK, power, control, and responsibility are quite heavily concentrated in London, where the central or national government has its home. In France, power is also concentrated at the centre, with the national government in Paris dominating the political scene.

The differences between these two kinds of system are best explained through a discussion of federal versus unitary political systems, two very different but equally important forms of organizing the nation-state in geopolitical terms. Both kinds of system present certain strong points and certain deficiencies, and good arguments can be made for each, in terms of efficiency, stability, and representation. The purpose of this chapter is to introduce you to these distinct ways of organizing the state, and to encourage you to consider their respective strengths and weaknesses, particularly in the Canadian context.

Indeed it is fair to say that if you do not understand the nature of federalism, and in particular Canadian federalism, you do not understand Canadian politics at all. So many of the most pressing issues in Canadian politics, government, society, and economics today are directly affected by, or linked to, the particular brand of federalism practised in this country. As we will see in this chapter, Canadian federalism is unique, problematic, complex, and constantly changing. It is therefore vitally important that we study and understand its workings. The fact that federalism is such a 'living' issue in Canada also makes it a surprisingly exciting and dynamic area of study.

Distributing Power within the State: To Centralize or Share?

A key element for a clear understanding of the workings of different political systems is the actual physical or geographical distribution of authority. All political units, despite their ideological underpinning, must distribute the activities and functions of government within their territorial boundaries. The degree to which a political system parcels out political authority — or, conversely, keeps that authority in one place — is largely a result of **decentralization**.[1] Governments that desire to manage most of political decision-making and influence within one geographical position may seek to create a single, supreme locus of power. On the other hand, many states seek to divide power and responsibility among geographical positions. The two primary compositions of government in this regard are federal and unitary arrangements. Elsewhere in this text, we have discussed the concept of **sovereignty**,[2] which is the legitimate authority given to a government to rule a political unit. It is useful to think about sovereignty when we compare unitary and federal systems, and where sovereignty is 'located'. In unitary states, with a strong central government, sovereignty is concentrated in the national government (although in some cases some powers may be given to sub-national authorities in a unitary system; this is referred to as **'delegated authority'**).[3] In federal states, sovereignty is divided between the national government and the sub-national governments (provinces, states, or *länder* in Germany).

The historical evolution of most countries in the international system, at least until the second half of the twentieth century, resulted in the progressive concentration of power in the hands of central governments who were unwilling to share that power with the geographic regions that made up their territory. By creating **unitary**[4] states, political authority was not divided, and control made

Decentralization
process whereby power and authority is taken from the central government and conferred to non-central (for example, state, regional, or provincial) governments

Sovereignty
recognition by other political authorities that a government is legitimate and rightful for a political community

Delegated authority
situation where some powers may be given to sub-national authorities by the national government in a unitary system

Unitary systems
political systems that concentrate political authority and powers within one central government, which is singularly responsible for the activities of the political unit, both domestic and foreign

Centralization

concentration of power in a single body, usually the principal government

Federalism

form of governance that divides powers between the central government and regional governments; often, particular roles and capacities are given to the regional governments

Confederalism

political system of divided powers where added power is given to the non-central governments, and limited authority and power is conferred to the central government

easier. In fact the concentration and **centralization**[5] of political power was a central goal for most states as they established themselves in the modern era (that is, since the seventeenth century). The need to consolidate internal control over territory by the monarchs of Europe led them to build institutions and systems of command that maximized their ability to dictate policy, to tax, and to mobilize the populations of their countries. This process of centralization of power had two goals: first, to defeat and suppress internal rivals to power, and second, to strengthen the state vis-à-vis neighbouring states.

In other states, however, the only way to consolidate distinct geographic, ethnic, and cultural areas into one political body was through a form of power-sharing. By guaranteeing certain rights and areas of responsibility to the constituent parts, the central government could garner internal support for the broader project of state building. This system, known as **federalism**,[6] was certainly the case for Canada and for the United States. Each of these countries, formed out of various former colonies of Great Britain, needed to bring together diverse entities under one flag and one political control. By creating a political structure based on power-sharing between the central or national government and political authorities at the level of the provinces or states, these two countries were able to pull together different political units with diverse interests and concerns, and ensure a measure of unity that would otherwise have been impossible.

Some countries have gone even further than federalism in the sharing of power. **Confederalism**[7] is when a group of regional or constituent governments give some powers to a central government; in many ways, confederalism is the opposite of unitary government. Confederal systems, such as that created in the United States in its early years (1781–87), give important powers to the constituent parts, and the regions may be said to dominate the central or national government. The central government depends heavily on the regions for its authority and legitimacy and maintains only limited powers for itself. In short, in a confederal system, no final authority is given to a central government to override the wishes or authority of the regional systems. Although one often hears reference to Canada as a 'confederation', it is, in fact, not. At the time of 'confederation' in 1867, the powers given to the provincial governments in Canada were vastly inferior to those of the central government in Ottawa. Canada was then something of a highly centralized 'quasi-federal' state. Since then, Canada has further 'federalized', although most final powers are still given to the central government. The European Union (EU), with its concentration of limited authority in Brussels, and retention of final political authority in the governments of the states that make up the EU, is an example of a confederal arrangement, where most decision-making is still contingent on the activities and will of member states (see Box 6.4). Although this chapter focuses on unitary versus federal systems, the confederal model remains an interesting and important alternative to which we will make reference in the pages to come.

Unitary Systems

It is important to bear in mind that both unitary and federal systems are created and maintained largely as a result of the constitutional authority accorded to the geographical positions of power. Unitary political systems are those that concentrate political authority and powers within one central government. The central government in a unitary system is singularly responsible for the activities of the political unit, both domestic and foreign. Further, though other 'levels' of government may exist, such as city or municipal authorities, they fall under the jurisdiction of the central unitary government.

Unitary governments, then, have a single, central authority responsible for making, interpreting, and enforcing laws, and for representing the political community abroad. An overwhelming majority of the states that exist in the international system today are unitary states. This reflects the desire to centralize power in many countries to overcome opposition, and it is also a manifestation of the perceived need to increase efficiency and effectiveness in the decision-making process and the business of implementing that policy. By centralizing power, national governments maintain closer control over the gamut of political activities, and, in theory, are able to respond more quickly and on a national scale to specific challenges and problems. Proponents of unitary government argue that this not only makes governance easier for the state, it also benefits citizens who do not, therefore, have to wait for a prolonged national debate to take place, and it also guarantees a more harmonized delivery of government services across the national territory.

This is not to say, of course, that the central authority in a unitary system will carry out each and every task related to government. In France, for example, one of the world's most centralized and unitary systems, certain powers are left to the *departments* (of which there are 90, grouped into 36 regions) and also to the municipalities, which play an important role in daily life for a vast majority of French citizens. In Britain, some powers are left to the counties and towns, and even at a lower level to the villages (through the system of parish councils).

Some unitary systems have taken steps to divide power among more than just the central government. Political arrangements where power is given to regional authorities, but are not constitutionally or legally bound, are referred to as **devolution**[8] systems. Within a 'devolved' framework, some authority is given to regional governments, but the power to oversee, dismiss, or entrench these authorities is still held by the central government. The decision in 1997 by the British government in London to give limited authority to Scottish and Welsh legislatures is an example of devolution. A state may choose to devolve power to its regions in order to respond to calls for greater autonomy, or in the interest of increasing efficiency and effectiveness in the policy process. The devolution of power in Britain responded to calls from Scottish and Welsh citizens for greater local control over policy, and for the need for a strengthening of cultural identity.

However, in all of these cases, the national government has overriding authority, and where powers have been formally devolved, they can be called back, or recentralized, if the national government so chooses. This has happened at various times throughout history, with the most recent example being the direct rule of Northern Ireland from London during the period from 1973 to 2007 (see Box 6.1). This is possible because the powers of the regional or municipal bodies are either not protected in the constitution of the state, or the central government can easily override or change the constitution. Many criticisms have been levelled

Devolution
political system where some authority is given to regional governments, but the power to oversee, dismiss, or entrench these authorities is still held by the central government

at unitary forms of government over the years. One of the most common is that they are somehow less 'democratic' than other forms of government because the central government does not respond to the wishes of different groups living in different regions, instead formulating national policies that may or may not reflect the wishes of people across the country. According to this argument, it is much easier for authoritarian governments to exist when power is centralized and concentrated in the hands of the national authority. Although this argument makes some sense in theory, in practice it holds little weight. Many of the most centralized systems of government in the world, including the British and French models, coincide with countries that are bastions of democracy and liberal political behaviour and thought. The extent to which a state is democratic or not is affected by a wide range of factors and the level of centralization of power is only one of them.

Closely connected to the first point is the second criticism, namely, that a centralized form of government cannot possibly be in touch with the needs of people across the national territory. This argument suggests that the closer consultation that comes from devolved or decentralized government makes them much better equipped to know what is happening within the regions, and to respond to them. The next criticism comes from those who argue that because the central government is out of touch with local wishes and needs, and because of the lack of strong local institutions, unitary government will be less effective and efficient in its implementation of policies. As we have already seen, this is also one of the arguments *in favour* of unitary government, namely, that it will be more effective and efficient.

The final set of criticisms about unitary government concerns culture and diversity. A serious charge against unitary systems is that they do not reflect the cultural diversity present in most modern states, and that they result in the hegemony and dominance of one culture over the others. In other states, where one ethnic grouping dominates other minorities, highly centralized government can be blamed for further restricting minority rights, especially if those minority ethnic groups are concentrated in specific geographical regions. This is a particularly grave issue, of course, in multicultural societies, although it applied in the case of countries such as the United Kingdom and France even before the arrival of large numbers of immigrants. In the case of the UK, the central government in London was for years accused of favouring English (and in particular southern English) preferences and needs ahead of those from Scotland, Wales, or Northern Ireland. What's more, the dominance of English perspectives was blamed for a lack of understanding of the true nature of regional problems.

As noted earlier in this chapter, devolution of power is increasingly proposed as a solution to many of these problems of unitary government, thereby decentralizing power, albeit on a reversible basis. Such devolution allows the central government to maintain control of the most important issues from a national perspective, while allowing the regions to take more responsibility for the issues that mean the most to them on a daily basis. Still, even with devolution, the central government dominates all other jurisdictions within the national territory.

6.1

Home Rule in Northern Ireland

The Northern Ireland Assembly in session. Northern Ireland is involved in a changing relationship with the central government in Westminster.

Source: Parliamentary copyright images are reproduced with the permission of Northern Ireland Assembly Commission.

The history of Irish relations with its powerful neighbour Great Britain is a long and tortured one, in which Ireland has been dominated in both economic and political terms. For a long time subjugated to British rule, in 1922 Ireland achieved independence, after the fighting of what was essentially a war of independence against the British. Northern Ireland, a grouping of six counties in the north of the country also known as Ulster, briefly became part of the Free Irish States before returning to a special position within the United Kingdom of Great Britain and Northern Ireland. From 1922 until 1972, Northern Ireland operated under a system of autonomous regional government, or Home Rule. This was suspended when violence between Catholics and Protestants in the province became uncontrollable for the local forces, and Britain assumed a position of Direct Rule from Westminster. For 35 years, during the period that Irish and Northern Irish call 'the Troubles', Northern Ireland's identity as an autonomous entity within the unitary system of the United Kingdom was lost. With a war being fought between the forces of the Irish Republican Army (IRA), a group that wanted to bring about the reunification of Northern Ireland with Eire (Southern Ireland), and the British government and loyalist groups within the territory, Home Rule became impossible.

However, in the early years of the twenty-first century, things had improved in the province to the degree that the British government offered the option of re-establishing autonomous government in Ulster. The Northern Ireland Act introduced a renewed Northern Irish Parliament at Stormont, the Parliament Buildings in the city of Belfast, and the formation of a Northern Ireland Executive as well. At the same time, Westminster devolved significant powers to Parliaments in Scotland and Wales. The

6.1 Continued...

Northern Ireland Assembly has considerable influence over local issues, although a large number of the most important areas of policy-making remain under the heading of **'reserved matters'**,[9] meaning that they may at some point be transferred to the region at a later date, or **'excepted matters'**,[10] meaning that they will remain permanently under the control of the central government in Westminster. Reserved and excepted matters include constitutional questions, economic policy, fiscal policy, foreign and defence policy, and energy.

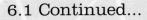

Reserved matters
powers not given to the Northern Ireland Assembly, but that may be transferred to the region at a later date

Excepted matters
powers not given to the Northern Ireland Assembly, and that will remain permanently under the control of the central government in Westminster

Länder
'states' in German

Federal Systems

Although a majority of states in the international system have adopted the unitary, centralized form of government, a small number, with Canada a prominent example among them, are organized according to the federal model. At its core, federalism seeks to divide powers between the central government and regional governments. Legal authority is given to the 'non-central' governments to act on behalf of citizens. Often, particular roles and capacities are given to the regional governments; for instance, in Canada education is a provincial responsibility, paid for in part from transfer payments from the central federal government in Ottawa.

Generally, federal states are territorially large, lending a functional nature to regional authorities. States such as Canada, the United States, Germany, and Australia operate under the federal system in part because powers and responsibilities are distributed to provincial, state, or '*länder*' ('states' in German) governments, which work in conjunction with the central government. Federal states also are often marked by linguistic or cultural differences, making non-central governments more responsive to the individual needs of constituent parts. Further, different levels of government have different powers in both political and economic matters. Historically, many federal states evolved as a response to the needs of organizing themselves for mutual defence and mutual economic gain, on the one hand, and maintaining their regional identities and interests on the other. Canada is a perfect example of this, as we will see later in this chapter.

Power is divided in such a way that each level of government, be it federal (national), provincial (or regional), or even municipal (municipal governments answer to the provincial level), maintains the final say over the areas under its control. These powers will be enshrined in a constitution, guaranteeing freedom from interference by other levels of government. This is not to say that all areas are controlled by only one level of government. Indeed, as is the case in Canada, co-operation and cost-sharing between different levels may be normal and necessary in some areas. The division of powers between federal and regional levels differs from country to country, but it is fair to say that, in general, the central government maintains control of most functions relating to defence and foreign relations, of overall, national economic planning, over trade and currency issues. At the levels of the provinces or states, there is the final say over issues of more local importance, such as health care, education, and social policy. The level

The US

The United States of America, as can be discerned from its very name, is a federal country that has seen an evolving dynamic relationship between the federal and state-level governments throughout its history. Arising out of a loose confederal structure of British colonies, the founding American states were anxious to not cede excessive power to the central government. This drove them to insist on a formal division of powers between federal and state level governments in the constitution and, even at the level of the federal government, to protect their position by ensuring strong representation in the Senate (where each state has two senators). In the constitution, the federal government is granted certain express powers, such as the right to declare war, and to regulate trade between the states, but the spirit of this was to show that the states were ceding powers to the federal government, rather than vice versa. The theory of 'dual federalism' holds that states and federal governments are co-owners of US sovereignty, and thus state consent is needed for all federal government actions not covered by the express powers. The states were believed to retain all powers not granted expressly to the federal government, but this was rapidly proven false. In fact, early debates between the federalist and anti-federalist parties showed that many in the US believed that the states had given over too much power to the central government and should try to take it back.

As time moved on, however, the US political system became more and more centralized, and this came to be a contributing factor in the US Civil War (1861–65), as Southern confederate states attempted to break free of the control of the national government. Of particular importance was the issue of the right of individual states to continue to allow slavery. Nonetheless, with the Northern victory in that war, the federal government was further strengthened and, with an expansion of federal powers in the twentieth century due to increased taxation, increasing demand for government services, and the impact of the World Wars, today it continues to dominate the US political scene.

of decentralization of power varies from federal system to federal system. We can think of two extremes within federalism: one, where the regional governments dominate (peripheralized or decentralized federalism) and one where the national government dominates (centralized federalism). In some systems, such as those found in Canada and Switzerland, the national or federal government has given up important powers to the provinces or regions. In others, such as Russia and Mexico, although the constitution accords considerable powers to the states, the culture of the centralization of power means that it is the federal government that holds onto overwhelming power.

It is important to remember that the decision to create a federal system came, in most cases, not from the belief in some lofty idea of political justice, but rather from political expediency. Distinct and diverse geographical units were convinced to combine their forces and surrender part of their control in exchange for guarantees of protection and security from the new federal power. The advantages

6.3

Switzerland

Switzerland's particular brand of federalism is fascinating in many ways. First, Switzerland's political system is unique in that it adopts direct democracy, which is the direct exercise of citizen voting on almost every major issue in the country. Through referenda and plebiscites, Swiss citizens can give their opinion and judgement on a wide range of policy matters on a regular basis. Further, Switzerland is the only country in the world to have an executive branch that is led by a collective presidency, the Swiss Federal Council, which is formed of seven members nominated by the Swiss Federal Assembly.

But the federal–canton relationship is what is directly relevant for our purposes here. Founded as a country in the thirteenth century, Switzerland brought together a loose grouping of cantons or regions that reluctantly agreed to share power with a central authority. However, they only agreed to do so under the condition that the federal government was not given the ability to dominate them or limit their powers. As the country expanded, incorporating new areas, the loose configuration held together. The influence of a French invasion (1798) and a civil war (1847) pushed the cantons to integrate more fully and move from a confederation to a federation, giving increased powers to the central government. However, the guiding principle for the cantons has always been to surrender only as much autonomy as necessary, and to maintain as much independence as possible.

Today the cantons maintain a high degree of independence, governing issues as diverse as education, public health, citizenship, natural resources, policing, and cantonal taxes. This last point is important: by giving the cantons the ability to raise sufficient financial means, the constitution guarantees their autonomy from the central government, allowing them to maintain the diversity of the country more easily.

of economies of scale also played a role in many cases; by combining into one, larger economic entity, the regions were able to take advantage of synergies and access to markets and raw materials that would otherwise have been essentially foreign. In the case of the United States, the individual states only reluctantly gave up power to the federal government, reserving control over a large number of issue areas, but transferring authority over military and defence, foreign policy and foreign trade, and other areas of national interest to the federal level.

It is interesting that the particular division of powers embodied in the constitution at the time of the federal union will begin to take on a very different appearance as time passes and new political and economic realities emerge. What may have seemed unimportant areas of decision-making power at the time of union may in fact become hugely important as time goes on, both in terms of their financial impact and in terms of political significance. As we will see in the case of Canada, when the regions came together to form the country of Canada in 1867, the areas of education, health care, and natural resources seemed rather low-level issues. By the middle of the twentieth century, however, these issues had attained a much greater and more central role in the lives of Canadians.

6.4

The European Union: A Modern Confederation

In Chapter 9 we will learn more about the European Union (EU), but it is worthwhile looking briefly at the entity in this chapter as an example of a confederal structure made up of sovereign entities that have agreed to surrender certain elements of their sovereignty to an overarching central government in Brussels. Since 1957, the process of European integration has involved two main processes. First, there has been the 'widening' of the European Union, involving the expansion of membership, incorporating new member states. Second, the European Union has experienced a 'deepening' process, whereby the member states have become increasingly integrated in political, economic, and social aspects. Both of the processes concern us here. By incorporating new states, the European Union has seen a remarkable transfer of sovereignty from a large number of countries to its central decision-making structures. The deepening process has meant that these structures have grown in importance and power, and now stand as real actors on the European and indeed global political stages.

But all of this process has been tempered by the reluctance of states to surrender too much sovereignty. How much is too much is of course a tricky question, and the answer varies from country to country. However, the insistence of states to maintain their autonomy, and not to give over absolute control to Brussels, reminds us first of the confederal structure discussed earlier in this chapter, and also of the experience of Swiss confederalism and now federalism.

One of the major advantages of federalism put forward by its proponents is that governments will be much more closely in contact with the needs and desires of citizens because of the proximity of authority to those it seeks to rule and serve. It is also argued that the federal model much more effectively upholds democratic institutions and practices by giving the people another level at which to hold governments accountable. In reality, much of this depends upon the nature of the federal system. Whereas in Canada and the United States there is a high degree of decentralization of power to the provinces and states, in Russia, also a federal system, power remains highly concentrated at the centre and democratic practice is questionable. Mexico offers an interesting example in this regard: even though there is a relatively extensive set of powers credited to the state governments, the federal government has maintained an overwhelming dominance over the regions, due in large part to the existence of one-party rule in the country for over seventy years. Indeed, even after the country had become more democratic and one-party rule had been ended, Mexico continued to be a country in which power was highly centralized, largely because of the fiscal (taxing and spending) capacity of the central government (see Box 6.5).

One of the major criticisms of federalism is that it becomes difficult to maintain political stability when political control of a country is divided in this way. By sharing power over important functions, it is hard to ensure equal provision of services (in both quantity and quality), levels of economic prosperity, even

6.5

The United States of Mexico

Interestingly enough, all three member countries of the North American Free Trade Agreement (NAFTA) are federal states. Yet each one is different, and Mexico stands out as the most centralized of the three. Mexico's full and proper name is **Los Estados Unidos de Mexico,** or the United States of Mexico, and this gives a clue to the federal nature of the country. Indeed, according to its constitution, the 31 states of Mexico have considerable powers and autonomy, and each state has its own constitution, legislative assembly, and elected governor. However, largely due to the political and economic history of the country, Mexico remains highly centralized, with overwhelming power being exercised by the federal government from the Federal District of Mexico City. The major cause of this centralization is that for over 70 years one political party, the Partido Revolucionario Institucional **(PRI),** stayed in power at the federal level and dominated the country's politics, governing most of the states as well. By limiting the autonomy of the states as well as their powers of taxation, the federal government was able to control and coordinate almost all aspects of political life in the country.

Since the 1990s, however, this has begun to change. As the dominance of the PRI weakened and was then lost, significant variation has emerged across the country, with rival political parties ruling different states. As they have broken from the control exercised by the federal government, they have begun to exercise more autonomy on a wide range of issues. Disparities in levels of economic growth have also played a role, with the richer northern states gaining greater autonomy due to their increased governmental incomes. For more on Mexico's politics, see Chapter 10.

Los Estados Unidos de Mexico
United States of Mexico

PRI
Partido Revolucionario Institucional (Institutional Revolutionary Party) of Mexico

public security, across the national territory. These inequalities will lead to envy and discord if left unchecked, and may push federal systems to fall apart. A number of federal systems have ended in this way. The former Yugoslavia was a most unsettling example. Its constituent parts went to war with each other in the 1990s after the federal union fell apart under the strains caused by ethnic tensions and inequalities among them. The conflictive forces created by inequalities within a diverse population will need to be countered by some kind of coordination by the national or federal government, if such an unhappy outcome is to be avoided.

In summary, therefore, it is difficult to say whether federal systems provide a better model than their more centralized, unitary counterparts. Much depends on the nature of federalism, its degree of decentralization, the political culture and institutions that guide it, and the homogeneity of the country concerned.

Canadian Federalism: An Evolving History

Before British North America became the country we now know as Canada, it was a grouping of different territorial units bearing diverse socioeconomic, geographical,

6.6

India: Centralized Government in the World's Largest Democracy

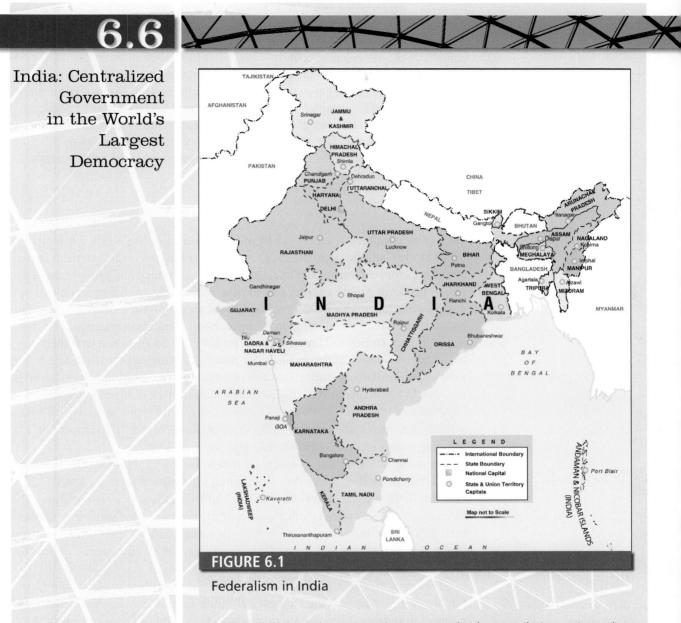

FIGURE 6.1

Federalism in India

As the world's second most populous country (with a population estimated at over 1.1 billion people), and the seventh largest country in the world measured in territorial extension, India presents a fascinating case study of federalism. It is the world's largest democracy and is highly diverse, in ethnic, religious, linguistic, and economic terms. How then to maintain stability and unity in such a large and diverse country? Part of the answer lies in the particular form of federalism operating in India. The country has traditionally experienced strong regional tendencies, both before independence and since, and the Indian federal model was actually based originally on the Canadian experience. Formed of 28 states and 7 union territories, the federal government plays a strong centralized role, although the states still exercise significant autonomy (the union territories are governed directly by

6.6 Continued...

the federal government). Despite significant further centralization of power in the 1970s and 1980s, due to political emergencies and internal conflict, the states are important players in Indian politics.

Most importantly, the states are formed around linguistic and ethnic concerns. The reorganization of the Indian state in 1956 redrew political boundaries and formed the new states along mainly linguistic lines. This has helped the states to develop their own cultural identities, and has promoted the diversity of India. This, in turn, has helped to accommodate concerns about dominance of the regions by the central political authority, while still allowing the federal government to act in the interests of national unity.

and political aspects. The British had tried to assimilate the French-speaking, predominantly Catholic population of Quebec into British North American society after the victory of General Wolfe in Quebec in 1759, which had brought the entire region of North America under British rule. But significant differences remained, and the French-speaking peoples worried about the suppression of their culture, language, and especially their religion. The process of integration began in 1841, with the uniting of Upper and Lower Canada (today Ontario and Quebec respectively) into what was known as the Province of Canada. By bringing these two entities into a closer political union, institutions and processes of coordination began to emerge that would eventually lead to the creation of Canada as a modern country.

Nonetheless, after 1841, the differences between Upper and Lower Canada actually grew, especially because of the rapid population growth in Upper Canada, bringing with it economic growth and increased expectations. A more permanent and equal solution to the problem needed to be found. However, it is important to remember that, while they dominated the political scene in British North America in the nineteenth century, Upper and Lower Canada were not alone. The Maritime provinces were smaller, poorer entities, looking for some way to make their economic futures more secure. And the vast expanse of land to the West and to the North of Upper and Lower Canada represented an enormous opportunity if efforts could be well coordinated.

However, just as important as the internal considerations for the future Canadian provinces was the concern with their mutual security. Throughout the nineteenth century it became increasingly clear that the survival of British North America was far from assured. After the British defeat in the American War of Independence, the United States posed an ever-present threat in terms of either invasion or annexation. Although the War of 1812 resulted in a more stable environment and a more institutionalized bilateral relationship between the United States and Britain, as the century wore on, two factors came into play. The first was that Britain's focus shifted from the Americas to its new colonies in Africa and especially in India. Britain not only recognized the American Monroe Doctrine (which excluded European intervention in the Western hemisphere), it also signalled that its Canadian territories were far from a priority. By uniting into a closer political project, the Canadians could strengthen their defences against possible invasion.

Why Ottawa?

The choice of Ottawa as Canada's national capital may seem strange to many: it holds neither a central geographic position in the country, nor is it an economic or financial centre. Before Confederation, Ottawa was just a good-sized town on the border between Upper and Lower Canada, whose major source of income was the logging industry. It held no special place in the political affairs of the nation. Why, then, was it chosen to be the nation's capital?

In fact, the choice was made by Queen Victoria from England and, although a number of apocryphal stories exist about the way she made the choice (by sticking a pin in the map at random; because of her penchant for art from the Ottawa area), the fact is that the Queen's advisors chose the city for a number of strategic reasons. First, it was relatively far removed from the border with the United States, making it easier to defend and protect in the event of an invasion from the south. This was a key consideration given the still-fresh memories of the War of 1812. By a similar logic, it was a town that was adequately supplied with fresh drinking water that could not be tampered with by the Americans, and was well defended by the forests surrounding the city.

But more importantly than that, the city reflected the traditional division of power between French- and English-speaking peoples in Canada and served as a reminder of the need to balance the interests of the provinces. Sitting almost equidistant between Toronto and Quebec City, and right on the border between Quebec and Ontario, Ottawa seemed an adequate choice in terms of helping to placate fears of the dominance of one group over the other.

The second factor was the experience of the American Civil War. As the American federal union was placed under increasing strain by the calls of the southern states for a *looser* rather than a tighter union, Canadian elites saw the need for a more formal arrangement between the regions of British North America if they were to avoid either the possibility of a civil war or a gradual deterioration of relations between them. Already in 1837 both Upper and Lower Canada had been subject to rebellions that had raised the spectre of deeper armed conflict in the country.

What was needed on both fronts was a formal project of union that would bring economic, political, and military benefits, while at the same time preserving the individual identities of the geopolitical units. It was this dilemma that faced the men who came together in the 1860s to negotiate and design the political future of Canada. These individuals, later to be known as the 'Fathers of Confederation', included John A. Macdonald, who was to become the first prime minister of Canada. Macdonald, a lawyer, had been influenced in views of the future of the country by his experiences during the 1837 rebellions, when he had given legal assistance to Americans who had participated in raids on Canadian territory. This helped him to appreciate the vulnerability of Canada's geographical position, and the need for stronger defences.

In 1864, Macdonald, the leader of the Conservative Party of Canada, came together with George Brown (who led what was later to become the Liberal Party) and George-Étienne Cartier's Parti Bleu from Lower Canada to form the Great Coalition. This grouping of the country's major political forces allowed for the relatively rapid negotiation of articles of confederation between the Canadian colonies through three conferences, the first at Charlottetown in September 1864, the second at Quebec City in October of the same year, and the third in London, England, in 1866. Upper and Lower Canada, New Brunswick, and Nova Scotia agreed to form a united country. However, both Newfoundland and Prince Edward Island opposed confederation, and there was also significant opposition within the Province of Canada itself, though it remained in the minority. Each of the provinces that accepted the union did so for reasons of self-interest. Upper Canada supported the union because its leaders saw opportunities for economic growth and trade, Lower Canada because the union promised to protect its language and culture, and the Maritime Provinces saw the potential for benefiting from the wealth of the Province of Canada and also for protection from foreign aggression (largely from the United States).

In 1867 the agreement that had been negotiated was presented to the British parliament in Westminster, and the Constitution Act of 1867 (also known as the British North America or BNA Act) was passed, creating the Dominion of Canada. Upper and Lower Canada were split from each other and renamed Ontario and Quebec respectively. Although Canada did not immediately become a fully independent country (its powers over foreign policy were in fact limited until the 1931 Statute of Westminster), it began to adopt the shape and institutions that we recognize today. In terms of the relations between the provinces and the federal government in Ottawa, the arrangement that emerged from the Charlottetown and Quebec conferences was interesting. Rather than giving the provinces a dominant position vis-à-vis the federal government, Ottawa held the strongest hand in terms of constitutionally mandated powers. The provinces were left with areas of responsibility that in the second half of the nineteenth century were not considered to be priorities for government, such as education and welfare. The federal government was given everything else. This preference for centralized power in Canada reflected the fear of repeating the American experience of the Civil War, where the states had pushed for an expansion of their powers relative to the federal government.

The Division of Powers

The Constitution Act of 1867 specified a number of areas of 'sole jurisdiction' or exclusive responsibility for the provinces of Canada. They included control over property and civil rights (meaning, in those days, relations between private citizens), prisons, hospitals and asylums, charities, and municipal institutions. They were also given exclusive control over education, allowing them to create whatever educational structures they saw fit. Again it is important to remember that, while these are all seen as central functions of government today, in 1867 they were seen as being much less important. Provinces were also granted, in section 92 of the Act, two **concurrent powers**,[11] in agriculture and immigration. This means that control is shared between provincial and federal levels of governments in these areas. In other words, it is a common area of jurisdiction where both may enact laws.

As for the federal government, section 91 of the Constitution Act outlined the extent of its powers. First, in the **Peace, Order, and Good Government**[12] (POGG) clause, all other powers not specifically given to the provinces were reserved for the federal government. Section 91 goes on to list a number of examples of issues that are to be treated exclusively by the federal government, including the military and defence, the regulation of trade and commerce, and fisheries (it is important to remember how important the fisheries industry was in Canada in financial terms in the nineteenth century). In addition, the postal service, census and statistics, navigation and shipping, Aboriginal peoples and reserve land, and the criminal law were specifically given over to the control of the federal government.

A crucial question was that of taxation and government income. Government services and activities are incredibly expensive and require significant income generation if they are to be effective. When the Articles of Confederation were negotiated, provinces were given only limited powers of taxation. They were restricted to only 'direct taxation' in order to raise revenue for provincial policy activities. What this means has been a recurring question in the history of Canadian federalism, and has been reviewed numerous times by the Canadian judiciary. Today, most provinces generate their income through personal and corporate taxes, sales tax, and through licensing and royalties. The federal government, on the other hand, was granted very wide taxing powers. According to section 91 of the Act, the federal government may raise revenues by any mode or system of taxation, including direct taxation, such as income or corporate taxes, and indirect taxation, such as duties and fees.

Most intriguingly, however, the Constitution Act also gave the federal government special powers for controlling the provinces and overriding their mandates. The first of these was the power of **reservation**,[13] which allowed the lieutenant governor of a province (a position appointed by the federal government) to put provincial legislation up for consideration by the federal cabinet, which could then approve or reject the legislation. Secondly, any piece of provincial legislation could be rejected or vetoed by the federal cabinet through its power of **disallowance**.[14] Lastly, the federal government was given **declaratory power**[15] that could be used to take control of any local project if it decided that this would be for the greater national good. Convention now dictates that the federal government does not use these powers, but in the early days of the federal system they served to emphasize the dominance of the central authority.

An important question that often comes up when studying the history of Canadian federalism is why the Constitution Act came to be known as a 'Confederation Agreement' and why the founders of Canada are known as the 'Fathers of Confederation'. Canada is clearly not a confederation; rather, it's a federation or federal system. Why, then, the name? The answer lies in the fact that the term refers to the act of coming together to form a federal system rather than the system itself. Confederation, in this sense, is more abstract, since it refers to the process of creating a federation; 'entering into confederation' meant joining a federal body. The founders of Canada never intended the country to be such a loose union

Concurrent powers
when control is shared between provincial and federal levels of governments

Peace, Order, and Good Government (POGG)
clause in the Canadian constitution that specifies that powers not specifically given to the provinces are reserved for the federal government

Reservation
when provincial legislation is put up for consideration by the federal cabinet

Disallowance
when provincial legislation is rejected or vetoed by the federal cabinet

Declaratory power
federal government power to take control of any local project if it decides that this would be for the greater national good

Table 6.1 Federal vs. Provincial Powers

	Federal	Provincial	Shared
Legislative Control Over...	regulation of trade and commerce, postal service, census and statistics, the military, navigation and shipping, sea coast and inland fisheries, Indians and reserve land, and the criminal law, as well as international treaties, taxation (wide range: direct and indirect), unemployment insurance	hospitals, asylums, charities, municipal institutions, prisons, property and civil rights, education, taxation (limited, only direct)	agriculture and immigration, old-age pensions, amending the constitution if this change concerns one or more provinces, natural resources (although federal still has more power here), and direct taxation (through federal–provincial/ territorial taxation agreements)
Inter-governmental Interaction	Department of Intergovernmental Affairs, First Ministers' Meetings	Department of Intergovernmental Affairs, First Ministers' Meetings, Council of the Federation. First created in 2003, the council is a provincial/territorial forum constituted by the premiers of each province and territory in Canada.	
Federal Control Over Provinces	*Reservation:* This allows the lieutenant governor of a province to reserve provincial legislation for the consideration of the federal cabinet. *Disallowance:* Even if the lieutenant governor granted assent to a piece of provincial legislation, the federal cabinet could subsequently disallow it through this power. *Declaratory power:* to place any local work or undertaking, which it deemed to be for the general advantage of Canada, under its control.		

as a confederal system; indeed, the Canadian form of federalism that emerged after 1867 was in fact much closer to the British unitary system of government. Nonetheless, it is true that Canada is one of the more 'decentralized' federations.

The Evolution of Canadian Federalism

This was a situation, however, that would not stay static. Throughout Canadian history the balance of power between the federal and provincial governments has been changing, and although the national authority has always maintained the upper hand, so to speak, there has been significant variation through time in the level of autonomy on the part of the provinces. Partly this has come from their expanding role in the lives of citizens, as the issues under their control have grown in importance. This also has to do in part with their increasing ability to raise revenue. Although in the early days of confederation the provinces were limited to only direct taxation, in recent times they have been able to find new sources of income from indirect taxation as well. But it is also important to remember that the federal government has played a role in determining the level of autonomy afforded to the provinces. During the Great Depression of the 1930s, for example, the provinces became increasingly dependent on the federal government for financing, which gave the central government increasing influence over them. During the First and Second World Wars, the federal government again increased its power relative to the provinces as it sought to unify the country and mobilize citizens for the war effort. During these periods we can talk about **centralized federalism**.[16]

At other times, however, a spirit of co-operation and coordination of policy has governed relations between the two levels of government. Such **co-operative federalism**[17] was particularly important in the postwar period as economic growth was accompanied by an expansion of the Canadian population and a sense that the federal bargain was one that involved increasing benefits for both sides. Even in the areas of shared responsibility, relations between federal and provincial authorities were largely cordial and positive.

Since the 1960s, however, there has been a more conflictive relationship between the provinces and the federal government. This period has come to be known as **executive federalism**,[18] as the provinces have attempted (often successfully) to achieve greater autonomy from Ottawa, and the federal government has resisted or imposed a price on such autonomy. For example, in the 1990s Ottawa reduced its own spending on social programs, forcing the provinces to take on a greater fiscal responsibility, such as increasing their levels of taxation, if they were not to go bankrupt.

The question of finance has always been central to Canadian federalism. As the demands for provincial services increased, especially with the improvement in health and education services in the early twentieth century, provinces found themselves without sufficient funds to provide for these increasingly expensive areas. As a solution to this problem, the federal government provided **conditional grants**[19] that gave the provincial authorities the necessary funds but put controls and conditions on how the monies could be spent. This, of course, signified a considerable imposition by the federal government, but the provincial authorities had little choice but to accept. The fiscal manifestation of the federal bargain is a feature that continues to mark Canadian federalism to this day. In later years the idea of conditional grants would disappear but the basic problem of how to finance provincial programs remained.

To compound the problem, not all provinces, of course, have equal capacities for raising revenue. Ontario, traditionally a rich province due to its industrial base and its strong services sector, has throughout most of Canadian history been seen as a 'have' province, whereas the Maritimes have a long history of being poorer and

Centralized federalism
process whereby federal government increases its power relative to the provinces

Co-operative federalism
co-operation and coordination of policy between the federal and provincial levels of government

Executive federalism
a generally conflictive relationship between the provinces and the federal government when provinces attempt (often successfully) to achieve greater autonomy from the federal government, which resists such attempts

Conditional grants
funds given to provincial authorities but with controls and conditions on how the monies may be spent

therefore 'have not' provinces. Because of this, the federal government has for a long time engaged in a program of transferring funds from the richer 'have' provinces to their poorer 'have not' counterparts. (More recently, of course, Ontario has struggled to maintain its 'have' status — and has even been a 'have not' — as a result of severe cuts to the manufacturing sector.) By taxing citizens and businesses in the rich provinces and then transferring part of that income to the poorer regions of Canada, the federal government aims to preserve both a minimal level of equality in the provision of services and also to cement the country through perceived mutual interest. This program of **equalization payments**[20] is, of course, highly contentious for the richer provinces of Canada, who complain that their economic prosperity is being drained away to parts of Canada that are either not well run in economic terms, or simply economically unsustainable.

Determining who has the power to tax, and how it affects the economy and political life in Canada in multiple ways, requires collaboration between the two levels of government. If both provincial and federal governments were to tax the

Equalization payments
compensation given to more needy regions in a political system in order to create a general state of parity

6.8

Fiscal Federalism

© Copyright Simon Fraser University

The issue of who gets what from the federal budget is a constant source of tension in Canadian politics.

As we have shown in this chapter, one of the fundamental questions related to federal political systems is that of revenue for the provinces or states. Unless significant flexibility is given to the provinces by the federal government in this area, they will either be limited in what functions they can carry out, or they will depend on financial transfers from the central authority. In Canada, this has been a contentious question since Confederation, because the provinces have to fulfill their obligations in terms of providing services as well as maintain autonomy from the federal government.

In the period following the Second World War, the federal government established its dominance over the provinces by assuming all tax collection activities and

6.8 Continued...

then transferring money to the provinces through **transfer payments**. These came in the form of conditional grants to the provinces, in which the federal government could determine exactly in which way the funds should be spent. In the 1970s, as provincial influence and demands (inspired by Quebec) grew, the federal government agreed to **unconditional grants**, block payments that could be spent by the provinces in any way they saw fit. Under this rubric also came equalization payments, funds transferred from the federal government to the poorer provinces to try to bring greater equality in the standard of living of all Canadians from coast to coast. The idea of equalization payments has always been controversial; back in the 1930s and 1940s, the richer provinces openly opposed the idea and continue to complain about the system today, but it is a fact that such payments have been responsible for bringing about a fairer and more equal society across Canada.

same sector of the economy at high levels, competitiveness would be damaged. Further, if one level decides to raise taxes to increase government revenues at the same time the other level cuts taxes in an effort to increase citizens' spending power, then they would find themselves at cross-purposes. Just as importantly, the ability of some provinces, such as Alberta, to raise large amounts of public revenue through royalties and taxes on the natural resources sector creates a problem of inequality between the provinces — of envy from poorer entities and of a reluctance on the part of Albertans to continue what they perceive as 'bailing out' the rest of Canada.

Financial transfers from the federal government have consistently come under scrutiny and revision. In 1977 the Federal/Provincial Fiscal Arrangements Act, for example, offered the provinces block grants to finance education and health care, involving minimal interference from Ottawa. This may have seemed to be a positive move for the provinces, giving them greater autonomy, but it also established their sole responsibility and therefore financial liability for these programs, programs that were rapidly becoming more and more expensive to uphold. What's more, the federal government was able to retain some degree of influence over the nature of health and education spending through legislative manoeuvring. Since 1977, this arrangement has been modified a number of times, with the provinces consistently complaining that the federal government is trying to push ever-greater financial burdens their way.

Given that there needs to be ongoing consultation and coordination between the two levels, how do the provincial and federal governments interact? In addition to day-to-day informal contact and consultation between bureaucrats at provincial and federal levels, primary responsibility for coordinating relations is assumed by the executive branches. Therefore, the federal/provincial/territorial First Ministers' Meetings (FMMs) have evolved to become the highest profile means of contact. There is no regular schedule for the FMMs, and they very much depend on the national political agenda. They have become more frequent at times when the federal system is under stress due to economic crisis or the Quebec question, such as during the 1970s and 1980s, but they have also been held to discuss specific policy issues, such as health care. Further, ministers' meetings have

Transfer payments
funds given by the federal government to provincial governments on a conditional or unconditional basis

Unconditional grants
payments from the federal government that may be spent by the provinces in any way they see fit

also taken place where the respective ministers for a specific area from the federal, provincial, and territorial governments come together to coordinate actions. In order to serve these interactions, the Canadian Intergovernmental Conference Secretariat (CICS) was created in 1973 to be a permanent administrative support for intergovernmental co-operation, and this has served to significantly strengthen co-operation in institutional terms.

In addition to the 10 provinces, of course, Canada also has three territories. Their position within the Canadian union is somewhat different, coming closer to a unitary system. Territories have no inherent, constitutionally designated jurisdictions, only what is given to them by the federal government, and are therefore far less autonomous. (We discussed the territories in some detail in Chapter 4.) Nonetheless, each of the territories of Canada has significant devolved powers, and each has its own legislative and executive branch of government, and participates in multilateral intergovernmental conferences alongside the provinces and the federal government.

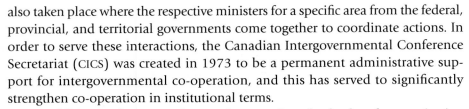

6.9

Canadian Dept. of Mines and Resources/Library and Archives Canada/PA-021722

Natural Resources

Natural resources have long been a source of wealth and economic development across Canada.

Provincial control over their natural resources has always been a fundamental element in their portfolio of rights and responsibilities. In the early days of Confederation, the forests and wildlife of Canada presented significant economic opportunities in terms of timber and animal pelts respectively. However, the true importance of this control would only become apparent in later years with the arrival of the oil industry to Alberta and other provinces.

6.9 Continued...

Based upon its royalties and taxes on oil production, Alberta has managed to become the richest province in Canada and has become an international power through its importance in global oil and gas markets. In the first decade of the twenty-first century, as global oil prices soared, Alberta received hundreds of thousands of new immigrants, from abroad and from other parts of Canada, people who were attracted by the employment opportunities connected with the oil and gas sector, and especially by very high wages. Although such dependence on oil and gas revenues means that Alberta's fortunes rise and fall with global prices in this area, the province has used its newfound wealth to invest in a wide range of social, business, and educational programs to diversify its economy and prepare itself for the future.

The 1980s and 1990s were marked by a number of constitutional conferences in which the provinces attempted to achieve what they saw as a more equitable distribution of power with the federal authorities. The Constitutional Accord, Meech Lake Accord, and Charlottetown Accord of 1982, 1987, and 1992, respectively, sought to redefine the federal–provincial bargain. Increasingly, the provinces have learned to coordinate their positions, presenting a more unified front in the negotiations with the federal government. This has made it more difficult for the federal authorities to pressure the provinces into an agreement.

These conferences, however, are better remembered for a different issue, namely, that of Quebec nationalism, and it is to that particular challenge to Canadian federalism that we now turn.

Quebec and Canadian Federalism

No issue excites political sentiments in Canada more than the question of Quebec's proper place in the federal system. Should Quebec be treated the same as every other province in the country, should it hold a special status, should it seek some form of new sovereignty association with Canada, or should it seek outright independence? These are just some of the options that have emerged over the years, as Quebec and the rest of Canada have struggled to accommodate the province in such a way as to satisfy both the requirements of Canadian federalism and the desire of Quebecois Canadians to protect and promote their identity.

The Quebec question has been a prominent one since the early years of the Canadian federal system. As we noted earlier in this chapter, the choice of Ottawa as the capital of Canada had much to do with placating Quebec's fears of being dominated by English-speaking Canada. But the question of protecting the French language and Quebecois culture go far beyond the simple selection of the capital city. It is fair to say that the history of Canada is marked with numerous incidents and policies where the use of French and Quebecois culture itself have appeared to be under threat, often through anti-French legislation passed by the federal and provincial governments. It is therefore entirely understandable why Quebec nationalists believe that their rights and aspirations for political self-determination would be better served either by independence or a new form of looser federal relationship with Ottawa.

Quebec has attempted to renegotiate its status within Canada on a number of occasions, seeking a new federal deal through conferences at Meech Lake, Charlottetown, and of course at the constitutional accord negotiations, where Quebec refused to accept the repatriation of the constitution under the conditions given at the time. Nonetheless, to date, a satisfactory final solution has not been found. One reason for this is that Quebec itself is divided within; although a majority of Quebecois believe that the province and its citizens have a distinct identity, repeated opinion polls and referenda have shown that there is no clear majority in favour of any new federal arrangement to deal with this concern.

The lingering question of Quebec is a recurring strain on Canadian federalism. The prospect that the second largest and one of the founding provinces might leave the Canadian union, dramatically altering the balance of economic and political power within Canada, and fundamentally changing Canadian cultural identity, is almost unthinkable for many.

It is here, though, that federalism shows both its strengths and weaknesses. First, we can say that, because of the greater regional autonomy provided by the federal structure in Canada, Quebec has been better able to develop its sense of a distinct identity, to establish language laws and government recruitment practices that have strengthened the place of francophones in the province and, indeed, in Canada as a whole. The provincial government, mainly under Parti Québécois (PQ) rule, has also been a strong adversary of the federal government. The PQ has worked alongside the federal Bloc Québécois party to demand more for the province from the federal arrangement. These factors have served to spur the movement calling for more autonomy, and maybe even independence. However, the inherent flexibility of federalism also allows for innovative approaches to dealing with the Quebec question without necessarily dissolving the Canadian union. The federal model applied in Canada has traditionally been quite centralized, and it is quite conceivable that more power could be transferred to the provinces (all of them, not simply Quebec) without permanently damaging the existence of Canada as a unified country. Other states, such as Switzerland for example, have given increased powers to their regions while still maintaining national unity.

It is important to remember here that, although Quebec's status is by far the most contentious question facing Canadian federalism, other regional challenges exist. The continued depressed economies of the Maritime provinces and the rise of the Western provinces have placed significant strains on Canadian unity. The Maritimes have found themselves left behind, in economic terms, in the late twentieth and early twenty-first centuries, and have called for greater investment by the federal government in their economies to raise living standards. On the other hand, Alberta's rising wealth and British Columbia's increasingly influential position within Canada have meant that they are more assertive in interprovincial and provincial–federal relations, challenging the traditional dominance of Ontario and Quebec. However these challenges are resolved, debates over federalism will continue to be a central feature of Canadian politics long into the future.

Conclusion

As this chapter has shown you, the political distribution of power within the national territory is one of the most important factors in determining the nature of the state. The choice between unitary and federal (or even confederal) systems will be based on a number of factors, including territorial extension, regional and cultural diversity, political traditions, and concerns of effectiveness and efficiency. Centralizing power in a unitary government has been the form adopted by a vast majority of countries in the world today, as a way of overcoming social divisions and maximizing the capacity of the state to implement policy on a national basis. The federal system, however, offers the alternative of providing closer contact between citizens and government, of tailoring government policy more closely to regional needs, and of encouraging diversity within the nation.

In Canada the federal experiment has been successful for more than 140 years. Based on the need to unite diverse political entities for their mutual benefit and protection, federalism in Canada is a living system that is in constant flux. The place of Quebec is clearly the most controversial and contested piece of the federal jigsaw puzzle, but so far the system has been flexible enough to accommodate the provinces' concerns, albeit in a less than perfect way. Rest assured, as a Canadian political scientist, federalism will be a major element for the duration of your studies.

Self-Assessment Questions

1. What is the difference between unitary, federal, and confederal states?
2. What are equalization payments and why are they necessary?
3. Which do you think would work better in the Canadian context — the current quasi-federal structure or a looser confederation?
4. Explain why some countries choose unitary and others federal systems.

Weblinks

Canadian Federalism
www.pco-bcp.gc.ca/aia/index.
 asp?lang=eng&page=federal

Equalization Payments
www.fin.gc.ca/fedprov/eqp-eng.asp

Health Canada
www.hc-sc.gc.ca

Indian Government Website
india.gov.in/govt.php

Powers of the National and Provincial Governments
www2.parl.gc.ca/Sites/LOP/AboutParliament/
 Forsey/powers_of_govt_01-e.asp

Provinces and Territories of Canada
www.canada.gc.ca/othergov-autregouv/prov-
 eng.html

Further Reading

Bickerton, James. 'Regionalism in Canada.' In *Canadian Politics*. Ed. James P. Bickerton and Alain-G. Gagnon. 3rd ed. Toronto: Broadview Press, 1999.

Filippov, Mikhail, Peter C. Ordeshook, and Olga Shvetsova. *Designing Federalism: A Theory of Self-Sustainable Federal Institutions*. Cambridge: Cambridge University Press, 2004.

Guy, James J., *People, Politics and Government: Political Science: A Canadian Perspective*. Toronto: Prentice Hall Canada, 1995.

Howlett, Michael. 'Federalism and Public Policy.' In *Canadian Politics*. Ed. James P. Bickerton and Alain-G. Gagnon. 3rd ed. Toronto: Broadview Press, 1999.

Nye, Joseph S., Jr. *Understanding International Conflicts: An Introduction to Theory and History*. 6th ed. New York: Pearson Longman, 2007.

Potter, Jonathan. *Devolution and Globalisation: Implications for Local Decision-Makers*, Paris: OECD, 2001.

Robinson, Ian, and Richard Simeon. 'The Dynamics of Canadian Federalism.' In *Canadian Politics*. Ed. James P. Bickerton and Alain-G. Gagnon. 3rd ed. Toronto: Broadview Press, 1999.

CBC News Clips

Visit the companion website for *Politics: An Introduction* to listen to news clips from the CBC radio archives.

7 Political Participation: Elections and Parties

LEARNING
OBJECTIVES

After reading this chapter, you will be able to:

* explain the importance and significance of voting

* distinguish between different forms of electoral systems

* understand the importance of campaign financing and the need for regulation

* explain the importance and role of political parties

* debate the referendum as a special element of democracy

* apply voting, elections, parties, and referendums to the Canadian case.

Introduction

By this point in your studies you will be aware that politics surrounds us. At local, national, and international levels, politics is one of the determining forces in our lives. Very often, however, this seems to be a force over which we have little control, one which is directed by elites and by rich and powerful groups in society. Wars in foreign countries, decision-making in the nation's capital, the process of integration in Europe, are all outside of our control. In this way politics is something that happens to us, but in which we do not directly participate. But how might we be involved in this process of participation? Are we truly removed from the 'political' in our daily lives, or do we actually have an influence in the manner of decision-making that we all would agree affects us in a most basic manner? Furthermore, how might this involvement in the political process serve to improve our lives?

The purpose of this chapter, and the one that follows, is to introduce you to the various ways we become involved in the political process, and how this participation actually affects our lives and well-being and those of our communities. Politics cannot be separated from citizens, and there are several ways in which people may affect their political community, either as individuals or as members of a group. Politics is like any other form of **socialization**[1] — the process of organizing in a social manner — and we are faced on a daily basis with politics. In fact, these two chapters are primarily about the political and social organizing of citizens. Participation in a political unit, we argue here, is a product of the manner in which we are socialized.

The material introduced here builds on the ideological and institutional knowledge you have gained in the previous chapters. In many ways, participation

Socialization
process whereby individuals act in a social manner; the creation of social and political authority and rules to regulate behaviour so as to permit operation of social units

is the most consequential aspect of political studies because it is only through understanding involvement in the political process that we can come to understand the larger issues of 'who gets what, when, and how'.

In this chapter we will study the different ways in which citizens can become directly involved in the political process through voting in elections, membership in political parties, and also in decision-making. In many respects this chapter deals with the issues that most of us think of first when we think of politics and things political, and, of course, they form a fundamental part of democracy, a system that involves us directly in choosing our governments.

Democracy and Voting

As you already know, democracy can take many forms and differs from country to country. However, at an abstract level we can differentiate between two basic forms. **Direct democracy**,[2] as we will see later in this chapter, employs direct citizen involvement in the decision-making process through the referendum, where all eligible citizens express their opinions and preferences on issues of policy. However, since it would be nearly impossible for every member of a society to be a direct part of the decision-making process all the time (the life of a politician is, after all, a full-time job), most political systems use what is referred to as **indirect democracy** or **representative democracy**,[3] where citizens' opinions and preferences are defended and articulated by elected representatives. Indirect democracy, then, uses **elections**[4] to decide who will be given the authority to make decisions on behalf of the entire political grouping. For most people in most countries at most times, elections are the most direct forum through which individuals in the political system may affect the decisions made for society as a whole.

In modern liberal democracies such as Canada, most citizens who have reached the age of majority (adults) take part in an array of elections. Voting consists of eligible citizens showing their preference for an individual who puts him- or herself forward as a candidate for government. Voters express their preference for candidates by casting a ballot, that is, marking their preference on an official piece of paper, and then putting that paper into a predetermined ballot box, to be counted later by electoral officials. Elections represent that aspect of the voter-government relationship where individual citizens have the opportunity to choose politicians who best meet their interests and preferences. This occurs at both federal and provincial, and also at municipal levels. Yet while this is the most direct way that we might affect the political system, electoral systems do not come without conditions. Every electoral system, despite its composition, sets out formal restrictions on this choice, indicating who may vote and through what means.

It is notable that electoral systems, though considered to be generally open and liberal today, once were highly restrictive. Most conspicuously, the right to vote (**suffrage**)[5] was not always an open affair. Historical systems discriminated based on gender (usually only males were allowed to vote), on age (often only certain age groups were given the right), on economic status (requiring, for instance, individuals to be employed or own land, or other valuable resources, in some cases), or even literacy (thereby eliminating those who were not educated

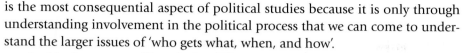

Direct democracy
political system in which citizens are directly involved in the decision-making process

Indirect democracy
political system of representation in which citizens elect a delegate to act on their behalf

Representative democracy
political system in which voters elect others to act on their behalf

Election
a form of choosing governors whereby individual citizens cast their vote for candidates running for office

Suffrage
granting of the right to vote

from the right to vote). These restrictions were slowly relaxed over time, but for women and some minority groups, it was still impossible to partake in the voting process until well into the twentieth century. On the other side of the coin, restrictions were put in place governing who could legally run for election. Most of the time the laws regulating who was allowed to vote also pertained to who was allowed to stand for election; often the laws surrounding election candidacy were more stringent than those for voting.

Today we allow most adults over the age of 18 to vote in elections in Canada, but this raises the question, why 18? What is it about an 18-year-old that makes them more deserving of the vote than a 17-year-old, or for that matter, a 7-year-old? Generally, states have taken the decision to assign the voting age based upon the age of majority, when people are considered to be fully responsible adults. When democracies first extended the vote to the general public, the age of majority was set at 21, but was reduced to 18 in most countries during the twentieth century. In recent years a debate has begun in some countries over reducing the voting age to 16, and in fact in Austria, in 2007, this occurred. In Britain, however, although an active debate exists over the issue, and although lowering the age has drawn significant regional support (particularly in Scotland), the national voting age remains 18.

Every country also has its own laws applying to candidates who are designated to run in constituencies. Membership in political parties in some countries governs whether an individual is permitted to stand for election; if he or she is

7.1

Who Gets to Vote?

In most democracies we assume that all citizens participate in voting and elections. However, we also commonly accept that there are exceptions. In Canada, for many years, prisoners were excluded from voting. Indeed, the Canada Elections Act specifically prohibits them from taking part in the electoral process. However, in 2002 a case was brought before the Supreme Court arguing that prisoners deserve equal treatment as Canadian citizens. The court's decision in this landmark case, known as *Sauvé v. Canada*, declared that the Canada Elections Act of 2000 violated the terms of the Canadian Charter of Rights and Freedoms, and was therefore unconstitutional. Since 2002 all adult Canadians have held the right to vote (in an earlier case in 1988, the mentally ill were accorded the right to vote).

The question of age and maturity, however, is more controversial. As we noted, it is common practice to exclude citizens under the age of majority from voting. In 2005, however, two young women from Alberta — Erin Fitzgerald and Christine Jairamsingh — tried to bring a case before the Supreme Court of Canada to allow citizens under age 18 to vote. Noting that the Charter of Rights and Freedoms states that 'every citizen of Canada has the right to vote in an election of members of the House of Commons or of a legislative assembly', Fitzgerald and Jairamsingh argued that such language should be interpreted to permit all Canadians, regardless of age, to vote. The court refused to hear the case, but this is an issue that is sure to reappear in the not too distant future.

not a member of a party, they may not be allowed to run. In Mexico, for example, in a high-profile case in 2005, independent candidate, intellectual, and former foreign minister Jorge Castaneda was denied the right to run for the presidency because he lacked an official party affiliation. On the other hand, states such as Canada do not have party requirements, so 'independents'[6] can run in elections.

Elections take place in constituencies, or the geographical units in which the voters are separated and within which candidates compete for votes. Most political systems try to create an equitable system of **constituencies**[7] (or 'ridings' as they are sometimes known) to accurately match where the majority of the population lives, thereby giving more elected representatives to densely populated areas, such as urban cities, and fewer to sparsely populated regions, such as rural ridings. Electoral systems further set out the rules regarding where voting occurs, who is given authority in ridings for ballot collection and counting, and, **enumeration**[8] (surveying who lives in which ridings), and how votes are actually converted into seats. The process of enumeration can be highly sensitive in some countries, as the manipulation of constituency boundaries may be used by politicians to affect electoral outcomes. Throughout history, political boundaries have been altered for political gain; in Britain in the past **'rotten boroughs'**[9] existed where areas with very small populations and electorates were given equal standing with normal-sized constituencies. **'Pocket boroughs'**[10] tended to have very small electorates whose votes were controlled by (or in the pocket of) the major local landowner. As we noted above, in Canada, rural ridings generally have smaller populations, and thus electorates, than their urban counterparts, but Canadian electoral law allows for this. In the United States the process of altering election boundaries is known as **'gerrymandering'**[11] (see Box 7.2) and is highly controversial. It seeks to group together or divide groups of voters in order to maximize or reduce their power, depending on the situation. By dividing up ethnic minorities into multiple voting districts, for example, their influence over electoral outcomes may be reduced. Alternatively, by grouping together certain minorities who share similar political preferences, they may be guaranteed dominance in the district or constituency. In Canada, too, constituency boundaries have been altered in order to affect election outcomes; however, the 1964 decision by the federal government to delegate the drawing of constituency boundaries to Elections Canada, an autonomous agency, has largely solved the problem.

No doubt one of the most critical problems facing election systems today is **voter apathy**. This is the condition where individuals simply decide not to vote or even bother to follow the election process, because they believe for one reason or another that elections do not affect or influence them, or that they have little influence over outcomes. In some countries, such as the United States, voter turnout is a major challenge, and it is considered a 'good' turnout if over half of registered eligible voters actually cast a ballot. In recent years all major democracies have engaged in public awareness and education campaigns designed to get more people to the polls at election time, with a particular focus on young people. Programs like 'Rock the Vote' (see Box 7.3), have achieved some success in the United States and have been imitated around the world, but it is a constant struggle to maintain voter engagement. It is easy in modern society to discard the

Independents
candidates for public office belonging to no political party

Constituencies
territorial or geographical localities (ridings) represented by a politician chosen through the electoral process

Enumeration
the process of determining the number of individuals eligible to vote in a constituency

Rotten boroughs
in Britain, areas with very small populations and electorates that were given equal standing with normal-sized constituencies

Pocket boroughs
in Britain, areas where very small electorates were controlled by (or in the pocket of) the major local landowner

Gerrymandering
controversial method of grouping together, or dividing, groups of voters in order to maximize or reduce their power

Voter apathy
condition in which individuals do not vote, or do not follow the election process, because they believe elections do not affect or influence them, or that they have little influence over outcomes

7.2

Gerrymandering

THE GERRYMANDER.

The reshaping of electoral districts to guarantee election results is an old phenomenon.

The origins of the term 'gerrymandering' are to be traced back to 1812 when the Governor of Massachusetts, Elbridge Gerry, signed into law a piece of legislation that reshaped electoral districts in such a way as to benefit his party at the next election. A local newspaper, the *Boston Gazette*, examined the new electoral boundaries, noted that they resembled a mythical salamander or small dragon, and put the governor's name together with the shape to produce the word 'Gerrymander'. The term has been in use since that date and continues to excite political controversy.

Rock the Vote

Founded in 1990, Rock the Vote is a non-governmental organization (NGO) that is dedicated to convincing young people of voting age to participate in elections. Though it was started in Los Angeles in the United States, it has spread throughout the world and is active in many elections. The organization states its mission as 'to engage and build the political power of young people in order to achieve progressive change in our country.' Using music, new technologies, and mass media, Rock the Vote not only encourages voting among the young, but also voter registration, and ongoing participation in the important political debates of the day. Further, it has programs that engage high school students in political issues to prepare them for their impending participation in elections.

role that casting a **ballot**[12] plays in our systems of government; the multitude of issues facing individual citizens often seem overwhelming, and the real role that we might play in the political process frequently seems small, indeed. Still, voting is an essential part of living in a liberal democracy. What's more, it is all too easy to forget the struggles that millions went through to earn the right to vote. Whether from oppressed minorities, or from the lower socioeconomic classes, people throughout history have fought and risked injury, imprisonment, and even death to gain the right to vote. The **suffragette** movement (see Box 7.4), the anti-apartheid movement in South Africa, and democracy movements around the world struggled for years to achieve what many of us today take for granted. It seems irresponsible not to exercise that right when you consider what others have gone through to earn it for themselves.

Studies show us that voting preference, and indeed the tendency to vote itself, is highly determined by one's position in society, level of education, family background, and chosen profession. Those in the higher echelons of society, with higher levels of education and with a family background of political participation, are much more likely to vote. This threatens to create an underclass of people who see little point in voting or other forms of political participation, and this is clearly not healthy for democracy. Therefore, in order to encourage voter participation, it is essential that society provide adequate and reliable information flow about the political parties and individual candidates who are standing for election. In recent years this has become easier in many ways with greater access to information through the media and Internet. However, it has been argued that there is in fact too much information available and that this confuses the public and increases voter apathy.

What is certain is that **voter turnout**[13] (the number of voters who show up to the polls on election day) has been steadily dropping since the middle of the twentieth century across the Western democracies. One solution that has been attempted in a number of countries is to make voting compulsory for people of voting age. Under this system of **compulsory voting**,[14] used in countries such as

Ballot
card used to cast a vote

Suffragette
female advocate of women's right to vote

Voter turnout
number of voters who show up to the polls on election day

Compulsory voting
system in which citizens have a legal obligation to vote in elections

7.4

The Suffragette Movement

Suffragette leader Emmeline Pankhurst was arrested by British police.

© The Print Collector/Alamy

Until the twentieth century, women in most parts of the world were prevented from voting. Even in the world's pre-eminent democracies, such as Canada and the United Kingdom, women were very much treated as second-class political citizens. However, as noted in Chapter 3, the rise of feminist thought in the nineteenth century and increasing demands for equal treatment led to the Suffragette Movement in Britain, Canada, and the United States. Led by such visionaries as Emmeline Pankhurst (Britain), Emily Howard Stowe (Canada), and Susan B. Anthony (United States), the movement used a program of civil disobedience, violent resistance, and hunger strikes to influence public and elite opinion. Though initially dismissed as dangerous revolutionaries, these pioneers were responsible for bringing full political participation to women in their countries and leading the movement for equal political rights across the world.

Australia, Brazil, Peru, and Turkey, citizens have a legal obligation to vote in elections, and may be fined or even imprisoned if they don't. Voters do not necessarily have to express a preference for one candidate or political party over another; they may spoil their ballot (by filling it in incorrectly) or may choose none of the options included on the voting paper. It is argued that this system encourages greater citizen participation, greater citizen awareness of political issues, and will bring higher levels of legitimacy to elected governments because they will represent a majority of eligible voters. Arguments against compulsory voting claim that voting is a right, not a duty, and as such it is wrong to force unwilling citizens to vote. It is also claimed that forcing people to vote may actually make them resent the political process and thus damage democracy.

At the other end of the scale, some have argued that voting should become a privilege rather than a right. According to this rather extreme position, potential voters should be tested on their knowledge of political parties, candidates, their **election platforms** (their positions on political issues and their political intentions), and the basic workings of the political system before being allowed to vote. It is unlikely that any liberal democracy would ever implement such an approach, because it eliminates the right to vote, something that is an essential part of democratic systems.

Election platforms
positions of political parties or individuals regarding issues and political intentions

Types of Electoral Systems

Having established what voting is, and how voters are organized into political districts or constituencies, we must examine the different types of electoral systems that exist in the world today. There are two basic forms of electoral systems that allow for the conversion of votes into seats in the legislature, or alternatively winning the presidency. The **simple plurality**[15] system involves the election of the individual who obtains the greatest number of votes. This system is also called the 'first-past-the-post'[16] system, alluding to a horse race where the winner 'passes the post' with the most votes. In this system, the winning candidate or party wins all the seats associated with a particular district or constituency; there is no reward for finishing second. It is quite possible that in any given constituency, a candidate may lose by only one vote out of thousands, and yet gain nothing from this result.

The system is well-known for harming the chances of small political parties. Well-established parties that already have a strong voter base will be able to win seats and potentially to form a government. However, a party that garners, say, only 10 per cent of the vote is unlikely to win any constituency and will therefore find it difficult to raise its profile on the national stage. This, then, tends to reinforce the position of the established parties and hinder the rise of new parties.

Under some circumstances, the result of a simple plurality system is the election of a **minority government**,[17] where the party that receives the most number of seats might still not receive a majority (more than 50 per cent) simply as a result of the number of parties involved. The party that receives the 'most' seats, then, might not receive the 'majority' of support. However, it is quite common for a party to receive a majority of seats (more than 50 per cent) but not more than 50 per cent of the overall vote, or the majority of the vote. In this case, though the governing party may in fact be in a majority situation, it cannot say that it received the majority of votes. This will pose a serious challenge to the authority and legitimacy of the government and may reduce its capacity to govern.

Simple plurality
electoral system (first-past-the-post) where the winner receives the most (but not necessarily a majority of) votes

First-past-the-post
electoral system (simple plurality) where the winner receives the most (but not necessarily a majority of) votes

Minority government
government by party that received the most, but not a majority of, votes in an election

Two-round system
see Run-off system below

Run-off system
a form of electoral system in which a first round of voting takes place and the two (or three) candidates receiving the most votes pass to a second round of voting to determine an outright winner

Proportional representation
electoral system in which seats are designated according to the parties' popular vote; used in countries as a whole in order to institute proportions between votes allotted for all the parties

Party list
voting system in which voters in multi-member constituencies choose from a list of candidates; parties are rewarded with a percentage of the seats available in each constituency

Single Transferable Vote (STV)
voting system in which voters cast their ballot in multi-member constituencies, expressing their first and second choice for candidates; second choices may be transferred and counted if all seats are not filled in first count

Finally, a winning majority government might not receive any seats at all in certain regions, given the peculiarities of individual riding preferences. This poses a challenge for governments because they may not have widespread support across the national territory, but still attain a majority of seats in the Parliament or Congress. This will inevitably lead to questions about the nationwide legitimacy of a government, and calls for greater consultation with the parties that dominate specific regions.

Regardless of this, the tendency of the first-past-the-post system to create majority governments is applauded in some quarters. These proponents of the system argue that majority governments give more certainty, stability, and stronger direction to government, without the need for constant negotiation and brokering that is common with minority governments who need to seek the co-operation of other parties in order to be able to pass legislation.

Overall, we might say that the simple plurality system is highly efficient because it quickly and easily determines the winner in each constituency and at the national level. However, it suffers from the problem of leaving smaller parties underrepresented and minimally involved in the business of government. What's more, the system faces the problem of legitimacy because governments may not have the support of a majority of the electorate or of all regions of the country.

To overcome some of these problems, some countries that employ the simple plurality system choose to supplement it with a second round of voting. This **two-round system or run-off system**[18] (as it is more commonly known in the United States) involves the elimination of all but the two leading candidates after the first round of voting. In the second round, all voters get the chance to pick their preferred candidate from the reduced list. This ensures that the winning candidate can claim that he or she has the support of a majority of all participating voters, thereby increasing the legitimacy of the government. This system is employed in a number of countries, including France, Brazil, Ghana, and Indonesia.

The other basic category of electoral system is called **proportional representation (PR)**,[19] whereby voters have a better chance of seeing their preferences count. There are a number of different forms of PR in use in the world, but each attempts to create a more direct link between the number of votes cast and the number of seats won for each party, where seats are designated according to the parties' popular vote. The first, known as the **party list**[20] system, relies on multi-member constituencies where the political parties submit a list of candidates. The voters express their preference, and the parties are rewarded with a percentage of the seats available in each constituency. So, in a four-member constituency, a party receiving 50 per cent of the vote will win two seats, a party receiving 25 per cent one seat, and so on. There are two forms of the party list, one where voters express their preference for the party (closed list) or another where voters define which candidates they prefer (open list).

The second form of PR is called the **Single Transferable Vote (STV)**[21] system, in which voters cast their ballot in multi-member constituencies, expressing their first and second choice for candidates. During the first count of the votes, all candidates who receive sufficient votes will be elected. If all seats are filled, then the process stops. However, if seats are left unfilled, then the second choices of voters who picked the winning candidates are transferred and counted. After this process has been completed, the remaining seats are likely to have been filled. In the event that all seats have not been filled after the second count, the candidates with the least votes are eliminated and the second choices from their ballots are transferred.

Proportional representation is a better assessment of the likes and dislikes of voters. It also gives more of a chance to minor parties that otherwise would be ignored or eliminated in a simple plurality system of voting. On the other hand, proportional representation downgrades the relationship that constituents have with their individual representatives because so much in the election rides on the weight and influence of the parties involved. This is particularly true of the simple or national party list system, where the candidates are not linked directly to any constituency. In any case, proportional representation — despite its flaws — is often used as an example of what the Canadian system of elections might aspire to in an effort to overcome the problems associated with the simple plurality system.

There is a third form of proportional representation, the **additional member**[22] system, which mixes the plurality system with elements of PR. In each constituency the voters elect a representative and also cast a vote for a political party. These second votes are counted at the national level and additional seats in the Parliament or Congress are distributed among the parties according to the percentage of votes received. This system, it is argued, mixes the best of the simple plurality system with the benefits of PR. It maintains a link between representatives and their constituencies, while at the same time allowing smaller parties to establish themselves and gain experience. It is in use in countries such as Germany, the Republic of Ireland, and Mexico, and in the regional Parliaments in Scotland and Wales.

Political Parties

The need for organization has been a recurring theme throughout this book and is fundamental in politics. We have seen the organization of the state according to its different functions and according to geography, and we have seen the organization of voting systems. Within the political system, the organization of individuals and their representatives according to their ideologies and preferences is also important. The most common form of organizing is through **political parties**.[23] Parties are first and foremost driven by the desire to control government through the election of members of their group. Although interest groups may be concerned with a particular issue or sector of a political system, the function of political parties is to present a clear perspective regarding the manner in which a political system is administered. In brief, political parties are organized groups that place members as candidates for election with the expressed goal of governing the political system.

Earlier in this chapter we discussed suffrage, or the process of gaining the right to vote. The rise of political parties actually was directly related to suffrage, since as larger and larger groups of people were given the right to vote, there was a coinciding need to organize the interests of these new voters in some institution. Parties, then, arose as a result of the need in society to represent the views of sectors of public interest. In some countries parties were formed primarily

Additional member
mix of simple plurality and proportional representation voting; voters elect a representative and also cast a vote for a political party

Political party
organization that seeks to gain and maintain political power

around single issues, such as federalism (and anti-federalism) in the US in the eighteenth and nineteenth centuries, or around the question of the monarchy or slavery in Britain in the eighteenth and nineteenth centuries.

For many voters, political parties seem to emerge only when there is an election. This is not surprising, given that political parties first and foremost exist to coordinate and organize the opinions of party groups in a formal and institutional manner. However, parties do have a broader role in the political process. Aside from the capacity they have in society, they also have a direct role to play in the legislative setting. Parties allow for the grouping of elected members into coherent clusters, and provide for governmental direction, as well as opposition in the daily activities of the legislature.

Parties are created and operate on the basis of a set of beliefs or attitudes; these are referred to as **ideologies**,[24] or the underlying ideas for a political and economic system. And, just like in the case of electoral systems, or as we will see regarding interest groups, political parties and their level of influence in society and government varies from country to country. In many states in the international system, for instance, only one political party is allowed to form the government. These are called **one-party systems**. Most of the former communist systems that existed under the Soviet era are representative of this form of government. There are still examples of one-party states today — Cuba, North Korea, and Myanmar.

In liberal democracies, on the other hand, political parties are permitted to compete with one another for support from the electorate. These are referred to as **competitive party systems**,[25] and there are a number of varieties. These systems may comprise two competing parties (a **two-party system**),[26] or more than two (a **multi-party system**).[27]

However, these classifications tend to be alterable, depending on the prevailing interests in society. The United States, for example, is often acknowledged as a two-party system, but in the 1990s, the relative dominance of the traditional parties — the Republicans and the Democrats — was challenged by the upstart Reform Party (not to be confused with the Reform Party of Canada, which was a separate party). Similarly, the United Kingdom is often characterized as a two-party system, dominated by the Labour and Conservative parties. Yet this portrayal does not take into account the role of many other parties, including the influential Scottish National Party, or the Liberal Democratic Party. The simple plurality system at work in both of these two countries, however, helps to maintain the dominance of the two main parties, and it seems that there is little chance of a serious challenge to use of the term 'two-party system' in the US and UK.

In a similar vein, the role and influence of some parties in multi-party states is not always clear. In Canada, for instance, there are several significant political parties — the Liberals, New Democratic Party, the Greens, Bloc Québécois, and the Conservatives. Yet only two of these — the Liberals and Conservatives (and its predecessor, the Progressive Conservative Party) — have actually formed a federal government (there were a few examples of 'Unionist' governments made up of both Liberals and Conservatives). Should this mean, then, that the other parties are not as significant? Should the fact that the New Democratic Party has formed provincial governments, but not a federal government, give that party a different

Ideology
set or system of ideas that form the basis of a political or economic system and provide guidance and direction for political leadership

One-party system
political system in which only one political party is allowed to form the government, or compete in elections

Competitive party system
electoral system found in liberal democracies in which political parties are permitted to compete with one another for support from the electorate

Two-party system
competitive party system marked by two competing parties

Multi-party system
competitive party system with more than two parties

level in the Canadian party system? In fact, developments in the Canadian political party system are really no different than in any other state. Political parties tend to rise and fall in their level of support among the public based on a variety of societal concerns, and the major issues in the civic debate.

There are several types of political parties. **Cadre parties**[28] refer to those parties that are created and directed by a small elite group, and tend to control much power within legislatures. The history of cadre parties extends back to the initial process of suffrage, as powerful elites sought to maintain the control over government that they stood to lose with the influx of many more voters in the political system. By forming parties that they controlled, the relative influence of huge masses of voters in society was offset by the continuing dominant role played by elites in party organization. **Mass parties**,[29] on the other hand, were formed partly to combat the influence that cadre parties had in government. Mass parties are organized in society at large, rather than within government. They exhibit a large public influence by placing a great degree of power in the membership, rather than in the hands of a small minority elite. **Umbrella parties**[30] tend to cover a wide range of ideologies and beliefs in society, and are formed and run with the idea of incorporating as many different groups in society as possible. Umbrella parties have been of particular importance in countries such as Mexico, where single-party rule for decades necessitated the absorption of many social and economic groups under the 'umbrella' of the Partido Revolucionario Institucional (PRI). **Militia parties** are a third example, and are often found in military governments or communist systems. These party types have an extremely centralized leadership system, and place great requirements on members. Militia parties often are led by martial leaders, and are frequently found in one-party systems.

Political parties have many prominent functions in society. First, they play a **recruitment function**, in that they help to bring new voters into the political process. Parties create a link between government and the people, since government members are usually members of parties that also include private citizen participation. Therefore, in theory at least, party leaders and government members will be attentive to the concerns of other members of the party. Parties also form a method of arranging and categorizing interests in society, as individuals that choose to join — or at least support — parties are essentially making an ideological choice, as well. Party support, then, gives us a sense of how the electorate feels about the role of government in society, and the approach that administrations should take. In a more functional way, parties are a basic way for private citizens, even if they do not support a party at large, to register their backing for individual potential representatives. Related to this is the role that political parties play in the education and instruction of future politicians and political actors. As institutions, parties embody established structures that might be used to train party workers and upcoming leaders. Once parties are elected to power, they are crucial in creating and upholding the direction, approach, and organization of government. In this way, parties determine not just the immediate bearing for an administration, but also a 'template' for future ones, and future supporters.

Political parties play a fundamental role in organizing political activity. They perform a variety of functions, from recruiting voters to training candidates to

Cadre party
party created and directed by a small elite group; tends to control much power within legislatures

Mass party
party organized in society at large, rather than within government, and having public influence through power of membership, rather than in the hands of a small minority elite

Umbrella parties
political parties that cover a wide range of ideologies and beliefs in society, with the idea of incorporating as many different groups in society as possible

Militia party
party system with a centralized leadership system; often having martial leadership, and frequently found in one-party system

Recruitment function
role played by political parties to help bring new voters into the political process

fundraising for election campaigns to consulting with society. In many ways parties are one of the central organizers in our political systems. First of all, parties organize legislators within the Parliament or Congress, coordinating their positions, disciplining those who go against the party line, and negotiating with other political parties. This is particularly important when the party in question is in opposition. In this situation, the party leaders will need the organizational and disciplinary capacities of the party to organize members effectively in their opposition to government initiatives and policies.

How can parties discipline their members? In several countries, parties employ a specific party member to enforce discipline. This person is known as 'the Whip' or 'Chief Whip'. The whip works to guarantee that all party members vote according to the preferences of the party, particularly on issues of central importance. In the UK, the term 'whip' refers not only to the individual responsible for discipline, but also to describe the level of importance of particular votes in the House of Commons. A 'one line whip' indicates in a non-binding way to the party members what the party preference is. A 'two line whip' indicates that members must attend the vote, although it does not commit them to voting one way or another. The strongest indication of party preferences is the 'three line whip', which binds party members to attend the vote and to vote a certain way. A member who chooses to disobey a three line whip can expect to be heavily sanctioned by the party. A particularly effective method is through threatening to expel non-conformist members, or by refusing to give them the party's endorsement in upcoming elections. When in government, parties may do the same thing, although a government's patronage powers will likely be a more effective tool.

Parties also help the democratic process by broadening consultation with society. By engaging in dialogue with the community at the local level, there is a greater chance that issues of importance to the community find their way into the halls of power. Over the years, parties have been responsible for pushing a wide array of issues onto the legislative agenda, from civil rights to environmental protection to immigration reform.

The registration of voters is another crucial function that is performed by political parties in many countries. Clearly, it is in their interest to help as many potential supporters as possible to register to be eligible to vote, and thus parties work hard, particularly close to election time, to facilitate voter registration. On the day of the election itself, parties also assist voters in getting to the polls, driving those who may not have their own transportation or who are unable to make it there on their own, and phoning registered voters to remind them of the importance of making their vote count.

As you may have guessed by now, political parties are today highly organized, professionally run organizations. They have full-time staff, extensive databases, and widespread networks that can be called upon when necessary. This all requires the party to raise sufficient funds to be able to carry out their functions. In many countries, the state provides funding for major political parties to enable them to do this. In addition, parties will raise funds from other sources, both in the form of membership dues and charitable contributions.

Political parties also play a central role in raising funds for the electoral process. By calling on their extensive network of party members and supporters, both individuals and organizations, parties are able to raise hundreds of millions of dollars to pay for the work of getting their members elected. This raises some controversial issues, as we will see in the upcoming section on campaign financing.

Election Campaigns

Election cycles are set at different frequencies in different countries. In the United States the presidential elections happen every four years, on the first Tuesday of November. In Mexico, the presidential election occurs every six years (a period known as a *sexenio*), with elections occurring during the first week of July. However, in countries such as Canada and the United Kingdom, there is a maximum period set before an election must be called. In both countries it is set at five years, but a government may choose to call an election at any time during that period. This gives the government a significant advantage because it can pick a time when it is enjoying high levels of public support, call an election, and dramatically improve its chances of re-election. This can, of course, backfire: if a government appears too arrogant and opportunistic, it may end up losing support.

Once an election has been scheduled, political parties play a central role in organizing campaigning and in determining policy positions. Candidates need to be chosen by the parties, and this can occur in a number of ways. In some countries a central party committee chooses candidates for specific constituencies. In others, such as the United States, potential candidates for the presidency or Congress must compete against other potential candidates to win the party's official nomination. In the election campaign itself, conflict between the parties may get particularly intense. Throughout history parties and candidates have used 'smear tactics'[31] and 'negative campaigning'[32] against each other (see Box 7.5). By highlighting mistakes, infringements of the rules and other negative issues, and in particular character flaws of the opposing candidate, one candidate may hope to turn the electorate away from his or her opponent. Increasingly, we can observe the use of negative and aggressive television and media advertising, or **'attack ads'**.[33] Again, however, this can be risky, as the public often reacts badly to such negative tactics, particularly if it emerges that the allegations are not true.

But even aside from this, there are a host of concerns about awareness of issues and platforms taken by the candidates themselves. In an environment where candidates recognize that they will only be given a short 'sound-bite' in the media, and where voters are literally inundated with information, it is difficult, if not impossible, to truly have a meaningful discourse about the issues or policies that are taken by candidates.

As a result, the process of electioneering in modern society takes on a paradoxical dimension: candidates reduce what they say into digestible commentary and pursue marketing strategies to appeal to voters. Voters, on the other hand, complain not about getting the information they need, but about not having the time to absorb what is being presented to them! Increasingly, elections become

Attack ads
negative and aggressive television and media advertising by one political party or organization against another

7.5

Negative Campaigning

In 1993 the Progressive Conservative Party used Liberal candidate Jean Chrétien's partial facial paralysis as a campaign strategy. The strategy failed.

Elections often bring out the uglier side of politics and politicians. In recent years the use of negative campaigning and attack ads in Canada has become more common. In the 1993 federal election, the Progressive Conservative Party launched an advertising campaign that appeared to put emphasis on Liberal candidate Jean Chrétien's partial facial paralysis. The public reacted very negatively to this kind of tactic and the Progressive Conservatives lost votes. In 2006, it was now the turn of the Liberal party to employ such negative campaigning, suggesting in their publicity that Stephen Harper was an authoritarian who might impose martial law on Canada. Again the tactic backfired and the Liberals suffered at the polls.

Of course negative campaigning is actually nothing new in politics. In the US presidential campaign of 1800, where vice-president Thomas Jefferson ran against the then president John Adams, Jefferson's campaign team insulted Adams publicly, saying he had a 'hideous hermaphroditical character, which has neither the force and firmness of a man, nor the gentleness and sensibility of a woman.' Adams' campaign responded by calling the vice-president 'a mean-spirited, low-lived fellow, the son of a half-breed Indian squaw, sired by a Virginia mulatto father'. In this case Jefferson's attacks were to prove effective and he narrowly won the election.

rather superficial contests that focus on personal qualities and presence, rather than issues, platforms, and policies.

Campaign Financing

One area of the elections process that has become particularly controversial in recent years is how parties and candidates finance their bids for public office. Candidates are spending more and more on their campaigns: high costs amount from television, radio, and press advertising, extensive travel and appearances at high-profile events by the candidate to ensure the widest possible media exposure, as well as the staff required to run an effective modern political campaign. In the case of the US, hundreds of millions of dollars are spent by the leading contenders for the presidency (see Box 7.6). Although this figure is extreme, across the world election campaigns have become exorbitantly expensive affairs.

In order to be able to raise the funds necessary to fight a competitive and hopefully successful campaign, parties and politicians need to turn to powerful and wealthy groups in society, beyond the party membership. Because of the high costs of election campaigning, candidates seek contributions from a diverse array of sources, both from individuals and from groups, as well as from corporations. It is in this situation that private interests seek to influence the political process through their financial contributions. These contributions raise the specter of wealthy groups or individuals buying political favours in exchange for substantial contributions to the campaign coffers. Of course such a trade-off is vigorously denied by both politicians and those who contribute to their campaigns, arguing that contributions merely reflect the desire of a particular group or individual to see a candidate (re-)elected.

Because of this problem many countries have put in place legislation that limits the amount of money an individual or group can contribute to a campaign, and demands transparency and accurate and detailed accounting of all

7.6

Campaign Finances and the 2008 US Presidential Campaign

In recent years there have been a growing number of questions raised by lawmakers and the public over the nature and implications of contributions to election campaigns. Nowhere has this been truer than in the United States of America, where the scale and intensity of election campaigns exceeds any other country. After the 1996 presidential election campaign, in which the Democratic Party came under increasing scrutiny because of questionable methods used by fundraisers (and also because of the sources from which large contributions came), the US has been engaged in an active debate about how to fund elections.

The sheer amount of money that was raised by the two candidates in the 2008 presidential campaign is astounding. The losing candidate, John McCain, raised over $368 million and spent a total of $333 million. The winner of that election, Barack Obama, raised over $745 million and spent $730 million. Total spending by all candidates in the US in 2008 came to $1.324 billion! When evaluating how enormous this sum is, we should contrast it with the total spending by presidential candidates in the election of 1976. In that year candidates spent $66.9 million in total.

contributions and spending. In other countries the state provides financing to political parties, proportional to the number of candidates they intend to run and provided they achieve a certain minimum percentage of the popular vote. Nonetheless, elections provide an opportune moment for private interest groups and corporations to buy the support of candidates. As long as an aspiring office-holder intends to seek re-election at some time in the future, she will be tempted to exchange political support for sizeable campaign contributions. Though this is hardly the rule in the political systems of most democratic states, it remains a serious concern. In Canada, changes to the electoral finance law in 2003 set the limit for individual contributions to political parties and individual candidates at election time at $1100, but there is an active ongoing debate about ways to ensure that wealthy groups and individuals do not circumvent these rules.

One way in which some interest groups circumvent limits on contributions is to organize their own campaigns on behalf of a candidate, buying press space or media time in which they express their support for an individual, independent of the official campaign. Some such television, radio, or newspaper commercials do not even feature the name of the candidate in question, choosing instead to negatively influence the public against the opposing candidate(s). Because such media exposure is often the most expensive element of an election campaign, doubts must also be raised about the legitimacy or ethical nature of such assistance.

An important distinction to be made in the area of election campaign contributions is that between 'soft money' and 'hard money'. The first of these terms refers to funds given to the party as a general or non-specific contribution, whereas the second refers to monies donated to the party or candidate specifically for the purposes of fighting an election campaign. This distinction has come to be of particular importance in recent years in the United States, and it has become clear that the line between the two kinds of donation is very often blurred, a problem that makes the issue of campaign financing that much more complex.

Direct Democracy and the Referendum

Up until this point in the chapter we have been learning about the workings of democracy in its representative, or indirect, form, where intermediaries are chosen by the people to carry out the business of politics. We noted earlier that, in an ideal world, politics is a full-time job that requires professionalism. There are times, however, when political systems call on the direct voice of the people to determine outcomes. Rather than let political parties and elected representatives decide for the people, the people themselves are asked to decide. It is in these situations that **direct democracy** occurs. Citizens of voting age are asked to express their opinions on a particular policy in an official vote, the results of which will determine whether or not that policy is adopted by the government. Such a vote is known as a **referendum** or **plebiscite**.[34]

The best-known example of a country where this occurs frequently is Switzerland. Citizens are asked to vote on issues on a regular basis, and the

Direct democracy
political system in which citizens are directly involved in the decision-making process

Referendum
when citizens vote to express their opinions on a particular policy, the results of which will determine whether or not that policy is adopted by the government; also known as a plebiscite

Plebiscite
when citizens vote to express their opinions on a particular policy, the results of which will determine whether or not that policy is adopted by the government; also known as a referendum

outcome of these votes is then passed onto the states, or cantons, in Switzerland. If a majority in favour of a measure is achieved in both the referendum and among the cantons, then it becomes federal law. In the European Union, referenda have been used to determine individual state policy regarding further integration, as occurred in 1992 with referenda over the Maastricht Treaty or in 2005 over the creation of a European Constitution.

To many it may seem as though this direct involvement of the citizen in the workings of the democratic system is admirable, that it strengthens democracy and encourages exactly the kind of participation that we have been reading about in this chapter. However, referendums can be controversial because they can be manipulated and twisted by politicians to help them reinforce their grip on power. In the contemporary world, the case of Venezuela stands out. President Hugo Chavez brought in a new constitution for the country in 1999 that requires a referendum for any constitutional change and for recalling elected officials. Opponents of Chavez argue that he has used referendums since then to modify the constitution and overcome organized opposition by rival politicians and political parties. Chavez himself argues that he is only doing what the sovereign people of Venezuela tell him to.

Direct democracy will become more and more viable in the future as modern communications technologies make it more feasible for citizens to express their preferences instantaneously and in real time. You can imagine a not too distant future in which every household is linked through the television, Internet, or video games console to a central computer that registers citizen preferences on a wide range of everyday political issues. Whether or not citizens will become better educated, more informed, and less apathetic is another question.

Elections and Political Parties in Canada

We have already made mention of a number of important features about voting and elections in Canada. Almost every Canadian citizen over the age of 18 has the right to vote, and there is a maximum period of five years between federal elections. Canadian elections are well organized and are generally considered to be free and fair, and employ the simple plurality system of determining election winners. Since the first general election at the federal level in Canada in 1867, the Liberal and Conservative Parties have dominated Canadian politics, although other parties have achieved success at the provincial level, or have made up the official opposition. This situation has been reinforced by the first-past-the-post system used in elections in Canada, making it difficult for smaller parties to win sufficient numbers of seats to challenge for government.

It is important to note, however, that Canadian elections and political parties are involved in a process of ongoing development and evolution. It was not until relatively late into the twentieth century, for example, that full suffrage was achieved. The federal government and some provinces excluded Native Canadians and some ethnic groups from voting as recently as the early 1960s, and women were only given the right to vote in Quebec in 1940 and in Newfoundland in 1948. Now, however, suffrage is universal for adults over the age of 18.

In Canada, however, as in most countries, there are rules about who may stand for elected office in the legislature. Candidates in federal elections must be eligible voters, which means that people under the age of 18 or foreigners may not stand. Prisoners may not stand for office and anyone who has been convicted of an election-related crime is barred from office for a number of years. Neither senators nor provincial or territorial parliamentarians may be federal MPs in the House of Commons at the same time; neither may judges, Crown (public) attorneys, or elections officers.

The situation of political parties too continues to evolve. In particular, the right side of the political spectrum has experienced considerable change in recent years. During the 1990s a new conservative political party, the Reform Party, grew in importance and split right-wing political support, helping the Liberal Party to maintain a dominant position. However, a merger between the Reform Party's successor, the Canadian Alliance Party, and Progressive Conservatives produced a new Conservative Party of Canada, enabling the new party to unite the right and win power in 2006. Of course, the leader of the Canadian Alliance, Stephen Harper, went on to become the leader of the Conservatives and the first Conservative prime minister of Canada since Kim Campbell's short-lived term in 1993.

We have also seen the emergence in Canada of parties that have quite specific regional support. For instance, in the Canadian federal election of 1997, the dominant party in Quebec was the Bloc Québécois, and in Alberta, the dominant party was Reform. In both of these cases, these parties received both a majority of votes, and seats, yet neither formed the federal government; that title went to the Liberal Party. These two parties, then, have been referred to as 'regional parties'[35] because of their strong provincial strength but weak national presence. For a period in the 1990s, the Bloc Québécois was the second largest party in the Canadian Parliament, creating the rather strange situation where a regional party that was seeking separation from Canada was Her Majesty's official opposition.

Canada's system of election financing, embodied in the Election Expenses Act and the Canada Elections Act, provides state subsidies for candidates who achieve 15 per cent of votes, allows candidates to raise private funds, but places limits on total spending and requires candidates to provide detailed accounts of all monies received and spent. These regulations came into operation in response to problems experienced by political parties in generating enough funding and also public outrage over scandals involving just the kind of influence-buying behaviour discussed earlier in the chapter. As we noted above, the limit on individual contributions was set at $1100 in 2003, and no group or union contributions are allowed. However, the provinces set their own rules for provincial elections, and the strictness of these rules varies widely.

In terms of direct democracy, in Canada the referendum has been used on a number of occasions, but rarely at the federal level (the most recent being the national referendum over the Charlottetown Accord in 1992). Most famously in the Canadian case, the people of the province of Quebec have voted on the question of Quebec's future in Canada, and this gives us a good example of some of the problems associated with referendums. In 1980 the question posed to Quebecois was whether or not they wanted to negotiate a relationship of 'sovereignty association' with the rest of Canada, meaning that Quebec would achieve sovereign status but still remain connected to Canada, in some way reminiscent of a confederal relationship and incorporating free trade relations, a common currency, and common external trade tariffs. This proposal was rejected by 60 per cent of the population, but by offering the citizens of Quebec a question with a simple yes/no answer, the referendum did not allow for different or intermediate points of view to be expressed. What's more, the question itself was worded in such a way as to maximize the potential for a 'yes' vote. A similar situation occurred in 1995 when the question now posed was over the *possibility* of negotiating a sovereignty association agreement. This time the proposal was rejected by a slim margin of 50.6 per cent to 49.4 per cent, with a strong majority of francophone Quebecois voting in favour. This left almost 50 per cent of the population unhappy with the outcome, further prolonging the uncertainty about the future of the province.

Conclusion

This chapter has introduced you to some of the most important issues surrounding formal political participation, through voting, elections, and political parties. Voting was presented as a fundamental element of any democracy, and the primary form of political participation available to the average citizen. In indirect democracies, this means the election of representatives who will act on behalf of the interests of the citizen. An alternative form of participation that exists at different times in different places on different issues is direct democracy using the referendum, where the individual citizen has the opportunity to directly influence the policy process. We also looked at political parties as one method of aggregating individual interests and concerns into large public forums. While political parties are primarily created in order to seek political power, they also serve multiple functions in society and in the political system, organizing sometimes diverse actors into recognizable groups, and helping to engage citizens in the political process.

Self-Assessment Questions

1. Should voting be made compulsory in Canada?
2. Should people be tested on their political knowledge before being allowed to vote?
3. Why is it important to regulate campaign financing?
4. Is direct democracy a good alternative to the representative democracy we have today in Canada? Why?

Weblinks

Bloc Québécois
www.blocquebecois.org

Conservative Party
www.conservative.ca

Elections Canada
www.elections.ca/home.asp

Green Party
www.greenparty.ca

Liberal Party
www.liberal.ca

New Democratic Party
www.ndp.ca

Rock the Vote
www.rockthevote.com

Your Members of Parliament
http://webinfo.parl.gc.ca/
    MembersOfParliament/
    MainMPsCompleteList.aspx?TimePeriod=Cu
    rrent&Language=E

Further Reading

Farrell, David M. *Electoral Systems: A Comparative Introduction*. Houndmills, UK: Palgrave, 2001.

Gunther, Richard, José Ramón Montero, and Juan J. Linz, eds. *Political Parties: Old Concepts and New Challenges*. Oxford: Oxford University Press, 2002.

Kitshelt, Herbert, and Steven I. Wilkinson, eds. *Patrons, Clients, and Policies: Patterns of Democratic Accountability and Political Competition*. Cambridge: Cambridge University Press, 2007.

Norris, Pippa. *Electoral Engineering: Voting Rules and Political Behavior*. Cambridge: Cambridge University Press, 2004.

Reilly, Ben, and Andrew Reynolds. *Electoral Systems and Conflict in Divided Societies*. Washington, DC: National Academy Press, 1999.

Schaffer, Frederic Charles, *The Hidden Costs of Clean Election Reform*. Ithaca, NY: Cornell University Press, 2008.

Stoker, Gerry. *Why Politics Matters: Making Democracy Work*. Houndmills, UK: Palgrave Macmillan, 2006.

Taagapera, Rein, and Mathew Soberg Shugart. *Seats and Votes: The Effects and Determinants of Electoral Systems*. New Haven, CT: Yale University Press, 1989.

CBC News Clips

Visit the companion website for *Politics: An Introduction* to listen to news clips from the CBC radio archives.

8 Political Socialization and Culture

LEARNING OBJECTIVES

After reading this chapter, you will be able to:

❋ explain why political culture is a fundamental element in any political system

❋ understand the importance of society and socialization in determining political culture and identity

❋ understand the role of education in politics

❋ explain why public opinion matters and how we measure it

❋ know the role of the newspapers, television, and radio in politics

❋ recognize what are civil society and non-governmental organizations (NGOs)

❋ know the importance of interest groups and lobbying

❋ discuss the process of consultation between government and society

❋ analyze political socialization in Canada.

Introduction

In the previous chapter we saw how formal citizen participation can be organized through elections, political parties, and referendums. These are the forms of participation that we most commonly consider when we think of politics, but there are many more ways for citizens to participate in political life. In this chapter we will examine less traditional forms of political activity, including some that have become very important and highly controversial in recent times. One of the purposes of this chapter is to introduce you to multiple forms of political expression and to show you that you do not have to wait for an election or referendum to 'become political', nor do you have to join a political party to gain a political identity. In many ways we are all socialized into becoming political animals to different degrees throughout our lives. What's more, you will see how unelected groups and actors in society have extensive influence over the political process.

The Process of Political Socialization

As we now know, each of us as citizens exists within a particular society and political system. We have the opportunity to participate in the political process through political parties, elections, and referendums. But there are a host of other ways in which we exist as political beings, and in which we may participate in politics in less formal and less traditional ways. As we saw in Chapter 1, politics surrounds us and many of our actions take on a political significance when viewed in that context. By forming interest and protest groups, by choosing one source of political information over another, by organizing discussion groups on the Internet on political themes, by refusing to buy certain products because of the way they are produced, and by simply engaging in debate and dialogue over political issues, we are participating in this broader political reality. That is why we need to look beyond the more limited boundaries of formal political action and participation, to understand how societies and individual citizens can and do play an important role in politics.

Political Culture

Though we may not be fully aware of it, there is a set of attitudes, beliefs, and values that underpins any political system. These attitudes, beliefs, and values may come in a variety of forms, be they religious, cultural, linguistic, or class-based, but they all contribute to the general outlook we, as citizens, have regarding our political system and our relations with each other and the rest of the world. These attitudes, beliefs, and values are referred to as our **political culture**.[1] Our political culture — any political culture — is an integral part of the process of political socialization that we will describe in this chapter. Think about the views that you might have about the role of your government, and your rights and freedoms that are constitutionally guaranteed as part of your citizenship. These rights and freedoms allow you and others to freely group with others, to express your views without persecution, to pursue your own religious beliefs, and to have an open and free system of information and communication. Now imagine life in an authoritarian state where these rights and freedoms are denied you. The political culture of an authoritarian state will be necessarily different than your own, largely because of the type of system in which the culture exists. Political culture is an important element of our community, our tradition, and our function of identity as citizens.

Political culture, then, refers to the underlying fundamental political values of a society. These values are not set or predetermined, rather they evolve over time. However, at any given moment they help to determine the scope of viable political options, they influence political processes and public policy, and they shape political views and opinions. If asked, it would be difficult for us to give an exhaustive list of the values that make up our own political culture, but most of us would be able to identify certain political values that we recognize as being part of Canadian political culture.

Political culture
set of attitudes, beliefs, and values that underpin any political system

Political culture is also activated by and influences political activities. For instance, the relative freedom of the media, the role of interest groups and political action committees, the influence of parties, collective bargaining among unions and corporations, and the relationship between constituents and elected officials are all affected seriously by the prevailing political culture in a political system. Just as different political systems exist, whether they are liberal democracies or authoritarian states, presidential or parliamentary systems, federations or unitary countries, so does the distinctive political culture in every country affect the desires and hopes for citizens.[2] The North American Free Trade Agreement, the future for Quebec in the federation, the legalization of narcotics, and Aboriginal rights and land agreements are examples of contentious areas of public policy in Canada. But most issues of governmental policy in Canada are not so contentious because of the prevailing political culture in Canadian society that concedes to the legitimate role of the federal government in decision- and policy-making.

8.1

The Symbols of Canada as a Form of Political Socialization

© kawisign/iStockphoto.com

The beaver is one of several national symbols in Canada and serves to highlight elements of Canadian identity.

The use of symbols to create and nurture loyalty, social cohesion, and obedience is nothing new. For centuries monarchs, religious organizations, and the state itself has used such symbols to create a sense of identity among their subjects, members, and citizens. Often this takes place in such a subtle way as to be unnoticeable. The singing of the national anthem, the use of the flag, the wearing of a national emblem on clothing — all these are ways in which we are indoctrinated into the national identity.

You have probably been exposed to Canadian national political symbols since your birth or arrival in this country. The ubiquitous nature of these symbols and their effective use by both government and business mean that we

8.1 Continued...

are constantly being reminded, consciously or not, of our membership in this particular political community.

The symbols of Canada are unique and idiosyncratic. The current flag, for example, was adopted only in 1965. For many years the Canadian red ensign (a red flag with the union jack and the Canadian royal coat of arms) had been used. The search for an official Canadian flag had begun in 1925 but was abandoned and then taken up again later; after a fervent national debate, the red-and-white design with a maple leaf was chosen in 1964 and officially inaugurated on 15 February 1965. Red and white reflected the official colours of Canada (in use since Victorian times but officially proclaimed in 1921) and the maple leaf had been a symbol of Canada since the 1700s. It was used for many years as a symbol of the Canadian Armed Forces and had been worn by Canadian athletes since 1904.

The beaver was chosen as an official symbol of Canada when it was recognized as 'a symbol of the sovereignty of Canada' in an Act of Parliament that received royal assent on 24 March 1975. The beaver may be thought of as a strange choice; other nations choose lions, eagles, or dragons to represent their sovereignty. But the beaver is once again uniquely Canadian. It reflects the importance of the fur trade in the early economic development of Canada and in recent years has come to be seen as bearing Canadian attributes: it is modest, ingenious, hardworking, persevering, and constructive.

A non-visual symbol of importance is the national anthem. Written in the nineteenth century in French, the lyrics reflect the idea of Canada as a nation 'strong and free'. It generates feelings of belonging (our home and native land, true patriot love) and of defence (we stand on guard for thee). These lyrics, however, have experienced various incarnations, with the current version being approved by Parliament in 1972 and accepted as Canada's national anthem.

The use of these symbols in official ceremonies, at sporting events, and in particular in schools, is part of the process of political socialization that permeates throughout Canadian society, and which for the large part goes unnoticed and unquestioned by citizens.

In the 1960s, political scientists Gabriel Almond and Sidney Verba proposed three distinct categories of political culture. The first, which they named 'parochial', refers to a political culture in which citizens feel removed from the central decision-making processes of the country, and in which they have little influence over those processes. Part of a parochial political culture is a lack of interest in politics, for the simple reason that citizens are uninformed of political processes and feel there is little chance of shaping outcomes. The second category is known as 'subject political culture,' in which citizens are subjected to the decisions of central government without much consultation, without much involvement in the decision-making process, and without much chance of influencing outcomes. Here citizens may be informed, but they do not play an active role in politics on a regular basis. The last category was named 'participant political culture' by Almond and Verba, and is one in which citizens play an active role in the political process, influencing outcomes on a daily basis, and engaging in a constant dynamic relationship with political authorities. Each of these categories is, of course, a simplified version of reality, but they are useful in analyzing political systems around the world. Nonetheless, they will never be able to give us a detailed, complex understanding of the particular political culture of any country, which instead requires in-depth examination and description.

Political culture matters because it forms a central part of the political environment within which we, as citizens, and the political authorities at all levels, behave and participate in politics. As such, it provides us with both incentives and disincentives for distinct forms of behaviour. However, political culture is open to change over time, as we can observe by the rise of such political values as democracy, tolerance, and respect for minorities over the past hundred years.

Political Socialization

Political socialization is the process through which individuals are educated and assimilated into the political culture of a community. This can happen in both formal and informal ways. First we must look at the formal education system that exists in any given country, and the lessons, values, and symbols that are passed on through that system to children. By singing the national anthem, by pledging allegiance to the flag, by being taught a particular version of the nation's history, children are being socialized into the national political culture. If you remember back to your elementary and high school days, and think of how often you were exposed to the Canadian flag, the national anthem, and lessons extolling the achievements of great historical figures (Samuel de Champlain, Wilfrid Laurier, John A. Macdonald, or Nellie McClung, for instance), you can begin to see how important education is in this process. When we remember that provincial educational authorities generally set the curriculum, we can also see how political authorities can exercise influence over the socialization process. In countries such as Britain, where there is a national curriculum, there is potential for a more harmonized process of political socialization of young people.

At the university level the influence of the classroom remains important, but we also see the central role played by student organizations, peer groups, and activism. As a student of politics you may or may not be active in a political way, but on almost any university campus around the world the opportunities for participation and for political learning and socialization are abundant. Traditionally, university campuses have been centres for protest and dissidence, although in recent years in countries like Canada, this has been less and less the case.

But socialization goes far beyond the classroom and the formal educational system. In fact the primary agent of political socialization is, of course, the family. The information that we receive from our parents, the level of political debate in the home, and the views of our parents, are all fundamental factors in shaping our views and our attitudes towards politics. Although it is natural for children to reject the views held by their parents, studies have shown that there is a considerable degree of continuity in the beliefs passed from parents to children.[3] This applies not just to voting preferences and support for political parties, but also to a wider range of basic values that will affect political beliefs and actions throughout an individual's life. Think of your own experience and ask yourself how much your family, your parents, guardians or siblings, or aunts and uncles influenced your own political views. And, of course, we should not just stop at political values and beliefs. Moral and ethical values will play a key role in influencing your political attitudes, as well as basic life lessons concerning work, religion, sports, and charitable activities.

Once we recognize the importance of family, the importance of socio-economic status must also be taken into account. A person's belief system and values will be fundamentally influenced by the economic and social opportunities that are made available to them. To give a simplistic example, someone who makes a good enough income to fit into a tax bracket where they have to pay a higher rate of taxes is less likely to be in favour of a progressive taxation system where the rich pay a higher percentage of their income in taxes than someone who makes less money.

A further influence on political socialization comes from the geographical region in which one lives. The predominant political views of the local society in that region will play an important role in determining what an individual comes to believe. The importance of community versus the individual, traditional versus modern values, and the element of identity will all be significant factors. In Canada the regional component of political socialization is obvious. In provinces such as Alberta a less interventionist political culture exists than in provinces such as Saskatchewan. In Quebec, we cannot understand political socialization without the elements of language and identity. In the north of Canada and in particular in the territories, Aboriginal cultures and values play a role in the process of political socialization.

One of the most important agents of political socialization today, however, and one that we will spend considerable time discussing, is the media.[4] By controlling and shaping the flow of information received by citizens, newspapers, radio stations, television channels, and Internet sites are increasingly determining factors in the process of shaping views and attitudes. The media is a particularly important agent of socialization when we remember that it has an effect not only on children and young people but also on the political attitudes and beliefs of individuals of all ages. But especially in their formative years, people are susceptible to the media as a way of shaping their basic beliefs and attitudes towards politics. Again, here we can see how the state itself can play a role through state-controlled media outlets, such as public television and radio, and through government ministry websites that regulate the flow of information. We will come back to a more thorough examination of the media in a later section of this chapter.

Public Opinion

Participation can also come in the form of expressing an opinion in public discourse.[5] This is a way for citizens to proclaim their views regarding the activities of their government in a sanctioned and legitimate manner. Public opinion refers to

Opinion poll

investigation of public opinion conducted by interviewing a sample of citizens

the patterns of opinion found among the public when **opinion polls**[6] are taken by polling firms.[7] These polls have acquired importance in recent decades not only as measures of public views and preferences, but also in the run-up to elections and in the formation of public policy. In the first of these instances, polling firms such as Gallup, Zogby, Ipsos, and MORI have played a key role in measuring public sentiment during election campaigns, measuring public support for incumbent politicians and the candidates for office who are running against them. This helps us to keep track of the popularity of candidates, and to track the impact of policies and public statements. But it has also become controversial because it has meant that in some countries, there appears to be a permanent election campaign underway, with polling firms testing public opinion with regard to candidates on a near-constant basis. Further, questions have arisen over the capacity for opinion polls to influence election outcomes, and in some countries opinion polls relating to elections have been prohibited in the days leading up to a major election. The fear is that the public will be influenced by the results of opinion polls, with some deciding not to vote because the election may seem a foregone conclusion with one party dramatically out-polling its rivals.[8] Alternatively, some may decide to change their vote, given the apparent dominance of one party or candidate over the others.

With regard to the formation of public policy, governments have increasingly turned to polls to measure the impact of proposed policies on public opinion. This has been questioned for its potential to push governments towards populism, designing policies not for their effectiveness or efficiency, but rather because they will win the government popular support. This threatens to change the role of government, from one in which it provides for the needs of a population, to one where it pampers whims and desires. This becomes a particularly sensitive issue in the months leading up to an election, with the government holding back from potentially unpopular policies (such as raising taxes or cutting public services) to increase its support.

Often our public opinions might seem to be so straightforward and accepted that we do not even recognize them as opinion. For instance, our attitudes towards our system of tolerance, economic openness, and free expression may simply be seen as accepted attitudes regarding our relations with our government, but they are actually part of the opinion we hold about our entire political system. Our public opinion, then, might be quite constant, depending on the issues involved. On the other hand, our opinions might be changing, depending on our age, where we live in the country, our economic status, or level of education. For example, someone who has recently lost his or her job will no doubt form a very different opinion regarding job creation, benefits, and unemployment benefits than when he or she was employed.

Public opinion is also influenced by the strength of the views held. Religious beliefs, for instance, are a strong indicator of public opinion; this is one reason why pollsters and public opinion firms ask respondents to indicate their religion as a means of identifying the views held. Attitudes towards issues such as abortion and church schools, therefore, are heavily influenced by the relative strength of the individual's religious views and beliefs. Other issues, such as public works projects and the creation of national parks, are not likely to be affected by the intense opinion that influences other issues.

There are many political scientists who devote their professional lives to the study of public opinion, and in these people we see a true crossover between the world of academia and the real world of politics. Experts in public opinion use their skills and experience to analyze the results of opinion polls and interpret their results, not only to the broader public through the media, but also to governments, businesses, and political parties. Partly because of the demand for such analysis, there has been a dramatic growth in this area of political science in recent years, particularly in the United States.

The Media and Politics

Perhaps the most pervasive element of information in our modern society is the media. When the United States and its allies invaded Iraq in early 2003, the military forces involved took the decision to embed journalists, from television, radio, and newspapers, among the troops as they moved through Iraq. In this way the world was able to follow the conflict on a seemingly first-hand basis, and was continuously informed of progress and setbacks in the war. This example shows both the importance of the media as a source of information and as an agent in the process of political socialization, but also demonstrates how the media can become an unwilling servant of government as a channel for the official dissemination of political messages. The control of information flows in the Iraq war by the US military (among other authorities) highlighted many of the challenges of maintaining a free and open media in the modern world.

The importance of the press and the media has been recognized since at least the early nineteenth century. Thomas Carlyle, quoting Edmund Burke, commented on the importance of the **fourth estate** (the first three estates being the clergy, the nobles, and the commoners), arguing that it had acquired an importance that matched, if not surpassed, the other three. The fourth estate, in an ideal world, is supposed to act as another check on the power of government, as a watchdog to ensure that public authorities do not go beyond their mandates and abuse their position of power.[9]

Fourth estate
media; other estates: clergy, nobles, commoners

The media has become the most organized form of information in our society. Twenty-four-hour news channels, international correspondents, and a seemingly endless barrage of newscasts, print media, and Internet dispatches afford us, as ordinary citizens, a view of the world that was simply not available to previous generations. Our generation has more access to information than any previous generation, and at times we feel as though we are overwhelmed, and confused as to which news source we should turn to in the search for reliable and honest reporting.

For with the advent of all this information comes important drawbacks. News reporting, like any other form of information outlet, is a competitive environment. It is expensive for media organizations to maintain correspondents around the world, and to employ the technicians and professionals to produce and transmit the broadcasts. News reporting requires advertising revenue, and revenue operates in a very aggressive market, with several options available. As a result, news

8.2

Citizen Kane

In 1941, Orson Welles portrayed Charles Foster Kane, a newspaper magnate who attempted a foray into politics, in the movie *Citizen Kane*.

In 1941 the actor Orson Welles directed, produced, and starred in an epic film documenting the life of Charles Foster Kane, a fictional newspaper and media magnate who became a multi-millionaire and had a profound impact on American life. The film was a thinly veiled study and critique of the true life of newspaper and media magnate William Randolph Hearst, who dominated the US newspaper business through the middle part of the twentieth century. Despite receiving critical acclaim (it is often referred to as the greatest movie ever made), the film almost did not see the light of day. Hearst was so outraged by the depiction of himself in the movie that he offered the film studio, RKO Pictures, $800,000 to burn every copy they had made. When RKO refused, Hearst prohibited any of his media outlets from even mentioning the film, which

8.2 Continued... contributed to disappointing box office revenues. However, in the long run, Hearst and Kane have become inextricably linked and the film stands as a fascinating treatment of media control.

organizations must constantly be aware of the share of viewers, listeners, or readers that they attract, in order to lure advertisers and their funds. The result is that newscasts are often not as informative or inclusive as they might be. In order to capitalize on a relatively small market, given the number of media outlets offered to potential viewers, listeners, and readers, news organizations 'package' their news much like a network television program in order to lure and captivate an audience. This means that some stories, and particularly those that are deemed uninteresting or tedious, are given rather short shrift, while even the most riveting issues of the day are bundled into a summary piece with titles, graphics, and main players.

The media also is a two-way street. Just as with opinion polls, political decision-makers take note of what is being reported in newspapers, television, and on the radio in order to recognize and anticipate the concerns of citizens. Thus, the concern over opinion polls noted in the previous section of this chapter can be applied here: if policy-makers are worried primarily about the media impact of a particular decision, then questions of effectiveness and efficiency will be relegated to the second order of importance. What's more, by making decisions about what gets reported principally, what is left to the margins, and what is not reported at all, news organizations actually affect the course of public debate and participation in society.[10] We citizens, after all, can only respond to what we hear. This gives enormous influence to the media in its different forms.

For these reasons, questions of control of the media acquire a special significance. First of all, we need to think about the relationship between government and the media. We must ask which media outlets are owned by the government, which outlets are controlled by the government (due to the exercise of political influence), and which outlets are dependent on the government for information flows. It is here that the independence of the media becomes significant. Earlier in this section we noted the importance of the fourth estate as a potential check on the power of government. In order to exercise that function, it needs to be independent from government control, have independent sources of information (that is, not only those that come from the government), and have competent, experienced, and capable journalists who can both conduct investigative reporting and provide insightful commentary on major news stories.

But a strong, independent, and competent media is not enough. Throughout history, private control of most countries' media outlets has been concentrated in very few hands. When you look at the world's major news sources today, you will see that there is a notable concentration of ownership of newspapers, television channels, and other news sources. Perhaps the best example of this in the modern world is that of Rupert Murdoch and his control of News Corporation, a multinational multimedia conglomerate that controls newspapers, radio, and television stations across the globe. These news outlets offer a particular

perspective on world events, what we call the **editorial line**, which is the political or ideological bias of a newspaper, or television, or radio station. In the case of Fox News channel, for example, it is clear that there is a right-wing political bias, particularly in the case of US politics, with a definite preference for policies coming out of the Republican Party. In Canada, the media has often been accused by political groups and parties on the right of having a left-wing or Liberal bias. Part of the complaint stems from the fact that the CBC, the country's major television and radio news source, is government-owned.

Editorial line
particular perspective on world events offered by news outlets

8.3

Rupert Murdoch and News Corporation

Rupert Murdoch's News Corporation is one of the most powerful media entities on earth.

The concentration of control in the media business is nowhere more apparent than in the case of News Corporation. A media conglomerate that has interests in the broadcasting, newspaper, publishing, Internet, and entertainment industries, News Corporation began with a single newspaper (The News) in Adelaide, Australia, in 1990 and the vision of one man, Rupert Murdoch. From this humble origin, Murdoch expanded his corporation's activities and interests to the UK, US, and around the globe, also broadening the business into new areas and technologies. A quick survey of the global reach and concentration of ownership by News Corporation today is astounding. Of particular importance is the firm's control over news sources, and the editorial line that is exercised over the choice of news stories and the form in which they are presented. Most famously, News Corporation owns Fox Broadcasting Company and Fox News, which has come to be vilified in many circles as providing a strongly biased, right-wing slant on news in the US and around the world.

But News Corporation is just one example of this impressive concentration of ownership in the media. Around the world the news and information are being fed to us from a very limited number of sources. This raises questions about the independence and reliability of the news we receive, and about the political power wielded by the owners.

8.3 Continued...

The modern media, then, represents an exceptionally important actor in our modern political systems. News organizations contribute to the substance of public debate, influence that debate based on the manner in which the story is reported, and ultimately give us the opportunity, nevertheless limited, to learn about events in our nation and abroad to which previous generations would not have had access.

Civil Society and Non-Governmental Organizations

In recent years considerable attention has been given by both academics and policy-makers to the growing role of private citizen groups in day-to-day politics. The increasingly high profile of **non-governmental organizations** (NGOs) such as Greenpeace, Amnesty International, Transparency International, and Médecins Sans Frontières (Doctors without Borders) in issues of international importance, as well as the rising importance of a host of smaller organizations at the national and local levels, has brought to light a broader reality of political life and intercourse than we had considered in earlier times.[11] Civil society organizations, and NGOs in particular, stand as intermediaries between governments and private citizens; generally issue-specific, they represent diverse groups of individuals and seek to organize them in such a way as to maximize their impact on the policy process and in the execution of non-governmental activities.[12]

First we must ask, what is civil society? Civil society is a term used in academic and policy circles to refer to the actions and organization of private citizens around shared goals, interests, and values. It is incredibly diverse and embraces sports, politics, hobbies, belief systems, community groups, development, labour movements, self-help groups, and business associations. Essentially, any group that is not a part of the apparatus of the state, or which operates without interest in gaining political office, can be included in the definition of civil society. Generally, however, in political studies we think of civil society organizations in terms of non-governmental organizations or NGOs. These most commonly tend to be oriented towards the areas of advocacy, political pressure, and economic and social development.

We find civil society organizations everywhere in modern society, whether it is in the area of environmental protection, the promotion of human or civil rights, or the defence of lifestyles, traditional or modern. NGOs provide an opportunity for many citizens who are disillusioned with traditional politics to get involved, to express their views, and to participate in the public sphere. In recent years in Canada, NGOs have been particularly active in the areas of human rights, drug policy, and climate change.

It would be easy to suppose that NGOs and civil society in general are a relatively modern political phenomenon. However, in many Western societies, NGOs have been active in the public sphere for hundreds of years (thousands if we take into consideration faith-based NGOs), although they were not recognized by that

Non-governmental organization (NGO)
non-profit group organized on a local, national, or international level

name. Think of the importance of trade unions, for example, since the nineteenth century in redefining labour relations and winning important victories for workers' rights, or of women's organizations that have struggled for over a century to win the vote, civil rights, and gender equality in the workplace.

8.4

Civil Society and Globalization

Many civil society organizations have been criticized for their undemocratic and unrepresentative nature.

In recent years, one of the most vocal, high-profile, and best-organized civil society movements has been the anti-globalization movement. Now a regular feature at all major international summit meetings between government ministers or heads of government, the movement had its origins in 1988 with demonstrations against the International Monetary Fund (IMF) and World Bank at their annual meeting in Berlin, Germany. From that time, the anti-globalization movement has grown in size and activity, incorporating protests, hunger strikes, and email and Internet campaigns. Although the movement in fact incorporates a large number of different groups and organizations, in recent years an umbrella organization known as the Peoples' Global Action network has been used to bring together diverse causes.

8.4 Continued...

The anti-globalization movement focuses its efforts against the manifestations of global capitalism, that is, against organizations such as the World Trade Organization (WTO), the IMF and World Bank, the Group of 8 (G8), and multinational corporations (MNCs). One company that has been a particular target over the years has been McDonald's Corporation, with the bombing and vandalizing of restaurants.

However, despite its high profile in the media, the anti-globalization movement has achieved very little. It has failed to derail any major conference, and has not succeeded in halting the spread of global capitalism or the signing of international free trade agreements. A more serious charge against the movement is the fact that it is amorphous, undemocratic, and ultimately not accountable to the society it claims to represent. This criticism can be laid at the feet of civil society organizations more broadly and becomes more important as they play a more significant role in the policy process.

The Participation of Private Actors in the Decision-Making Process

In this section we will discuss the interaction between political authority and societal actors in the formation of policy. An understanding of this interaction is vitally important if we are to get a comprehensive grasp of the dynamics of political participation and of the policy process itself. Governments clearly need the involvement of non-state actors, such as interest groups, businesses, and labour unions, if they are to make policies that are not only politically palatable to key groups, but also functionally viable.

In contemporary political systems in Europe and North America, governments and bureaucracies do not simply formulate their policies in a vacuum. Instead there is often an intense system of consultation and collaboration with important economic interests and actors within the nation. Governments rely on the expertise of private actors in a multitude of areas so that policies can be designed and implemented in such a way as to be more efficient, and more broadly accepted. Such consultation takes place in all levels of government; in Canada and most countries this is most clearly seen in industry consultations in the area of economic policy. In the banking sector, for example, banks are closely consulted before any new regulations affecting their activities are applied. In the area of safety and public health standards, the government will consult with a host of private-sector actors, from industry, academia, branches of government, and civil society organizations.

There is a danger, of course, that the government will depend too much on the opinions of one group over another, and this is particularly problematical if regulatory policy is too heavily influenced by private business, especially if the industry concerned attempts to skew regulation so that it increases profitability yet sacrifices other goods such as safety and soundness, or public welfare. In areas such as finance, or high-technology industries, there is often a serious inequality in the level of expertise between policy-makers and industry representatives. This can make it extremely difficult for governments to design efficient policies without the help of the actors they seek to regulate. In this case concerns can be raised about the independence of government policy-makers and also about the effectiveness of economic policy.

These concerns are particularly important in the area of environmental regulation, where large corporations such as oil companies can afford to hire expensive lawyers and teams of scientists to 'prove' that their economic activities will have only a minimal impact on the environment. Because governments rely on information in the policy process, and because specialized information is expensive, such large corporations have an advantage over environmental protection groups in their influence over government.

The issue of expertise in the policy-making process is of particular importance in developing countries. There governments are especially handicapped in their ability to negotiate with corporations because of the extra financial constraints they face. Large multinational corporations in particular are able to dominate the governments of poorer countries in negotiations over investment and regulation because they are able to utilize both the best personnel from that particular country and indeed expert personnel recruited from all over the world.

A final point that must be made here is that different states allow different levels of business and other interest group participation in the policy process. As we have seen, some political systems encourage more citizen participation than others, and the same is true of business involvement. Peter Katzenstein, in a 1978 work entitled *Between Power and Plenty: Foreign Economic Policies of Advanced Industrial States*, examined the domestic political structures of six states and examined the impact on their foreign economic policies. The key determinant that emerged from the study was that states' foreign economic policies were shaped to a significant degree by the amount of access they allowed major interest groups (most importantly those representing industry, trade, and finance) to the policy-making process. Katzenstein's study found considerable variance between the six states, not just in the amount of access but also in the way that access was organized. Such examinations of the role of economic actors in the policy process remain an integral part of political economy to this day.

Interest Groups

Interest groups
groups in a political system that seek to either alter or maintain the approach of government without taking a formal role in elections or seeking an official capacity in government

Although civil society and NGOs cover a huge area of non–state-based political activity in modern society, it does not embrace everything. We must also be aware of the role played by interest groups.[13] Increasingly in our society, interest groups have affected decision-making and the 'approach' taken by government. In many ways, interest groups are similar in their effect to political parties; however, interest groups may be distinguished from political parties in that they are not concerned with controlling who runs for election representing certain parties. Rather, interest groups are primarily concerned with influencing the decision-making process, though not through direct means, as politicians may. Therefore, interest groups are an integral part of the 'political community' of policy-makers discussed earlier in this chapter.

Interest groups are also called pressure groups or political action committees (PACs).[14] These groups seek to either alter or maintain the approach of government without taking a formal role in elections or seeking an official capacity in government. Just as political parties differ from country to country, interest groups have varying degrees of importance depending on the country in which they exist. In some countries such as Japan, interest groups are not usually given a substantial role in decision-making by government leaders. Though there may be some attention paid to the concerns raised by the groups, the more traditional form of government in that country — which places a higher degree of importance on the customary and formal delineation of authority in society — limits the influence that these groups might have. For the Japanese decision-making process, greater attention and value is placed on the opinions and interests of formal corporate and business interests in Japan (more attention is given to this in Chapter 9). On the other hand, various other countries, such as the United States, place such high relevance on the role played by interest groups in the decision-making process that there are even laws regulating the formal role that the groups might have in the pattern of government–society relations.

There are a number of different types of interest groups. Political action committees are conglomerations of several groups that have combined their resources to more effectively influence the decision-making process.[15] Associational and non-associational interest groups, respectively, are closely related to, or not connected with, particular political objectives. Ad hoc interest groups are called anomic interest groups and do not have a standard organized composition. Instead, these groups are formed to deal with short-term issues and concerns.[16]

Interest groups attempt to convey their point of view primarily through lobbying, which refers to those activities undertaken by groups in order to get their perspective and views across to political decision-makers: petitions, meetings, hearings, demonstrations, and so forth. Often interest groups will hire professional 'lobbyists' whose job it is to carry on these activities on behalf of the group. Later in this chapter we will return to the issue of lobbying, and the important function it performs in the articulation of citizen views in government decision-making.

There are competing views regarding the presence and role of interest groups in liberal democracies. Interest groups, it must be kept in mind, are not inclusive; that is to say, they do not represent the views of all or even a majority of citizens. Rather, they are in place to bring attention to concerns that some sectors of the public find important. This tends to draw criticism from some who view interest groups to be the voice of the elite in society, and not representative of all. Not all groups in society, after all, have the means or are capable of forming organized groups and hiring lobbyists to try to alter the approach of government. So, there are those who view interest groups as corrupting the true purpose of democracy, which is to represent and account for the views of all.[17]

Yet there are those who consider interest groups to be an integral part of democratic society. They argue that there are not enough formal avenues for individual citizens to vocalize their concerns or views in the governmental process.

Pressure group
group in a political system that seeks to either alter or maintain the approach of government without taking a formal role in elections or seeking an official capacity in government

Political action committees
conglomerations of several interest groups to more effectively influence the decision-making process

Associational interest group
interest group closely related to particular political objectives

Non-associational interest group
interest group not closely related to, or not connected with, particular political objectives

Anomic interest group
ad hoc interest group that does not have a standard organized composition; formed to deal with short-term issues

Lobbying
method by which business/interest groups apply direct pressure to the executive, legislative, and bureaucratic branches of government

Pluralism
society in which several disparate groups (minority and majority) maintain their interests, and a number of concerns and traditions persist

Voting is a relatively infrequent event, and does not allow citizens to do anything more than simply choose a representative. And joining a political party may not be satisfactory for others. According to this view, then, interest groups allow for a more informal role in the approach of government. Those who view interest groups to be a positive force in society argue that true democracy is **pluralist**, where a number of groups and concerns are expressed; interest groups, then, are a functional and indispensable arena for citizen action.[18]

To take the view of this latter group (those that consider interest groups as essential in democracies), let us assess the broader function of interest groups a step further. Whereas it might be true that interest groups are created to deal with the particular concerns of members of the group, we should recognize that interest groups play a bigger purpose in society. Interest groups are a basic means of tying the function of government to that of groups in society. In this way, interest groups are a 'bond' between the formal and informal segments of our society that influence the approach of our political systems. Interest groups provide a 'feedback' loop for government, because they funnel information back to their members and the public at large.[19] Further, given their level of expertise, these groups provide essential information to decision-makers themselves. Interest groups can be particularly important for members of the public service, who are responsible for accounting for the views of the public, and providing all necessary information to decision-makers in the legislature and the executive.

When we stop to consider the real impact interest groups have on the political process, substantial contrasts to voting behaviour and political party involvement emerge. Unlike the immediate consequence that voting or parties demonstrate in the political domain, interest group influence is not as easy to measure. There are, after all, many different interest groups competing for attention and influence, and the opinions that they put forward may be changed substantially by the time governments set out to make decisions. However, there are some factors that help define the relative success and sway that these groups have. First, if the opinion of the group tends to match that of government in some way, the level of importance placed on the group will rise. Second, interest groups will have more influence if there is an absence of a real contending perspective. Finally, the level of stability of the group is important. Groups that have experienced lobbyists, plentiful resources, and an organized structure are more likely to have the ear of government at any level.

In sum, interest groups are one of the most important means of real influence that citizen groups have in the governmental process. Interest groups are becoming increasingly influential in democratic societies, largely as a result of their level of organization, as well as the considerable expertise and substance that they bring to the process itself.

Lobbying

One of the most important and increasingly common ways in which business/interest groups interact with the policy process is through lobbying, where they apply direct pressure to the executive, legislative, and bureaucratic branches of government. The roots of the word 'lobbying' are disputed, some arguing that it derives from the hallway of the House of Commons in the British Parliament, where constituents could meet with their representatives and demand their support for legislation. Others have suggested that it came into use in the early nineteenth century with reference to the lobby of either the New York State Capitol building or the Willard Hotel, both places where private citizens and interest groups could directly pressure legislators. Whatever the word's origins, lobbying has become an integral part of the reality of modern politics in democratic and even non-democratic systems.

How is lobbying carried out? First, it can be an activity in which the interested party, either an individual or a group, directly meets with those involved in the policy process and attempts to secure the support of these individuals. Second, and increasingly this is the norm, individuals or groups contract a representative, a professional lobbyist, who understands and who has contacts within the political process. Lobbyists do not always go by the title itself, often preferring to label themselves public relations experts, lawyers, or consultants.

Earlier in this chapter it was mentioned that information is a crucial element in the area of political participation, with private citizens needing access to information so that they can make informed choices. With lobbying the process is reversed. Here it is the legislator who needs access to information in deciding how she or he will vote on an issue. Similarly, bureaucrats often find themselves under pressure from lobbyists when they are drawing up legislation or deciding how to implement it.

Lobbying has a mixed reputation. First, it can be seen as a vital part of the policy process, ensuring the representation of diverse views and ensuring also that relevant information is taken into account in decision-making. On the other hand, however, lobbying can be seen as an example of the undue influence of some groups at the expense of others, where well-organized, often wealthy or economically powerful groups buy the support of influential members of the policy process.

A key word here is 'expense'. Lobbying is not a cheap business, and groups may pay upwards of tens of thousands of dollars to engage the services of a professional lobbyist for one issue. Some large corporations keep a lobbying firm on contract full-time, so that the firms' interests are continually represented in the political process, an enterprise that can cost them hundreds of thousands of dollars annually. This expense puts lobbying out of the financial reach of most individuals and groups in society, and thus we have to ask whether or not lobbying is truly compatible with the pursuit of democracy in modern political systems. Does lobbying allow certain groups to have a disproportionately high level of influence over the political process? Or is this simply the best way for decision-makers to take the views of interested parties into account? Here we have to ask whether political favours are being bought in exchange for material rewards, either financial or in kind. If so, then lobbying certainly crosses the line between acceptable and unacceptable behaviour. But what about the personal relationships that are built up between lobbyists on the one hand, and legislators, bureaucrats, and members of the executive branch, on the other? Do they contravene the principles of democracy? Can lobbying be seen as a mere extension of corporate hospitality activities, where one corporation courts another, offering tickets to sporting and cultural events in an attempt to secure a business contract? Or do we have to draw a distinction between the world of business and the world of politics?

From the other side of the fence, the opponents of 'clean coal' have employed different media outlets to get their point across. A famous television spot (which can be viewed at www.thisisreality.org) put forward by The Reality Coalition (a coalition of organizations including the Alliance for Climate Protection, Sierra Club, National Wildlife Federation, the Natural Resources Defense Council, and the League of Conservation Voters), and efforts by other environmental organizations, have tried to counter the public relations campaign by the coal industry. Directly related to these questions is the issue of the 'revolving door' between the

8.5

Climate Change and Public Relations: The Cases of Wind and 'Clean Coal'

© Braden Gunem/Alamy

The debate between traditional and green sources of energy involves intense public relations campaigns.

As evidence of the human causes of climate change mounts, states, societies, and businesses are searching for new ways to produce energy in ways that do not release as many greenhouse gases into the atmosphere. Clean, green, and renewable energy sources such as wind energy and hydroelectric power are one obvious option, but some of the more traditional sources of energy are trying to reinvent themselves, both in the technological sense and in terms of their public image. In the United States this effort has taken on a very public dimension with press and television media spots outlining the advantages of 'clean coal' over other sources. The photograph in this box was to be seen across the Washington, DC, area in the summer and fall of 2009, as the coal industry attempted to convince US government officials and congressmen and -women that coal was the best option available. The campaign has also used the Internet to get its point across, through websites such as www.cleancoalusa.org, to stress the benefits of the fuel and potential of clean coal technology.

world of politics and lobbying. Insiders who have learned the inside workings of a national political system and who have built up a network of contacts are in great demand with professional lobbying, consulting, or public relations firms. Their influence is an invaluable addition to the tools possessed by consulting firms in the struggle to be heard in the policy process. In addition, governments (and certainly political parties) can benefit from the expertise of individuals who have experience in the world of public relations and communications. Doubts can be raised about the benefits of such a revolving door, however. Is inside knowledge of government business a commodity that should be traded like any other form of specialized knowledge? Or is it something different, special, because it confers such an advantage on those who can pay for it?

One last point about lobbying that ought to be made clear is that governments employ lobbyists themselves. This occurs when authorities at one level seek to influence policies at another, for example, municipal or provincial governments that seek to influence federal policy. Perhaps more important than this is when national governments contract lobbyists to represent their interests in another country. Most commonly this occurs when foreign governments seek to influence policy in the United States, but the phenomenon exists around the world with foreign governments taking advantage of local expertise to lobby the national government. A very important example of such lobbying took place in the early 1990s when the Mexican government employed Washington-based lobbyists to secure congressional approval for the North American Free Trade Agreement (NAFTA), countering the anti–free-trade forces in Washington, led by presidential candidate Ross Perot.

Policy Communities

As should now be clear, policy is not made in a vacuum. Politics and policy-making involve a variety of actors, both within and outside government. If we are to fully understand the ways in which policy is made, particularly in the economic realm, we have to identify the group (or groups) of actors who participate in that process. William Coleman and Grace Skogstad, in their 1990 book *Policy Communities and Public Policy in Canada*, employed the concept of a **policy community** to understand as the making of policy. A policy community can be understood as a collection of actors who have a direct or indirect interest in the issue area. These actors will have different levels of influence over the policy process, but they each play a significant role, even if they do not apply pressure directly to policy-makers.

This concept is useful because it allows us to identify key actors in politics, and to encourage us to include individuals and groups that we would not normally take into consideration. So in the formation of government policy concerning climate change, the non-governmental groups involved in the policy process would include scientists, industry representatives, and NGOs such as Greenpeace and the David Suzuki Foundation. There is, of course, no natural limit to the size of a policy community or to the kind of actors that get involved. Policy communities

Policy community
collection of actors who have a direct or indirect interest in an issue

are of particular importance in open political systems, but we can also use the idea to examine closed or authoritarian systems. Policy communities will exist even within a military dictatorship, as the armed forces governing the country consult with industry and other elites to smooth the business of government.

Corporatism

A significant challenge for capitalist countries over the past one hundred years or so has been to avoid direct clashes between what may be seen as, and sometimes are, opposing interests. For what makes sense to the owners and controllers of industry may be anathema to those who work in their factories and corporations. The idea of price controls and the minimum wage, for example, will be more popular with the representatives of labour than with producers and employers. Increasing the maximum number of hours to be worked in one week, on the other hand, may be favoured by industry but vigorously opposed by labour unions. Such controversial policies provide ample opportunity for conflict and economic disruption, strikes, or maybe even the departure of private industry to other countries where the business climate is more favourable. It may be preferable, therefore, for government policy to be formulated in such a way as to minimize the level of conflict between opposing interests.

In several countries of Northern Europe and Scandinavia in the 1970s an alliance developed among government, business, and labour that came to be known as corporatism. This approach to governance entails close co-operation and coordination between these three organizations, in the expectation that such activity will bring more stability to the political economy and also that it will produce a larger degree of consensus, making economic and social policies more acceptable to important constituencies in society.

One of the most powerful arguments in favour of corporatism is that it will include and benefit a broader section of society than more traditional pluralist systems, where elites tend to dominate the policy process. However, that self-same criticism can be levelled against corporatism itself because selected agencies of business and labour are chosen to represent the views and interests of the wider business and labour communities. There is a tendency for business representatives to favour big business in the demands they place on government, whereas the representatives of labour have tended to favour the larger, more powerful unions. Perhaps more worrying has been the accusation that both business and labour representatives 'climb into bed' with each other and the government, and tend to compromise the interests of those they represent. Of equal concern is the issue of corruption, the danger that the leaders of business and labour will seek individual rather than collective gains, sacrificing the interests of their members in return for personal reward. [20]

In the 1980s and 1990s the corporatist approach to economic and political management fell into disrepute in some countries of Europe, particularly in Great Britain. Largely, this was in response to the feeling that organized labour had gained too much power and was jeopardizing the long-term economic interests

Corporatism
approach to governance that entails close co-operation and coordination among government, business, and labour in the expectation that such activity will bring more stability to politics

of the nation. However, as we will see in Chapter 9, quasi-corporatist arrangements still exist in Japan, and also in other Asian countries. Indeed, such close co-operation among government, labour, and business has been seen by many as one of the fundamental reasons for Asian economic success since the 1950s.

Canadian Political Culture and Socialization

Canada has a political culture that, broadly speaking, reflects many of the features of European culture. It is founded on the rule of law, which gives certainty and predictability to processes and to individuals. Democratic processes and institutions are seen as fundamental, not only in the national Parliament and federal elections, but also at the provincial and local levels. The existence of elections bodies at both federal and provincial levels and the emphasis given to democracy in all levels of education highlights this. In recent years the concepts of transparency in political, legal, and administrative processes has become an important feature, alongside accountability. These elements can be seen in the increasing scrutiny of government activities and accounts, and the role of the media in providing citizens with access to reliable information.

Canada can also be said to have a preference for gradual, peaceful, somewhat evolutionary change, rather than the sudden, violent revolutionary sort. This can be seen throughout Canadian history, from its emergence as a post-colonial dominion, to its gradual assertion of full sovereignty, to its piecemeal redistribution of political power among the provinces and regions.

But beyond these elements of political culture, we can say that there is a well-established connection in Canada to the ideals of negotiation and compromise, with a strong tendency towards respecting minority views. This is closely tied to the very modern values of tolerance and respect for diversity (both in terms of culture and opinion). The contemporary manifestation of this is obviously in the idea of multiculturalism, but we can see that in fact tolerance goes back a long way in Canadian political history and has been reinforced by the Westminster parliamentary model.

The Canadian Charter of Rights and Freedoms is an essential element for us in marking out individual rights and liberties in the Canadian context. At various points in this book we have already made reference to the Charter, and the way in which it has been used to question, correct, or overturn government policy. It continues to define much about political culture, and is closely connected to debates concerning rights for minority groups, for example.

Perhaps above all else, we can say that three terms sum up the heart of Canadian political culture. 'Peace, order, and good government' continue to define the core values of Canadian politics in the twenty-first century. It is surprising how a phrase first used in the 1867 Constitution Act continues to have relevance and meaning today, and how often it is quoted in political dialogue and debate.

The process of socialization in Canada is similar to that taking place in many modern liberal democracies. The teaching of basic elements of civic culture and history in elementary and secondary schools, the use of the mass media by government to emphasize the importance of core values, and the process by which new immigrants to Canada are asked to take courses acquainting them with Canadian history, culture, and society are all obvious ways in which socialization takes place on a daily basis. But the media plays a role too, as well as civil society and (at times) business in the development and reinforcement of those core values and identity.

Conclusion

This chapter has introduced you to the diverse forms of politics outside of the formal electoral and political party process. It also established the process of political socialization as a precursor to any kind of political participation. We are all socialized in a particular political culture that embodies certain values and ideals about politics. Our attitudes and disposition to the world of politics is shaped by the socialization process of our society, the exposure to family, community, institutions, government, and more and more by the media. This process is far from neutral and reflects the distribution of power within society and the political and economic systems.

This chapter also introduced you to civil society, interest groups, policy communities, and the model of corporatism as diverse methods of aggregating individual interests and concerns into large public forums. By now, then, you should be aware of the multiple forms of participation that are available to you as a citizen and the ways in which you can become involved. It is up to you to decide if, when, and how you engage in this dynamic world.

Self-Assessment Questions

1. What are the defining features of Canadian political culture?
2. Where do you get most of your political information and why?
3. Find out who owns your local newspapers. Are they part of a national news chain?
4. What is a policy community?
5. What is the difference between an NGO and an interest group?
6. What are the basic features of corporatism?

Weblinks

The Symbols of Canada
www.pch.gc.ca/pgm/ceem-cced/symbl/
index-eng.cfm

**Free Press: Reform Media; Transform
Democracy**
www.freepress.net

Diversity and Multiculturalism
www.pch.gc.ca/pc-ch/sujct/divers-multi/
index-eng.cfm

Lobbying Data for the US
www.opensecrets.org/lobbyists

**Office of the Commissioner of Lobbying of
Canada**
www.ocl-cal.gc.ca/eic/site/lobbyist-lobbyiste1.
nsf/eng/home

Further Reading

Almond, Gabriel, and Sidney Verba. *The Civic Culture: Political Attitudes and Democracy in Five Nations*. Newbury Park, CA: Sage Publications, 1989.

Althaus, Scott L. *Collective Preferences in Democratic Politics: Opinion Surveys and the Will of the People*. Cambridge: Cambridge University Press, 2003.

Asher, Herbert B. *Polling and the Public: What Every Citizen Should Know*. 2nd ed. Washington, DC: Cogressional Quarterly Press, 1992.

Berger, Suzanne, ed. *Organizing Interests in Western Europe: Pluralism, Corporatism, and the Transformation of Politics*. Cambridge: Cambridge University Press, 1981.

Dahl, Robert. *Polyarchy: Participation and Opposition*. New Haven, CT: Yale University Press, 1971.

Gamson, William, and David Meyer. 'Framing Political Opportunity.' In *Comparative Perspectives on Social Movements: Political Opportunities, Mobilizing Structures, and Cultural Framings*. Ed. Doug McAdam et al. 3rd ed. Cambridge: Cambridge University Press, 1996.

Inoguchi, Takashi, Edward Newman, and John Keane, eds. *The Changing Nature of Democracy*. Tokyo: United Nations University Press, 1998.

Linz, Juan J. 'Totalitarian and Authoritarian Regimes.' In *Handbook of Political Science*. Ed. Fred I. Greenstein and Nelson W. Polsby. New York: Addison Wesley, 1975.

Middlebrook, Kevin. *Dilemmas of Political Change in Mexico*. San Diego: Center for U.S.–Mexican Studies, UCSD, 2004.

Milner, Helen V. *Interests, Institutions, and Information: Domestic Politics and International Relations*. Princeton, NJ: Princeton University Press, 1997.

Mingst, Karen A. *Essentials of International Relations*. 3rd ed. New York: W.W. Norton, 2004.

Norris, Pippa. *Electoral Engineering: Voting Rules and Political Behavior*. Cambridge, MA: Cambridge University Press, 2004.

Olson, Mancur. *The Logic of Collective Action: Public Goods and the Theory of Groups*. Cambridge, MA: Harvard University Press, 1971.

CBC News Clips

Visit the companion website for *Politics: An Introduction* to listen to news clips from the CBC radio archives.

9 Politics in Developed States

LEARNING OBJECTIVES

After reading this chapter, you will be able to:

❋ have a clearer idea of the practical application of political concepts to country studies

❋ understand the important linkage between politics and the economy in 'development' as well as the links between domestic economy and foreign economic policy

❋ know how to compare and contrast the political systems of Canada, the United States, Japan, and the EU

❋ recognize and identify some of the most important issues facing developed nations today.

Introduction

Previous chapters in this book have introduced you to several important aspects of contemporary political studies, governance, political ideas, and the way we get involved in political life. By now you should feel fairly comfortable with most of the major political concepts and the way political scientists use them. In this chapter, we will apply those concepts and ideas in a series of case studies. Here, we will think a bit about the 'developed world,' or those high-income nations whose economic and political progress have given them certain advantages over other nations in the world. We will consider the differences between these nations and those of the 'developing world', which we will return to in the following chapter.

This chapter begins with a presentation of some of the major themes and issues facing the political economies of advanced industrialized states. This section will provide an overview of the development of advanced economic interaction after the end of the Second World War. These years, often referred to as the postwar era, were crucial in the development of institutions and regulations governing global politics and the global economy.

Interestingly, though in many ways industrialized nations have areas of mutual concern and interest, they are still a diverse lot. Each of these countries has had its own strikingly unique experience of political and economic development.

In order to demonstrate this, we'll look at some specific country study cases: the United States, Japan, the European Union (which is not a state but a group of states), and Canada. In Chapter 10, we will look at some cases of politics and economics in the developing world.

Developed world
industrialized nations, including Western Europe, North America, Japan, Australia, and New Zealand, that are part of a structurally integrated system of global capitalism

Developing world
less developed nations that are not part of a structurally integrated system of global capitalism

Postwar era
period after World War II; since 1945

9.1

Bretton Woods and Political Order

'Bretton Woods' is a short-form name for the United Nations Monetary and Financial Conference held in Bretton Woods, New Hampshire, in July 1944.

The UN Monetary and Financial Conference at Bretton Woods, New Hampshire, in 1944 charted a new structure for the global economy. Some aspects are still in place today.

Forty-four nations were represented at the conference, invited by US president Franklin Roosevelt to gather to discuss the future of the international economic order. Institutions that still exist today, such as the International Monetary Fund and the World Bank, were conceived at these meetings. The International Trade Organization failed, but the General Agreement on Tariffs and Trade, and then later the World Trade Organization, managed to fulfill most of the trade-related goals of the conference participants. Bretton Woods was instrumental for the postwar order, since it saw the creation of a foreign exchange market system (where different currencies were linked to one another), a system of financial lending and assistance, and US leadership for the new global order.

We have looked fairly extensively at Canada and the United States in other parts of this book. You will recall that earlier chapters explained the important distinctions between parliamentary and presidential forms of government and used the Canadian and American case studies as examples of each. We learned in that section that the political structures in these seemingly similar countries are actually very different, though the broader goals and objectives of the states themselves in fact may be quite the same. We also examined the federal system in Chapter 6 and highlighted the particular experience of Canada, and to a lesser extent the United States. In this chapter we will delve a little deeper, and pay close attention to the economic sphere. We will see here that the two countries are closely entwined, and that the economic dimension of the bilateral relationship is the most significant element of their combined mutual relationship.

Japan and the EU represent distinctive and important examples of alternative paths for economic development. One, Japan, took a focused approach to international trade and commercial relations, and the other, the EU, saw strength in **regional integration**. Because of specific circumstances (explained later in this chapter) that constrained the activities and development of the Japanese economy, its shift from a country decimated by war to a global economic powerhouse is particularly striking. Japan represents a different mode of capitalist development and maintains a rather individual democratic experience, leading to a very separate level of growth and prosperity in the international economic system.

The EU is the best example of political and economic regionalism today. Following World War II, Europe saw another option for peace and prosperity by formally uniting to combine the strengths of each into one for all. The early days of the EU weren't as encompassing as today, but over time it developed into the most advanced and sometimes controversial example of regionalism. Given that Japan and the EU have not been given as much attention as the United States or Canada in previous chapters, more time will be spent here on their political and economic history and development.

What Are Developed States?

The story of the developed world is as economic as it is political. But attention to the **political economy**, or the interrelationship of politics and economics, of advanced nations is still a relatively recent phenomenon in political studies.

As recently as the early twentieth century, the physical security of states was the predominant sector of interest for analysts of state affairs. Indeed, it was not until the mid-twentieth century that the significance of economic welfare of states became a major arena of analytical examination in political studies. The rise of the **welfare state**, where governments sought to aid the efficiency and development of their countries through social spending and programs meant to benefit citizens' way of life, became undoubtedly the single most important development in industrialized states after the end of the Second World War. As a result of growing trade and investment, international economic interaction among states has become the norm in the international system today. This is largely because of the development of national economies in the states themselves, and of the expansion of economic freedoms for individuals and corporations.

Not all nation-states are the same in the international system of politics, and no two have the same attributes. That is fairly self-evident, even when we look at countries that are similar. People who have travelled in Europe or Asia, for example, or even those of us who have spent some time in the United States

---

Regional integration
economic or political integration in a defined territorial area

Political economy
approach that views political and economic spheres as harmonious and mutually dependent perceptions of the world; relationship between people, government, and the economy

Welfare state
political system that creates the means for individual protection and quality of life, such as health care, employment insurance, pensions, social programs for the elderly, children, and unemployed

9.2

Political Economy

Before the modern term 'economics' became popularized, political economy was used to describe the study of buying, selling, production, and labour in a political system. Writing in the late 1600s, Sir William Petty was among the first to advocate a 'laissez-faire' (to 'let be') approach to government.

Although others, such as Adam Smith, are better known, Sir William Petty is considered by many to be the architect of modern political economic thought.

Other early political economists, including Adam Smith and David Ricardo, took on a similar perspective, while still others, such as Karl Marx, had competing views about the proper relationship between governments and markets. Political economy examines the links between human behaviour and decision-making and the institutions of economic governance. It assumes that one cannot separate the two fields. Today, political economy takes an interdisciplinary approach to the political–economic relationship, and its offshoot, international political economy, looks at this relationship at the global level.

9.3

One World?

The term 'Third World' is really quite dated. First used in the immediate postwar years, the Third World was labelled as a way to distinguish a group of developing states that were not aligned to either the United States or the Soviet Union. The First World referred to the industrialized countries allied with the United States, and the Second World meant those communist states tied to the Soviet Union. As this period drew on, however, the term came to describe a very large and diverse group of nations. Countries such as South Korea and Singapore, quite developed in their own right, were labelled alongside other more challenged nations such as Ghana and Bangladesh. To confuse matters further, once the former countries of the Soviet Union, and its allies, converted to democracy and economic free markets in the 1990s, the term 'Second World' largely disappeared, yet the Third World continued in use. There are, of course, no apt descriptors of such a wide array of countries, yet like so many other concepts in political studies, the 'Third World' has taken on a short-form meaning for a very complicated issue.

Gross domestic product (GDP)
total value of goods and services produced in a country in one year

DC
developed country

Industrialized world
nations including Western Europe, North America, Japan, Australia, and New Zealand that are part of a structurally integrated system of global capitalism

North
industrialized nations including Western Europe, North America, Japan, Australia, and New Zealand that are part of a structurally integrated system of global capitalism

First World
industrialized nations including Western Europe, North America, Japan, Australia, and New Zealand that are part of a structurally integrated system of global capitalism

Post-industrial
developed economies that maintain a high-technology, or high-value, economy

and have seen the difference between that country and Canada, can attest that all countries have their distinguishing features.

Development is no different. The 'developed' world refers to that group of nations with a high level of economic development, a high **gross domestic product (GDP)** per capita, an industrialized economy, and advanced stages of political and social development. Developed countries are sometimes referred to as DCs, as an acronym, or the **industrialized world**, the **north**, **first world**, or **post-industrial**.

Dividing the world into such categories is a relatively new practice. Following World War II, imperial states gave up their colonies, leaving many new independent countries in difficult economic conditions. Chapter 10 will look at **colonialism** and **post-colonialism** in greater detail.

A History of the 'Developed World'

Before the end of World War II, it seemed that the dominant form of state interaction was not economic interchange but rather war and conflict among political actors. The lack of routine economic interaction among political actors had a direct effect on the physical well-being of states and their governments. In the **interwar period** (the years between the First and Second World Wars, 1919–39), a state of **autarky**, or non-interaction and isolation among states, was the defining feature of political relations.

Making matters worse was the fact that the state of general non-interaction in the economic sphere — coupled with a confusing and ever-changing array of rules put in place by different governments at different times — did not just limit itself to the largely (or seemingly) benign realm of economics. In fact, this autarkic system was a major contributor to the more widespread dynamic of suspicion and distrust that existed among states in the international system. Further, a lack of coordinated economic relations was one of the major contributing factors leading to the Second World War. Increased economic competition led to economic conflict, and this contributed to the downward spiral into violence.

Not surprisingly, the leaders of states at the close of the Second World War sought a mechanism to avoid the state of autarky that had contributed in such a major way to the First World War a decade earlier. The resulting agreements (and there were many, dealing with a variety of spheres, ranging from finance and banking to development and reconstruction, from international loans and currency stability to trade) first and foremost sought to avoid the conditions that all had come to agree had played such a serious role in bringing about the Second World War.

The development of advanced industrialized economies after the end of the Second World War took place in a variety of forms. Some nations, including Canada and the United States, were largely protected from the direct effects of damage from the war, such as the sheer devastation felt in the European and Asian states. For example, at the close of the Second World War, the United States alone was responsible for over half of all global production.[1] Although this number may seem astounding, it is not altogether surprising, given the level of reconstruction that was required in Europe and Asia. Simply put, the United States did not have to rebuild its industries and infrastructure the way that European countries did, and as a result enjoyed a high level of immediate strength in the economic arena. Yet this very high level of relative productive output in the United States declined as economies in Asia and Europe began to rebuild and re-establish their pre-war capabilities. Nonetheless, the United States did maintain the world's largest productive output, and remains the world's largest economy today. The fact that the United States and Canada were largely insulated from the direct effects of the war's devastation allowed these two countries to very quickly establish a foothold in the world economy, and indeed in all spheres. Other states, such as Japan, had to deal with the cost of rebuilding, in addition to the challenges of the new international economy.

Post-Industrialization and Political Authority

As you have learned in previous chapters, governments have two very simple goals in the contemporary world. First, they seek to ensure the physical security of their borders and people. Security has always been the central objective of any political unit throughout history, because a community that is not secure cannot seek a better way of life. Once security is achieved, states may pursue goals that benefit the welfare of constituents. Programs that we have come to expect in our day-to-day lives, such as employment benefits, health care, and government funding for social policies are impossible for governments to pursue without being able to first secure the state against internal insecurity or possible attack or incursion by foreign parties.

Colonialism
exploitation of weaker country(ies) by stronger one(s), for political, strategic, or resource interests

Post-colonialism
following a period of colonial rule

Autarky
condition of complete self-sufficiency and isolation from the rest of the system

Interwar period
the years 1919 to 1939 between World Wars I and II

It is important to keep in mind that the growth of the modern social welfare state (providing benefits to citizens in order to improve efficiency and competitiveness) is a relatively new development. In fact, if we were to study the major policy questions facing nations before the Second World War, we would find that issues pertaining to physical security, concerns of alliances and possible conflict with foreign parties, and internal stability would fill the daily docket of governmental mandates in advanced industrial nations.

The growth of a modern global economy, and the postwar creation of a set of institutions and organizations to help govern peaceful economic relations (the **Bretton Woods Agreement**, detailed more fully in Chapter 13) allowed states to concentrate not only on the security of their people and territory, but also on the benefits that might be allocated to citizens in order to improve their way of life. This is not to suggest that governments suddenly became altruistic for no cause: there was a perception that supplying these programs and benefits would improve the general ambitions of governments in an environment of increasing economic mutual dependence and openness. The pressure to create a welfare state, then, was understood to be in the best interest of national governments. Industrialization facilitated the allocation of social benefits in advanced states, leading to the globalized economy we experience today. With this in mind, this chapter now turns its attention to the individual political economy of each of its case studies: the United States, Japan, the European Union, and, first of all, Canada.

Cases

Canada

Canada is a federal parliamentary democracy with divided responsibilities: some powers are given to the ten provinces and three territories, and other powers are given to the federal government in Ottawa.[2] Canada's basic law is its constitution. Ultimate power and authority resided in the United Kingdom until 1931, when Canada officially received its autonomy with the passing of the Statute of Westminster in the British Parliament. Still, any changes to the Canadian constitution had to be approved by Britain until the **repatriation** of the constitution in 1982 brought full authority for decision-making to Canada.[3]

The British monarch, represented by the Governor General in Canada, remains the official head of state. Though there is no set term for the Governor General, it is usually five years; the Governor General is appointed by the monarch on the recommendation of the prime minster. The head of government is the prime minister, who is leader of the dominant party in Parliament, and is responsible for creating and leading the federal cabinet. **Parliament** is split into two houses, the Senate (with 105 members) appointed by the Governor General on the advice of the prime minister, and the House of Commons, with 308 members based on a representative-by-population allocation grounded on a popular vote system in the constituencies.

Senators, who represent provinces rather than smaller constituencies, have to meet certain criteria, including being at least 30 years old and owning property valued at $4000 or more, and they are appointed 'for life', but only serve until

Bretton Woods Agreement

postwar system of fixed exchange rates and heavy controls on private banks and other financial institutions so that their roles in international finance would be limited

Repatriation

to restore or bring back to a native land

Parliament

legislature in Westminster form of government

they are 75 years old. Legislative bills may originate in the Senate (though not those that require appropriating funds, or 'money bills'), but usually the Senate is used to review legislation coming from the House of Commons. Although it has the power to veto a bill, this is rarely done. Changes and suggestions, however, are often made, and quite frequently adopted.

Most legislation in Canada originates in the House of Commons, where its members represent individual 'ridings' from across the country. The number of **Members of Parliament** (MPs; Senators are MPs, as well) in the House change depending on results from each census, which come every 10 years. Although ridings are now added based on population, unique assessments of representation done at the time of Confederation mean that some small provinces, like Prince Edward Island, have a disproportionately high number of MPs for their population.

In recent years Canada has had to deal with the phenomenon of minority governments, where the governing party (the one that received the most seats in Parliament) does not have a majority. Both major parties — the Liberals and the Conservatives — have had minority governments in the past decade. This has happened in part because of the number of parties competing for votes in elections, but also because of shifting allegiances among Canadians for particular parties. The growing popularity of the Bloc Québécois in Quebec, for instance, shows the level of support in that province for a party that seeks political independence from the rest of Canada.

Canada is best described as a liberal plural state with a diversity of interests that reflect its regional, cultural, and socially plural population, as well as its linguistic duality (English and French). Canada's parliamentary democracy places a great deal of concentration of power over political and economic affairs at the level of the executive. The prime minister is responsible for powers of appointment in the Canadian government. Cabinet ministers, also appointed by the prime minister, are the individuals in government with the most real power over the state, with support bureaucracies responsible for goal articulation and the implementation of policy.

Canada is a resource-rich country, with easy access to air and space, as well as the high seas. These geopolitical attributes give Canada a comparative advantage in global relations, thanks to both access to needed resources, as well as the infrastructure to trade these resources with the outside world. Consequently, Canada has maintained strategic alliances with the United States and the American hemisphere, Europe, and the Asia Pacific rim. Economically, Canada is part of the '**North Atlantic triangle**' of Canada, the United States, and the European Union — so named because these three partners represent the most significant and strategic modes of interaction for each other.

Canada's economy is diversified, which means that it benefits from not only import–export trade with its partners, but also from high-technology trade, foreign direct investment (both by Canadians abroad and from foreigners in Canada), and membership in crucial economic organizations. Fully two-thirds of Canada's GDP comes from its foreign trade, which means that its overall economic health very much depends on a favourable international trade and commercial environment; Canada is by no means an 'independent' economy, and

Member of Parliament
representative of voters in a parliamentary system

North Atlantic triangle
geographic region of Canada, the United States, and the European Union; most significant and strategic modes of interaction for each other; historically, refers to the relationship between Canada, the U.S., and Great Britain

requires continued and consistent relations with its partners in order to maintain its welfare state programs and quality of life.

Much of Canadian politics and economics is driven by its close relationship with the United States. This is not to suggest that Canadian politics is not autonomous from the United States, but rather that the interdependent (mutually dependent) relationship between the two has necessarily led Canada to coalesce many of its policies with its southern partner. Also, the two countries share similar cultural values, democratic principles, and an adherence to market capitalism.

Canadian power and influence in domestic and foreign political relations is largely a function of its influence among and with greater powers as well as its emphasis on group membership. On the first point, Canada is most commonly considered a **middle power** because of its influence and close relations with the United States; unlike other comparable powers such as Australia or the Netherlands, Canada has an inordinately close and strategic relationship with the world's only remaining superpower. However, despite what we might commonly think of as Canada's reliance on the United States for its economic vitality, Canada is neither a satellite nor a dependent state. In fact, Canada retains a great deal of autonomy in its policy-making, and is often at odds with the United States on key issues, such as west-coast fishing, economic relations with Cuba, or the war in Iraq. Canada's middle-power status, then, is not just a measurement of Canadian power, but rather is representative of Canadian attributes in policy-making, as well as its style and history of domestic and foreign relations.

On the second point — group membership — Canada is a world leader in its emphasis on the importance of international organizations and institutions to help guide political and economic relations. Canada is a member of many diverse organizations that include cultural and linguistic groups such as *La Francophonie*; economic associations such as the North American Free Trade Agreement (NAFTA), the Asia–Pacific Economic Cooperation (APEC) body, the Organisation for Economic Co-operation and Development (OECD), and its constituent body the Development Assistance Committee (DAC); political organizations such as the United Nations (UN) and its component bodies, the Organization of American States (OAS) and the Organization for Security and Co-operation in Europe (OSCE); strategic alliances such as the North Atlantic Treaty Organization (NATO), and the North American Aerospace Defence Command (NORAD) partnership with the United States. Canada does not join and stay with these organizations lightly. There is a much higher purpose for membership in such groups. Though respected in the international community, Canada, as a middle power, is simply unable to create and alter the rules and regulations that pertain to nation-states and their interaction. Institutional membership allows Canada a degree of *independence* in its policy-making, since it is able to assert its views and opinions in groups, and often is able to affect the international agenda and decision-making of other states. This has real repercussions for Canada's international relations.

Middle power
country that does not have great power or superpower status but has significant influence in international relations

The United States

Countries are usually created out of a cause, or a motivation: revolutions, a new ideology, or the recognition of a distinct people are examples. Certainly, the 'motivation' behind the creation of the United States of America came with its Declaration of Independence from Great Britain in 1776, the resulting revolutionary war of independence fought with Great Britain, and its official independence, formalized in 1783. The USA became one of the first new republics in the late eighteenth century, with political authority through the people with representative government. For the next century or so, the United States continued as a federal union of quasi-sovereign states, and a useful collective authority. That changed in 1861 with the American Civil War, when eleven 'Confederate States of America' (Southern slave-owning states) broke away from the Union to try to form a separate country.

The resulting war, which lasted until 1865, became the new defining period in US politics, and the outcome was a new attention to unity and indivisibility. Despite lingering animosities that would run well into the twentieth century, the United States became, once and for all, a nation.

In comparison with the rest of the world, the United States is the fourth largest country with the third largest population. Native Americans came to the land that is now the United States more than 12,000 years ago. Today, fewer than 2 per cent of Americans are Native Americans or Hawaiians. Europeans first landed there in the fifteenth century, but large-scale European immigration really took place in the mid-1800s, followed by waves from Asia and Eastern Europe later in that century and then further Asian and Latin American immigration in the twentieth century.

The United States is a democratic federal constitutional republic, meaning that its political system is democratically governed, with ultimate authority in its central

9.4

Slavery and the American Civil War

The American Civil War (1861–65) is just one example of a 'civil' war, where citizens of a state war with each other over the political authority of the government or to change the government. Although there may be outside influences in a civil war, the main players are citizens of the same state. The American Civil War is undoubtedly the most famous, partly because of its ferociousness (with over 620,000 dead, it had the highest casualty rate of any American war), but also because of its lasting effects on one of the most influential countries of the nineteenth century. Eleven of the American Southern states declared their independence from the north in a new 'Confederate States of America'. Although there were other contributing causes to the war, such as immigration, religion, and the economy, by far the largest issue was slavery in the Southern states. Abraham Lincoln stated in 1858 that he was committed to the extinction of slavery, and his election to the presidency in 1860 convinced many observers that war was imminent, particularly after South Carolina seceded from the Union, followed by six other states. The war indeed began in 1861 and lasted until 1865. The American Civil War left a lasting sense of division between north and south that still resonates to some degree today. Yet it also firmly established the principle of US freedom and rights, granted to all slaves in Lincoln's 1862 Emancipation Proclamation. US historians suggest that the horrible experience of the Civil War forged a new direction for the country, and a clearer sense of unity and common purpose.

government and political powers that are divided among its 50 states, one district (District of Columbia, DC), and the federal government in Washington. Modern federalism, in fact, owes much to the United States. When the US was formed, several of the states did not want to see such a concentration of powers in Washington. But the counterargument was that reasonable government would need a strong central authority. The compromise — a balance between ensuring existing powers of the states and granting some oversight to the central government — was the federal system: a division and **separation of powers** that was constitutionally defined.

The American political system is unlike the British parliamentary model. It represents one of two major examples of revolutionary **republicanism** (France is the other one). Breaking from the Westminster parliamentary tradition, American politics was based on a definite separation of powers among the levels of government, with a firm role to be played regarding the review of each other's actions — the '**checks and balances**' of the American system. The American executive is headed by the president, who is both head of government and head of state, and the cabinet. The legislative branch of government is bicameral, with an elected upper house (Senate, with 100 members), and lower house (House of Representatives, with 435 members).

The US constitution, which entered into force in 1789, is the world's oldest written constitution. (You can refer back to Chapter 5 for more information about written constitutions.) As discussed elsewhere in this text, the constitution is considered the basic law for a country, and is a 'living document' in that it can be altered over time. In the US case, this has been done twenty-seven times, most recently in 1992. The US Bill of Rights, which is much like the Canadian Charter of Rights and Freedoms, is laid out in the first 10 amendments to the US constitution. These amendments spell out the basic individual and collective rights of all US citizens.

The American system relies on the input and involvement of all citizens in a form of **indirect democracy**, which denotes the representation of views of citizens by elected officials. The United States is a federal democracy, which means that decision-making and authority is divided among different layers of power — national, state, and municipal. American politics separates executive (or presidential) power from that of the legislature (the bicameral Congress, which is separated into the House of Representatives, whose members serve a two-year term, and the Senate, where members have a six-year term) and the judiciary (the courts). And then there is the bureaucracy, which could well be referred to as the fourth level of government, given its important role in the definition of policy-making and implementation.

The separation of powers in the US is the single most important defining aspect of its politics. Unlike other countries, such as Canada, that 'fuse' the powers of the legislature and the executive, the drafters of the US constitution ensured that power would be divided. As a presidential democracy, the president is chosen in a separate vote on election day. Electors actually vote indirectly, because the president is formally elected by the **electoral college**, which is a group of 538 officials from each state (based on population) who are voted for by the electorate and who then directly elect the president and vice-president. To win the election, the president must gain a majority of these college votes. The president is elected to a four-year term, and may only hold office for two terms.

Separation of powers
division of powers among several institutions in government (e.g., legislature, executive) to avoid concentration of authority

Republic
political unit in which supreme power is held by the people or elected representatives of the people

Checks and balances
system of inspection and evaluation of different levels and branches of governments by others

Indirect democracy
political system of representation in which citizens elect a delegate to act on their behalf

Electoral college
in United States, officials chosen from each state based on population who then directly elect the president and vice-president

The American judicial system still retains vestiges of the British legal system but with a strong tradition of judicial review of legislative acts. Supreme and federal court judges are appointed by the president, and approved by the Senate, while lower court judges are elected by citizens. Supreme Court judges have the responsibility to ensure that no government legislation violates the US constitution, and they have the right to override both the Congress and the president. This is known as **judicial review**, which gives ultimate power of interpretation to the Court.

It may seem odd for such a large political system, but just two major political parties have dominated American politics since the US Civil War. The Democrats have traditionally occupied the more 'left-leaning' side of American politics, with the Republicans to the 'right' of the political spectrum. In the real world, the two parties are actually rather close — at least compared with more radical political movements — in terms of most of their platforms, ideology, and political practice. Other political parties exist, and some have had some influence, but these two have controlled most of American politics in the modern era.

> **Judicial review**
> power of the courts to interpret the constitution, varying from the ability to resolve disputes between levels of government in federal systems to the ability to annul legislative and executive actions outright

9.5

Ross Perot and the Reform Party

Two parties have dominated American politics for most of the post-Civil War years. That changed a bit in 1992 when Texas businessman H. Ross Perot ran for the presidency against incumbent Republican George H.W. Bush and Democrat Bill Clinton.

Ross Perot, seen here in California in 1992, almost singlehandedly made third parties relevant in the United States in the 1990s.

Clinton won that election with 43 per cent of the vote, but Perot took 19 per cent, a startling percentage (Bush received 38). After that election, he formed the Reform Party (no connection to the Canadian Reform Party of 1987–2000), and

9.5 Continued...

ran again in the 1996 election. He received 8 per cent of the vote in that election. Perot's 1992 success surprised those who considered the US a bastion of two-party politics, but since that election no third party has had a similar level of support from the electorate.

In terms of political culture, US politics reflects a lot of what Canadians might recognize: freedoms (religion, speech), democratic values, the essential equality of citizens, and respect for authority. Traditionally, the US has been thought of as a melting pot of immigrant cultures, which blends all into something new and different: Americans. But the United States is actually a very diverse country. Like other multicultural countries, pockets of different traditions, languages, and cultures dominate different parts of the nation. For instance, Hispanics (peoples of countries formerly ruled by Spain in Latin America) now represent more than 15 per cent of the total US population. The old idea of being 'an American' has given away to a more diverse notion of nationality.

Regarding American economics, we see a prime example of liberalism, market freedom, but with government regulation. The United States is commonly seen as the 'home of capitalism', a place where the market reigns supreme. But the US economy became the world's largest thanks to a combination of private initiative and effective government management by agencies at the federal and state levels. Today the US economy is the world's largest by far, with a gross domestic product of over $14 trillion. Japan and China are rivals for second place, with GDPs of $4.5 trillion and $4.3 trillion, respectively. While the US doesn't have the same predominant role it played in the years following World War II (more on that in Chapter 13), it still is the most important economy in the world, with the dollar as the basic global currency unit and a concentration of such a large number of global manufacturers and financial institutions.

In addition to regulating and managing the economy, the US government is also a consumer of enormous dimensions. Each year the US federal budget involves over US$1.5 trillion in spending. This gives the government enormous influence over the economy, and again raises the possibility for lobbying and pressure over the awarding of government contracts. It also gives the United States government the option of providing a large stimulus to the economy, if it should choose to. For instance, in 2008 and 2009, the US government spent hundreds of billions of dollars in an effort to stimulate the domestic economy.

The United States spends more than any other nation on R&D (Research and Development), and one element of its global dominance has been the spread of American multinational corporations (MNCs) throughout the world (see Chapter 13 for more details). Through this global corporate reach, American brands and companies have extended far more than just products and services. Indeed, American products have a cultural impact as well: McDonald's, Nike, IBM, General Motors, and Citibank — just to name a few — have enormous visibility far beyond American shores. For better or for worse, this extends American culture to a wider global market. A trip to any major city throughout the world would quickly reveal the influence of American products and culture.

From an economic standpoint, the American capitalist economy means that the production and distribution of goods and services in the American system relies on private, rather than public or government, profit-making and capital. Though this might seem rather obvious when we speak of the American economy, they are really elemental properties of the system of accumulating and distributing public goods in the United States.

As explained in greater detail in other parts of this text (see, for instance, Chapter 13), the international economy as we know it today is a tightly entwined dynamic that relies tremendously on relations of many different actors. However, there is no doubt that the most significant actor in the modern global economy is the American one, both for its leadership role, and lead economic position. Of all the economies in the international system, the United States is most intertwined with the rest.

The United States took on the role of undisputed leader in the international system in terms of both military and economic power at the close of the Second World War. Then, it had the world's largest military force, and was responsible for over 50 per cent of global production. At that time a series of international institutions, organizations, and **regimes** (rules and decision-making procedures) was created to guide decisions taken by states. The idea here was not so much to strip countries of their sovereign power, but rather to give an important role to international institutions so as to provide a peaceful way to alleviate potential conflict. Importantly, the new international system of institutions needed a leader to uphold the structure, and to provide a military and economic guarantee. That leader was the United States.

It was significant that the United States was chosen to be the leader of the international economic system at the close of the Second World War. Most of the former international leaders — the colonizing powers of Europe such as Great Britain, France, Belgium, and Germany — were simply so weakened at the close of the war that they were unable to uphold their position in the global order. And, while it might seem clear to us that the United States would be chosen to act as the leader of the new system, it was not without some resistance that this decision was taken. As part of what became known as the **Transatlantic Bargain**, the former great powers of Europe conceded to American leadership in exchange for an agreement on the part of the United States that it would uphold the economic and military stability of Europe, as well as the rest of the Western world. The United States remained the unquestioned leader in the international system, retaining the position of **hegemon**, or principal power among states.

But by the 1970s, the American political economy, as well as its position in the international system, looked very different than it had in previous decades. The United States was in an economic downturn, and a global economic **recession**, or a serious decline in economic activity, productivity, and prosperity made matters worse. It took a decade before the US economy rebounded, and in the 1980s a **neoconservative** movement under President Ronald Reagan brought with it a reduced role for government in the economy, and far greater emphasis on private capitalism.

Regimes
rules and decision-making procedures

Transatlantic Bargain
postwar arrangement whereby former great powers of Europe conceded to American leadership in exchange for United States support of economic and military stability of Europe

Hegemon
one country with inordinate capability to uphold and protect the system

Recession
decline in economic productivity or affluence; specifically, a decline in GDP for two or more consecutive quarters

Neoconservative
advocate or in favour of return to conservative values or policies

By the 1990s some economists thought that the dominance of the US economy was eroding. Other countries, such as Germany, Japan, and (later) China, posed real challenges, and the US found itself overextended and greatly in debt. During this decade, strength in the US economy righted much of the imbalance felt in Washington, but there was no doubt that other actors, such as these other countries as well as global corporations and institutions, were playing a much more significant role than in the past. Even though the US is unquestionably the most powerful economy in the world today, its relative position is very different than it was after World War II. It now shares much of global decision-making, and no longer is considered the undisputed leader it once was.

It would be fair to say that the United States has undergone significant challenges over the past decade. First, the 2001 terrorist attacks in Washington, Pennsylvania, and New York against innocent American citizens left many feeling vulnerable and uncertain. The policies of the Bush administration changed substantially on September 11, 2001, as that relatively new government took on the 'war on terrorism' that would frame so much of US domestic and international policy for the rest of the decade. A war unlike any other, it brought allies closer to the United States, then quickly repelled them. Political challenges in the new century became multifaceted: managing an economy under siege, building public confidence and security, and — most importantly — fighting two wars concurrently, in Afghanistan and Iraq.

Partly due to the costs of these wars, and thanks also to an economic downturn, the financial stability of the 1990s gave way under the Bush administration to government deficits and growing debt. The balance of trade with other countries became more negative, with a growing trade deficit as the US imported more goods than it exported, and its powerful currency fluctuated with a shifting economy. By decade's end, the new Obama presidency was in the throes of the worst recession in 80 years, and facing the need to spend billions on bailouts and stimulus packages to revive — or at least save — an economy in peril.

Nevertheless, the United States is one of the very few states in the international system today that can lay claim to a global sphere of influence. Despite the challenges facing its economy — and those challenges are severe — the basis of the US economy will ensure its influence in the world for many years to come. The rest of the world is reliant on the United States for a huge percentage of global production, innovation, and finance. However, the influence of the United States extends beyond the economy: it remains an exemplar of democracy and political freedoms, its culture has been widely accepted around the world, and the country remains a global leader in international relations.

Japan

Japan is located in the North Pacific in one of the most volatile and robust regions in the world. On the one hand, Japan is surrounded by potentially belligerent countries, such as North Korea and China. Other countries in Japan's larger geopolitical region, such as India and Pakistan, also present a source of insecurity. Japan's emergence in the latter half of the twentieth century as the world's second largest economy has given that nation a clear economic, if not political, leadership role in this growing region.

Japan's well-being relies on close and amiable relations with partners. Slightly smaller than the American state of California, Japan's terrain is mountainous and rugged. Its arable land comprises only 11 per cent of total land mass, and permanent crops in Japan total only 1 per cent of its territory. Japan, by necessity, is a trading nation. Japan is an almost ethnically pure state, with over 99 per cent of its population ethnic Japanese. It is almost impossible to become a Japanese citizen unless one is born to Japanese parents; this is not to say that others may not work or live in Japan — many ethnic Koreans do, for example — but citizenship is reserved just about exclusively for Japanese only.

Japan is a constitutional monarchy with a bicameral legislature. The monarch — the emperor — has had a largely symbolic role to play in Japanese politics since the modern Japanese constitution was implemented in 1947. Although this role is not unlike the Canadian Governor General, Emperor Akihito (born in 1933; acceded to the throne in 1989) today still maintains a high degree of reverence in Japanese society as a result of links to a time when the emperor was considered a deity on earth.

The **Diet**, or Japanese Parliament, is divided into the House of Councillors and the House of Representatives. Though the Japanese political system is a multi-party one, the Liberal Democratic Party, or the LDP, has largely dominated domestic politics since 1955. That changed in 2009 when the centre-left Democratic Party of Japan (DPJ) took more than 300 of 480 seats in the lower house, unseating the LDP as the ruling party.

Unlike the United States and Canada, Japan's domestic politics, as well as its global position, underwent severe changes and alterations in the latter half of the twentieth century. From regional great power, to defeated nation, to global economic presence, Japan has seen its power and influence shift drastically in a short period of time. It is particularly remarkable that in this short time frame the Japanese political and economic presence became such a global force, now second only to that of the United States. In spite of these massive changes (in such a short period of time), Japan's extensive history has had a significant effect on its current politics, as we will see in the following.

Japan has one of the oldest and most sophisticated political and economic histories among the advanced industrialized nations. Early written historical records in Japan, which date to the eighth century AD, relate the story of the emergence of the Japanese state, which took its first steps to nationhood in the fifth and sixth centuries. For two centuries prior to that Japan was ruled by the Yamato tribe, which had divided the island chain into hereditary units called *Uji*. It is worth noting that the belief system of this early civilization served as the foundation for *Shinto* — or 'the way of the gods', which as Japan's traditional religion emphasizes the need for humans to live in harmony with nature and the environment. By the seventh century some aspects of the political system of the Chinese T'ang Dynasty (618–907) were also introduced to Japanese civilization.

Throughout this early period the Japanese political system was highly centralized. As often happens with such a system, particularly when it is able to

Diet
Japanese Parliament

remain relatively isolated and unchallenged, the political leadership weakened and power was decentralized. Feudal Japan emerged as a result of the decadent rule of the Fujiwara, whose political system borrowed heavily from that of China. Throughout the tenth and eleventh centuries the power of the central government declined as the prominence of provincial powers grew.

With independence from the direct influence of the Chinese in the eleventh century and a simultaneous surge in population growth, the Japanese feudal economy began to prosper. As was the case in the West, the mounted warrior aristocrat was a key element of this society. By the twelfth century they were responsible for the management of tax-free estates called *shoen*, and were charged with the defence of their territories from marauders.

Although power was decentralized to provincial authority, the imperial court at Kyoto was still generally recognized as the governing authority for judging land claims and awarding government positions. However, the aristocrats were responsible for their own security; this was unlike European feudalism where the nobility could always appeal to the king or any other higher authority for assistance. This requirement of self-protection encouraged several groups to band together, and two became particularly powerful. The *Taira* and *Minamoto* comprised branches of the imperial family and both managed to garner the support of a strong military following. In the mid-twelfth century the central authority, even as limited as it was, came to be called into question. Wars started to become the common way of settling various disputes between groups of nobles.

It took until the late sixteenth century before national unity was finally restored, and was maintained from roughly the mid-seventeenth to the mid-nineteenth century. Reunification and the peace that came with it fostered change, growth, and the mobilization of the Japanese economy. This period also witnessed the start of the decline of the prominence of the warrior class in Japanese politics and society.

It was at this time that deeper relations were forged with European states. Towards the end of the eighteenth century both the Russians and the British tried to increase their economic interactions with the Japanese. Japan was also recognized as a useful water- and coal-replenishment station for American whaling ships and ships involved in the trade with the Chinese province of Canton. However, the Japanese of that period remained highly isolationist and resisted all attempts by the United States, Britain, and Russia to coax them into a trade deal. They were largely successful too, at least up until the mid-nineteenth century.

In July 1853 an American fleet under Commodore Matthew C. Perry entered Tokyo Bay. Perry presented a letter from the president of the United States to Japanese officials demanding that Japan open itself to trade with the Americans. The Japanese agreed to open two small ports to US ships and establish an American consulate. Many conservatives in Japan were vehemently opposed to this concession, but the leadership saw that, with the threat of imminent attack by the Americans, it had few alternatives. Other treaties were soon reached with Britain, Russia, France, and the Dutch. By the 1860s it was becoming increasingly clear to most Japanese that their country was fast achieving the same semi-colonial status that China had received.

In 1871 the class system was abolished, a declaration of equality was made, and all land became centralized under the empire. The finance ministry soon became the core of the government and a banking system was created. Japanese banks were initially decentralized like those in the US, but were later redesigned and centralized based on the model of Belgian banks. The unification of Japanese currency also occurred in 1871 with the development of the yen.

The government also recognized the need to industrialize and develop a railway, postal system, and port facilities. The Japanese were also quick to develop their own mining and munitions industries in order to fulfill their mandate for a strong military. Another important step was the recognition of the need to develop an education system and to learn about technology and industrialization from other countries. Students were sent abroad to study the Navy and the Merchant Marine of Britain, the army and medical sciences in Germany, local governmental systems and law in France, and business methods in the US.

Political development took another step forward in 1881 with changes to the legislature, including a modern cabinet system through which central executive control could be exercised, and a civil service system. Both the cabinet and civil service system have remained largely unchanged since their establishment. Also at this time, a Japanese constitution was drafted. One of the most important aspects of the Japanese constitution was that it reinforced the sovereign authority of the emperor.

The Japanese constitution included a bill of rights of sorts; however, the rights of the people remained subordinate to the rule of law, which was aimed at preserving the state and, more specifically, the emperor. The constitution also introduced limited democracy to Japan as a House of Representatives was established in 1890.

It was generally believed that the efforts of the Japanese leadership to modernize and develop Western forms of government would earn the respect of Western states and help place Japan on more even footing with them. This was in fact the end result of these changes. By 1899 the British had given up their extraterritorial claims in Japan (which had been established in 1856) and other Western states soon began to do the same.

The Japanese came to be a strongly unified people. This island nation had previously been isolated for more than two hundred years, with a people who shared a strong sense of self-identity. These factors, combined with the absence of any significant ethnic or religious tensions among the Japanese, contributed to a highly nationalistic sentiment among the people. This sense of nationalism contributed to the creation of the Japanese Empire throughout the 1880s and 1890s. In addition to consolidating control over the entire island chain, the Japanese government also managed to take control of the island of Taiwan and the Korean peninsula. Competition for control over the Liaotung Peninsula and Manchuria, where the Russians already had a strong presence, was the initial source of conflict in the Russo-Japanese war of 1904–5.

Japan took advantage of the alliance it had established with England in 1904 by declaring war on Germany in 1914 and seizing control over German colonies in the East. Throughout the interwar period Japan began to distance itself somewhat from the West in an attempt to fall back into its isolationist cocoon.

Later, Japanese militarism began with the swift and total conquest of Manchuria in 1931. Japanese policy rapidly shifted from one of isolationism to one of expansionism on the Asian continent. This period of heightened nationalism and expansionism, which obviously continued into World War II, serves as the basis for much of the mistrust and animosity on the part of other Asian states towards Japan even today.

Japan was devastated at the end of World War II. In addition to being attacked by atomic bombs at Hiroshima and Nagasaki, the country's economic infrastructure was decimated by the demands of the war. For seven years between 1945 and 1952 the Americans occupied Japan and played a significant role in rebuilding the country, both economically and politically. For their part, the Japanese were surprisingly accepting of the Americans, particularly once they saw that the Americans had a genuine interest in helping to rebuild the country. In the aftermath of the war, concepts such as nationalism became taboo, and the Japanese had little interest in rebuilding their military, regardless of the fact that they were prevented from doing so. Instead Japanese and American energies were focused on the redevelopment of the economic and civil infrastructure of the country.

The postwar years represent the most remarkable period in modern Japanese economic history. As a result of the redrafting of the Japanese constitution — the foundation for its basic law — and its tight alliance with the United States, Japan was restricted from organizing or budgeting for an offensive armed forces. However, the restrictions placed on Japan regarding its domestic military ability actually permitted a large degree of independence in economic matters. Given the opportunity to concentrate on matters of a non-security nature, the Japanese government began a strategic effort to rebuild its domestic economy and industry, and to engage in sectors of the international economy that would aid in its reconstruction efforts.

Perhaps the most significant medium for this development was the creation of the federal Ministry of International Trade and Industry (MITI). This ministry was, and still is, responsible for the orchestration of domestic economic ventures and targeting within the international environment. It was MITI that was responsible for the strategic marketing of Japanese technology and consumer electronics worldwide. Partly because of the **corporatist** model of government in Japan, which allows for the integration of business interests, unions, and government officials in decision-making, MITI was very successful in both identifying emerging consumer and corporate markets in the industrialized world and in distributing its goods globally.

The broad policy implemented and followed by the Japanese in the postwar years was a combination of three basic elements: to establish an essentially non-interventionist role in international affairs; to support the United States as hegemon in the global system, and to deepen links with the Americans; and to focus on the domestic economy of Japan as a means of reassembling power and influence. This came to be known as the **Yoshida Doctrine**, and was a largely successful policy of domestic attention and international interaction. It was also a firm break from the more entangled and involved role Japan had played, particularly in the Asian sphere, in previous eras. The postwar order, then, saw the role of Japan in a far different light.

Corporatism

approach to governance that entails close co-operation and coordination among government, business, and labour in the expectation that such activity will bring more stability to the political economy

Yoshida Doctrine

postwar Japanese political and economic policy to establish a more non-interventionist role in international affairs, support the United States as hegemon in the global system, deepen links with the Americans, and focus on the domestic economy of Japan as a means of reassembling power and influence; named after Japan's postwar prime minister, Shigeru Yoshida

9.6

The Jutan Corporation

The Jutan Corporation is a very good example of the influence of Japanese economic strategy, the growth of multinational corporations in a modern political economy, and the changing nature of corporate ownership in an interdependent global environment. Jutan was originally set up as a Japan-based manufacturer of electronic consumer goods, with several different name-plates under its corporate identity. Citizen, Electrohome, and Candle, for instance, were names of electronic product lines offered in Canada, often competing with one another in the same stores for the same customers. All the lines were managed and run by the same larger corporation, which had a series of manufacturing plants throughout Thailand, Malaysia, Singapore, Taiwan, Korea, and China. Having several names under the same corporate banner allowed Jutan better access to consumer markets by covering more market share with different 'brands'; this gives shoppers the feeling that they are competitively buying, when in fact a decision to opt for another brand may still yield profits for a company like Jutan. As a multinational corporation, the manufacturing is farmed out to less expensive labour markets in the Asian rim. In what may be an increasingly rare twist in multinational behaviour, Jutan was purchased by a Canadian corporation, Jonic International, in 2004. (This is interesting for another reason, because Electrohome, one of the product lines under Jutan, was originally a Canadian electronics company.) Jonic's new assets from Jutan were then subsumed under the new Redmond Group of Companies. These assets were then purchased in 2007 by Synnex Canada, a company that licenses branding for products that are often produced in a generic fashion and sold as separate lines, much like Jutan did in the first place!

It is somewhat ironic, therefore, that Japan became such a leading international participant in trade and commerce. Though its economy and national infrastructure were obliterated as a result of the Second World War, Japan quickly came to challenge the United States as a regional economic forerunner in the Asia–Pacific rim, and became the second largest single-nation economy in the world after the United States.

The reasons for Japanese economic success in the postwar and post-Cold War eras are numerous, but there are several that are particularly irrefutable. First, Japan's careful planning and strategic marketing have contributed to long-term regional and international strength. Rather than attempting to immerse itself in existing sectors — such as primary resources or heavy manufacturing — Japan instead targeted future and emerging markets that were not already saturated or inundated with existing participants.

Second, self-imposed regulations on international investment, for instance, kept credit and wealth at home, and discouraged the foreign ownership of domestic enterprises. A very high domestic savings rate was achieved, giving the Japanese economy impressive financial resources with which to manoeuvre. Later, as the Japanese domestic economy grew, the government relaxed laws on domestic and international investment at a time when investment opportunities increased, leading to another period of growth in Japanese multinational interests abroad, as well as international investment in Japan.

Third, Japan made critical assessments of its domestic abilities and needs. For instance, Japan must import most of its domestic food, energy, and resource needs. Strategic assessments, then, allowed the Japanese government to set objectives in regards to goods and services that needed to be imported, versus those in which Japan held a crucial pre-eminence, such as manufactured goods and high technology.

Fourth, Japan benefited from the international liberalization of markets, openness in trade and commerce, a reduction in tariffs, and the careful integration of national modes of economic interaction and interdependence. Japan's position of predominance globally allowed it to ensure that others adhered to the rules, while taking advantage of the system and its own politics. Corporatism in Japan allows business involvement in government decision-making, which benefits private businesses and corporations here, but government through the direct input in and observation of private economic players in the Japanese system. This resulted in a more efficient relationship, and a legitimate way that the Japanese government could take certain advantages of the global economic order.

The distinctiveness of the Japanese economy is a fifth reason for its success. Its distinctive political history, culture, and domestic economy means Japan reaps the benefits of international openness, institutions, and world markets, yet does not position itself on the import side to the same degree that other trading nations do, or must. Though a strong player in an international environment of openness and liberalization, Japan has often been criticized as being a **protectionist** state that would seek to uphold its domestic interests at all times over the health of the international economy — even though it benefits greatly from the international economy. Further to this is the Japanese tradition of *keiretsu*, which is the vertical integration of large industrial groups, permitting like-minded groups to bind together to influence the policy process in Japan.

In the 1990s, the Japanese government was faced with a problem. A deep financial crisis struck the country in the early part of that decade, breaking several banks that had earlier ranked among the largest in the world. This banking crisis was matched by a crash in the real estate market, which had become hugely inflated in the 1980s. For the first time since the Second World War, the Japanese economy began to shrink as corporations and individuals faced bankruptcy. For many Japanese this crisis challenged the assumptions they had come to take for granted concerning Japan's economic dominance and efficiency. Political instability followed, and for the first time in decades the Liberal Democratic Party lost power (1993), albeit temporarily. Because Japan was the world's second largest economy, the crisis exacerbated a deep economic crisis in Asia (in Thailand, Indonesia, and South Korea in particular) as the Japanese market for Asian exports shrank.

This crisis underscored the importance of Japan in the international economy. Although Japan began to show growth in 1999, it recovered some strength only to decline again in the early 2000s with other industrialized nations. After

Protectionism

tendency of countries to safeguard their own economic sectors or industries using tariffs, quotas, or other forms of trade and investment legislation

Keiretsu

a business group or set of companies found in Japan that work together in decision-making and production to provide increased benefits for all

9.7

Japan's Influence on Business–Government Relations in Asia

In many Asian countries the relationship between business and government is a very close one, with a high level of interaction between the state and large corporations. The goal of this co-operation is to produce both economic stability and higher levels of international competitiveness. In South Korea such a relationship existed and appeared to work very well until the financial and economic crisis of 1997–8. The largest industrial and business conglomerates, families of corporations known as *chaebol*, worked closely with the government in the formation of domestic economic, trade, and investment policies. Many analysts saw this as being one of the great advantages of countries such as South Korea, allowing them to harness the power of the national government to assist in the development of competitive industries, and also ensuring the collaboration of big business in achieving the goals of the government, both domestic and international.

When the deep financial and economic crisis of 1997 hit South Korea, these long-standing assumptions were rapidly reconsidered. For it emerged that the relationship between government and big business had been, perhaps, too close.

a decade of slow recuperation, the Japanese economy slumped dramatically with others in 2008 with the onset of the global recession. Many pundits used the Japanese descent and rise in the 1990s and 2000s as an example of how to 'fix' the global economy; whatever the likelihood of using Japan as a template for economic restoration, this example shows the close interdependence of many economies in the world today: the sufferings of one often spell a similar experience in other interrelated economies.

Japan is an excellent example of how an ancient system of politics can be significantly altered to fit another era. Of course, the post–World War II experience in Japan could only have happened with the specific circumstances stemming from the war and its outcome. The urgent need to revamp a political and economic system in that country, coupled with its close relationship with the United States, allowed Japan to take advantage of strategic changes in the global system and quickly become a major force in the new wave of globalization taking place. It would be difficult, if not impossible, to completely replicate Japan's experience, because it presents a unique and circumstantial case. Yet there are other cases where exceptional conditions have led to political and economic success, even if that success likely could not be repeated elsewhere. Similar to Japan, the European Union offers another example of a way to do things differently in modern politics.

The European Union

The European Union (EU) is a dynamic and advanced example of regional integration. Other regional bodies look to the EU for an example of success and failure. Ideas like a common currency, or expanding into Eastern Europe, seemed

North American Free Trade Agreement (NAFTA)
agreement whereby Canada, the United States, and Mexico have opened their markets to each other

Asia–Pacific Economic Cooperation (APEC)
group for promoting open trade and economic co-operation among Asia–Pacific economies

unlikely half a century ago, but now are part of the new Europe. Other groups, such as the **North American Free Trade Agreement (NAFTA)** and the **Asia–Pacific Economic Cooperation (APEC)** body, exist, but none have the same combination of deep integration coupled with a fascinating evolution of politics, economics, and institutional structures.

The EU is made up of twenty-seven European states, in Western, Northern, Eastern, and Southern Europe. However, the EU does not include the 'whole' of Europe; many other countries have applied to join, and still others have decided to remain out. The EU was previously known as the European Community (EC), and before that the European Economic Community (EEC), and before that the European Coal and Steel Community (ECSC).

Europe is much more than geography; its long history has given it a cultural and political identity as well. While the idea of 'Europe' is ambiguous, to say the least, the modern conception of Europe can be found in the revival of classical learning during the Renaissance. In this context, Europe was perceived as the geographical and cultural heir to the Roman Empire. But this did not symbolize a single political domain. Even today its boundaries do not rest on any clear-cut geographical divide. The Ural Mountains were once designated as the eastern boundary of Europe, but since the end of the Cold War and the demise of the Soviet Union, this frontier has expanded. The most recent wave of EU enlargement, for instance, includes many former 'East Bloc' countries, and Russia is now more 'European' than during the latter half of the twentieth century.

Today, in many countries of the European Union, immigration from the West Indies, Africa, and Asia has produced an ethnic mix more diverse than at any time since the decline and collapse of the Roman Empire. By the same token, emigration from Europe since the fifteenth century has spread various European identities across the globe. All of this is to say that it has never been possible to define 'Europe' or 'Europeans' in culturally or ethnically homogeneous terms.

The 'European Movement' appeared in the years between World War I and World War II (1919–39). After World War II, British prime minister Winston Churchill spoke of a 'kind of United States of Europe' to create unity and avoid another continental war. As time went on, political actors used the European Movement to deal with the reconstruction of Europe for largely the same purposes that Churchill envisioned: peace and prosperity in the region.

David Mitrany proposed the theory of '**functionalism**' to describe this movement.[4] Mitrany argued that countries on their own could not respond to the problems associated with modern economies; rather, a collective approach was necessary to provide a full range of social and welfare services. These needs would be accomplished by functionally specific international organizations (hence the term 'functionalism') that would be independent of governments, or that would enjoy a great deal of functional autonomy. The final goal was peaceful economic development. This **institutionalism** is, in essence, the basis of the EU system.

Much of the political impetus for European integration emerged before World War II ended, when countries began considering ways to deal with the ongoing conflicts of the major powers. Increasingly, the idea of a unified Europe found widespread popular support among diverse political perspectives. Importantly,

Functionalism
collective approach by countries to provide full range of social and welfare services through functionally specific international organizations

Institutionalism
belief in utility of institutions to provide collective goods

9.8

Will Turkey Join the EU?

Joining the European Union is no easy task, but Turkey has had a rougher time than many other aspirants. That is despite the fact that Turkey has done everything it should to be favourably considered. An 'associate member' since 1963, Turkey first formally applied to join in 1987, when the EU was still the European Community.

FIGURE 9.1

The EU and Turkey

Turkey (represented here by its red flag with a white crescent moon and star) continues to seek membership in the EU (represented by the circle of gold stars on a blue background), causing great debate about the extent of enlargement for the Union, and what really constitutes 'Europe'.

It is also a member of the Organisation for Economic Co-operation and Development, the North Atlantic Treaty Organization, the Council of Europe, and the Western European Union. Its application was first recognized in 1999, and it has been suggested that it will be at least 2013 before its membership is complete. A largely Islamic country, Turkey is a secular state, and is a close ally of the United States. However, its desire to be part of the EU has been one of the most controversial issues facing the Union today. Critics of Turkey's possible membership say that it hasn't done enough on human rights and democracy. While supporters see Turkey offering an important link to the Islamic world as well

9.8 Continued...

as Asia (since Turkey straddles the easternmost parts of the European continent), some leaders, such as France's Nicolas Sarkozy, have remarked that Turkey 'has no place inside the European Union'; when he was president of the Convention on the Future of Europe, Valéry Giscard d'Estaing stated that allowing Turkey to join 'would be the end of Europe'. Austria and France have both indicated they would not support Turkey's membership. Since accession to the EU requires the unanimous support of all EU members, it is difficult to envision an easy path for Turkey in its European aspirations.

Treaty of Paris
European treaty of April 1951 that created the European Coal and Steel Community (ECSC)

European Coal and Steel Community (ECSC)
first institutional version of European integration (1951) involving Belgium, the Netherlands, Luxembourg, France, West Germany, and Italy

the influence and policies of the United States were crucial: the US saw European co-operation as the solution to the problem of European security and the revival of the European and international economies. It also offered a way to avoid a future war, and the likely involvement of the US once again.

Behind European integration is the idea that intergovernmental institutions could facilitate greater co-operation among countries, and hence less chance of future conflict. Today, the EU is 'run' by six main institutions, each with a specific role (see later in this chapter). In addition, other lesser bodies also serve the institutional system of the EU. Importantly, it is not a government; rather, the European Union is an international organization that consists of sovereign states.

This institutional system was formed in April 1951, when the **Treaty of Paris** created the **European Coal and Steel Community** (ECSC) among the original six signatories (Belgium, the Netherlands, Luxembourg, France, West Germany,

9.9

Why Brussels?

The real influence brokers in the European Union are the large economic and military powers of the United Kingdom, France, and Germany. One might expect, then, that the 'home' for the EU would be in one of those capital cities. However, you would have to go to Brussels, Belgium, to visit most of the institutions of the EU. Part of the European Parliament, the Council of the European Union, the European Commission, and the European Council are all located in Brussels, the capital of Belgium. Although other cities, including Strasbourg in France and the country of Luxembourg, have seen European institutions set up, Brussels pushed hard beginning in 1958 to be seen as the location for Europe's new structures. Brussels was seen as the best compromise: a modern city close to most major capitals; space for institutional growth; a thriving urban centre; good relations with member states; and no ulterior motives. This is a good example of the advantage of being small, and having good-quality relations with others. As the EU has expanded, so has the impact on Brussels, where a third of its citizens are non-Belgians. About one hundred thousand people work for the EU or EU-related business, and billions of euros flow into the local economy every year.

and Italy). The ECSC established a **common market** (as distinct from a free trade arrangement or customs union), in coal, coke, iron, steel, and scrap. At this time the coal and steel industry was still regarded as the foundation of an industrial economy. The ECSC came into operation in July 1952. The unique feature of the ECSC was the degree of **supranational** authority that it gave to its main institutions. Later, in 1958, these six countries created the **European Economic Community** (EEC) and the **European Atomic Energy Community** (EURATOM) with the **Treaties of Rome**. The EEC established free trade in both industrial and agricultural products, set out prospects for a complete common market among the signatories, and created a **Common Agricultural Policy** (CAP), which provided economic benefits to agriculture in all countries in order to permit stable pricing and profits for agricultural producers.

As soon as the ECSC was introduced, talk began about expanding the group from the original six. There have been seven 'enlargements' to the EU since 1951, with 27 countries in total today. Most importantly, these processes confirmed the importance of internal trade and political relations over those with non-EU members. But, in addition, successive enlargement and integration among EU members forced the outside world to adjust their own policies. As the EU expanded and deepened, so did our ideas about economic integration. For instance, one of the strongest reasons for the North American Free Trade Agreement (NAFTA) was its 'response' to deepening trade relations in Europe. Expansion has not been a smooth process, and often changes have been prompted by outside events such as new applications for membership, changes in the policies of major outside powers such as the United States, the collapse of Communism in Europe, the reunification of Germany, and the economic and political development of former communist countries.

There are six main institutions in the EU today: Parliament; Council; European Commission; Court of Justice; Court of Auditors; and the European Central Bank.

Although the Treaties of Rome established the Parliamentary Assembly, it was only in 1987 that the title was legally recognized. Members of the **European Parliament** (MEPs) are elected directly by citizens of EU member states. Rules for these elections are determined by the individual states, and are held every five years. The European Parliament consists of 785 members; representation roughly reflects differences in the size of members' populations, although the smaller countries are overrepresented on a proportional basis. MEPs are elected on the basis of multinational party affiliations rather than on the basis of nationality. The Parliament is located in Strasbourg, France; additional plenary sessions and committee meetings are held in Brussels, Belgium, and the Parliament's General Secretariat (its administrative offices) is in Luxembourg.

The Parliament has three main roles. First, it shares with the Council of Ministers (described later in this chapter) legislative power. Second, it is responsible for democratic supervision over all EU institutions, particularly the commission (discussed later in this chapter). Third, the Parliament has authority (again with the Council) over the EU budget, with the power to adopt or reject the budget. Like legislatures in national governments, this 'power of the purse' gives the Parliament influence and control. However, neither the commission nor the Council of Ministers can be considered 'responsible' to Parliament in the sense of the Westminster model. A

Common market
an economic arrangement among states intended to eliminate barriers that inhibit the movement of factors of production — labour, capital, and technology — among its members

Supranational
international organization or union where decision-making is shared by all members

European Economic Community (EEC)
second institutional version of European integration (1958) involving Belgium, the Netherlands, Luxembourg, France, West Germany, and Italy

European Atomic Energy Community (EURATOM)
community created to govern atomic energy in Europe, entered into force in 1958

Treaties of Rome
European treaty of 1958 that created the European Economic Community and the European Atomic Energy Community

Common Agricultural Policy (CAP)
European Union program that provides economic benefits to agriculture in all countries in order to permit stable pricing and profits for agricultural producers

European Parliament
parliamentary assembly for the European Union

bigger problem facing the European Parliament is the lack of public interest in the body, with voter apathy being a significant factor in elections.

The **Council of the European Union** is the main decision-making institution of the EU. Its membership is made up of ministers from the EU national governments, based on areas of concern; for instance, health, industry, transportation, or social affairs. The most important body of the council is the European Council, comprising the heads of state and government and the president of the European Commission. The European Council is responsible for setting up and overseeing the broad agenda of the council as a whole. All 27 member states are represented at council meetings, but the particular ministerial representation is dependent on the topic under discussion. Major issues, including common foreign and security policy, taxation, and asylum and immigration, normally require unanimity. Other issues are decided upon by a simple majority (usually procedural decisions), or by 'weighted' majority voting. The bigger the country's population, the more votes it has. But the number is not strictly proportional: it is adjusted in favour of smaller states. The weighted voting formula is designed to ensure that the five largest members cannot outvote the seven smallest.

The **European Commission** is responsible for implementing activities mandated by the European Parliament and the Council. The 27 commissioners are nominated by national governments and appointed by unanimity for a renewable term of five years. They are to act independently of national governments and to further the interests of the EU as a whole. The commission functions as the initiator of policy proposals and the executive arm of the EU. It is responsible for ensuring that treaty provisions and EU rules are implemented and observed. One of its most important functions is to negotiate, on behalf of the EU, economic agreements with non-members, either bilaterally or in multinational bodies such as the World Trade Organization (WTO). The commission is not a bureaucracy but the executive arm of the EU. It is served by an international secretariat, located mostly in Brussels (some are in Luxembourg). The secretariat employs about twenty-four thousand people, many of whom are translators, since there are 11 official languages, and 9 new languages have recently entered the EU.

Comprising 27 judges (one judge per country), the **Court of Justice** makes certain that EU legislation, which is also known as 'Community law', is evenly and fairly interpreted and applied in all member states. It has the power to settle legal disputes between member states, EU institutions, businesses, and individuals. The court adjudicates, at the request of a national court, on the interpretation or validity of points of EU law. At the request of an EU institution, member state, or individual citizen of the European Union, it can declare void any legal instruments adopted by national governments, the commission, or Council of Ministers which is incompatible with EU law.

Based in Luxembourg, the Court of Auditors comprises 27 members (one from each country) appointed for six-year terms. It functions as the financial watchdog of the EU. The court reports annually on the implementation of the EU budget, and examines whether revenues and expenditures have been handled in a lawful and proper manner. The court may issue special reports on specific questions and deliver opinions at the request of other EU institutions. In co-operation with national audit authorities, it can carry out investigations in individual member states. (For comparison, in Canada the Auditor-General performs similar functions.)

The European Central Bank, or the ECB, was set up in 1998 to prepare the EU for its new single currency, the euro. Since the euro came into circulation on 1 January 2002, the ECB, located in Frankfurt, Germany, has been responsible for framing and implementing the EU's economic and monetary policy. Members of the EU 'euro area' or 'eurozone' and their central banks, together with the European Central Bank, make up what is called the 'Eurosystem'. The ECB works with the European System of Central Banks (ESCB), which covers all the EU countries, including those that have not adopted the euro. The ECB is independent, meaning that both member states and EU institutions cannot try to influence the ECB or the national central banks. To maintain the euro's stability, the ECB is tasked with dealing with price stability in the EU, and safeguarding the euro's purchasing power. It does so by controlling money supply (monetary policy) and monitoring price trends in the euro area.

Other important institutional agencies of the EU include: the European Economic and Social Committee (EESC), an advisory body designed to give various economic and social interest groups an influence on EU policy; the Committee of the Regions, an advisory body composed of representatives of Europe's regional and local authorities ensuring that regional and local identities and prerogatives are respected; and the European Ombudsman, who deals with complaints from citizens concerning maladministration by an EU institution or body. The complicated politics and interrelationships between the various institutions of the European Union operate on transnational, transgovernmental, and international levels. Moreover, the decision-making process involves a whole network of transactions and official contacts that cut across lines of national jurisdiction.

Two major developments over the last twenty years bear mention. First there was the establishment of the Economic and Monetary Union (EMU) and common currency, and second, the establishment of a common market. A common currency was discussed as early as 1969, but didn't get much attention until the creation of the European Monetary System (EMS), which fixed exchange rates among members, in 1979. Not all joined the EMS, however; in the 1990s, a common currency received renewed attention, and the European Monetary Union and the new euro currency were established in 1999. Currencies of those nations joining the system (16 of the 27 states: Austria, Belgium, Cyprus, Finland, France, Germany, Greece, Ireland, Italy, Luxembourg, Malta, the Netherlands, Portugal, Slovakia, Slovenia, and Spain) were removed from circulation, and replaced by the common currency which is now managed by the European Central Bank (ECB) in Frankfurt, Germany.

Second, a common market was created with the ratification of the **Single European Act** in 1987. This removed 'non-tariff barriers' to the free movement of goods, services, capital, and labour in 1993. Examples of such barriers include national preferences in government purchases, different national safety standards and product specifications, different criteria for professional qualifications, exchange controls, and a myriad of other barriers to the practice of the four freedoms. In the years since, the EU has established itself as the most ambitious example of a multinational common market in existence.

Single European Act
European removal of 'non-tariff barriers' to the free movement of goods, services, capital, and labour

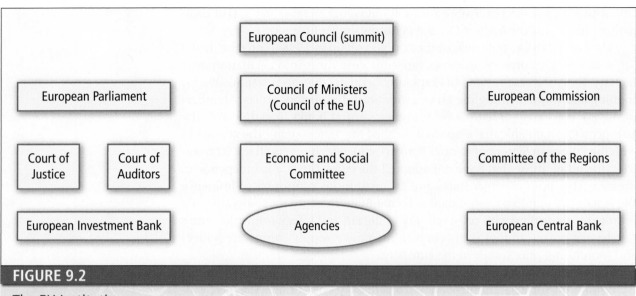

FIGURE 9.2

The EU Institutions

Like any governmental organization, the many institutions of the EU are interrelated. Each carries out its own specific task, such as legislation, policy-making, and judicial interpretation.

Throughout the process of integration in the EU, politics have been the driving force. Not only is it about the politics of who gets what, when, and where, both at the national and sub-national levels, but also about the contemporary role of nation-states and the redefinition of what Europe is, and the future for the region. How the EU operates is driven by the vital interests of these historical nation-states. Today, it may be said that it is not so much the survival of the member nation-states that is at issue, but what their role will be in a highly interdependent Europe, and what will be the terms of their co-operation.

Conclusion

The years following World War II brought significant challenges to the developed countries. First, the reconstruction effort concentrated much of the resources of those countries, then the growing integration of their economies took on a whole new approach with the rapid enlargement of the welfare state. This new interdependent relationship between the economy and the political structure of the country became more outward-looking as nations increasingly relied on one another for trade and commerce. Economic stability and growth is a key element of a modern state's political stability and reputation internationally. Increasingly, countries have focused on the welfare goals of their citizens as the need to concentrate entirely on military and defensive security has been less important than in the past. As we will see in the following chapter, developing states have their own set of concerns, which are often quite different from those of the developed world. Yet one of the lead themes that binds both developed and developing nations is their focus on growth and change in an increasingly competitive environment.

Self-Assessment Questions

1. How did countries change their view of security and economics after World War II? What does this mean for security? Can developed countries afford to ignore issues like national security?
2. Japan and the EU offer two different modes of developing political and economic systems in a very competitive global environment. Is one more successful than the other? Could other countries easily adopt either of these strategies?
3. American hegemony has changed a lot since the end of World War II. Is it still fair to say that the US is a global leader? What has changed? Are there real challengers to US power on the horizon?
4. The EU is based on its institutional foundation. Do these institutions threaten the sovereignty of its member states? Is the EU headed to a form of 'statehood'?
5. Canada's political and economic system is intricately tied to the United States. Does this threaten Canadian independence? In what ways are Canadian domestic and foreign affairs different from its neighbour to the south?

Weblinks

Europa: European Union Online
http://europa.eu/index_en.htm

Japanese Government Links
http://web-japan.org/links/government/index.
html

Information on September 11 Attacks from cbc.ca
http://www.cbc.ca/news/background/sep11/

Further Reading

Brooks, Stephen. *Canadian Democracy: An Introduction.* 6th ed. Don Mills, ON: Oxford University Press, 2009.

Caramani, Daniele, ed. *Comparative Politics.* Don Mills, ON: Oxford University Press, 2008.

Clemens, Walter C., Jr. *America and the World, 1898–2025: Achievements, Failures, Alternative Futures.* Houndmills, UK: Palgrave Macmillan, 2000.

Hayes, Louis D. *Introduction to Japanese Politics.* 5th ed. Armonk, NY: M.E. Sharpe, 2004.

O'Connor, Karen, and Larry J. Sabato. *American Government: Continuity and Change.* New York: Longman, 2008.

Ravenhill, John. *Global Political Economy.* 2nd ed. Don Mills, ON: Oxford University Press, 2008.

Yeşilada, Birol A., and David M. Wood. *The Emerging European Union.* 5th ed. New York: Longman, 2010.

CBC News Clips

Visit the companion website for *Politics: An Introduction* to listen to news clips from the CBC radio archives.

10 Politics in Developing States

LEARNING
OBJECTIVES

After reading this chapter, you will be able to:

- define the terms 'development' and 'developing'
- compare and contrast the political and economic challenges facing developing countries in the early twenty-first century
- assess the importance of democratization
- identify some of the links between political and economic development.

Introduction

Countries in the process of political and economic development face many of the same problems and challenges as those we consider to be 'developed'. Issues of justice, equality, economic growth and stability, and inflation, all feature in the political debates and conflicts of states in Latin America, Africa, Asia, and Eastern Europe. Governments, citizens, and corporations in developing countries, however, confront a wide range of challenges that the nations of Western Europe, Scandinavia, North America, and Japan have already overcome, or are unique to political and economic development in the early twenty-first century. These problems include overpopulation, disease control, capital flight, environmental degradation, democratization, public order, and the creation of a viable infrastructure.

Less Developed Countries (LDCs) countries that may be characterized by the following: low levels of per-capita income, high inflation and debt, large trade deficits, low levels of socioeconomic development, a lack of industrialization, or undeveloped financial or legal systems

In this chapter we will examine the political and economic systems of **Less Developed Countries (LDCs)**, and in particular two leading LDCs, Mexico and China. These countries face many different challenges between them, but also some that they share in common.[1] Each has taken a markedly different development path, and the road to development has presented them with obstacles large and small, short- and long-term, national and international.

Such problems at the beginning of the twenty-first century pose a strong challenge to the stability and well-being of the world's developing countries but they also provide the student of political economy with a myriad of interesting research cases. As we will see in this chapter, the dual challenges of political and economic development are linked, and many developing countries face a difficult situation in which they must stabilize their economies, an often painful process for ordinary people in economic terms, at the same time as they try to consolidate democratic practices and the legitimacy of their regimes.

A word should be said about the terminology used in this chapter. The poorer countries in the system have been referred to in a number of ways. During the Cold War, they were known by some as the **Third World** (after the First World of Western industrialized states and the Second World of the communist bloc). Others (quite inaccurately in geographic terms) divided the world into **North** (the wealthy countries) and **South** (the poorer states). Financial analysts and economists today talk of **'emerging markets,'** poorer economies with potential for future growth. This chapter, however, prefers to use the terms 'LDCs' and 'developing countries'.

What Is Development?

For many years development was seen in a purely economic sense, implying growth and industrialization of the economy and little else. Gradually we have come to see the problems of development in a multi-dimensional manner, accepting that progress must be understood in more than one way and that truly developed societies must provide more than just economic benefits for their members. Citizens should be involved, for example, in the decisions that affect their futures, either through group representation, direct democracy, or perhaps decentralization of power. The governing of society should be less arbitrary and more rules-oriented, guaranteeing due process of law and security of person. Of course economic growth should be a priority, but it has become obvious to us that the issue is far more complex. Questions of distribution, stability, and ensuring that growth is compatible with the protection of the environment are fundamental in building a sustainable development path.

Political and Social Development

The issue that has come to dominate discussions of political development in recent decades is that of democracy. Since the end of the Cold War democratization has been seen by both national and international authorities and organizations as a priority for underdeveloped countries, a political liberalization to go hand in hand with the progressive (and in some cases rather rapid) liberalization of their economies. But the spread of democracy throughout the world is but one feature of political and social development. LDCs are often young states, many having been created since the end of the Second World War and the retreat of **colonialism** (see later in this chapter), and lack well-established government institutions. What their societies seek in their development paths are essentially the political values (justice, order, freedom, etc.) described in Chapter 2. One of the most common values sought by developing country governments is legitimacy. In some cases the short history of their countries as independent states makes it difficult for governments to achieve true legitimacy in the eyes of the people. In

Third World
largely Cold War categorization of less developed nations that are not part of a structurally integrated system of global capitalism

North
industrialized nations, including Western Europe, North America, Japan, Australia, and New Zealand, that are part of a structurally integrated system of global capitalism

South
categorization of less developed nations that are not part of a structurally integrated system of global capitalism

Emerging markets
poorer economies with potential for future growth

Colonialism
exploitation of weaker country(ies) by stronger one(s), for political, strategic, or resource interests

10.1

The Human Development Index

Instead of focusing exclusively on the size of a nation's economy, or even on the size of the economy per person, the United Nations decided that it would use a broader indicator of national development that took into account a wide range of relevant factors. The United Nations Human Development Index (HDI) uses a combined measurement of income, life expectancy, and literacy to determine the level of individual development granted by national economies. These factors are chosen because they increase an individual's freedom to direct and control their own life. The index gives a rating to each country, and the closer that number is to one, the more highly developed it is according to the HDI. Countries such as Iceland, Canada, and Japan frequently appear at the top of this list with ratings above 0.95, but most of the world's LDCs fare less well. Countries such as China feature in the middle of the list (0.772), but Niger comes in at number 182 overall, with an HDI rating of only 0.34. It is noteworthy that all but one of the bottom 20 countries on the list are African states.

Table 10.1 Human Development Index 2009: Top 20 Nations vs. Bottom 20

Top 20 Countries (High Human Development)	Bottom 20 Countries (Low Human Development)
1. Norway	163. Côte d'Ivoire
2. Australia	164. Zambia
3. Iceland	165. Eritrea
4. Canada	166. Senegal
5. Ireland	167. Rwanda
6. Netherlands	168. Gambia
7. Sweden	169. Liberia
8. France	170. Guinea
9. Switzerland	171. Ethiopia
10. Japan	172. Mozambique
11. Luxembourg	173. Guinea-Bissau
12. Finland	174. Burundi
13. United States	175. Chad
14. Austria	176. Congo (Democratic Republic of the)
15. Spain	177. Burkina Faso
16. Denmark	178. Mali
17. Belgium	179. Central African Republic
18. Italy	180. Sierra Leone
19. Liechtenstein	181. Afghanistan
20. New Zealand	182. Niger

Source: UNDP (United Nations Development Programme). 2009. *Human Development Report 2009: Overcoming barriers: Human mobility and development.* New York: Palgrave Macmillan.

others it is not the brevity but rather the turbulence of their history that makes legitimacy an elusive goal.

Democracy, of course, is one way to achieve legitimacy in the eyes of both national and international societies. By including all adult citizens in the electoral process, by allowing voters to choose their government rather than having it imposed upon them, a democratic political system helps to guarantee its own survival. As we will see, however, in both countries studied in depth in this chapter, democratization is a complex and controversial issue. Democracy is difficult to institute in society, as the experience of democratization in Western Europe in the eighteenth, nineteenth, and twentieth centuries demonstrates. It requires the overthrow of established power elites and the creation of strong institutions that guarantee democratic representation. Primarily, of course, it requires the presence of a liberal ideology that will drive individuals and groups to fight for democracy.

It should not be thought that democracy acts as a cure-all for the political challenges faced by developing countries. Democracy, on its own, cannot rectify deep social divisions, for example, nor can it guarantee justice. It cannot eliminate the use of violence as a means of exercising power, nor the political advantages conferred by wealth. Democracy does not imply stability or even security. Neither should it be thought that it is necessarily the best-suited system for all societies. Most of human political history has been un-, even anti-, democratic. The norm throughout history has been repression of the many by the few, of might equalling right. Even those societies (tribal or otherwise) which have been egalitarian in nature have been based on the group or family rather than the individual. Many societies today still hold the group in higher regard than the individual and may thus not be ideally suited for democracy as practised by European and North American states.

On the other hand, liberal democracy appeals to us for the reasons we saw earlier in this book. Morally it makes sense to us as North Americans to accord every individual member of our society the same right to decide their political future. A commitment to democratic values means seeking peaceful resolutions to conflict before resorting to violence. Democracy, when applied in its Western form, means including groups and minorities, not excluding them, a quality that leads to a higher probability of stability and sense of community. Just as importantly, the history of many developing countries demonstrates that non-democratic regimes find they are unable to hold on to power either sooner or later, even if they are not then replaced by democratic regimes.[2]

As we saw in Chapter 9, democracy works in developed countries such as Canada, the United States, Japan, and in Europe because of the political institutions that enforce and implement the principles of democracy. Institutions such as a competitive party system, Parliaments or Congresses where elected representatives may not only voice the concerns of the electorate but also influence the policy process, electoral commissions that ensure that elections are run according to universally accepted rules and regulations, all encourage the use of democratic and non-violent means of resolving political conflicts. As we will see in the case of Mexico, an independent federal elections commission is essential if elections are to be free and fair, as is the involvement of observers from other countries and from international organizations.

If democracy is going to work and become embedded in a country's political culture, it is surely crucial that the electoral system function effectively. This means choosing a system that adequately represents the views and interests of significant minority groups and parties, while at the same time ensuring stability and a government's ability to both pass and implement legislation.

A free and independent media establishment is one of the private institutions that are desirable if democracy is to function effectively, yet in most LDCs this has remained an elusive goal. Governments in some countries control television, radio stations, and newspapers with little viable competition, whereas in others there are severe restrictions on reporting with censorship regulations that allow the government to control the flow of information. China is a perfect example of this. Not only does the Chinese government control the flow of information, it also censors the arts to prevent criticism of its own activities and has been active in censoring access to the Internet (see Box 10.2). For many developing countries there is still a shortage of access to reliable information and independent evaluation of the government and political system. However, as technology has become cheaper, and televisions and radios more commonplace, there has been a positive effect on both the spread and consolidation of democracy.[3]

But of course not all political institutions are concerned with democracy, though they can help to consolidate its place in society. The structure of political parties greatly influences the ability of the state to formulate and implement policy.[4] Other institutions help governments to rule. A well-run, professional, and independent bureaucracy will grant the government the expertise it needs to govern a country efficiently and effectively. A mature, rules-based, and egalitarian legal system will ensure equal and predictable treatment for a country's citizens and help to resolve private conflicts peacefully.

Human rights

rights granted to people on the basis of being human, not to be denied by governments; includes rights to life, liberty, religion, information, as well as economic, social, political, legal, and constitutional rights

10.2

The Beijing Olympics and Internet Censorship

In 2008 the eyes of the world fell on Beijing, China, as it hosted the summer Olympic Games. This was an opportunity for China to show the world how far it had come in terms of economic, political, and social development over the past 30 years. The infrastructure, planning, and the Games themselves were a huge success, generating enormous global television audiences. However, early on in the Games it became clear that the Chinese government was censoring journalists' access to the Internet in the official media centre. In its bid to host the Games in 2001, the Chinese government had promised to give journalists 'complete freedom to report' from the Games; however, when the time came, journalists found they were unable to access Internet websites related to **human rights** issues, Chinese politics, or Tibet. Despite international outcry at the censorship, and some slight changes in the level of censorship, journalists were never able to attain complete, unrestricted access during the Games.

A reliable, predictable, egalitarian, and transparent legal system is essential, of course, for the achievement of legal justice. Attaining justice is a vital element of political and social development because without it the government will face constant opposition from those treated unfairly by the system. Increasingly, the search for justice in LDCs is focused on the respect for human rights as understood by international society. A high level of **human rights abuses** is a strong signal that a country is socially and politically underdeveloped (though developed countries also commit such offences from time to time). Both of the countries studied in depth in this chapter have consistently been under international scrutiny for their human rights records in recent years, although each has used different methods to deal with this.

The legal system of a country can also be an important weapon in the defence against corruption. This particular problem has come into high profile in recent years as international aid agencies have linked their programs to efforts to reduce the influence of corruption in developing countries. There is an important connection between anti-corruption policies and democracy, of course; a system's benefits cannot be universally shared and enjoyed if they are reserved for those with economic, social, or political influence. The legal system must be seen to apply equally to all if all are to have respect for that system. Likewise, for government and the bureaucracy; without free and equal access to these institutions they will not be seen as legitimate. [5]

Restraining the non-legitimate use of violence is a further political challenge for developing countries. Around the world national governments fail to control all of their territory or face significant challenges from rebel or guerrilla groups. In Africa, Asia, and Latin America such groups threaten not just the sovereignty of states but also their survival in their present forms. The existence of rival military factions in a country may signify military weakness on the part of the government, but more importantly it denotes a lack of universal legitimacy. The same can be said of governments who fail to keep public order in their cities and towns. When there is rioting and widespread disrespect for the rule of law, governments must take measures (through either reform or suppression tactics) to ensure that the social and political systems survive.

A perennial issue for many LDCs has been the role of the military in politics. Where the military has not been placed under strict civilian control in a state's constitution, and thus restricted to a legitimate and restrained role in national affairs, there has been a tendency for the military to intervene in the political life of developing countries, especially during times of political, social, and economic crisis. Most such interventions claim to be in the broader national interest, and often military leaders argue that such actions are necessary to restore the right conditions for democracy to be successful. Many military coups are carried out on the principle that military rule will be temporary; yet most have retained control over politics much longer than they first promised.

Another concern involving the issue of force is territorial integrity. Although almost all developed countries have held their present geographic boundaries for extended periods of time, many developing countries are involved in border

Human rights abuses
maltreatment of human rights

10.3

Colombia: The War on Drugs and the FARC

Ingrid Betancourt (centre right) was released from captivity during a crackdown by the new president, Álvaro Uribe.

Colombia is a developing South American country that faces a host of challenges relating to economic and political development. However, Colombia has become synonymous over the past decade with the twin problems of drug trafficking and armed insurgency, seriously challenging the integrity of the Colombian state and the prospects for sustained development. Fundamental to understanding the problems of development in Colombia are the high levels of inequality that have marked the country's history.

The last decade of the twentieth century saw a progressive deterioration of government control of large areas of Colombian territory because drug cartels and rebel groups attacked government forces and corrupted government officials. However, in 2002 a new president, Álvaro Uribe, came to power and immediately launched an all-out offensive against left-wing rebels, in particular the Fuerzas Armadas Revolucionarias de Colombia (FARC), and against the drug lords. The Uribe government, using a multi-pronged attack involving intelligence, military action, and international co-operation, has achieved significant successes against both the drug cartels and the FARC, securing the release of long-term hostage Ingrid Betancourt. With considerable military assistance from the United States through Plan Colombia — an anti-drug initiative from the Bush administration — the government has beaten back rebel groups. Though armed rebel groups continue to be active throughout the country, the FARC has been vanquished from most urban areas and appears to be on the verge of collapse. The war on drugs continues but the Uribe government's determined approach looks to have turned the tide for the Colombian state.

disputes and conflicts with neighbouring states. It was 1998 before Peru and Ecuador settled their border dispute, a conflict that had continued for more than 40 years.[6] India and Pakistan continue to come to blows periodically regarding the region of Kashmir, over which they both claim sovereignty. Partially this is the result of the complex and often messy situations left behind by withdrawing colonial powers. If we examine the case of Africa, borders were drawn during colonial times without significant references to tribal or ethnic distribution, and this has resulted in a number of prolonged conflicts since the end of the colonial period. The war in Biafra, Nigeria, between 1967 and 1970, the war between Eritrea and Ethiopia, and the conflict between Somalia and Somaliland all stand out as legacies of colonialism and the messy end of that period. Partially, however, the problem also arises as national leaders seek to consolidate their domestic power and influence by unifying the electorate and important domestic constituencies behind a national cause involving conflict with a neighbouring state. As long as its territorial boundaries are disputed, there will probably be an enhanced role for the military in the political life of the nation. What's more, it is likely that a developing country will be forced to divert valuable resources away from other more deserving and productive purposes.

One such productive purpose, which has unfortunately remained a secondary goal in a large number of LDCs, is public education. The majority of developing countries have failed to develop effective systems of public education, and this hinders not only economic development but also the development of mature political and social institutions. The problems of instituting a comprehensive system of public education are enormous; not the least of them is the fact that in most LDCs child labour is very common, and indeed necessary for many families, if they are to generate sufficient income.

Another vital social issue is that of health care. Modern health care systems are incredibly expensive to run, absorbing more than 10 per cent of the GDP of countries such as Canada. LDCs, which have much smaller economies and tax bases, and generally much larger populations, are in no position to provide comprehensive health care at the level found in the developed world. This means that the majority of LDC citizens face a life plagued by the worry of ill-health and disease, which in turn has an enormous cost for the economy.[7] To compound the problem there is the fact that Sexually Transmitted Diseases (STDs) such as AIDS, and insect- and water-borne diseases such as malaria and cholera, are much more common in the developing world. For many countries in Africa, AIDS has become a threat not just to individuals and families, but also to the strength of the country as a whole.

One last issue that has risen in importance in recent years concerns questions of gender. Whereas women in the developed world made many important strides towards gender equality in political, social, and economic spheres in the twentieth century, in most LDCs women continue to face a far more difficult future than men. Not only do women earn much less than men for similar work (which, of course, also remains the case in most developed countries), many women are also denied reliable access to the vote, health care, and education.

10.4

AIDS and the Developing World

Due to the effect of weak education and health systems, the countries of the developing world have been harder hit by the global AIDS crisis than their developed counterparts. Infection rates are higher, treatment is relatively more expensive and largely unavailable, and social stigma and prejudices regarding the disease are more widespread.

The continent that continues to be hardest hit by the spread of the AIDS virus is Africa. There the infection rate is rising daily, and there seems to be little that health authorities, both national and from international organizations such as the World Health Organization (WHO), can do to stop its spread. Part of the problem stems from a lack of education, part from cultural values preventing the use of condoms, and part from economic realities. In Africa many men are forced to travel far from their homes to find work, spending months away from their families at a time. While separated from their wives, these migrant workers will have sex, more often than not unprotected sex, with local prostitutes. Because so many men have sexual relations with the same prostitutes, the rate of infection is very high indeed. These men then go back to their wives and families, to whom they pass on the disease.

In recent years some progress has been made in tackling the problem of treatment as developing countries such as Brazil, South Africa, and India have broken international patents on medicines to produce cheaper, generic versions of the drugs. This has helped treat those already infected, although the infection rate is still frighteningly high.

Table 10.2 The Problem of AIDS

Adults and Children Living with HIV (2007)

Global	33,000,000
Sub-Saharan Africa	22,000,000
East Asia	740,000
Oceania	74,000
South and South East Asia	4,200,000
Eastern Europe and Central Asia	1,500,000
Western and Central Europe	730,000
North Africa and the Middle East	380,000
North America	1,200,000
Caribbean	230,000
Latin America	1,700,000

Source: UNAIDS 2008 Report on the global AIDS epidemic (available at http://www.unaids.org/en/KnowledgeCentre/HIVData/GlobalReport/2008/)

10.5

Education, Gender, and the Oportunidades Program

A major challenge facing most developing countries is that of education. Throughout the developing world children drop out of education at an early age, not finishing their studies and leaving them ill-equipped to deal with the challenges of the modern world. The problem is particularly marked for girls. Parents often keep their daughters at home to help with household chores or to work in the fields because they believe that education is wasted on women.

In 2002, the Mexican government initiated a new social program called Oportunidades (Opportunities) aimed at getting more children to stay in school until at least the end of the secondary education system. By paying mothers a bonus depending on the age of the child and their attendance record in school, the program has been highly successful in boosting school attendance. An interesting, though controversial, aspect of the program is that mothers receive more money from the state if their daughters continue to attend school than they would for their sons. This has helped to drastically increase female school attendance. Serious questions remain, however, over the quality of the education received and whether the program is making a real difference in women's lives.

Economic Development

The economic development of LDCs is a highly contentious issue, and no sure path to economic development has been found. While some LDCs, in particular the **Newly Industrializing Countries (NICs)** of Asia, experienced high levels of growth from the 1960s to the late 1990s, developing countries in other parts of the world were unable to repeat that particular development path.[8] In the 1980s and 1990s the dominant philosophy of economic growth has been liberal, but its results are as yet uncertain. Debates continue to rage in most developing countries about the wisdom and benefits of free markets, open economies, and less government involvement in the economy. The future of economic development still seems to lie in liberal models, but questions continue to be raised about their sustainability (see later in this chapter).

Nor should it be thought that economic growth is enough to secure development. A number of other conditions must be met if economic growth is to have a positive impact on living standards. The first and most obvious of these is that the economy should grow at a rate higher than that of the population. If the population grows faster than the economy, the benefits received by the individual will gradually decline. Further, benefits and costs of economic development should be equitably divided up among society's members, if widespread support for the program of development is to remain.

Just as important for the long-term economic development of a country is the concept of sustainability. **Sustainable development** is a term that came into widespread use in the 1990s, and it marked a wholly new approach

Newly Industrializing Countries (NICs)
countries benefiting from external trade relationships, growing export markets, and burgeoning industrial development

Sustainable development
model of economic growth that seeks to use renewable resources so as not to destroy the environment in which human beings have to live

to the dilemma of development. Sustainable development recognizes that many models of economic growth result in severe environmental degradation and the use of non-renewable resources. Although such models may succeed in kick-starting economic growth and the process of development, they are unsustainable in the longer term. Sustainable development seeks a model of economic growth that does not rely on non-renewable resources and does not destroy the environment in which human beings have to live. Essentially it is a development path that does not compromise the ability of future generations to meet their own development goals. This is, of course, a very simple and logical calculation, at least in theory. The application of the principle of sustainable development has proven much more complex because strategies based on this concept have tended to be more expensive and have been slow to produce tangible gains.

Economic development has to be sustainable in other ways. First, it must be sustainable in the sense that it does not produce cycles of boom and bust, as the history of Mexico's economy demonstrates. Economic growth should ideally be more steady and progressive, producing smaller gains in the short term but greater benefits in the medium and long term. The chosen path of economic growth should also be politically sustainable. This generally means ensuring that the benefits of economic growth are widely dispersed and that the population in general experiences an improvement in its standard of living. Connected to this issue is the commonly observed **Kuznets Effect**. This economic formula demonstrates that as a country develops economically, income distribution will become more unequal before it becomes more equal. This means that it in the short to medium term, developing countries are likely to experience a widening gap between rich and poor. This has been one of the main criticisms of Mexico's liberal model of economic development, and as the country becomes more democratic, it becomes a greater problem for the Mexican government. China,

Kuznets Effect
economic formula that demonstrates that as a country develops economically, income distribution will become more unequal before it becomes more equal; named after Simon Kuznets, the Russian-American economist who formulated this concept

10.6

The Brundtland Commission Report and Sustainable Development

In 1987 the World Commission on Environment and Development (the Brundtland Commission) issued its report, entitled *Our Common Future*. In this report the commission prescribed a development path for LDCs that did not 'compromise the capacity of future generations to satisfy their own needs'. The report outlined the concept of sustainable development, that is, a form of development that does not rely upon the use of non-renewable resources and that does not destroy the environment in which we need to survive as a species.

Though this seems an uncontroversial proposal, many developing country governments have seen it otherwise. They have argued that the notion of sustainable development is another way that the wealthy countries have tried to pass the costs for environmental protection onto the poor in the international system, while those same wealthy countries long ago destroyed their own forests and have pumped billions of tons of pollutants into the earth, oceans, and atmosphere.

too, faces this problem, and it may become a political problem in the twenty-first century as the gap between rural and urban populations widens.

Since the mid-twentieth century the developing world has attempted both integration with and isolation from the wealthy countries and the international system. Purely national development proved too slow and inefficient for most LDCs in the postwar period, and this was one of the factors that propelled them to attempt liberalization and opening of their economies in the 1980s. However, the international financial and economic crises that hit many LDCs in the second half of the 1990s caused a re-evaluation of openness and, in particular in some parts of South America, governments and societies have turned away from liberalism to more socialist economic models.

The Link between Political and Economic Development

One of the most perplexing and challenging aspects of development studies is the analysis of the connection between political and economic development. Often the argument is made that sustainable economic growth and stability cannot be achieved without stable democratic institutions. Almost as often we hear that workable democracy cannot be achieved without first obtaining high rates of economic growth.[9] Certainly the connection has often been made between economic liberalization and democratization, particularly in the aftermath of the end of the Cold War and the dual transitions in Eastern Europe.

Yet the relationship between these two spheres remains elusive. There does appear to be a connection between economic development and progress and more stable democratic institutions. In those countries where socioeconomic inequality reaches high levels, democracy is often under threat. But some analysts have argued that undemocratic regimes may actually be better suited to the business of reforming and modernizing an LDC economy, most often making reference to Chile's experience under General Augusto Pinochet, or as we will see in this chapter, in China since the late 1970s. The argument here is that economic liberalization and reform incurs high levels of social and political costs, and an autocratic or authoritarian regime is better equipped to deal with the pressures arising from these costs. These two examples, however, do not seem to be representative. A more thorough examination of LDCs demonstrates that democracy in those countries actually contributes to stability, and stability to the prospects for economic growth.

Population Growth

One of the perennial challenges for most developing countries is the size of their populations and, more importantly, the rate of population growth. Many LDCs experience a doubling of their populations every 30 to 35 years, and that is with an annual growth rate of around 2 per cent. If the population growth rate

10.7

The Politics of Population: Nigeria

Due to the ever-present tensions between the regions and ethnic groups of Nigeria, the question of regional population size has been a perennial issue of contention. In 1962 the government carried out a census to determine the correct distribution of political power and financial resources. This became a heavily contested issue and the importance invested in the census was reflected in its results, and the reaction to those results. First, the census showed that the South had grown rapidly in size to the point where it now surpassed the historically more populous North. Second, it quickly became clear that the figures for the Eastern region were inflated. In response to this the North announced that it had overlooked 8 million people in its region, a number sufficient to restore its numerical superiority.

When the census effort was repeated a year later, the outcome was even more ridiculous. The results showed that the population had increased by over 80 per cent since the last census ten years previously, but still with a Northern majority. Despite this incredible outcome, the North's political forces managed to secure official acceptance of the census, thus guaranteeing them higher levels of support from the federal government.

is closer to 3.5 per cent, then the population will double every 25 years. This can cause immense strains on the economic system. If the standard of living of the average citizen is to improve, the economy must grow at a rate faster than that of the population. New jobs, new housing, and education must be provided for all of these new people. The issue of population control is, of course, a highly contentious one. The use of barrier methods of birth control is still limited in many countries (particularly in Africa and Latin America) for cultural and religious reasons, and overcoming these obstacles has proven incredibly difficult. China, as we will see, achieved considerable success in limiting population growth in the latter part of the twentieth century, but this was only done with the use of policies that were repressive and highly intrusive into the private lives of its citizens.

One of the costs of population growth comes in the form of government services. Providing health care for a rapidly expanding population is enormously costly. So is providing public utilities such as potable water and electricity. Rapidly expanding populations also lead to massive movements of human populations, both within a country and outside, in the form of migration. As can be seen in the case of Mexico, this leads to strains on government services and also on Mexico's relations with its northern neighbour, the US.

As much as population growth is a problem, it can also eventually become a strength too.[10] China's enormous population will constitute the world's largest national market at some point in the first half of the twenty-first century, and this will give China increased economic influence in the international system. India's population is growing even more rapidly than China's, and its recent burst of economic growth has turned it into a force with which to be reckoned.

The Role of International Organizations

One final word that must be said about development in general concerns international aid and development organizations. The international aspect of development has become more and more important to LDCs in recent years. Most prominent have been the World Bank and IMF, whose lending activities have been essential to the rescue of developing country economies in Asia, Africa, and Latin America. Though the IMF is not officially a development organization, its financial facilities are used almost exclusively by LDCs.

A strong and credible criticism of international development organizations in recent history has been that they try to impose neoliberal, free-market policies upon LDC governments. In many of the developing world's crises during the past 30 years we have seen the IMF and the World Bank forcing free-market policies on these countries, even when they are not prepared for the high levels of competition that ensue.

China: The Politics of an Emerging Global Power

China is the world's most populous country with roughly 1.3 billion inhabitants and it will, at some point in the twenty-first century, have the world's largest economy. China is a nuclear power and occupies one of the five permanent seats on the United Nations Security Council. During the past 30 years China has achieved very high and sustained rates of economic growth. China has managed to pull hundreds of millions of its own citizens out of poverty, and has provided a strong stimulus for economic growth at the global level.

Yet for all of these qualities, China still faces some serious and deep-rooted problems. A large percentage of its citizens remain in poverty. China's political system remains highly undemocratic, and there appear to be few signs of it becoming democratic in the near future. Health care and environmental protection are still woefully underdeveloped, and there are significant ethnic and regional tensions across the country.

This section studies the politics of China and addresses the major challenges lying ahead for the Chinese people and their government. It shows us a country that is indelibly marked by its history, and in which reform of the economic system has not been accompanied by real political change.

Chinese History: The Heritage of Imperialism and Revolution

Long before the countries of Western Europe had organized themselves into coherent nation-states that we would recognize today, the Chinese empire had united a huge territory and many disparate peoples under one system of government, using the strong arm of military force to bring them peace, prosperity, and innovation. During the more than two thousand years of imperial rule, China developed a mode of government that was highly authoritarian, willing to use violence to suppress dissent, and which stressed the value of the group over that of the individual. This governmental and cultural tradition continues to exert a strong influence on modern China, though at the dawn of the twenty-first century the pervasive values of Western culture are knocking hard at China's door.

The end of China's imperial history came with an armed uprising in 1911 and 1912. This ushered in a long period of civil war in China, in which regional warlords struggled for supremacy and in which two parties, the Nationalist Kuomintang Party (KMT) and the **Chinese Communist Party** (CCP), a party committed to Marxist revolution, struggled for control of the country's government.[11] During a brief alliance in the late 1920s, the KMT turned on the CCP and slaughtered hundreds of thousands of its supporters. After that, the CCP split into two competing factions. The more successful of these was led by Mao Zedong (sometimes written as Mao Tse Tung and also known as Chairman Mao); it turned away from the traditional focus on the working class and towards the rural peasant class, a group that made up over 85 per cent of the Chinese population. Mao created the People's Liberation Army (PLA), a guerrilla army made up of poorly equipped peasants that was at first unable to withstand the KMT's professionally trained soldiers, but which in time became the country's dominant military force.[12]

Before and during the Second World War China was occupied by Japanese forces, and this invasion of Chinese sovereignty discredited the KMT in the eyes of the Chinese people. With the close of that war, the civil conflict resumed and this time the CCP defeated the nationalist forces. By 1949 the KMT and its supporters withdrew to the nearby island of Taiwan, and the People's Republic of China was born with Mao as its leader. Communist ideology governed policy in the People's Republic, with Mao developing his own branch of communist thought, one based on constant vigilance against the forces of capitalism and the bourgeois or middle classes. In practice this brought a turbulent and bloody post-revolution history to the country.

China's economy grew rapidly in the period from 1949 to 1976, an achievement brought about by a series of policies in which the government played a central role. From 1949 to 1958 the government used Soviet-style policies of industrialization that had been employed in Stalinist Russia but which were ultimately not well suited to China's mostly agrarian economy. From 1958 to 1962 Mao instituted the **Great Leap Forward**, a program of economic policies designed to revolutionize rural production by replacing private ownership of land with communes, in which all agricultural production was to be sold to the state.[13] The chaos that ensued from this program resulted in the loss of, in some estimates, 25 million lives from starvation and malnutrition.

As horrific as these figures are, they represent only one of the more unpleasant features of Mao's rule over China. Up until his death in 1976 Mao and his followers used terror tactics to maintain control and to weed out dissident factions. Most infamous was his program of the Cultural Revolution, in which Mao oversaw

Chinese Communist Party (CCP)

governing political party in China, founded in 1921 as part of revolutionary movement

Great Leap Forward

Chinese program of economic policies designed to revolutionize rural production by replacing private ownership of land with communes, in which all agricultural production was to be sold to the state the creation of Red Guard units throughout the country, units that were aimed at eliminating any subversive bourgeois or capitalist elements in Chinese society. During this program of repression, between 3 and 20 million people were killed.

The Origins of Modern China

One political party, the CCP, has dominated China's politics, and there are few prospects of a viable opposition emerging from outside the ruling party. Politics as they transpire in China can only be understood if one understands the internal struggles and processes within the CCP. Even before the death of Mao Zedong in 1976, Chinese political and economic development was determined and shaped by such divisions, as witnessed by the struggle between the Red faction, a radical Marxist group led by Mao himself, and the Expert faction, a more pragmatic grouping led by the Chinese president, Liu Shaoqi, and the future leader of China, Deng Xiaoping. Though the Red faction was victorious in this struggle and Mao imprisoned or executed many of the leading members of the Expert faction, it was the ideas of the latter group that would come to dominate Chinese development at the end of the twentieth century.

When Mao died in 1976 his passing was marked by a power struggle within the CCP for leadership. Mao's widow and three of his most radical supporters, known collectively as the Gang of Four, were held up as scapegoats and blamed for the horrors of the later years of Maoist rule. Hua Guofeng, Mao's immediate successor, had the Gang of Four arrested. Hua was soon replaced by Deng Xiaoping, and much of the old CCP cadre was weeded out.[14] Maoist policies and ideology were officially discredited, and the modernization of China began apace.

Yet the internal divisions within the CCP did not end there. Chinese development since the early eighties has been defined by the struggle within the communist party between those, like Deng, who favour a rapid transition towards a market-oriented economy, and those who prefer to see a slow and gradual movement in the same direction. A radical return to communist production has long since ceased to be a viable alternative for the CCP and China, and adherents of such Maoist policies have no voice in the politics of modern China.

How is the CCP organized? First of all it must be noted that the party is massive in size, with over 50 million members, so that it reaches down through every level of Chinese society. It is organized hierarchically from the national level down through provincial and local levels, with the Politburo and Standing Committee at the top of the CCP's structure. It is in these two bodies that the major policy directions and important day-to-day decisions are determined. Though the National Party Congress (NPC) officially serves as the highest authority in the CCP, it plays a relatively minor role in legitimizing rather than directing government policy, and the only other body at the national level which performs an important function is the Central Committee, which serves as a representative body for the members of the CC and votes on major policies. Having said this, the NPC has at times played a role in displaying popular discontent with government policies, as happened in the debate over the Three Gorges dam in 1992, which took place shortly after the Tiananmen Square massacre. Though

10.8

The Tiananmen Square Massacre

One of the most memorable photos in history: a lone protestor stands in front of Chinese tanks during the Tiananmen Square demonstrations.

The economic boom that China experienced since Deng Xiaoping began his program of economic reforms brought not only increased wealth to the country but also new political problems. These problems involved calls for democratization and greater choice in the political arena, but also complaints brought on by a growing income gap between rich and poor, and between rural and urban populations. The result of this growing discontent was a mass protest in the summer of 1989 in Tiananmen Square in the heart of the nation's capital, Beijing. For several weeks the square was occupied by protesters, whose most vocal demands concerned the opening up of the Chinese political system. Coming as it did at the same time as the end of the Cold War in Europe, many Western observers predicted that this would mark the beginning of a similar political transition in China.

The reality, as it turned out, was quite the opposite. On June 4, Chinese tanks rolled into the square, destroying protestors' barricades and killing several hundred of them. International condemnation of the massacre was immediate, yet the Chinese government neither expressed remorse nor gave any sign of reforming the nation's political system.

the government is not directly accountable to the NPC, the NPC elects the Central Committee, and the government will face pressure from that body to respond to discontent manifested in the Congress.

This last example points to an often neglected fact of Chinese politics, namely, that pluralism exists in the system, albeit in a very different form to that which we find in democratic systems in Canada and other advanced capitalist nations.

Though the most important officials in the CCP do not depend on popular re-election for their mandates, they must always be mindful of their power bases in other areas, such as the military and important sections of the communist party. In her 1994 study of the liberalization of the Chinese economy, *How China Opened Its Door*, Susan Shirk[15] demonstrated this point by examining the way in which economic reform depended upon support from within the government and party structure, as well as upon China's quite decentralized federal structure, for its success. The role of internal party support for economic reforms was of particular importance during times of political instability and especially during leadership struggles, she found. As we learn more about the internal workings of the CCP, we should expect that this way of explaining Chinese politics will take on increasing importance.

Chinese Economic Reform

We tend to think that the emergence of a market-oriented economy in China only really began in the 1990s with the end of the Cold War. In fact the process began long before the fall of the Soviet Union was ever envisaged. The reform of the centrally planned Maoist economy of the 1970s began in earnest almost as soon as Mao had died. Deng Xiaoping, who had proposed economic reform in the 1960s and been imprisoned for his audacity, led a steady process of introducing market-oriented practices to economic management in China.[16] From the late 1970s onwards the Chinese government began decentralizing production and economic decision-making, giving more power to the provinces, which served as an incentive for them to increase productivity. A further step in the early years of economic reform was the institution of rural enterprise reform in 1979, when the system of collectives was gradually replaced with a system giving responsibility to household farms. These households were entitled to hold on to the profits they received from their agricultural production. Though they still had to sell their required quota to the state, these farms were allowed to sell any surplus goods at free-market prices, thus giving them the incentive to increase productivity. This incentive appears to have worked well, as productivity increased rapidly in the early 1980s.

Following on from rural reform, the Chinese government in the 1980s focused on expanding the non-state sector and increasing inter-firm competition in the economy. This program resulted in large increases in private sector employment and in productivity and competitiveness. Throughout the later eighties and 1990s there were further market reforms and the gradual opening up of China's economy to foreign trade and investment with the implementation of the **Open Door policy** and the creation of **Special Economic Zones** (SEZs).[17] By the end of the century China was experiencing the highest levels of foreign investment in the world, and was seeking membership in the World Trade Organization, the global trading regime.

The Chinese government, however, maintains active involvement in the economy. In addition to its role as economic planner and manager, the government also acts as banker and entrepreneur, continuing to control many

Open Door policy
approach taken by Chinese government starting in the late 1970s to introduce the Chinese economy (and by extension political system) to the Western world

Special Economic Zones
regions in China with different economic regulatory controls and more independence meant to spur economic growth

state-owned industries. Large-scale privatization of Chinese industry had still not occurred by the end of the 1990s, but mergers and joint ventures with foreign multinational corporations (MNCs) had dramatically changed the shape of the Chinese economic landscape.

China has also been highly successful in controlling one of the most import-ant areas of growth for most LDCs, that of the population. By limiting its citizens to one child per couple, the government has been able to contain population expansion to within reasonable limits. The methods used by the government, however, go against most Western conceptions of the right to privacy and free-dom of choice. The government has severely limited the individual rights of many Chinese men and women, and this may in the future be unsustainable. On the positive side, real income growth throughout history has resulted in lower reproduction rates, so this problem may in time solve itself.

The results of China's economic reforms are that the country has consist-ently experienced the highest rates of economic growth in the world, surpassing even the Asian Tigers (i.e., Hong Kong, Singapore, South Korea, and Taiwan) with annual rates of growth around 10 per cent. China's economic strength and sound management ensured that the country weathered the Asian economic crisis that began in 1997 without having to devalue its currency or experiencing high levels of capital flight.

Future Challenges for China

In the twenty-first century, China's prospects may at first look promising, but the country faces many challenges in both the political and economic spheres. Politically the government must face international condemnation of its human rights record at the same time as an increasingly wealthy middle class will likely demand greater freedom of choice in the political sphere. Human rights continue to be a problem for the Chinese government, and it faces significant international opposition to its policies concerning political prisoners, labour camps, and free-dom of expression. The political protests that culminated in the Tiananmen Square crackdown are also likely to resurface, and the government will once again be faced with the choice between tolerance and repression. A policy of tolerance would be more popular with foreign governments and human rights groups, but it may encourage further questioning of the Chinese political system as a whole, threatening the hold that the CCP has over the country.

In the economic realm, the challenges that face China today are still considerable. The reform of the Chinese economy must be seen as a work in progress that must continue to bring tangible benefits to key constituencies in China if it is to remain sustainable. The government must increase agricultural prices and public investment in agriculture if production levels are to rebound to the levels they reached in the 1990s. Rural poverty also remains a problem, and the government of Jiang Zemin should not forget Mao's lesson that the key to Chinese political power lies with the peasantry. The government must also continue to modernize the country's infrastructure, building roads, bridges, and electrical networks to support a modern economy. However, all of this costs

10.9

Taiwan

The exile of Kuomintang forces from mainland China in 1949 led to the birth of a new state in the international system, Taiwan or Chinese Taipei. The United States and its allies immediately recognized Taiwan as the legitimate government of the whole of China, denying recognition to Mao's communist regime. Since then the mainland Chinese government has campaigned successfully to have itself recognized as the legitimate voice of the Chinese people. However, it has also campaigned continuously to limit the recognition of Taiwan by other states in the international system, and has used the threat of force to attempt to destabilize and weaken the strength of the government in Taipei. In recent years these threats reached new heights, with the Beijing government firing missiles towards the island. This brought about an immediate response from the US government, which has committed itself to the defence of Taiwan.

Taiwan is more than just a cause of tension in the China Sea, however. Since 1949 it has become a highly successful economy, industrializing at a rapid rate and dramatically raising the standard of living of its people. However, it has done so with the help of an authoritarian political system that has consistently limited political freedoms. Ironically, the Chinese government itself has looked to Taiwan as an example of how to implement a capitalist economic system without democratization.

huge amounts of money, and the government will be forced to find additional sources of revenue by reforming the nation's tax system, a move that could prove highly unpopular.

China as a country will also have to face other growing pains. As some regions grow faster than others, political tensions will emerge and calls for redistribution will either have to be ignored, thus further aggravating these tensions, or placated, risking the alienation of wealthy provinces. Ethnic problems have already reared their head in the Western provinces, particularly in those with large Muslim populations. The government will either have to provide sufficient economic benefits to these people or use the PLA to suppress rebellion. Lastly, China has to face the responsibilities of becoming a regional power and decide if its future lies in encouraging regional co-operation or trying to dominate the weaker countries on its borders. It must decide what to do with Taiwan and how to define its relationship with the United States, which continues to be the most important force in the Pacific. The relationship with the US has become particularly complex in recent years as China has become the largest holder of US dollars in its national reserves, amounting to over $1.3 trillion. It is the largest holder of US national debt, and this gives it a privileged position. But it also exposes China to the dangers of devaluation of the dollar, meaning that its reserves and debt holdings would be worth less as time goes by. How China restructures its economic and political relations with the US is one of the key questions facing the world in the twenty-first century.

Mexico: The Challenges of Democratization

Perhaps more than any other developing country, Mexico highlights both the problematic link between political and economic development and the divorce between the theory and practice of political economy. Mexico is a democracy in which only one party has held power during most of its existence in its present form (though this may soon change).[18] Mexico has a presidential system which on paper is almost identical to that of the United States, yet in practice the Mexican Congress has acted as a mere rubber stamp to presidential policy initiatives. Mexico is an NIC and an emerging market, yet every time it appears to be getting close to achieving its goal of developed country status it seems to fall into economic crisis and has to begin the long climb back. Mexico is a country that, it is claimed, has the highest number of billionaires per capita, but that has regions where more than 50 per cent of its people live in extreme poverty.

History

Mexico was one of the first areas of the New World colonized by the Spanish in the fifteenth and sixteenth centuries, and the chaos of conquest was followed by an equally turbulent birth and adolescence as a nation. Mexico's early history saw the assimilation of indigenous and imperialist cultures, with much intermarrying between Spanish and native peoples. This is not to say that indigenous peoples fared better than their counterparts in Canada and the US; disease, war, and episodes of genocide all took their toll in the country. Unlike Canada and the US, however, Mexico was an incredibly rich colony for many years, promising unimaginable reserves of gold and silver to the conquering nation. As has seemed to happen throughout Mexican history, this wealth failed to produce lasting benefits for Mexico itself or for its people.

Mexico's history as an independent country began in 1821 with the end of the war of independence against Spain. Chaos and deep political instability followed, with a succession of weak presidencies. A disastrous war against the United States in 1848 and the secession of the state of Texas left Mexico with only half of its original territory, and the country found itself in an impoverished and uncertain situation. The solution to a part of these problems was found in the autocratic, authoritarian rule of Porfirio Díaz, who became president of Mexico in 1876. However, though he was highly successful in stabilizing the country and attracting foreign investment into Mexico, Díaz headed a gravely repressive regime, which was arbitrary in its rule and severely limited individual rights.

The reward for Díaz's repression came in 1910 when several groups rose up in revolution against his regime. Most notable among them was the band led by Emiliano Zapata, a peasant of both indigenous and Spanish heritage who sought to defend farmers and native rights against the central government. The revolution proved a long and bloody affair that resulted in the coming to power of the **Partido Revolucionario Institucional** (Institutional Revolutionary Party), or PRI, as it is most commonly known in Mexico. This party ruled Mexico for more

Partido Revolucionario Institucional (PRI)
Institutional Revolutionary Party of Mexico

than seventy years and, like the Díaz regime, provided considerable stability to Mexico. Unfortunately, it also shared some less desirable features with Díaz, such as repressing political opposition — an at times authoritarian style of governance — and limiting the freedom of the media.

Mexico's Political System

Mexico has, in theory, a highly democratic and inclusive political system that closely mirrors that of the United States, at least at first glance. The Mexican constitution sets up a federal system in which the powers of the president are balanced and checked by those of the Congress. Individual states (of which there are 32, including the Distrito Federal, or Federal District of Mexico City) are given considerable powers, something reflected in the official title of the country, Estados Unidos de Mexico, or United States of Mexico. Each state has its own elected state legislature and governor (the Distrito Federal having its own mayor, one of the most influential positions in the Mexican political system). In reality, however, the country's political system is highly centralized and has been since the revolution. The federal government controls most spending (over 85 per cent), with state and municipal governments (*municipios*) sharing the rest. To make matters worse, *municipios* depend on the upper levels of government for over 80 per cent of their income, having very few independent sources on which to draw.

This centralization in taxation and government spending has been compounded by the fact that many of the states of Mexico are desperately poor, whereas others (particularly in the north) have income levels close to those of some developed countries. The divergence in wealth and influence means that there is little unity among the states.[19]

As noted earlier, for many years one party, the PRI, dominated Mexican politics. The dominance of the PRI meant that the governing party was able to limit the independence of the states through **patronage**, or the awarding of key government positions to favoured and loyal supporters. Since 2000, however, and the coming to power of the Partido Acción Nacional (PAN or National Action Party), this kind of control has been weakened and the governors have begun to play an important role, not only at the state level, but also to once again be considered key national political actors.

Patronage
awarding of key government positions to favoured and loyal supporters

The Mexican Presidency

The Mexican presidency has traditionally been the focal point of power in the system. As chief executive and head of state, the president is given wide-ranging powers under the constitution, which creates the potential for presidential dominance of the other branches of government. In the past, with the domination by the PRI of national politics, the president has traditionally been responsible for almost all of the important legislative initiatives that are passed into law by the Congress. Thanks to long-running PRI dominance of both the presidency and Congress, legislation initiated in Los Pinos (the Mexican equivalent of the White House) has rapidly become law. Up until the 1980s this power was used by many Mexican presidents to alter the constitution; however, since that decade the PRI

Sexenio
six-year term for the
Mexican presidency

Political cohabitation
political co-operation
among parties without
forming a coalition

Political gridlock
lack of political progress
because of entrenched
differing of opinions

has been unable to obtain the two-thirds majority needed to effect a constitutional amendment, because of increased electoral competition.

The president in Mexico is popularly elected but limited to one six-year term (or *sexenio*). This limitation was created as a response to the Mexican experience of dictatorship under Porfirio Díaz in the late nineteenth, early twentieth century. For more than 70 years after the Mexican Revolution, every president was from the PRI (or its predecessor the PNR or National Revolutionary Party), but this changed in 2000 with the election of Vicente Fox from the PAN. Since then, power has been passed to another PAN president, Felipe Calderón; however, in 2006 the presidential election was incredibly close, with the candidate from the Partido de la Revolucíon Democrática (PRD), Andrés Manuel López Obrador, losing by only a few thousand votes. We now have the very real probability of the presidency alternating between different parties, thus strengthening Mexican democracy.

The Mexican Congress

Like the United States of America, Mexico's Congress is divided into upper and lower chambers, the Chamber of Deputies and Senate, respectively. Traditionally, however, unlike the United States, there has been very little division and conflict between the legislative and executive branches of government in Mexico because of the dominance of the PRI in both branches. However, in 1997 this changed when the PRI lost its majority in Congress, and **political cohabitation** between the Congress and presidency has become a reality.[20] This has made policy-making much more complicated in Mexico, sometimes leading to **political gridlock** between the two branches, but in general it has led to a stronger democratic system than before.[21]

Elections in Mexico

In 1988, with one-third of the votes counted in the presidential election, the FDN (Frente Democrático Nacional) coalition presidential candidate, Cuauhtémoc Cárdenas (before he joined the PRD), held a clear lead over the PRI candidate Carlos Salinas. At that point the computers tallying the votes lost power.[22] When power was restored, Salinas had gained the lead and went on to win the election, though by a very small margin. Though the PRI denied tampering with the election, and though post-election opinion polls suggested that Salinas would probably have secured victory regardless, the 1988 election highlighted the very real problem of electoral fraud in Mexican politics. Since then, the Federal Electoral Institute (Instituto Federal Electoral or IFE) has greatly improved its elections monitoring, thanks in no small part to support from international and foreign national agencies, both governmental and non-governmental. Until 2006, the IFE was recognized throughout Mexico as being an honest guarantor of free and fair elections. In fact it was so successful that the IFE has become an important international actor, participating in elections monitoring in other countries around the world. The role of IFE is crucial in Mexico because its work is the only way that elections have come to be seen as legitimate.

However, in the 2006 presidential election, the IFE's reputation came under attack. With widespread reports of electoral fraud, miscounting of votes, and

Carlos Salinas won the Mexican presidency in 1988 under suspicious circumstances.

entire ballot boxes going missing, the result of the election hung in the balance for months before the PAN candidate, Felipe Calderón, was finally declared the unequivocal winner. In the meantime, however, the IFE was accused of hiding evidence, of covering up illegal practices by the major political parties, of allowing the government to use the advertising of public programs as a thin cover for electioneering, and of generally failing to guarantee free and fair elections. Following this, the governing council of the IFE was changed and a new group of councillors took over. It remains to be seen if the IFE can recover its prestige.

The Mexican Economy

In terms of natural endowments, Mexico is one of the world's richest lands. The country has vast oil and gas reserves, huge forests, access to ocean resources on both the Atlantic and Pacific sides, and tourism opportunities that would make any country jealous. Yet because of mismanagement, exploitation, and corruption Mexico has been unable to take full advantage of these resources.

In the twentieth century national economic development was driven by the state for long periods. Between the revolution and the 1980s Mexico went through a period of rapid industrialization that raised expectations among Mexicans that they would one day join the ranks of the First World or wealthy nations. The Mexican government acted not only as economic planner and manager, but also as owner and director of many of Mexico's most important industries, most significantly and symbolically of PEMEX (Petróleos Mexicanos), the nation's oil company. The nationalization of such industries during the middle of the century went along with a large degree of state intervention in the economy as a whole, regulating both wages and prices. In this period Mexico experienced high levels of growth, particularly as a result of the policy of stabilized development in the 1960s.

PEMEX
Petróleos de Mexicanos — Mexico's national oil company

In the 1970s, however, economic development became much more complex in Mexico, despite the discovery of huge oil reserves in the Gulf of Mexico in 1976. The governments of Luis Echeverría (1970–6) and José López Portillo (1976–82) dramatically increased government spending and borrowing, mostly from foreign banks. This money was not spent wisely, however, and was used up in unproductive projects and public-sector wages. With the onset of the Latin American Debt Crisis (see Chapter 13) in the mid-1980s, the billions of dollars owed by Mexico created a national financial and economic crisis, which required the intervention of the IMF and World Bank to stabilize and later resolve. For Mexico, as for much of Latin America and the developing world, the 1980s was a lost decade, where very little positive economic growth was seen, living standards and real wages declined, and the enthusiasm and optimism of earlier decades evaporated.

Economic Liberalization and Openness

Beginning in 1982 with the Miguel de la Madrid *sexenio*, Mexico gradually opened and liberalized its economy, allowing foreign competition into the country and slowly removing the state from direct involvement in the economy. A key factor in this liberalization was the demand made by the IMF that the Mexican government improve the efficiency of its economy through policies of structural adjustment.

Portfolio investment
acquisition of shares (stocks) in a corporate actor for the purpose of profit; does not imply ownership

Foreign direct investment
investment in real foreign assets, such as domestic structures, equipment, and organizations

From a largely closed and state-run economy, Mexico has transformed itself into an open and relatively dynamic one. The role of the private sector has increased; foreign investment, both **portfolio investment** (short-term capital able to come into and leave a national economy with ease) and **foreign direct investment** (FDI), have grown dramatically, and Mexico has become an active proponent of free trade. On this last point, Mexico became the first developing country in the world to join a free trade association with developed countries when it signed the North American Free Trade Agreement (NAFTA) in 1992. Studies seem to indicate that this has benefited Mexico, guaranteeing the country access to the markets of Canada, but much more importantly the United States.[23]

The NAFTA was an important event for Mexico because it signalled once again that the country was close to First World status. President Carlos Salinas de Gortari, who pushed for Mexican membership in this organization and signed the treaty for Mexico, was determined to bring Mexico into a true partnership with the US, and the NAFTA marked the high point of that effort. Mexican hopes, however, were dashed at the end of 1994 when, less than 12 months after the NAFTA came into force, Mexico went into deep economic and financial crisis. Fortunately this crisis took much less time to stabilize and resolve than the Debt Crisis of the 1980s, but its effects on the general population were just as keenly felt. Since the crisis, which again required massive borrowing from the IMF to resolve, Mexico has continued with its liberal economic policies, examining privatization of many national industries, including PEMEX, and signing a series of free trade treaties. However, despite some important advances in terms of poverty reduction, Mexico's economy faces major challenges in the years to come. It has been overtaken by other LDCs, such as Brazil, India, and China, in terms of competitiveness and growth levels, and although Mexico has maintained financial and economic stability, it must grow more quickly and achieve better income distribution if the aspirations of its people are to be met.

The Future of Mexico

As Mexico enters the second decade of the twenty-first century its future is far from certain. Major problems endure, such as political and economic corruption, economic mismanagement, and human rights abuses, but at the same time there is reason to be hopeful. Democratization and economic liberalization are beginning to bring perceptible benefits to Mexicans, and the country appears to be handling the transition to a multi-party electoral system well, without sacrificing too much of its stability.

At the time of writing, however, Mexico faces a major challenge in the form of public security, organized crime, and drug trafficking. Large areas of the country have slipped beyond the federal government's control, with drug lords having bribed or threatened public officials to the point where there is no effective government. The Calderón administration, with significant help from the United States, is engaged in a full-scale war on drugs, with the military being used to patrol city streets in the north of the country and to conduct campaigns against the drug cartels. Mexicans themselves increasingly feel as though they live in a permanent state of siege, and the rising rate of kidnapping and violence in both cities and rural areas is alarming.[24] If the federal government fails to meet the challenge posed by the drug business, Mexico could slip into crisis and lawlessness, prompting a dilemma for the United States over whether to intervene to bring stability or not.

Conclusion

This chapter has introduced you to some of the myriad challenges that face developing countries as they enter the twenty-first century. China and Mexico have some elements of these challenges in common, such as the need to secure the support of key constituencies for economic reform, but at the same time they exist at different stages of development in widely divergent social, political, geographical, and economic settings. Part of the challenge for each of these countries, as for all LDCs, is to find their place in an increasingly interdependent world, and to seek out co-operative modes of development that harness the economic power of the developed states. They can only do this by understanding the nature of the international system, a system to which this book now turns.

Self-Assessment Questions

1. Why do you think there are rich and poor countries in the world?
2. Why have some LDCs been able to achieve sustainable growth while others have failed?
3. What is the link between political and economic development?
4. How important is democracy to political stability in your opinion, and why?
5. What should international organizations and foreign governments do to encourage democracy and respect for human rights?

Weblinks

Debt and Development
www.globalissues.org/issue/28/third-world-
    debt-undermines-development

Human Rights Watch
www.hrw.org

Poverty
www.globalissues.org/issue/2/causes-of-poverty

Transparency International
www.transparency.org

UN Human Development Index
http://hdr.undp.org/en/statistics/

UNCTAD
www.unctad.org

World Bank
www.worldbank.org

Further Reading

Balaam, David N., and Michael Veseth. *Introduction to International Political Economy*. Upper Saddle River, NJ: Prentice Hall, 2001.

Cohn H., Theodore. *Global Political Economy: Theory and Practice*. 4th ed. New York: Pearson Longman, 2008.

Dominguez, Jorge, and Michael Shifter. *Constructing Democratic Governance in Latin America*. Baltimore, MD: Johns Hopkins University Press, 2003.

Eisenstadt, Todd A. *Courting Democracy in Mexico: Party Strategies and Electoral Institutions*. Cambridge: Cambridge University Press, 2004.

Heywood, Andrew. *Political Ideas and Concepts: An Introduction*. New York: St. Martin's Press, 1994.

Lipset, Seymour M., and Stein Rokkan. 'Cleavage Structures, Party Systems, and Voter Alignments.' In *The West European Party System*. Ed. Peter Miar. (Oxford: Oxford University Press, 1990), 91–138.

Lustig, Nora. *Mexico: The Remaking of an Economy*. (Washington, DC: The Brookings Institution, 1992.

Miar, Peter. *The West European Party System*. Oxford: Oxford University Press, 1990.

Middlebrook, Kevin. *Dilemmas of Political Change in Mexico*. San Diego Center for US–Mexican Studies, USCD, 2004.

Mingst, Karen A. *Essentials of International Relations*. 3rd ed. New York: W.W. Norton, 2004.

Norris, Pippa. *Electoral Engineering: Voting Rules and Political Behavior*. Cambridge: Cambridge University Press, 2004.

Rueschemeyer, Dietrich. *Capitalist Development and Democracy*. Chicago: Chicago University Press, 1992.

Smith, Brian C. *Good Governance and Development*. Houndmills, UK: Palgrave Macmillan, 2007.

Shambaugh, David. *China's Communist Party: Atrophy and Adaptation*. Berkeley: University of California Press, 2008.

CBC News Clips

Visit the companion website for *Politics: An Introduction* to listen to news clips from the CBC radio archives.

11 International Politics and Foreign Policy

LEARNING
OBJECTIVES

After reading this chapter, you will be able to:

❊ see the unavoidable connections between domestic and international politics

❊ distinguish among the various approaches to and actors involved in international politics

❊ understand some basic concepts in international politics, including the nation-state, power, the international system, foreign policy, and interdependence

❊ explain the context of globalization on contemporary global politics

❊ recognize the role of foreign policy and decision-making in states' international relations.

International politics
also called international relations; the study of foreign policy and relations among states and other actors at the international level

Introduction

This chapter will introduce you to the substance and nature of **international politics**, one of the more prominent sub-fields of political studies. In many ways, the characteristics of international politics are quite similar to those of domestic politics. First, like domestic politics, actors in international politics compete in a structured environment for limited resources. Often this means that substantial inequity exists in the world, with people in some countries enjoying an advantageous way of life while others live in misery. Second, there are several different types of actors (military, economic, cultural, large and organized, small and diffuse, and so on) that have to relate mutually to one another. Different approaches can often mean competing approaches. Third, there is a very clear separation between those who have power and those who do not. This too contributes to the fundamental inequity that pervades the international system. Finally, just as in domestic politics, our main focus in analyzing international politics is to understand the allocation of public goods and benefits within the system and to explain the relationship among the main actors. Here, however, the 'system' is international.

Although there are some clear similarities between domestic and international politics, we need to examine the two levels separately, while at the same time recognizing that these levels are intertwined. International politics, then, introduces a new set of concepts and ideas that, while related to our basic notion of politics and political life, force us nonetheless to stretch the boundaries of relations to a global scale. In the real world of politics today it is often impossible to make this separation, as events at home have a direct effect on the global

11.1

Domestic and International Politics: The Elián Gonzalez Affair

When revolutionary leader Fidel Castro overthrew the government of General Fulgencio Batista in Cuba in 1959, relations with the United States changed radically, and immediately. But the plight of a six-year-old boy in Miami, Florida, 40 years later would fix the attention of Cubans and Americans, as well as people around the world, on the peculiar quandary Cubans face when they seek to come to the US. Thousands of Cubans fled their country after the revolution, and came to be known as the 'Golden Exiles', thanks largely to tales of success and prosperity in their new home. More Cubans attempted to escape to the US, resulting in an unofficial policy of the American authorities: 'wet feet/dry feet'. Caught on the seas (wet feet), they are sent back to Cuba; found on land (dry feet), they may stay and claim refugee status. In late 1999 Elián and his mother were part of a group of 14 who tried to make it to Florida's shores. Only 4 made it, saved by fishermen. Elián was turned over to a relative in Miami, but his father, who remained in Cuba, claimed he wanted him back. US authorities were left with a conundrum: send the boy back to his father, or allow him to stay with relatives in the US? Advocates for both sides of the argument made impassioned pleas, and the international community was fixated on the story in the early months of 2000, as expatriate Cuban groups made their arguments, and the old rivalries of US–Cuban relations were rekindled over Elián's fate. American Attorney General Janet Reno finally decided to send him back, but his Miami relatives threatened to use force to protect him. Heavily armed border patrol agents broke into the house Elián was kept in, and forcibly removed him, leading to anger in Miami's Cuban community, riots, and charges of excessive force.

The excessive force used to remove Elián Gonzalez created great controversy among the Cuban community in South Florida.

11.1 Continued...

This case represents a good example of domestic and international politics intersecting. Different communities in two countries advocated widely different courses of action; a little boy's predicament captured the attention of people around the world; and two governments — diametrically opposed in so many ways — were forced to seek some compromise in a scenario where domestic politics blended with international, and the other way around.

environment, and the opposite, too. But in our analysis of politics, we have to make decisions about the nature of our study: what will we study? What are the limits of our analysis? How can we compensate for the inherent limitations we face because of these decisions?

This chapter will discuss some of the primary areas of interest for international politics (or international relations) and foreign policy specialists. To that end, it will cover the nature of the **nation-state** in international affairs, the intricacies of the international 'system', different actors in international politics, some of the approaches used, globalization, and diplomacy. The intention here is to familiarize you with some of the main concepts, structures, and issues facing those who study international politics today.

International Politics, International Relations, Foreign Policy, and the State

Just as politics affects our everyday lives, sometimes in ways that we do not necessarily notice, international politics influences many of our day-to-day activities. Nightly news broadcasts let us see, often in immediate and vivid detail, the surprising closeness of our global community. Elections, wars, sporting events, entertainment, even local weather broadcasts are available to us almost on demand. Streaming information over the Internet — details from around the block or from the other side of the world — is made instantaneously available for us.

It is often said that we live in a '**global village**', where events happening on one side of the world have instant repercussions on the other. And, to a degree, this is true: the collapse of trading on a stock exchange in another part of the world, for instance, or news of the death of a prominent public figure, will surely have an effect — sometimes quite dramatic — on our more localized way of life. But we should be wary of phrases such as 'the global village', because we are also constantly reminded of the ways in which we are divided from the rest of the world, even as we connect in a greater fashion with it. That is to say, identifying oneself with a larger community also means separating oneself from other communities. This is most evident in the 'us versus them' mentality that frames so much of the substance of world affairs that we witness on a daily basis.

This, then, is one of the greatest paradoxes of the study of international politics: the world is increasingly disparate, yet somehow joined. Even as we learn more about relatively unknown parts of the world, or of different cultures and

Nation-state

autonomous political unit of people who share a predominant common culture, language, ethnicity, or history

Global village

term used to describe the 'shrinking' of the world, largely due to modern communications, into a more interconnected place where all people have a closer relationship and more frequent contact

Cliché Alert! The 'Global Village'

Like any other field, political studies is often the quarry of clichés, those overused terms that become less evocative as they are popularized. A prime example is the 'global village', a term used to describe an age of globalization, but ultimately meaningless when we really think about it. 'Global village' actually predates contemporary globalization, however. Canadian communications theorist Marshall McLuhan first used the term in the 1960s to describe the growth of technology, envisioning a world where information was universal and instant. But problems arise when we think about both words in the term. First, there's nothing truly 'global' about today's modern communications, economy, or politics. Select parts of the world, mostly the developed, advanced countries, benefit intensely while the rest of the world, largely developing states, may see some advantages, but are generally not anywhere near the same level as the developed states. Whether it's decision-making, economic growth, or communications, it is more regionally located than global. Second, a 'village' implies a small community of individuals. Those who are part of a village live in close proximity, and are social and familiar with one another. The World Wide Web, global organizations, and broader education may make us more knowledgeable about the rest of the world, and even a little more sensitive to other ways of action and thinking, but we live in an environment far apart from anything that resembles a 'village'.

peoples, modern international politics is also still very much about identifying oneself and one's community, often at the expense of others. There can be no doubt, however, that we are more aware of politics around the world today than previous generations. And that is one reason why international politics is such a popular field of political studies.

A word or two about labelling is necessary. In broad terms, '**international relations**' can be about almost any aspect of relations at the international level. In this sense, the 2010 Vancouver Olympic Games, the Toronto International Film Festival, or travel tours arranged in one country and held in another are as much about 'international relations' as are the **G8** meetings, NATO's talks with Russia, or international trade agreements such as the **North American Free Trade Agreement (NAFTA)**. International relations, in its broadest sense, therefore, is about all relations at the international level. However, it would be impossible to study all aspects of all types of relations in the international community. That would be an overwhelming task, with very little in the way of understanding of the broader political relationship among countries.

International politics is a better term for our goals here: to study the decidedly 'political' nature of relations at the international level. That stated, it should be kept in mind that those who study international politics are often referred to as international relations specialists; in fact, the sub-field is often called 'international relations', though is it not about all types of relations. Although there is clearly a difference between the two terms, they are usually used interchangeably.

International relations
also called international politics; the study of foreign policy and relations among states and other actors at the international level

G8
Group of Eight (formerly G7 — Group of Seven) major economic actors: United States; United Kingdom; France; Germany; Canada; Italy; Japan; Russia

NATO
North Atlantic Treaty Organization

North American Free Trade Agreement (NAFTA)
agreement whereby Canada, the United States, and Mexico have opened their markets to each other

Foreign policy
foreign diplomatic relations
and policies of a country
beyond its borders

Foreign policy is the third term that should be clear in our minds before moving forward. Foreign policy refers to the relationship states have to their external environment — policies created to govern state relations beyond national borders. So, if international politics is about the mutual relationship of two or more actors at the international level, foreign policy is essentially about the manner in which individual states present themselves to the international community. Foreign policy *is* policy, therefore, since it is the legislated, or legalistic, relations of a state in the international system.

Given its influence and power in the world, it is not surprising that the state is the most important actor in international politics. The state, for international politics, is a recognized political unit with a defined territory and people, and a central government administration responsible for administering. States are considered to be sovereign, meaning that no other international actor, not even the United Nations, can override their rights of self-determination and authority within their territory.

The modern notion of the sovereign state follows the collapse of the universalism of the Middle Ages. Medieval Europe under the Holy Roman Empire shared a religion, a culture, a written language, and, to a certain extent, political institutions. The religious and political reforms of the sixteenth century shattered this universalism and created a political vacuum that allowed for the emergence and development of modern sovereign nation-states. New ideas were born, challenging the previous notion that all held similar views or aspirations. Various political writers, including Hugo Grotius in The Netherlands, Emerich de Vattel in Switzerland, Italy's Niccolò Machiavelli, and Jean Bodin in France all wrote famous works on aspects of emerging states' power and legitimacy. By the time France's Montesquieu wrote that government should be adaptable to the needs and circumstances of its citizens, in *The Spirit of the Laws* in 1748, the concept of sovereignty was well accepted in law and in practice.[1] Montesquieu's monumental work not only made the case for change in government (rather than some form of fixed system, unbending to the changing will and wants of the people), it also detailed the various roles and authority different government institutions should have.

Sovereignty as we know it today emerged with the Peace of Westphalia in 1648. The 'Peace' came with the signing of two treaties, Osnabrück and Münster, which ended the Thirty Years' War and the Eighty Years' War, respectively. The states involved in the peace process were in what are modern-day Germany, Sweden, France, Spain, and the Netherlands, but none were modern 'states'. Rather, at that time there was an odd assortment of different types of political units and authorities, including imperial states, countries, city-states, and principalities, with no real sense of commonality. The outcome of Westphalia was the origin of the modern notion of state sovereignty, where governments were the ultimate authority within their borders, other states recognized their legitimacy, and external actors were not to interfere in the activities of internal politics elsewhere. Territorial integrity is still the benchmark of the 'Westphalian' system, which typifies the current global order.

In its modern sense, sovereignty means a monopoly of power over territory, people, and resources. The state (often in co-operation or conflict with other

11.3

Patriotism or Nationalism?

Related, but different, patriotism and nationalism are all too often used interchangeably. Patriotism means 'love of country' while nationalism is an ideology that revolves around ideas of nationhood, or the identity one feels for a larger community of individuals. While patriotism is necessarily limited to the country in question (think of the statement 'I am Canadian!'), nationalism is much broader, since it can be based on — but not necessarily reducible to — religion, race, culture, ethnicity, language, or even a form of government. When this identity takes on the role of a political movement to create a separate political unit, nationalism is born.

Most often, nationalism is peaceful. For instance, nationalist movements in Czechoslovakia at the end of the Cold War led peacefully to the new countries of the Czech Republic and Slovakia, and in Scotland and Wales, have produced just heated political debate and constitutional reform. This is not to say that the demands of these nationalist groupings have been satisfied, but the pattern has been one of peaceful resolution of conflict, rather than more extreme measures. Some other examples, however, have been anything but peaceful. Many of the conflicts that have dominated world headlines have involved disputes and fighting between different ethnic groups, such as those in Bosnia-Herzogovina, Rwanda, Burundi, East Timor, and Kosovo. Such conflicts led Harvard professor Samuel Huntington to argue in the 1990s that the next century would be dominated by what he called 'the clash of civilizations'. There are potentially thousands, if not tens of thousands, of ethnicities in the world. If each were allowed to form its own political unit, then the system of states that we currently know would be turned upside-down — imagine a system made up of thousands of micro-states. The consequences are immense for the stability of the international system, and for the institutions to which we have turned in recent history to provide stability and economic and political benefits. How could co-operation be organized among such a huge number of tiny states? More importantly, how could these states effectively provide for the economic and social well-being of their citizens? Would they be politically stable?

states) creates a boundary consisting of legal elements that prevent (within certain limitations) external interference and reinforce internal solidarity. Boundaries define the territorial extent of the jurisdiction of sovereign political-administrative units and are, therefore, legitimized by law and/or informal principles agreed upon by the people of the society. Because boundaries retain their significance only if citizens see them as valuable, it is to the state's advantage to influence public opinion to coincide with its objectives. By emphasizing patriotism and similarities within the state, and exaggerating the linguistic and cultural differences of outsiders, the state reinforces national territorial boundaries.

Some states used other methods to assert and maintain their authority, such as the use of force. **Authoritarian** states preserve their authority through the direct use of threats and fear among citizens and groups. As you may recall from

Authoritarian
form of political rule based on absolute obedience to a constituted authority

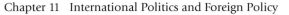

Totalitarianism

authoritarian political system that not only controls most social interaction, but is also marked by a desire by the government to force its objectives and values on citizens in an unlimited manner

the earlier chapter on types of governments, a variant of authoritarian regimes, **totalitarian** states, also seek a fundamental reordering of societal values and belief systems to match the wishes of the rulers.

The state has been questioned as the central unit of our analysis. Following World War II, for example, and particularly with the emergence of the United Nations and a greater internationalization of economic activities, many scholars and politicians alike proclaimed that the nation-state would be replaced. Fervent state nationalism was, after all, considered responsible for the horrors of the great wars (World War I, 1914–18; World War II, 1939–45). In reality, however, the prediction that the state would disappear has been proved wrong. The United Nations system now has 192 sovereign states in the international system, up dramatically from the roughly 50 states at the close of World War II.

In sum, the state is clearly the central unit of analysis in international politics, though it is not without its challengers and doubters. International politics in the late twentieth century is an increasingly complicated set of interrelated relations and actors, with a wide variety of goals sought by states, and levels of interaction.

International system

a system of two or more actors that interact regularly using established processes in given issue areas in the global arena

European Union

the economic and political union of 27 European states

Francophonie

international linguistic organization based on shared French language and humanist values

African Union

international organization founded to promote cooperation among the independent nations of Africa

Relative power

method of distinguishing the comparable strength of a political unit by contrasting it with another

Sub-systemic

international groupings or relations among states that do not include all actors

The International System

In simple terms, an **international system** may be any grouping of two or more states that have organized and regular relations with one another. In this sense, then, Canada, the United States, and Mexico, as members of the North American Free Trade Agreement (NAFTA), form an international system. So do the member states of the **European Union** (EU), the *Francophonie*, NATO states, or the **African Union** (AU). But we most often hear references to the 'international system' as the entire globe, encompassing every state in the world. This 'global' dimension, then, is the more common way that we may use the term, but it is not the only one. And it may not be entirely accurate.

The framework of the international system is one of the most important determinants affecting how a state achieves its goals. Actors in the international system (predominantly states, but also including other actors such as multi-national corporations and international organizations) are distinguished and divided on the basis of their **relative power**, or the way that their capabilities may be compared to those of another, or may be different from others. States that are militarily powerful, for instance, may have far more influence and effect in the international system than those states whose power is based on limited physical resources, because military power is more easily extended in the attempt to obtain objectives. Conversely, at different times, physical resources may be seen as more crucial. Waging war or mining minerals, a state's capability and relationship with others will vary.

Although all these actors are part of the international system (and also of **sub-systemic** groupings, such as NAFTA, which are made up of only some actors), we are still primarily members of individual political states rather than of the world community. Here again sovereignty, patriotism, and nationalism are all part of why the state is still so important. Structures and processes in states for decision-making have become more developed, and few political actors are willing to cede the same degree of authority or legitimacy to global institutions and organizations — even the United Nations — out of concern that this would diminish the role of the state and the concept of state sovereignty.

Some regional subsystems such as the European Union, NAFTA, and the **Asia–Pacific Economic Cooperation** (APEC) body are representative of a growing tendency in the international system not simply to hand power and authority over to non-state actors, but rather to work as a body of political entities — all the while retaining individual sovereign power — in order to achieve certain economic goals. Yet this shows that the international system may be international, but certainly not global. 'Global' international systems exist — think of the global natural environment, for example. And, to be sure, there is a global economic system. But far more common today are smaller organized bodies, still international in nature, but nonetheless limited to specific actors.

Actors in World Politics

By now it should be fairly clear to you that there are several different types of actors that are important in international affairs. Though we deal primarily with nation-states in international relations, there can be no doubt that other **units of analysis** on the world stage are important, too. And though we might consider some actors as having a degree of prominence over others, it is nonetheless essential to have a grasp of the competing influences.

First, we should start with the state. As mentioned above, sovereignty is one of the more consequential concepts in international relations. That is because actors that have sovereignty, and only states may be sovereign, are given certain rights and responsibilities that others simply do not have. For instance, only nation-states are permitted to enter into formal legal treaties or to wage wars with other states. These privileges extend back hundreds of years to the creation of the first political systems, which were not always states. States today are still the most important actors in the international system because of what we call **structural anarchy**, which simply means that there is no political authority greater than the sovereign state in international affairs. States exist in this condition of anarchy where there is no 'world government' (not even the United Nations) and are ultimately responsible for their own behaviour within their borders.

Other actors, such as the United Nations, are **international governmental organizations** (IGOs). These actors are larger conglomerates of nation-states that have grouped together for a common purpose. For instance, the United Nations was formed in 1945 to deal with problems that simply could not be dealt with by individual states — international insecurity, global indebtedness, and world hunger and underdevelopment, for instance. NATO, a military alliance, was formed in 1949 by states in North America and West Europe. It has since expanded dramatically. Members of these IGOs do not give up their sovereignty, but they do agree to work with other states to come to common positions on these and other issues. And — significantly — they agree to abide by the decisions of the

Asia–Pacific Economic Cooperation (APEC)
group for promoting open trade and economic co-operation among Asia–Pacific economies

Units of analysis
entities being studied in politics; the 'what' or 'whom' as the basis of analysis

Structural anarchy
in international relations, the assumption that no higher authority exists above the nation-state

International governmental organizations
institutions formed by three or more countries that have grouped together for a common purpose, including economic, social, cultural, or political

11.4

NATO

The North Atlantic Treaty Organization (NATO) was founded in 1949, uniting the countries of Western Europe and North America in the common struggle against Communism and the Soviet Union. For fifty years NATO stood face to face with the Warsaw Pact, its eastern bloc counterpart, and defined **security** relations between Western nations. With the end of the Cold War in the late 1980s, several analysts predicted that NATO would be dissolved, since its *raison d'être* had disappeared. The countries of Western Europe and North America, it was argued, would not be willing to pay the costs of a security organization that had become an anachronism.

In fact NATO, instead of becoming part of history, grew in size and membership. In 1993 NATO invited Eastern European states of the former Warsaw Pact to join with them in the Partnership for Peace (PFP), an initiative designed to increase co-operation in political and military affairs throughout Europe, to augment stability and remove threats to peace. Later, NATO pursued expansion to include Eastern European states. First in 1999, the Czech Republic, Hungary, and Poland were welcomed into the alliance. Further expansion in 2004 and 2009 brought NATO's membership to 28 members. Today NATO continues as a collective defence organization, meaning that states agree to mutually defend all members from external attack. Still the world's largest and most important security organization, NATO's new role is outside of the North Atlantic, beginning in 2003 with its mission in Afghanistan.

Security
freedom from danger or injury

International organizations
an international grouping, governmental or non-governmental, with activities in several states

Multinational corporations
corporate bodies that operate in more than one country

IGO, which means that, in exchange for group attention to common problems, the individual member states do sometimes surrender part of their autonomy and freedom of action for the common good.

Non-state actors sometimes form international institutions. Non-governmental organizations (NGOs), such as the Red Cross, Doctors without Borders, or Amnesty International, are groupings of like-minded organizations that all seek to work together on problems of a common nature, but without the direct input of governments in the decision-making process. This means that NGOs often have to work with governments, perhaps in the distribution of aid, for example, but the governments themselves are not part of the organization. Increasingly, NGOs are becoming more of a presence in international affairs, as a result of the growing nature of world problems that simply cannot be dealt with by states alone.

Aside from these two examples, which are both **international organizations (IOs)**, another type of non-governmental actor is the **multinational corporation (MNC)**. MNCs are business organizations with activities in more than one country. Many have operations in far more than just two countries, however. MNCs are unlike both IOs and states in that their constituency (that is, who they must answer to) is made up shareholders or members of a board.

MNCs are international corporations that seek to make a profit, like any other corporation, in the globalized economy. MNCs are now one of the world's most important actors, since there are so many (constantly growing, but over 250,000 'home' offices and affiliates worldwide), and because they have so much economic clout. Many MNCs are far more powerful than nation-states, and not just developing states. Exxon Mobil, for instance, has larger yearly sales than the entire **gross national product** (the total value of goods and services produced by a nation at home and abroad) of countries such as Finland and Hong Kong. This clearly shows the importance of these groups, especially when they invest

> **Gross national product**
> total value of goods and services produced in a country in one year, plus total of net income earned abroad

11.5

Human Migration

© igroup/iStockphoto.com

Signs such as this one are quite common along the United States–Mexican border, warning motorists that illegal migrants might be present on highways.

One of the challenges for states in the twenty-first century is to deal with the threat of mass human migration. The movement of huge numbers of people has been a threat to national governments for hundreds of years, as these new arrivals in a country absorb precious resources and contribute to political and economic instability. With the end of the Cold War, and the stability that it provided, Western European governments were forced to deal with the prospect of mass movements of citizens westward from the former eastern bloc in search of a better life. With the Kosovo conflict in 1999, Albania faced the prospect of hundreds of thousands of Kosovars seeking shelter and refuge from the violence, a situation that cost Albania hundreds of millions of dollars, financial resources it could ill afford. Human migration finds its starkest example on the southern border of the United States. In the states of California and Texas, in particular, the border with Mexico has been crossed by millions of undocumented Mexicans and Central Americans who seek employment and prosperity in 'El Norte'.

Signs like the one pictured above are common near the border, warning drivers to be on the lookout for persons, even families, who may run across busy highways

11.5 Continued...

in their attempts to elude officials. This has drawn a vehement response from many US citizens in the Southern states, who argue that illegal immigrants take away jobs and drain the social security and health systems. By way of response, the US government has erected high walls and fences and put in place border patrols to keep illegal aliens from entering US territory. However, the activities of the so-called 'coyotes', individuals who organize the illegal transport of immigrants into the US, continue to evade US restrictions. The coyotes, who charge thousands of dollars for their services, routinely abuse, rob, and maltreat their human cargoes.

in foreign economies, or negotiate with weaker states regarding access to local markets. We will return to the impact of MNCs on international relations in Chapter 13.

Finally, we cannot forget the influence and importance of people and groups.

We think so often of states, institutions, and organizations, but we forget that individuals often make a difference. Think, for example, of the influence of notable and well-known individuals such as the Pope, or the Dalai Lama, Bono, or Bill Gates. These people often can change the mindsets of millions of people, or even whole countries, based on the roles they play internationally, or the causes they take up. And groups of people, often short-lived or unorganized, regularly have an effect as well. Student protest groups in China, or agricultural workers in Europe, may come together for a brief period of time, but in that time they may affect the way we view the world.

We should keep in mind the array of actors that regularly affect and influence the course of world affairs. Though in this chapter most references will be to states, it is nonetheless critical to remember that there are several types of groups, with varying levels of influence and power, that consistently play a role in the international arena.

Globalization

World War II was an important watershed in international politics because it signalled the end of one era (the age of Empire and European domination) and brought about the leadership of the United States, and the rise of international institutions to help regulate an increasingly complex international system. The end of World War II also initiated a wider understanding of the type of relations considered to be important, moving from the almost singular attention to security to a wider definition of social and economic considerations. It also marked the beginning of the current age of **globalization**.

The end of World War II, and the period following it that came to be known as the **'postwar era'**, brought about major shifts in world economics, both in trade and monetary relations. The level of world trade had been gradually rising for several centuries, but after the war it greatly accelerated. In addition to non-political technological and economic factors, trade was encouraged by the belief that trade barriers had contributed to the economic collapse (world depression)

Globalization
the intensification of economic, political, social, and cultural relations across borders

Postwar era
period after World War II; since 1945

that preceded and (some argued) helped cause World War II. As a result, and in their own interest, many countries have agreed to remove tariffs and other trade restrictions. The result here was the creation of the **General Agreement on Tariffs and Trade** (GATT) and later the **World Trade Organization** (WTO), which absorbed the GATT together with other institutional arrangements. One result of greater trade is increasing economic **interdependence** in the world today since almost all countries have economies that rely on foreign markets and sources of supply.

Monetary relations were also considerably revamped at the end of the war, primarily at a 1944 conference at Bretton Woods, New Hampshire. The resulting monetary arrangements, known as the Bretton Woods system, were based on the gold standard and the strength of the American dollar. That system lasted until the early 1970s, when a number of factors, including the weakening of the dollar and the unwillingness of the United States to sell gold at a **fixed** (and no longer realistic) rate, brought the world to a new system of currencies that generally 'float'; that is, currencies are exchanged on the basis of supply and demand conditions. The Bretton Woods structure also included the **International Monetary Fund** (IMF), which was designed to help stabilize currency exchange rates by loaning countries money to meet international currency demands, thereby keeping the supply and demand stable.

The GATT and the IMF were two of the major institutions created in the immediate postwar era. (The other was the International Bank for Reconstruction and Development, the IBRD, or the World Bank.) These institutions will receive more attention in Chapter 13. This institutionalization was an important development in the new era. Nation-states agreed to permit co-operative governance of different aspects of the global economy such as trade, finance, and banking because the alternative — conflict — was so troubling. Twice already these states had gone to war and the possibility it could happen again was real.

The drive to create institutions in the immediate postwar period was in large part in recognition of the causes of World War II itself. World leaders in 1944 were concerned that the lack of regulation, integration, and normalcy of economic and political relations during the 1930s led some states, such as Germany and Italy, to react to what they viewed to be a system balanced against them. Those who met at Bretton Woods to deliberate a new monetary, commercial, and financial order felt that a new system of **multilateralism** (involving many states in a co-operative manner) was necessary to regulate and normalize a very fractious state of affairs. This was achieved through a systemic development of international organizations, institutions, and forums for deliberation that, it was hoped, would ameliorate any future conflict. In many ways, this new institutionalism was one of the main drivers behind the emerging process of globalization.

We hear about globalization daily, but few of us really understand what the term means, or what its significance is for us and others. A basic definition was given by Hans-Henrik Holm and Georg Sørenson in their 1995 book *Whose World Order? Uneven Globalization and the End of the Cold War.*[2] They defined globalization as 'the intensification of economic, political, social, and cultural relations across borders'. That is a very useful definition, but it doesn't really inform us

---

General Agreement on Tariffs and Trade (GATT) originally intended only as a temporary arrangement when the International Trade Organization (ITO) failed; became the world's permanent trade regime and was later subsumed under the World Trade Organization (WTO)

World Trade Organization (WTO) created in 1995 as a forum for promoting free trade between nations in goods and services

Interdependence 'mutual dependence'; a method of measuring dependent relationships among countries, based on the level of sensitivity and vulnerability one country has with respect to another

Fixed exchange rate system system in which states agree upon set values for their currencies in terms of other national currencies

Floating exchange rate system system in which market decides the relative values of national monies

International Monetary Fund (IMF) postwar institution designed to help stabilize currency exchange rates by loaning countries money to meet international currency demands, thereby keeping the supply and demand stable

Multilateralism integration or coordination of policies or decision-making by three or more nation states

about the broad nature of globalization. It also really tells us more about the outcome of globalization rather than the process.

Globalization is a process that has been underway since the post-World War II economic recovery of the European states, and has been driven primarily by economic interests, initially in the US, but later from all parts of the globe. Technology has clearly played an important role, too, and it would be remiss to ignore the role of states in encouraging, or at least not stopping the process.

Globalization has many attributes. It is not simply political or economic — but let us begin with **economic globalization**. The process of globalization has been driven by market forces, but has been encouraged by governmental actions. States have progressively removed barriers to the flow of goods, services, and capital across their borders, and the process of liberalization has thus boosted globalization. While this happened, financial institutions moved capital across national borders, engaging in lending, borrowing, and investment activities at previously unforeseen levels. Then, as the postwar era went on, MNCs sought out profit opportunities by expanding their production and sales basis to the international level, further linking national economies. In addition, groups of corporations have formed strategic alliances and joint ventures that have served to integrate national markets.

Globalization is also seen in sociological and cultural terms. In this sense, globalization refers to the emergence of a sense of global society and of global norms. The first of these elements means that across the globe individuals are increasingly associating themselves not only with their local or national societies, but also with billions of other individuals around the world. To say that one was a 'citizen of the world' used to be considered strange, but more and more it is being accepted as normal, at least to the degree that our everyday lives are certainly more affected by world activities than in the past. The emergence of global norms and cultural standards is underway, as communications become easier and faster and people around the world exchange opinions and experiences. The international consensus over human rights that came about at the end of World War II was a major step forward in this process. But we would be mistaken to simply believe that our greater connectedness means that we all see things the same way, or share the same global culture.

The political element is the last, and most controversial, of these facets of globalization. **Political globalization** refers to the emergence of political processes that span across national borders, and frequently circumvent them entirely. This is not merely the processes of international relations and diplomacy, which have been a part of our political reality for hundreds of years. Rather, political globalization implies that the influences on policy-making at both national and international levels derive from many different sources, and involve actors that reach across the globe. One example has been the creation of non-governmental organizations that are represented in many different countries, such as Greenpeace and Amnesty International. Another example is the global movement towards democracy that spread throughout the developing world in the 1990s. Political globalization ties national governments together through common pressures.

Globalization
the intensification of economic, political, social, and cultural relations across borders

Political globalization
political processes that span across national borders, and frequently circumvent them entirely

11.6

Cultural Sensitivity: The Movie *Australia*

North American moviegoers in 2008 who watched *Australia*, starring Nicole Kidman and Hugh Jackman, may have been a bit surprised to read the opening statement before the titles began: *Aboriginal and Torres Strait Islander people should be aware that this film may contain images of people who have since passed away and may cause sadness or distress.* The film's storyline hinged on the treatment of Australia's Aboriginal peoples, and many of the actors were of Aboriginal descent. Australian viewers may have been less surprised, because the statement at the beginning of the film is very similar to ones on websites, in books, and on television programs where Aboriginal persons appear. Australian Aboriginal and Torres Strait Islanders (the Torres Strait is located between Australia and Papua New Guinea) have deep cultural sensitivities regarding those who have died. In fact, the film itself deals with the matter of 'not speaking the name' of persons who have passed away. It is an interesting case of cultural globalization that a major Hollywood film addressed the matter of indigenous cultural sensitivities.

We can easily see, therefore, the way in which the end of World War II affected the international system, and the ensuing globalizing result. There can be no doubt that the very functions and purpose of relations among states radically altered after the war. However, perhaps the most important element of the post-war period was the emerging conflict between the United States and the Soviet Union: the '**Cold War**' — the strategic arrangement of states in the international system that existed from 1945 to 1991.

Although the United States and the Soviet Union were united during World War II in their attempts to stop German imperialism under Hitler, it would be wrong to assume that both countries viewed the world in the same manner or had the same attitudes about its direction. Very quickly after the end of the war, both sides began their pursuit of independent goals for the international system. On the one hand, the Soviet Union envisioned a world united in socialism, with centralized and controlled economies that would seek to redistribute wealth in a more equitable manner. On the other hand, the United States and its allies sought an international environment marked by economic opportunity, political free-dom, and international liberalism. These two antithetical approaches influenced all aspects of international politics during the postwar period.

This era was called the 'Cold War' because it was marked by rhetorical hostil-ities on both sides, which never erupted into violence or a 'hot war' that involved the two countries fighting each other. Further, the possession of great numbers of nuclear weapons by both sides, with sufficient power to destroy the world many times over, exacerbated the situation, and added to the sense of fear and distrust. (Chapter 12 will delve deeper into the problems with weapons and war.)

In brief, all aspects of international life — strategic, economic, cultural, and political — were deeply affected by the ideological divisions between the

Cold War
a period of rhetorical hostility not marked by violence; most often referenced to the period of 1945–91 that existed between the alliance systems centred on the United States and the Union of Soviet Socialist Republics (USSR)

Boycott

refusal to deal with another political community often involving banning of political, economic, or cultural relations

Détente

warming of relations

Rapprochement

reconciliation

Less Developed Countries (LDCs)

countries that may be characterized by the following: low levels of per-capita income, high inflation and debt, large trade deficits, low levels of socioeconomic development, a lack of industrialization, or undeveloped financial or legal systems

United States and the Soviet Union during the Cold War. Some aspects of global relations were more influenced than others, such as the way in which states sought military security through the forging of tight alliances with more powerful states. But even seemingly innocuous events such as the Olympic Games were victim to the Cold War animosity; in 1980 the United States and most of its allies **boycotted** (a refusal to deal with another political community) the Games, a decision mimicked by the Soviets in 1984, when the Games were held in Los Angeles. The Cold War, simply put, was the primary influence in world politics at this time.

The Cold War had a number of different phases. Immediately following World War II, tensions between the two sides brought about what has sometimes been referred to as the 'long decade' of the 1950s, marked by the first detonation of a Soviet nuclear device in 1949 and the corresponding American doctrine to 'contain' Soviet expansionism, to 1963, with the signing of the nuclear Limited Test Ban Treaty, considered by many to be the first real recognition by both sides that nuclear weapons escalation was out of control. The 1970s, on the other hand, were branded the decade of '**détente**' (a warming of relations), as the two sides sought a degree of **rapprochement** (reconciliation) with the other.

However, the election of Ronald Reagan in 1980, and his emphasis on a military build-up as a response to the perception of a Soviet threat, ushered in what was called the 'second' Cold War (in fact a continuation of the previous Cold War), with a return to colder and remote relations, and a corresponding renewed fear of nuclear war. Finally, the election of Mikhail Gorbachev as General Secretary of the Communist Party of the Soviet Union in 1985, and his program of restructuring Soviet politics and economics, brought about the beginning of the end of the Cold War, with a (symbolic, at least) end with the collapse of the Soviet Union itself, and its formal demise at the stroke of midnight on New Year's Eve, 1991.

Despite the changes to the international system after the end of the Cold War, a constant basic world reality is that the substantial majority of people and countries are poor. Chapter 10 dealt with this matter in some detail. To briefly recap, the vast majority of these countries are situated either near or below the equator, and they have become known as the South. In contrast, world wealth is concentrated in a few industrialized countries that lie in the northern hemisphere (the North). Although the absolute economic (and related social) conditions of the South are improving slightly, the gap between the North and the South is widening at an alarming rate. Since the 1970s the **less developed countries** (LDCs) have demanded a fundamental restructuring of the distribution of wealth and the end of trade and monetary policies that favour the North. The response of the North has been limited to date, and the question of Third World development and North–South relations will remain a perplexing and contentious aspect of international relations for years to come.

Compounding this increasing variance in economic opportunity is the more recent rise of the so-called newly industrializing countries, or NICs. Whereas we once had a fairly simple model of relative wealth in the international system

— basically the highly industrialized **Organisation for Economic Co-operation and Development (OECD)** member states and their partners versus the rest of the world — the relationship today is far more complicated. The past two decades have witnessed the rise of new, stronger economies, sometimes from states that were once considered 'Third World'. But, as a result of strategically positioning themselves in the international economic environment and liberalizing their economies, states such as China, Mexico, Malaysia, Singapore, Taiwan, Hong Kong, Thailand, Brazil, and Argentina cannot be considered simply LCDs anymore. In addition, the very uneven progression of economies in the former Soviet bloc (the countries of Eastern and Central Europe) has left us with a number of different levels of economic and political development today.

Though certainly not exhaustive, the preceding discussion gives us some insights into the nature of change in the international system. Indeed, one of the constant features of any international system is the transformation and variance of relations among the primary units of analysis. Politics is naturally a dynamic force in social life, and this dynamism is perhaps no more evident than in the international system. The fundamental alteration of the international system with the ending of the Cold War is an illustration of this tendency for substantial change in international politics, change brought on by globalization, and constantly affected by it, as well.

Globalization affects us all, but it affects some more than others, and the distribution of costs and benefits is far from equal. Individuals in some areas of the globe, in particular in the advanced capitalist democracies of North America, Western Europe, and Japan, are highly integrated into the process of globalization, taking advantage of advanced technologies and communications to maintain contact with the rest of the world. The increasing importance of the World Wide Web and email in the everyday life of citizens in these countries has led some to speak of the creation of an 'Internet society'.

The economies and political systems of these countries are also profoundly affected by globalization. Many developing countries, however, and in particular the rural regions of these countries, seem relatively unaffected by advances in telecommunications and the growth of the Internet. The daily lives of citizens in these parts of the world are, nonetheless, affected by economic globalization, as the values of the goods they produce and consume, of their national currencies and thus of their personal wealth, are moved upwards or downwards according to the activities of global markets.

In these sections so far we have discussed some important concepts, actors, and activities in the global arena. We've also examined in some detail the history and context of modern globalization. Not surprisingly, there are many different points of view on all of this; the ideological divisions of the Cold War present just one example of how serious these differences of thought can be. In the next section, then, we will consider some of the major theoretical approaches to studying international politics. Some of them will be familiar to you, since we covered a lot of theoretical ground in Chapter 3. But, given its global milieu, international politics approaches do take on a specific perspective.

Organisation for Economic Co-operation and Development (OECD)
international organization co-ordinating governments' approach to economic, social and governance challenges of a globalized economy

Third World
largely Cold War categorization of less developed nations that are not part of a structurally integrated system of global capitalism

Competing Approaches to International Politics

There are numerous theoretical orientations to the study of world politics, and even more variations within them. The main ones, however, can be roughly divided into three basic groups: realism, liberalism, and Marxism. These approaches can be separated for the purpose of discussion and analysis; in reality there aren't any neat lines separating each; in fact, many scholars and political leaders will use one or more approach, depending on the political needs of the time.

Power Politics: The Realist Approach

More than any other approach, realism assumes that states, as the primary actors in international politics, are driven by a desire for economic or military powers. Distrust and self-interest mean that co-operation is not likely, but rather the international system is in a constant condition of competition for power. There are many examples of historical works depicting the struggle for power in state relations. Over two thousand years ago, Kautilya, adviser to the first Maurya emperor Chandragupta of India, wrote, 'The possession of power ... in a greater degree makes a king superior to another; in a lesser degree, inferior; and in an equal degree, equal.'[3] This view, which summarizes that world politics is a contest for power, has continued to dominate the thinking of most of the decision-makers who practise international affairs.

During most of the post-World War II period to 1970, realist theory was also the main theme of academic international relations theory. Probably the most influential realist theorist of recent times has been Hans Morgenthau, who defined politics as a 'struggle for power'. His *Politics Among Nations*, published very soon after World War II, argued that human nature and societies are imperfect.[4] Therefore, conflict is an inherent danger. Given that reality, decision-makers should structure their policies and define national interest in terms of power. They should follow policies designed to maximize their power and should avoid policies that overstep the limits of their powers. Realists believe that political leaders can avoid war by not pursuing goals they do not have the power to achieve. It is necessary, therefore, to understand the goals and the power of your opponents, thereby not underestimating their abilities or threatening their vital interests.

Realism envisions the state as the key variable in the study of international politics. Other actors, such as international institutions or corporations, may become involved, but realists believe that the state will always wield the most power. Politics, for realists, is a struggle for limited resources in a competitive and non-co-operative environment. And the stronger will likely determine the nature and rules of the international system. This idea, too, has been around for a long time. Thrasymachus, a Greek sophist, or a teacher of rhetoric and philosophy, famously argued almost twenty-five hundred years ago in Plato's *Republic* that justice was the advantage of the stronger.[5]

Realism became the basic theoretical approach to international relations after World War II as politicians and academics alike came to advocate a relatively pragmatic approach to world politics, sometimes called **realpolitik**. This orientation argues that countries should practise politics on the basis of power, rather than morality. In the postwar period, this was largely about **balance of power** politics, where states strive to achieve equilibrium of power in the world in order to prevent any other country or coalition of countries from dominating the system. This can be done through a variety of methods, including building up your own strength, allying yourself with others, or dividing your opponents. Morgenthau's ideas were popular, given his emphasis on a practical approach to the limits of power and the inherent nature of competition in the world. Other thinkers presented Morgenthau's arguments in a more modern context, taking into account the conditions of the postwar order.

Most famous among these thinkers is Kenneth Waltz, whose *Theory of International Politics* became a mainstay in international relations theory almost as soon as it was published in 1979.[6] Waltz took a '**structural**' approach to international relations, arguing that the core ordering principle in the international system is **anarchy**, where no authority above the state can override sovereignty. Waltz thought that each state is effectively trying to do the same as others, to gain power, but all are constrained by the structure of the system, which limits the choices of individual states. This is ultimately more important than the moral choices (or lack of them) that actors may have. Waltz was one of the new realists, leading to a new school of thought known as **neorealism**, or **structural realism**, as Waltz would have it.

So, while co-operation is possible according to the realists, it is not always likely, given the level of suspicion and inherent struggles in the world. For realists, this is a never-ending situation: when one state achieves some degree of security, it only comes at the expense of another's, resulting in what realists call the **security dilemma**. The upshot is a generally self-centred and competitive world. Other approaches, however, take a different view.

Process and Co-operation: The Liberal Approach

Many scholars and policy-makers reject the idea that international affairs should or must be played simply according to the dictates of power politics. They suggest that the real world of politics demonstrates that co-operation is inevitable, because participants — states and otherwise — inevitably come to recognize that the **zero-sum game** of the world of the realists, where one has to lose in order for another to gain, is self-defeating and misdirected. Instead, **liberalism** suggests that the way the international system really works shows us that politics may take place in a co-operative manner, though not without competition.

Liberals have been criticized for being too idealistic in their approach. In fact, early idealists like Woodrow Wilson, US President from 1913 to 1921, were sometimes called idealists because of their positive view of a world united in its cause for human right and progress.

11.7

Wilson and the Failure of the League of Nations

Woodrow Wilson was president of the United States during a very important time in that country's history. In office during World War I, it was Wilson who brought the US into the war, and steered his country to a more assertive and active role in international relations. That didn't happen right away, however. First, he tried to remain neutral, but the US was ultimately drawn into the war as German aggression became increasingly impossible to ignore. As the war came to a close in 1918, Wilson described the American role as one in pursuit of progressive, rights-based principles of democracy, open trade, and diplomacy. His 'Fourteen Points', a speech he made to the US Congress in 1918, advocated democracy, free access to the seas, free trade, rights to citizens of colonized nations, and a series of independent rights to specific countries affected by the war. Although many other states did not agree with all Wilson's arguments, the Fourteen Points were nonetheless the basis of the Treaty of Versailles, which set out the conditions of peace between Germany and the allied powers. And a new international organization, the League of Nations, was formed on its basis. Reflecting much of Wilson's Fourteen Points, the new League of Nations was intended to provide a peaceful forum for its members, opportunities for free trade and diplomacy, and the basis for collective security, where members would be protected against possible forceful attack by others thanks to their alliance with the League. Although the League was actually formed, and lasted from 1919 to 1946, it never gained the legitimacy or impact intended. Oddly, one of the main reasons it failed was because the US never joined. Like any international treaty, it can only be considered binding when a nation's legislature passes it. In the case of the US, this meant that the US Congress would have to pass the legislation by ratifying it. Wilson was a Democrat, and opposition Republicans, especially Henry Cabot Lodge, refused to lend their support, arguing that the League would oblige the US to support situations it could not or would not want to uphold, including intervening if another member were attacked. The US never ratified the treaty, and therefore didn't join the League. Without the US as a member, the League was never considered fully effective, and it could not stop Japanese invasion of Manchuria, the rearmament of Germany under Adolf Hitler in the 1930s, or Germany's belligerent policies in Europe. After World War II, the League split up, and was replaced by the United Nations.

Positive sum
relationship between two or more entities where results, as a sum, are better as a result of that relationship

Later, liberals took a less idealistic perspective with the growth of institutions and co-operative behaviour, which they came to see as evidence that the world may be **positive sum** as nations can benefit from collective action in a way that would simply be impossible were they to act alone.

The liberal approach differs from realism in a number of ways. First, liberals do not believe that acquiring, preserving, and applying power is the essence of international relations. Instead, they argue that foreign policy should be formulated according to more collaborative and ethical standards. Second, the liberal approach also dismisses the charge by some realists that pursuing ethical policy works against the national interest; in other words, liberals suggest that ethical policy may in fact be in the national interest of states, rather than diametrically opposed to it. Third, the liberal approach believes that the world must seek a new system of order; they argue that it is imperative to find new paths to co-operate. Finally, in contrast to realists, liberals are prone to believe that humans and countries are capable of achieving more co-operative, less conflicting relations.

One of the most prominent fields of liberal international relations is **liberal institutionalism**, which really encapsulates these ideas about co-operative behaviour. Liberal institutionalists, such as Stephen Krasner, argue that the real world of collaborative interaction that is so evident in the many institutions that states join and work within shows the strength of liberal thought, and the weakness of theories like realism, which deny co-operative action.[7] Krasner pioneered research on **regimes**, which are rules and decision-making structures, suggesting that these forms of institutionalism create ways to distribute authority and control in international politics, but also give states incentives to work together.

Rejecting Realism: The Marxist Approach

In contrast to the liberal approach, which is reflective of the environment of the realists, the Marxist approach advocates a completely separate form of political interaction on the world stage. Marxists suggest that realism is really behind the current world situation, rather than the conditions of the world driving the theory of realism. In effect, they argue that the 'orthodoxy' that led to the dominance of realism also established the conditions of inequity and poverty worldwide. The Marxist approach concentrates not on the political nature of the state, but on the economic nature of the process of interaction. That is to say, the Marxists suggest that a more equitable distribution of ownership and goods would create an international political system of greater fairness and security.

The pure **communist** ideals espoused by Marx himself at the end of the nineteenth century envisioned the end of the nation-state, which he saw as an instrument of the oppressors against the oppressed.[8] The state, then, did not have a long-term role to play in Marx's vision. It really was not until the 1920s that Vladimir Lenin considered the nature of the international system from a Marxist approach, actually employing the state in a critical approach that denied the state as a viable unit. Nonetheless, Lenin saw the **imperialist** tendencies of industrialized economies as the 'highest stage' of capitalism and the most severe dimension of a fundamentally unequal system.[9]

Therefore, political scientists and politicians who operate from this perspective believe that economic forces and conditions play a primary role in international relations. Some analysts in this general group study political structure and process from the perspective of the control and distribution of economic forces. For them, the economic base (the modes of production) determines the **superstructure** (the political, legal, cultural, and religious justifications,

Liberal institutionalism
international relations theory that suggests that international institutions make co-operation more likely and advantageous

Regimes
rules and decision-making procedures

Communism
political theory, based on writings of Marx and Engels, that espouses class conflict to form a system where all property is publicly owned and each citizen works to his or her own best ability and is compensated equitably

Imperialism
extending one country's authority over another through conquest or political and/or economic control

Capitalism
economic system where production and distribution of goods relies on private capital and investment

Superstructure
political, legal, cultural, and religious justifications, structures, and practices

structures, and practices), which corresponds to a given economic system. They contend that a historically inevitable series of economic pressures and counter-pressures (**dialectical materialism**) will, and should, lead to the destruction of capitalism and the triumph of communism.

Perception and Politics

Often, however, world politics is based on **perception** rather than reality. Political developments are creations of the publics concerned with them. Whether events are noticed and what they mean depend on the observers' situations and the language that reflects and interprets those situations. A global economic or military problem, a political enemy, or a leader is both an entity and a signifier with a range of meanings that vary in ways we can at least partly understand. For example, in 1938, British prime minister Neville Chamberlain spoke of 'peace for our time' after meeting with German leader Adolf Hitler and signing the Munich Agreement. That agreement permitted Germany to annex the Sudetenland, bordering Czechoslovakia, in exchange for Germany's agreement not to move further. Germany did, of course, beginning with its invasion of the rest of Czechoslovakia, and this led to World War II. The Munich Agreement was called 'appeasement' by its critics, who suggested Chamberlain should have been stronger in his opposition to Hitler's aggressive expansion. But Chamberlain's perception was that Hitler would be satisfied with the Sudetenland, and war would be avoided. International politics is thus more than a matter of objective facts. It is a study of subjective judgments based on images of oneself and other international actors.

A final word on approaches here is necessary before moving on to the nature of foreign policy and its determination. Although the study of international politics is largely analytical, the 'scientific' dimensions of political science were reflected in a different approach to understanding international politics that gained influence after World War II. This 'scientific school' of political science is interested in recurring patterns and causal relations of international behaviour. Those who follow this approach, also called the **behaviouralist** approach, often use quantitative methods to arrive at and prove hypotheses that will explain both why certain events have occurred and under what circumstances they might occur again. They also often use cross-cultural analyses to test whether similar or divergent causal patterns occur between different political systems as well as over time.

Like realists, behaviouralists have little interest in advocating fundamental changes in the world system. Where they differ is that realists accept what is and often advocate that politicians should also accept and operate within the world of power politics. Behaviouralists, from their 'value-free' or 'scientific' perspective, are more disinterested in the good or ill of world politics. They tend to operate from a value-free posture, neither condoning nor condemning what is. They only describe what is and why and try to predict what will be. This value-free approach has been the source of some criticism of behaviouralism by those who contend that the problems and stakes of the world are too great to be studied dispassionately.

Dialectical materialism
Marxist notion that material forces affect politics through social and economic change

Perception
awareness or understanding through use of human senses

Behaviouralism
perspective that concentrates on the 'tangible' aspects of political life, rather than values; objective was to establish a discipline that was 'scientific' and objective

Diplomacy and Foreign Policy

Often when we consider international relations, whether we know it or not, we are really thinking about foreign policy. The US invasion of Iraq in 2003, for instance, had massive implications for international relations. States all over the world were forced to respond, to condemn or support, and the war itself affected global terrorism as well as the international political economy. But the invasion was a foreign policy decision: US president George W. Bush considered his options and ultimately decided that the best alternative was to invade. The US Congress authorized the military engagement in October 2002, before the invasion commenced in March 2003. So, was the war in Iraq international relations, or foreign policy? The simple answer is both.

Foreign policies are the diplomatic relations countries have with others in the international system. The word 'policy' is meaningful: foreign policy is legislated and authoritative. States do not simply 'do' foreign policy. Rather, there is an effective and understood process behind how it is made and how it is undertaken. The diplomatic element is crucial, as well. **Diplomacy** refers to proper international negotiation and discussions that take place on an official — and sometimes unofficial — level between and among states. Depending on the level of seriousness surrounding the issue (war, the economy, culture), different actors will be involved in the process. And the process itself will be vastly different depending on the issue at hand.

Diplomacy
international negotiation and discussions that take place on an official—and sometimes unofficial—level between and among states

11.8

Diplomacy Goes Awry: April Glaspie and Saddam Hussein

Sometimes even the most experienced diplomats fail to make their point clear. Most of the time when that happens, there are opportunities to correct the problem. In rare cases, however, a misguided phrase or a wrongly interpreted action can lead to bigger problems. In August 1990, Iraq invaded Kuwait in what was considered by almost all observers an aggressive use of force. Leading up to the invasion, there were signs that all was not well on the border between those two countries. Iraq had built up huge numbers of troops at the border, and had previously complained that Kuwait was slant-drilling for oil into Iraqi oil fields, and was demanding that Iraq repay money it had given to help Iraq fight its 1980–8 war with Iran. Tensions were high, and no one could be sure that Hussein, an unpredictable leader at the best of times, would not use his military against Kuwait. April Glaspie was the American ambassador to Iraq, and was instructed to meet with Hussein to discuss the military buildup. In her meeting, she pressed Hussein about why he had his military at the border, and expressed concern on behalf of the United States. Later, she said, 'We have no opinion on the Arab–Arab conflicts, like your border disagreement with Kuwait.' This statement, which she later argued was merely meant to convey the importance of Iraq settling its dispute with Kuwait through diplomacy in a manner independent from other countries — including the United States — getting involved, was interpreted by Hussein as a signal that the US would not intervene, and would likely only make a statement against the use of

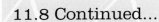

11.8 Continued...

force. Some analysts think that if Glaspie had been clearer about the US response, Iraq would not have invaded. But the US hadn't really considered its response at that time, except that it wanted to avoid war. Hussein ordered the invasion on August 2, which led to the international alliance against Iraq in Operation Desert Storm in 1991. Glaspie was widely blamed for not being clearer in her remarks to Hussein. But it is true that she urged him to find a peaceful way of solving the impasse. Defending her words as obvious to anyone, including Hussein, she later remarked, 'We foolishly did not realize he was stupid.'

Understanding foreign policy goes a long way to understanding the international system more generally, as much of what is done in the system involves states acting beyond their borders. Foreign policy varies, depending on the state in question and the circumstances of the policy. So, we should spend a bit of time reflecting on the forces behind creating foreign policy. Of course, in order to truly explain and understand the structure of relations among states, it is necessary to understand the political nature within states. And while we just do not have the opportunity here to review all nation-states and their particular political nature, there are some commonalities in the making of foreign policy.

Foreign Policy-Making

The actions of the state in making foreign policy are determined by several factors, of which international law is only one (and not the most significant) dimension. A state's actions in the international arena are determined by several factors. Some of the more important are: power, domestic capabilities, tradition, ideology, and perceptions of the national interest. These factors, admittedly, are rather imprecise; the national interest, for example, can mean whatever the person using the term wants it to mean, whether it is military gains, economic relations, or perhaps something more vague like reputation. In any case, these factors are determined to some degree by the following characteristics.

Geography

Geography, in terms of size and location in the world, is always part of the power equation. Canada, for example, is the second largest country in the world, and has a strategic location next to the United States. That means our resources and friendly relations will be of constant interest to the United States. Likewise, the location and economic strength of Germany in the middle of Europe means that it will remain a significant player in the European Union group of nations. But geography has its limitations. Unlike other attributes contributing to foreign policy-making, however, there is little a country can do about its geography! Canada's relatively low level of defence spending, for instance, is in part due to its location. Were Canada to be located in the Indian subcontinent, its military expenditures would be far higher.

There are other geographic issues affecting foreign policy. Whether a country is landlocked or a maritime state, its terrain, or its habitability are as much factors in a country's interests as relations with allies or economic strength. And the resources a country may have — closely related to geography — constitute a category of its own.

Natural Resources

A country's natural resources play an important part in establishing the power of a state. Some countries are close to being self-sufficient in terms of critical resources. For example, South Africa is almost completely self-sufficient in food production. The United States and Canada are two other examples of countries with vast resources, though they choose to import some for economic reasons. Still others have to rely on imports in such critical areas as sources of energy and food. Some countries such as Japan and Korea are able to offset relative shortages of natural resources by basing their economy on 'high technology', which is possible with a highly skilled labour force. Other countries, particularly underdeveloped countries, are under constant pressure to share or sell their resources at artificially low prices in order to receive other benefits.

Increasingly, countries are now concerned with access to resources, rather than outright ownership of them. In a highly interdependent world, it is simply not necessary for countries to have direct control over all the resources they need for their citizens. Rather, access — through trade — provides a more efficient way of realizing the resource objectives for countries. And despite all the attention paid to technological development in the modern economy (which is obviously very important), natural resources will always be essential. Countries will not be able to sustain their way of life without food, water, minerals, primary resources, and raw materials. Those states in possession of these attributes will have greater flexibility with their foreign policy objectives.

Population

Population is a major factor in determining the political, economic, and military power of a state. A very small population (particularly in relation to the size of the country) will prevent the state from being very powerful (unless the country occupies a strategic location and has other capabilities that offset its small population). On the other hand, a very large population that lacks an industrial base and suffers from food shortages will also lack the means required to exert power in the international world. Where that population lives (population density) will also affect a country's foreign policy decisions. Today, for instance, population growth in China and India, two countries with more than 1 billion citizens each, greatly affects their domestic and foreign policies, and also places strain on their development objectives.

Canada's population density shows an interesting example. It is widely known that, in large part due to the fierce climate, most Canadians live in the southern portion of the country. But it is perhaps less known that nearly 80 per cent of Canadians live within 160 kilometres (100 miles) of the United States border.[10] This fact is not that surprising, once we take into account the close economic relations the two countries share, as well as the natural development that took place as both countries gained independence from Britain and established their own very distinctive yet interrelated political systems.

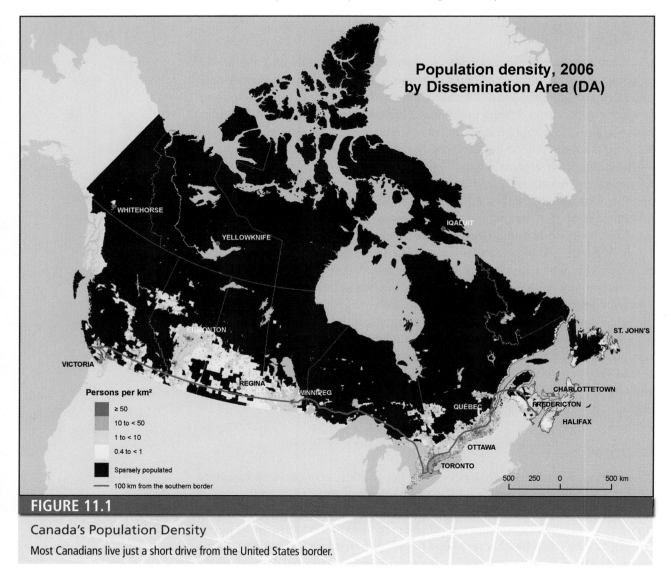

Population density, 2006 by Dissemination Area (DA)

WHITEHORSE
YELLOWKNIFE
IQALUIT
EDMONTON
ST. JOHN'S
VICTORIA
REGINA
WINNIPEG
CHARLOTTETOWN
QUÉBEC
FREDERICTON
HALIFAX
OTTAWA
TORONTO

Persons per km²
- ≥ 50
- 10 to < 50
- 1 to < 10
- 0.4 to < 1
- Sparsely populated
- —— 100 km from the southern border

500   250   0   500 km

FIGURE 11.1

Canada's Population Density
Most Canadians live just a short drive from the United States border.

Technological Development

The level of technological development in general and in the specific area of military technology (when combined with the strength of the military) will also contribute to the state's relative position in the international community. In some respects, technological innovation has become one of the most important indicators of economic strength; many of the states that have shown their ability to compete today, such as Japan, Taiwan, and South Korea, place a great deal of emphasis on strategically marketing their productive output within the world.

The relative technological development a country has will affect the degree to which a country may alter its foreign policy. Technology may have military spin-offs, for example, which will provide a country a level of security from attack. Economic development is greatly influenced by technology; more advanced states will enjoy levels of technology that provide a better way of life for citizens. On the other hand, the reverse will affect foreign policy, too. Countries that suffer from low levels of technological development will become more dependent on others for their security and economic welfare. Ultimately, technology can go a long way in providing independence and autonomy in foreign policy decision-making.

For this reason a primary goal of many developing countries in their foreign relations is to guarantee technology transfer, whereby they are given access to, or appropriate by legal or other means, technologies being used in the developed world. Since the 1960s this has been a priority for developing countries. As Chapter 10 shows in greater detail, countries such as China have been particularly successful in this regard in recent years.

Internal Political Structures and Processes

Even if two states have virtually the same geographical, resource, and technological attributes, there is little chance that their foreign policies will be the same. This is, quite simply, because politics always gets in the way! Of course, this can be beneficial or detrimental; there is no 'pre-determination' that things will go wrong when affected by politics. In any case, factors such as the type of political system and the degree of societal agreement about shared values and norms will have a significant effect on the outcome of foreign policy.

Take, for example, the case of foreign policy in Canada and the United States. In many ways these two countries share a lot regarding their foreign policy. Not all policies are the same, to be sure, but there are some general principles, such as democracy, multilateral behaviour, and open economic markets, that guide decision-making. But the decision-making process itself is much different, due to the nature of the individual political systems. The fusion of executive and legislative authority in Canada means that the creation of foreign policy goes through a different sequence than in the more directed and concentrated separation of powers model of the United States. That's not to suggest that either model is necessarily better, or that one gives less attention to a particular level of government, but rather that the systems themselves reflect distinctive histories, political development, and tradition.

Such questions as the nature of groups participating in the decision-making processes, performance of the system maintenance function, and the extent of support for the system will all shape the state's behaviour in the international arena. History, prevailing political ideologies, and dominant perceptions of national interest will also contribute to the direction of the state's decisions. The experience of some countries' relations with each other has left them historical friends or enemies. For example, the history of relations between China and Japan still make it very difficult for these two countries to overcome traditional hostilities, even though they trade freely with one another. Some countries have a long history of being 'world powers' (for example, France and Great Britain), whereas other states are relative newcomers on the international stage. Prevailing ideologies both from the outside and inside also give direction to foreign policy. As we have seen in this course in earlier chapters, there are various pressures and influences in the political planning of any state; this extends to the decision-making process and, in turn, foreign policy.

Finally, each and every state has some notion of what is in its best interest. Such notions transcend ideologies, elite behaviour, or any other considerations because they are embedded in the way of life of that particular polity. These are some of the main determinants of foreign policy operating independently of any particular decision or policy. Not all of these factors always determine a given policy outcome, but these factors are always a part of the decision-making process.

Canada and the World

We could never hope to encapsulate Canada's position in international relations in brief, but we can identify its main concerns: the economy, relations with the United States, and multilateralism. There are many other issues, of course, but for the most part all can be placed into these categories.

Canada is a trading state out of necessity. Security, sufficiency, and prestige for Canada come with a certain standard of life: a positive and robust economy. Canada has a small domestic market — under 20 million consumers. But its GDP of about (US)\$1.4 trillion ranks ninth among the world's economies. The domestic market in Canada is very small, with over 65 per cent of total GDP coming from trade. (Over 80 per cent of its trade comes from just the United States.[11]) Simply put, Canada produces more than its domestic market can buy. That means it must export to other markets to maintain its standard of living. Like most other major economies in the world, Canada is sensitive to the global trade economy, but its potential vulnerability is higher than other industrialized nations because of its dependence on global trade markets.

Given the amount of trade Canada has with the United States, one can easily see the high degree of dependence Canada has on its relations with its southern neighbour. According to the Canadian Department of Foreign Affairs and International Trade, Canada–US cross-border trade is over \$1 million every minute of every day. Add to this the over 200 million people who cross the border yearly, and it is clear that this is a strategic boundary for Canada.[12] Although it is a boundary, with the presence of border officials and in some cases armed personnel, it is a rather fluid one. Ever since the signing of the Canada–US Free Trade Agreement in 1988, and then the North American Free Trade Agreement (NAFTA), which went into effect in 1994, trade between the two countries has grown every year.

Canada's relationship with the United States is a broad one. They share membership in the North Atlantic Treaty Organization (NATO), as well as the bilateral North American Aerospace Defense Command (NORAD) system. These two defence agreements require each country to come to the aid of the other in case of attack. Canada's role in the war in Afghanistan, discussed in greater detail in Chapter 12, is the result of NATO invoking Article 5 of its Charter, which states that an attack against one is an attack against all (the attack in question was the September 11, 2001, terrorist attack against the United States by al-Qaeda). Though Canada's military is small by relative comparison, its main thrust is the defence of North America, pursued jointly with the United States. More broadly, Canada shares a cultural relationship with the United States. Though many Canadians would strongly defend their individuality, there is no doubt that many aspects of Canada's culture, including fashion, music, entertainment, art, and sport, are really quite interrelated with the United States. The upshot is an inescapable tie between the two countries on deep-seated issues of values, mores, and society.

Multilateralism, where two or more countries work together in a particular area, has been an important part of Canada's international relations, too. Historically, Canada's foreign policy always has focused on the role for international co-operation and organization as a means to achieve objectives. In the postwar era, institution building was strongly supported by Canada. It reflected Canada's evolving internationalism, which became an effective basis for enhancing its global influence. Collaboration, co-operation, and compromise through multilateral bodies such as the UN and NATO bore clear results over what surely would have been a greatly diminished role, had Canada been forced to act alone.

Canadian multilateralism following World War II emphasized co-operative policies with other actors rather than simply seeking individual goals, leading to the conventional opinion of Canada as 'helpful fixer'.[13] Canada's tradition of multilateral behaviour broadened to include all aspects of its foreign policy, including military, cultural, political, and economic affairs. Given Canada's power relative to larger states such as Britain and the United States, multilateralism certainly was its 'best option' for pursuing national and international interests.[14] In the Canadian experience, emphasis on multilateralism, in concert with its middle-power status (a term referring to those countries that do not have the largest military or economy, but still have significant influence in international relations because of their alliances, reputation, and diplomacy, or foreign policy behaviour) permits Canada to have its objectives achieved in the international system, even without being a 'great' power.

The conventional view of Canada's international relations is in part due to Canadians' own view of their place in the world. Peyton Lyon and Brian Tomlin have explored the conceptions and attitudes that surround Canadian 'roles' in world politics. 'Mediator', 'middle power', 'community-builder', 'peacekeeper', and 'bridge', Lyon and Tomlin suggest, characterize Canadians' self-perception of their influence in the international system.[15] To some extent, non-Canadians abroad also believe these characteristics are descriptive of Canada. Many Canadians have heard about Americans who have travelled abroad with a maple leaf stitched on their bag, knowing that the impression that they are Canadian would open doors where otherwise they might have been shut. It would be mistaken, however, for Canada to become complacent about its place in the world. Positive reputations come from positive accomplishments, and reputations may be lost if those accomplishments are not forthcoming.

Multilateralism
integration or coordination of policies or decision-making by three or more nation-states

Conclusion

International relations today take place in a frenzied and dangerous environment. Economic downturns, ethnic strife, terrorism and wars, environmental challenges and constant underdevelopment would lead anyone to conclude that the current state of world politics is not a peaceful scene. Instead of nations and peoples living together in harmony, the world is divided. The world drama has a cast of national and international actors at odds with one another, forever calculating what is good for them and then defining those ends in terms of universal justice and the common good of all humankind.

In this chapter we have examined the formation and development of the modern international political system. Filling the gap created by the breakdown of the Holy Roman Empire, dominant states within Europe developed a body of conventions and laws under the new Westphalian model by which to conduct interstate affairs. The prominence of and legitimacy of the nation-state is an important feature of the modern international world. Coupled with the sovereignty of the nation-state is importance of ideological, religious, and environmental concerns. These issues confound the ability of the state to bring about solutions independently of each other and lead to the creation of international organizations through which international co-operation can be achieved. Although there are always examples showing a lack of co-operation and understanding between states, there is also evidence that increasing demands for international peace, a solution to the arms race, and addressing a global pollution problem are resulting in new avenues of co-operation between states. The following two chapters will deal with some more areas of conflict and co-operation, international security, and economics.

Self-Assessment Questions

1. How might we distinguish among international politics, international relations, and foreign policy? In what ways do they overlap?
2. Why is the concept of state sovereignty held so strongly in the international system?
3. How did the Cold War of the post-World War II era shape and influence international politics?
4. What are the primary approaches to understanding international politics, and how do they differ? What is the role for the state in each of these approaches?
5. Does globalization create benefits or challenges for nation-states today?
6. What are the prospects for growing 'regionalism' in the international system? Do state actors have anything to fear in this regard?

Weblinks

North Atlantic Treaty Organization
www.nato.int

North American Free Trade Agreement Secretariat
www.nafta-sec-alena.org

The European Union
http://europa.eu/

African Union
www.africa-union.org

World Trade Organization
www.wto.org

International Monetary Fund
www.imf.org

North American Aerospace Defense Command
www.norad.mil

Organisation for Economic Co-operation and Development
www.oecd.org

Amnesty International
www.amnesty.org

Asia-Pacific Economic Cooperation
www.apec.org

Doctors Without Borders
www.doctorswithoutborders.org or www.msf.ca

La Francophonie
www.francophonie.org

Group of Eight
www.g8.utoronto.ca

Red Cross
www.redcross.ca

United Nations
www.un.org

World Bank
www.worldbank.org

Further Reading

Art, Robert J., and Robert Jervis. *International Politics: Enduring Concepts and Contemporary Issues*. 9th ed. Toronto: Longman, 2008.

Dougherty, James E., and Robert L. Pfaltzgraff, Jr. *Contending Theories of International Relations: A Comprehensive Survey*. 5th ed. Toronto: Pearson Education, 2001.

Hauss, Charles. *Beyond Confrontation: Transforming the New World Order*. Westport, CT: Praeger, 1996.

Mingst, Karen A. *Essentials of International Relations*. 4th ed. New York: W.W. Norton, 2007.

Williams, Phil, Donald M. Goldstein, and Jay M. Shafritz. *Classic Readings and Contemporary Debates in International Relations*. 3rd ed. Florence, KY: Wadsworth, 2005.

CBC News Clips

Visit the companion website for *Politics: An Introduction* to listen to news clips from the CBC radio archives.

12 International Security

LEARNING
OBJECTIVES

After reading this chapter, you will be able to:

✳ understand the nature of security and insecurity in international relations

✳ know the history and continuity of war among states

✳ understand enduring and emerging security dilemmas such as international terrorism and humanitarian intervention

✳ discuss methods to deal with conflict such as mediation, diplomacy, and conflict resolution

✳ explain the particular challenge Canada faces in its involvement in the war in Afghanistan.

Introduction

When people think of world politics they often imagine scenes of war and conflict. After all, a simple glance at any national newspaper shows headlines that reflect the darker side of our relations with other nations. Many notable observers share this more negative view. No less than Winston Churchill, who was British prime minister during the Second World War, wrote in 1932: 'The story of the human race is War. Except for brief and precarious interludes, there has never been peace in the world.' [1] Others support Churchill's view that the human race has always been prone to conflict. Canadian Gwynne Dyer wrote:

It can never be proven, but it is a safe assumption that the first time five thousand male human beings were ever gathered together in one place, they belonged to an army. That event probably occurred around 7000 BC — give or take a thousand years — and it is an equally safe bet that the first truly large-scale slaughter of people in human history happened very soon afterward.[2]

We can be certain of one thing: Dyer was correct that it would be impossible to prove his argument. On the other hand, it is difficult to imagine what other purpose would cause those five thousand males to gather at that time.

This might appear a rather bleak view of humankind, but it is quite realistic, given our history. Many long debates have taken place regarding the nature of human conflict, and whether it is a natural or learned characteristic. We certainly will not solve that controversy in this chapter — nor will we attempt to — but security in political studies is undoubtedly an important concern. In fact, we will suggest later that it is the most fundamental concern for political communities.

This chapter considers **security** in international relations. From a historical perspective, this has always been a primary concern for states, from ancient wars of empire to modern fears of terrorism. The methods of human brutality may have changed, and in many respects they have not, but the security of the state is still a priority. As a result, it is not surprising that wars and conflict get so much attention in international relations. Conflict is dramatic and it stimulates our thinking, reactions, suspicions, and our preparedness. It is not necessarily beneficial, although some good can come from certain forms and instances of conflict, but it captures our attention and stirs our thoughts. Large headlines in newspapers usually are reserved for bad news, and wars tend to fall into that category. Drama and uncertainty sells because we all — individuals and communities — worry for our own security. In that light, humans have not changed much over time.

Insecurity in the world is no doubt commonplace in our international system, and for many states it is a way of life. Nevertheless, most activities of states are actually aimed at preserving or improving the conditions of their citizens, and aiding peace among nations. Most of what states do does not fall in the category of front-page news; in fact, in contrast to the excitement of these events, the day-to-day operations of states are rather mundane: trade, diplomacy, and routine relations of states, for example. Yet these regularized activities are in some respects an ongoing effort to mitigate conflict in the international system.

Security and Insecurity

Security may be felt when there is a relatively low probability of threat or damage to citizens, government, territory, resources, wealth, and even values such as culture or identity.[3] However, security can never be completely assured for any state in the world, even the most powerful (consider, for example, the insecurity felt in the United States after the terrorist attacks of September 11, 2001). As discussed previously, conflict comes about when there are incompatible wishes concerning these values, particularly when groups of people are involved. And war can take place when these groups resort to the use of armed hostilities.

Individuals or even states can 'feel' insecure due to 'real' threats and violence, or the 'imagined' threat felt in the international system. Whether a nation is under direct attack from another, or whether it merely feels its values and culture are threatened due to the influence of another state in the international system, insecurity may indeed be present.

Of course, security is thought of differently today. Once, a state's security was almost completely based on its location and its proximity to potential allies and enemies. States in Western Europe, for instance, were constantly balancing the power of other alliances in an effort to avoid a situation where one side could be strong enough to challenge another with the threat of force. All of this is related to '**geopolitics**,' the relationship of political relationships to the geographical location of a state. Access to resources, beneficial or detrimental relations with neighbours, physical strength, population, and natural attributes all fall into the considerations of geopolitics.

Security
freedom from danger or injury

Insecurity
threat of danger or injury

Geopolitics
relationship of political relationships to the geographical location of a state

Geopolitics is still relevant today. Think of the geographical position Canada occupies in the world: close to the most powerful nation on earth (and Canada's closest ally), separated physically from some of the most dangerous regions in the world, and benefiting from one of the best standards of living thanks to its peaceful system of politics, large resource base, and educated citizens. Now, imagine if Canada were in the Asian subcontinent, or in the Middle East. In that scenario, Canada's relative security would undoubtedly be challenged by unstable regional politics, concerns over access to resources, and uncertainty about potential threats from neighbours. It would be a very different environment indeed for Canadians.

Even though today states are able to achieve certain goals — such as access to strategic resources — without necessarily having to actually possess the needed features required for those goals, geopolitics is still important in international relations. Some states, such as Japan, literally cannot feed themselves; in these instances, countries are unable to produce or obtain what is required for their very existence. However, in the modern world, states such as Japan need not have direct possession of such resources; they only have to have access to them. Such access is possible through trade and alliances with other states.

12.1

Human Security

Human security emerged in the 1990s as an alternative to traditional 'statist' security. At that time, prominent non-governmental activists such as Jody Williams of the International Campaign to Ban Landmines (ICBL) and politicians like Canadian Minister of Foreign Affairs Lloyd Axworthy sought an approach that focused attention on the security of the person, rather than the state. Human security created a fair amount of controversy in international security studies, with its assumption that an individual's protection comes not just from the safeguarding of the state, but also from access to well-being and quality of life. Human security entails the protection from threats that accompany aspects of non-territorial insecurity, such as environmental scarcity, human rights violations, genocide, and mass migration. Human security is often considered problematic for international security because it is more difficult to assess personal security than, say, an attack by one state on another. For instance, would someone be 'insecure' if they did not have access to social infrastructure, or health care? Some would say yes, others would disagree. But security has been contested for a very long time. We can define security in terms of military protection, meaning the defence of citizens, territory, and resources by military means. We can also think of it in political terms, such as the protection of government organizations and political ideology. Alternatively, economic security might be considered as the maintenance of welfare for citizens, and access to finance and markets. Societal security refers to the preservation of culture, social order, and communal identity. And environmental security signifies the conservation of natural ecosystems. All of these in some way impact the individual. In this way, we might say that any form of insecurity can be connected to human security.

International security is actually about the conditions caused by insecurity, since states in the international system are fundamentally concerned about their own self-preservation. A state is insecure if it is unable to provide for self-preservation (either for itself as a government, or for its citizens). Without security, any other goal of the state — such as economic prosperity and a better life for its people — would be impossible.

Insecurity can arise from a variety of causes. In simple terms, it involves threats to a physical place, person, or groups, or to important values felt by the community.

Or, these threats might emerge as pressures placed on individual or collective material welfare. That is to say, a better way of life, or prosperity, may be threatened due to conflict. Although the roots of these conflicts clearly cover a wide spectrum of threats, all of them can ultimately lead to more serious conflict, or even war. Finally, these threats may be directed at one's identity: how we define or identify ourselves.

Threats themselves, of course, also come in a variety of forms. Military threats involve physical harm. Economic threats relate to material welfare. Political threats deal with governance, control, and instability. Cultural threats are those directed at our values and way of life. Finally, environmental threats affect the conditions that sustain our communities.

It is evident, then, that security and conflict are complex dynamics involving much more than simply declaring war, or using armed force against another actor. Not surprisingly, given the wide variety of sources, conflict has always been present in international relations.

Part of the reason for the rising frequency of conflict is because of a condition in international relations that has been around for hundreds of years: **international anarchy**. 'Anarchy' tends to bring about images of chaos and destruction, a lawless environment of all against all, but this is not what we mean here.

Rather, anarchy refers to a fairly simple principle in international relations. Anarchy means 'no government', and since there is no 'world' government, the authority of nation-states is the most important power in the world. So, left with an international system that is anarchical, state security is left to the individual ability of states themselves, and the relations they have with others in the system.

The issue of anarchy at the international level is very important. On the one hand it allows states to be the ultimate authority in international relations, which means that citizens have an identifiable institution (that is, the state or government) that they can look to for protection, representation, and guidance. On the other hand, anarchy in the international system creates a security 'dilemma' for states.

Put in most basic terms, all states are potentially insecure, because the very attempt by one state to make itself secure makes other states less secure. This is known as the **security dilemma**. The underlying assumption is that not all states can be secure, given the limited resources and competing interests that exist. Even if states don't actively seek out conflict with others, the security dilemma suggests that conflict will ultimately arise. This is because, while one state maintains a military to protect itself, the presence of this military force could create tensions and insecurity for another state, since the other state might see the military

International anarchy
condition where there is no 'world government'; the sovereign nation-state is the highest authority in the international system

Security dilemma
conception in world politics that states are both protected by the existence of states, and threatened by them

12.2

Anarchy in the UK

In 1975 the Sex Pistols exploded on the British music scene, with a style that reflected disenfranchised youth living in the midst of an economic recession and chronic unemployment in that country. Considered front men for a burgeoning punk movement in the UK, the Sex Pistols and their 1976 single 'Anarchy in the UK,' from the album *Never Mind the Bollocks, Here's the Sex Pistols* (released in 1977), galvanized a counterculture and shocked the masses.

© CBW/Alamy

'Anarchy in the UK' was released to coincide with Queen Elizabeth's silver jubilee celebration.

The song's aggressive lyrics ('get pissed, destroy') and pessimistic take on British society conveyed both a hopeful and hopeless meaning: to the punk movement, the song typified its sense of disengagement and provided a vehicle for their collective anger and calls for change; for 'conventional' society, the song was a threat and a challenge to social norms. 'Anarchy' in the song came to take on many meanings: it was anti-establishment and anti-Monarchy, contained violent social commentary, and acted as a siren call for many similar bands in the UK and abroad. Lead singer Johnny Rotten (John Lydon) later said the song showed what energy he gained from living in poverty, and revealed that he used the word 'anarchist' because it rhymed with 'anti-Christ', which he sings at the beginning of the song. 'Anarchy in the UK' speaks of the 'coming' state of anarchy as an alternative to the broken social order at that time in England. It advocated the collapse of the political system through anarchism, reflecting the classic philosophical roots of political anarchism, which promotes the sanctity of individuals as self-determining and purposeful decision-makers. It also got a number of punks thinking about political criticism in their lyrics, and arguably spawned a movement that is still alive today.

presence as a potential threat against itself. As one state increases its security, another sees its security decrease.

Security in the twenty-first century is a complicated and multi-faceted dynamic: it is affected by modern technology and globalization, but still driven by the same geopolitical tendencies that have accompanied international relations for centuries. And, most unfortunately, the most violent form of conflict — war — is as much with us today as it ever was.

War in International Relations

International security is about much more than war. With human society comes **conflict**. We are less sure about whether it is so closely connected with humankind; that is a question pondered, but not answered, by generations of social scientists. We cannot know for sure if conflict is innate in humans simply because it is impossible to study humans away from civilization. All human groups form some type of civilization, and all civilizations deal with conflict in one way or another. Conflict may be rooted in problems over territory, access to resources, religion, culture and ethnicity, family or tribal relations, alliances we have formed, or economic prosperity. It may come as the consequence of one, or any grouping, of these causes. It is used as a means of achieving goals and solving problems in society. It may not seem like the optimal way to go about it, but it's always been an option, and is often very effective.

Conflict can come in many forms. Loosely defined as the opposition of incompatible wishes or needs of a person or group of persons,[4] conflict does not necessarily mean outright **war**, which involves armed hostilities stemming from conflict between social groups, which mainly means states.[5] So, to begin, we need to be clear that the terms do not mean the same thing, though they are intricately related. Whereas conflict can mean disagreements, debates, threats, and all sorts of other differences of opinion, war is a more serious consequence of conflict. There may be conflict without war, but not the other way around. Since war is always an option, we are concerned about conflict getting out of control.

Even the most stable and secure governments must still deal with conflict. Foreign and defence policies are the ways in which governments form responses to potential conflict in the world. And war must be considered 'policy'. Military theorist Carl von Clausewitz (1780–1831) is famously known for writing that 'war is the continuation of politics by other means'.[6] Clausewitz felt that war must be seen as a legitimate tool for states to respond to insecurity in the international system. This means, then, that war must have rules, and must be waged according to them.

Regrettably, history is full of examples of how frequently states are prepared to use this method in negative ways. There are several ways in which power is used in a 'negative manner' in international politics. First, states use their power, in particular military power, to coerce others to do as they wish. States protect their sovereignty by threatening to use military force in protection of physical territory. Second, demands against other states are frequently made with the stated or understood threat of military intervention in the case of non-compliance with

Conflict
a state of actual or perceived incompatible interests

War
use of armed forces in conflict with enemy

12.3

Just Wars

War may be among the most brutal of human actions, but that is not to say that it doesn't fall within some legal guidelines. Civilizations have always figured out new and innovative ways to attack and fight others, but efforts have also been around to try to stem the activities of war. The Law of Armed Conflict (LOAC), which is actually a collection of many laws, is meant to protect innocents in the waging of war: those caught in the crossfire, either literally or figuratively. *Jus in bello*, or laws in war, outline acceptable practices in war, as well as violations, including war crimes. The Geneva Conventions, for instance, are treaties governing standards of international law in warfare. Sovereign states agree to recognize these conventions as binding with regard to proper and acceptable actions of states engaged in war. Another set of international law deals with the acceptable justifications for war. *Jus ad bellum*, or laws of war, stipulate the acceptable use of force. A broader philosophical strain underpins this: just war doctrine. Stemming from teachings of the Catholic Church and Roman philosophy, just war theory considered the conditions necessary to make war acceptable. There are several different interpretations of just war theory, with many requirements. Six, however, stand out as consistent in most interpretations. First, there must be satisfactory conditions for waging war; just cause, for example, might emerge when lives may be saved only through the use of force. The 'right intention' for war, then, must be to right a wrong. Second, these just wars must be separated from those fought for aggression. Third, the war should address comparative justice. This means that to be just, the war must address a significant suffering felt by one side, meaning that one side should suffer more greatly than another. This greater suffering would suggest a 'right' by one side to use war to defend itself or its interests. For instance, were Country A to use state-sponsored terrorism to attack innocents in Country B, Country B might invoke comparative justice as a means of legitimizing the use of force and killing. Fourth, wars must be waged by legitimate authorities, and these authorities must use acceptable and lawful agents, such as militaries — not, say, terrorist organizations. Fifth, the war may not be futile. There must be a sense that it can be won. And sixth, it should be fought with proportional means, meaning that the use of overwhelming force such as nuclear weapons would only be considered were these means to be employed by the other side.

Whereas once in world politics the winning country simply dictated the aftermath, more recently laws of war have included *jus post bellum*, or the conditions regarding the termination and follow-up to war. These terms are considered necessary to provide for a peaceful and fair termination to war, including treaties, just treatment of combatants, provisions against unjust gains by the winning side, and avoiding vengeance.

the threatening state's objectives. Third, states threaten or use trade embargoes and physical blockades to influence the behaviour of other states. Fourth, states use purely military force in order to accomplish their goals.

However, there is another dimension to the use of state 'power' as it pertains to conflict management and resolution. States often use their powers of influence, gained through respect and authority in the international system, to avoid conflict or avert it from taking place. Often powerful states will send representatives to negotiate with other states, sometimes in cases where the powerful state has no immediate relationship, as a means of obtaining settlement. In addition, states sometimes use the threat of their power to persuade other states from taking actions that may be deemed detrimental to the international system.

Canadians might find it difficult to legitimize the use of war as a means of policy. Some would reason that warfare should be an obsolete policy, since far better courses of action are available to governments. But, for better or worse (and largely worse), war is still with us, and we must still strive to understand it.

There is great debate about whether humans are more 'war-like' today than in the past. Comparisons of historical studies of war and contemporary instances of war are controversial for a number of reasons. First of all, our written account of war today is far more detailed and accurate than in the past. Also, there are many more states in the world today, and as a consequence, we should expect the number of conflicts to rise, since the number of actors is larger than in the past. And, different interpretations of 'war' have existed throughout the ages: religious wars, civil wars, ethnic wars, guerrilla wars, world wars, for example.

Despite these difficulties, many analysts have attempted to number conflicts in the past as compared to the number that exists today. Although the totals in different studies tend to vary, it's generally accepted that the past 3200 years have seen more than three thousand violent conflicts.[7] Many research studies, from

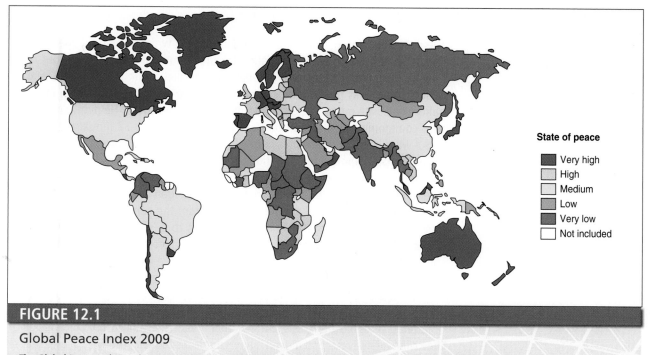

State of peace

- Very high
- High
- Medium
- Low
- Very low
- Not included

FIGURE 12.1

Global Peace Index 2009

The Global Peace Index ranks countries of the world based on their relative level of insecurity and security.

the Stockholm International Peace Research Institute (SIPRI) and the Correlates of War Project, have shown that the relative instance of war has increased since the end of World War II.

Although these numbers may not hold up to scientific precision, they do provide a basic benchmark for the instances of war in different periods. Many of these wars lasted more than one year. And many involved several countries at the same time. Some 'wars' are so contentious that even analysts cannot agree at times whether they count as wars or not. The point here is not about numbers; rather, it is about the rising incidences of violent conflict in the modern world.

Perhaps more worthy of note is not so much the sheer number of wars taking place today, but where they are happening. Since the Second World War, most wars in the world have taken place in the developing world — in South and Southeast Asia, in Central and South America, in Africa, the Mid-East, and Eastern Europe. Conventional wars taking place in Western Europe or North America are unheard of, although countries in these regions have taken part in wars waged elsewhere in the world. We can conclude from this that the more advanced and developed a region, the less likely violent conflict will occur there.

Further, the reasons why states go to war with each other tell us a lot about the use of conflict today. Although we live in an age of technology and globalization, wars today are fought for most of the same reasons as they were in the past: to create a state, in disputes over territory, to defend oneself or an ally, to maintain a governmental regime, or over ideology.

12.4

'Video Game' War, 1991

The First Gulf War in 1991 actually began in 1990 with the military operation Desert Shield, which was established to force Saddam Hussein's Iraq out of Kuwait. Iraq had annexed and occupied Kuwait illegally in August 1990, and Desert Shield was put together from over 34 separate countries as an international alliance meant to persuade Hussein to leave Kuwait. He didn't and the war, commonly called Operation Desert Storm, began on 17 January 1991. It was a war like no other. Seen instantly by millions of viewers around the world, images of precision-guided munitions and missiles (PGMs) and so-called smart bombs were carried by every major media outlet. The strange and eerily surreal video of tracer fire and bombs exploding over Baghdad on that first night made viewers feel at once involved and detached from the conflict. Commentators almost immediately began likening the images to a 'video game' where the player, or the viewer in this case, has an isolated and often unemotional relationship to the images on the screen. Viewers watched the war, but had no connection to it: they didn't see the death and destruction caused by the bombs and explosions, and the whole event had a sanitized quality to it. This wasn't a great surprise, as the US military had learned the hard way the lessons of permitting unfettered access to journalists in the Vietnam War. Then, uncensored pictures of the killing and devastation moved many Americans to reject the war. In the Gulf War, the reference to 'video games' soon became a form of criticism of the war

12.4 Continued...

and our impressions of it. More extreme references, like 'war porn', were used to describe the constant depiction of a war on the other side of the world, far from immediate effect on our lives. In 2003, with the Second Gulf War in Iraq, pundits resurrected the 'video game' metaphor. This time, there was a larger sense of reality, however. Secretary of State Colin Powell cautioned Americans: 'Remember, this is a real war — not a video game.'[8] In 1991, technology had given the US and its allies a huge advantage, where a war could be fought from a distance, with relatively little direct impact. It presented a false image of the conflict, a tidy war with few casualties, at least for the alliance.

As the saying goes, the more things change, the more they stay the same.

But of course there is more to conflict today than just what has not changed. The fact that so much of violence in the international system today is reminiscent of violence from the past tells us that international security today is a vital part of the study of international relations.

Terrorism

The terrorist attacks on New York, Washington, and Pennsylvania on September 11, 2001, were not, of course, the first case of international **terrorism**.

But the sheer magnitude of the attacks, combined with the fact that the target was the United States, the most powerful country in the world, caused our collective understanding of insecurity in international relations to focus on the problems of terrorism, and the very real threat that it poses to anyone, anywhere, and at any time.

Those attacks were the most severe acts of terrorism in history. Close to three thousand people were killed, immediate economic costs in the billions of dollars were incurred, and the more long-term effects led to a United States–led war in Afghanistan in 2001, then renewed conflict in Iraq in 2003. The attacks also had 'spin-off' effects, negatively affecting international economic markets, tourism and travel, relations among allies in Europe and North America, and causing serious questions to be asked about the future of international relations and American

Terrorism
strategy of violence designed to bring about political change by instilling fear in the public at large

The 9/11 attacks in the United States were the largest terrorist strikes in history and still have a broad effect on American foreign and domestic policies.

© Andrew Slayman/Artful Media LLC/Alamy

leadership in the world system. So many aspects of our lives, from the most banal (removing your shoes and checking the size of your toothpaste tube at airline security) to the more solemn (hearing of another Canadian soldier killed by a roadside bomb in Afghanistan) are the direct consequence of the events that day.

What made these terrorist attacks so of the essence for international relations was the fact that they were staged by illegitimate actors in the international system, caused such massive unrest, and completely altered the focus of the foreign policy of the United States, thereby affecting the entire global system. Prior to 9/11, President George W. Bush was facing an economic downturn, and citizens were wondering what his presidency, then only months old, would mean for the country. All that, and the focus of American foreign policy, changed in a matter of hours that morning. The US had been hit directly and on its own soil, and the approach we all take to terrorism (studying it, responding to it) would not be the same.

Unlike conventional threats or attacks made by states against each other, terrorism has a different set of causes, as well as different motivations and targets. Terrorism is a strategy of violence designed to bring about political change by instilling fear in the public at large.[9] This means that terrorism is more than simple criminal behaviour; it is politically motivated, and seeks change. The target is not necessarily a government, but rather citizens. The causes of terrorism are multi-faceted, too. Political, cultural, religious, social, and economic causes — and sometimes several of these at the same time — all can lead to terrorist attacks.

Terrorism is based on the idea (hence the 'ism' in terrorism, denoting a belief or an idea) that the kind of change desired by the terrorist can only be brought about with violence. Psychological studies inform us that terrorists are motivated to commit their acts of violence because they come to believe that they cannot cause change to occur using the 'conventional' or accepted modes offered in society. Violence, then, is seen as the only 'option' for terrorists, who believe that there is a real lack of political opportunity for them in existing political structures. They believe that these structures are illegitimate (just as we believe that terrorism is illegitimate) and have become disillusioned with the prospects for the change they desire. Those political structures cannot be changed to suit the terrorist, so they must be destroyed.

Terrorist organizations often are formed as the result of individuals who have a severe personal dissatisfaction with existing political structures, and want to participate in other, more violent actions. These individuals usually project their attitudes with others who feel the same way, thus creating terrorist groups.

It is crucial to keep in mind that these groups differ from others in their fundamental impression that the 'system' that is accepted by others (a government or society) is illegitimate, and must be attacked or destroyed.

Disgruntled groups often choose terrorism because it is difficult for governments to 'predict' when a terrorist act will take place. Also, the modes of terrorist actions are usually relatively inexpensive. For instance, the terrorists who struck on September 11, 2001, utilized box cutters, and commandeered airliners. For these reasons, it is extremely difficult for governments to respond effectively to, let alone prevent, terrorist acts.

12.5

Al-Qaeda

Al-Qaeda ('the base') represents a particularly nefarious example of globalization today. Rather like a corporation or an international organization, al-Qaeda has taken advantage of modern communications, transportation, finance, and technology to establish a truly twenty-first-century version of an ancient means of political violence. But unlike these other types of institutions, al-Qaeda is a terrorist group dedicated to eliminating any foreign influence in the Muslim world and creating a new Islamic political system. In many ways al-Qaeda is no different from other terrorist organizations: it seeks political change, uses violence, and targets innocent citizens in its ruthless attempts to alter the political system in which it exists. Aside from its most notorious 9/11 attacks (and an earlier, lesser-known attack on the World Trade Center in New York in 1993), it is also responsible for terrorist strikes in Turkey, Tanzania, Kenya, and Yemen. Formed in 1988, al-Qaeda rose from the ashes of the mujahedeen movement in Afghanistan, a group that fought the Soviet occupying forces, and which was initially backed by the United States. The mujahedeen went on to establish several different groups, with Osama bin Laden leading the newly formed al-Qaeda. Operations Desert Shield and Storm in 1990 and 1991 saw thousands of American troops stationed in Saudi Arabia, considered sacred due to its Muslim holy sites like Mecca and Medina. In 1996 he issued a fatwa against the United States, effectively declaring war. Bombings in Khobar, Saudi Arabia, then against the *USS Cole* off the coast of Yemen, and the bombings at US embassies in Tanzania and Kenya, signalled the seriousness of al-Qaeda's fatwa. Clearly, 9/11 was the organization's master stroke. Key to the group's success was its organization, containing a military wing, an internal financial system, a political and legal division, and even a public relations and media section. A truly 'global' organization, al-Qaeda has operations in dozens of countries.

Making matters even more complicated is the fact that many states in the international system — states that are recognized as legitimate by others — support terrorist actions. This state-sponsored form of terrorism is often used because it is thought that terrorism could achieve objectives where conventional military forces would not be practical, or effective. States such as Libya, North Korea, Afghanistan, Sudan, Syria, and Lebanon have all at some time been labelled 'sponsoring' states.

Terrorism will remain a particularly difficult problem for international security because it is a unique example of a threat in the international system. Responding to terrorism is made more difficult because treating it as a crime does not recognize the fully political nature of terrorist actions. Responding to terrorism under the conventions of warfare is also unfavourable because doing so might give the terrorist actions 'legitimacy' in the eyes of terrorist supporters, or other observers. Moreover, putting policies in place to dissuade terrorism often comes at the cost of civil liberties (such as the US Patriot Act). For instance, concerns about terrorist activities might lead overzealous authorities to disallow legitimate political protests.

Deterring and preventing terrorism, therefore, is easier said than done. Unlike other forms of insecurity in the international system, terrorism is particularly problematic. Simply understanding the causes of terrorism requires a full-bore overview of almost every aspect of international relations that could present answers to the question of why some individuals and groups feel severely ostracized or unable to accept what the rest of society — or even the world — feels is legitimate. On the one hand, there will always be those who feel marginalized, but that does not necessarily mean they will become terrorists. On the other hand, trying to establish 'root causes' of terrorism often leads to simplistic answers about why terrorists choose their approach in the first place. Unfortunately, terrorism will remain an option for individuals and groups that feel violence is the only way change will be brought about. This means that governments will continue to be challenged to respond to terrorist actions, and to try to protect their citizens from terrorism.

Humanitarian Interventionism

It is easy to see how countries 'intervene' in the affairs of others. Indeed, we've been discussing so many aspects of intervention in this book without even mentioning the term outright. But the nature of competing ideas, the need for trade and commerce, cultural relations, and global media all inevitably lead to some degree of intervention by someone or other. After all, just 'getting involved' with the affairs of another can be seen as intervention, even if it is a mild form of what we commonly see as forcibly getting involved. Intervention can be much more serious, however.

In international relations states are constantly intervening in the politics of others; it's really a natural part of the daily interaction of various actors on the global scale. But humanitarian intervention is of a different sort. Reflecting its name, this form of intervention involves the actions of one or many on behalf of those unable to care for themselves. Humanitarian intervention involves the interference in the affairs of a sovereign state with the intention of reducing the suffering felt by people in that country. And it is very controversial.

Intervention can be justified or legitimized for a variety of reasons, some more compelling than others. It is hard to find true examples of altruism in international relations, where states have acted selflessly in the interests of those needing help. Rather, interventions tend to occur when and where states seek to make some gains. Many, for instance, defended the Age of Empire as a necessary means of civilizing parts of the world that were considered barbarous. John Stuart Mill, for one, argued that it was the right and responsibility of civilized states to intervene in the interests of international morality.[10] Yet while in the modern era it is much harder to make the case that one group may be considered more 'civilized' than another, the basis for modern humanitarian interventionism is similarly based on many of Mill's ideas. The basic theory is still in place: one group is considered incapable or unable to provide the basic humanitarian needs for its citizens; worse, it could be that the group (a government, ethnicity, or community) is actively depriving its citizens of these needs.

12.6

Intervention Failure: Rwanda

One of the worst examples of humanitarian crisis began with an airline crash in April 1994. Rwandan President Juvénal Habyarimana and Burundi President Cyprien Ntaryamira were killed instantly when their plan went down under suspicious circumstances (it is known that the plane was shot down, but not by whom). At that time, the United Nations had a military force in Rwanda, the United Nations Assistance Mission for Rwanda, to police the ceasefire ending the Rwandan civil war. Canadian Lieutenant General Roméo Dallaire was in charge of the UN mission, and sought to protect Rwandan Prime Minister Agathe Uwilingiyimana, who was constitutionally next in line of authority. She and her 10 Belgian UN guards were killed, along with others that supported the peace agreement. Almost immediately ethnic Tutsis were sought out and murdered by Hutu militia groups, which aimed to eliminate completely the Tutsis in Rwanda. Stories of extreme brutality emerged over the coming months as between 800,000 and 1,000,000 Rwandans were killed. It is estimated that about 90 per cent of these were Tutsis. The UN troops were not allowed to intervene unless given express authority to do so by the UN headquarters in New York. Evidence of genocide was considered necessary before the peacekeepers would have been given the right to intervene. The UN in New York was fearful of negative reaction or being drawn into a protracted civil conflict without the resources or support to respond effectively. Despite the pleas of General Dallaire and others, the UN command refused to allow the peacekeepers to use force. Dallaire's peacekeepers were ordered to concentrate on removing foreigners and officials from Rwanda; meanwhile, thousands of Rwandans were slaughtered in many mass killings. Although he was ordered otherwise, Dallaire set up 'safe areas' where over 20,000 people were protected by the small military force the UN kept in the country. Still, many more died in what is now considered an avoidable human catastrophe. No less than former President Bill Clinton later stated that the US and the UN community should have recognized what Dallaire was warning was happening. Many agreed that even a small military force would have avoided the largest share of the mass murders. The Rwandan genocide led to a disaster hardly rivalled in modern history — in a few months perhaps a million dead, hundreds of thousands displaced or refugees, a failed state, and the exposed weakness of an institution (the UN) that was created in part to avoid this sort of occurrence. Rwanda and humanitarian intervention will always be linked due to this horrible example of the consequences of apathy.

The end of World War II and the global shock at the **genocide** committed during the Holocaust galvanized views regarding the necessity for collective action against any future atrocities. During that time, more than 6 million Jews, and millions of other peoples, including homosexuals, those with disabilities, and ethnic groups such as Romani and Poles were systematically exterminated by the Nazi regime of Adolf Hitler. Though the full extent of these horrors wasn't revealed until after the war, the collective guilt and shame felt by Allied countries

Genocide
deliberate and systematic killing of a group based on their ethnicity, nationality, culture, or race

that did not do all they could to stop the killings led to a new consideration for humanitarian intervention — the need to intervene to protect the unprotected.

Of course, to intervene in every case of human suffering would be practically impossible. Its supporters and detractors interpret humanitarian intervention differently, but it can be said that it assumes a moral responsibility to stop the killing of people, even in foreign countries. Perhaps the best recent attempt to codify humanitarian intervention was the International Commission on Intervention and State Sovereignty, established by the Canadian government in 2001 to examine and promote the concept and offer clear options for the international community. The resulting report of that commission, the Responsibility to Protect (R2P), captured the emerging theory surrounding the necessity for the global community to get involved when killings and major human rights abuses were known to take place.

This has had wide implications for state sovereignty, as we know it. Sovereignty, as you will recall, enshrines the rights of governments to act as the final authority within their borders. No other actor is supposed to have control over governments. The United Nations Charter upholds this principle. But it also upholds the preservation of the individual, and the accountability governments have to their citizens. Indeed, the United Nations as an organization is in many ways caught between these objectives: preserving the state yet protecting citizens. Critics of humanitarian interventionism point to this weakness: identifying a case where intervention is legitimate requires some subjective consideration. What might those considerations be? Regardless how rigorous the process may be, can we be certain that the true interests of people will be upheld, and that state governments will not act in their own self-interest? And, will intervention simply be another, more modern, case of imperialism, where the rich industrialized nations decide to intervene because poorer countries are thought to be ungovernable? Were this to be the case, Mill's 'thoughts' on intervention might be as vital today as they were in the nineteenth century.

Defenders of humanitarian intervention, of course, do not wish this to happen. They suggest that intervention is possible under more strictly defined conditions and in the interests of people, not governments. Major developments such as R2P help to redefine our thinking about when we must intervene in the affairs of others. Examples such as the Holocaust and the Rwandan genocide remind us that the sanctity of the sovereign state is not infallible, and that we have a collective responsibility to humanity, regardless of our national identity.

Peacekeeping, Conflict Management, and Resolution

Managing conflict in a globalized world is a more complicated matter than in the past. More states and issues, coupled with major advances in military weaponry, make conflict management an immediate concern for all states. Management and resolution can come in a variety of forms. In fact, war is a form of resolution: there's a conflict between two parties, a war occurs, one side wins, and the conflict is resolved. However, even the most cursory examination of this process shows real problems. One side will likely not be satisfied with the 'resolution', the other side may take advantage of its victory to punish its enemy, and in all likelihood the conflict will one day emerge again.

Other management tools are needed in modern international relations. Diplomacy, **negotiation**, **mediation**, and **arbitration** — these methods are less likely to cause adverse effects for any side, and offer the hope of peaceful resolution. But what if a conflict has already escalated to war? How to resolve, without total victory and loss for one side or the other?

Perhaps the best example of conflict management in the modern age, **peacekeeping**, presents a unique way to use military force not to resist attack or to attack others, but rather to enforce a ceasefire. Peacekeeping involves the use of lightly armed soldiers put in zones of active fighting. It can occur before or after outright hostilities have broken out, and its intention is to provide a forceful peace until a long-term resolution can be worked out. It is a method of conflict management, and in recent years has been broadened to include more robust activities such as peace enforcement, or peace building.

It has often been suggested that peacekeeping is a 'Canadian' invention. That is because Lester B. Pearson, a former external affairs minister and later prime minister, proposed the first real peacekeeping mission. The issue was over a potential conflict in the Suez Canal region in 1956. Egyptian President Gamal Nasser had nationalized the canal, leading France, the United Kingdom, and Israel to begin plans to attack Egypt in retaliation. Pearson suggested that the United Nations send an 'emergency force' to maintain a truce while a political solution was sought. The United Nations Emergency Force (UNEF) was a success, and ushered in a new, strong mandate for the UN.

The United Nations was formed in 1945 as a specialized agency of sovereign states. The UN has many roles — a political forum, a conflict mediator, a security organization, and an economic development institution. However, the primary objective of the UN is evident in the very first line of the Charter of the UN (which is rather like the 'constitution' of the UN, with which all members must agree before becoming members). The opening line reads in part: 'to save succeeding generations from the scourge of war, which twice in our lifetime has brought untold sorrow to mankind'. Clearly, the primary intent of the UN was to manage conflict.

Even before 1956, there were missions sponsored by the UN in Greece, India, and Pakistan, and the Middle East (after the Arab–Israeli War), where the United Nations Security Council sent observers to try to maintain peace amongst adversaries.

Peacekeeping is defined by the UN as the 'deployment of international military and civilian personnel to a conflict area, with the consent of the parties to the conflict, in order to: stop or contain hostilities or supervise the carrying out of a peace agreement'. Since 1948, there have been 63 peacekeeping missions sponsored by the UN, and there were 16 ongoing missions in 2009. Most of these missions were in Africa, Latin America, the Middle East, Southeast Asia, the North Pacific, Eastern Europe, and the Indian subcontinent. This is not surprising,

Negotiation
bargaining process among parties to seek commonly agreed upon resolution of dispute

Mediation
voluntary process using impartial party to bring about resolution of dispute

Arbitration
authoritative resolution to dispute made by impartial person agreed upon by all parties

Peacekeeping
military and civilian personnel in a conflict area used to stop or contain hostilities or supervise the carrying out of a peace agreement

since these are the areas most prone to conflict in the international system. Even though relatively safe countries such as Canada are not as concerned about conflict in their borders, they maintain an active interest in peacekeeping because of the 'interdependent' nature of international security. That is the idea that insecurity in one region might 'spill over' into other areas, drawing in nations that otherwise might not be involved.

There are criticisms of peacekeeping that are based on a variety of issues. Some worry about the role of an international organization such as the UN in a world of sovereign states. Others suggest that international peacekeeping has become overloaded, meaning that the UN cannot respond effectively to emerging security threats. Apprehensions about 'interoperability' — the ability of different armed forces to work together — and the communications between military and political agencies involved in peacekeeping also lead some to question the viability of peacekeeping. There are also concerns about how and where operations are defined and carried out. Finally, there are questions about the continued support of peacekeeping from Great Power nations such as the US, the UK, and China.

Despite these problems, peacekeeping remains one of the most positive contributions to international stability in the last century. As other organizations, such as NATO, and the African Union (AU), take on international peacekeeping as part of their mandate, there will inevitably be disputes between these agencies and the UN. Later in this chapter we'll look more closely at one operation that includes peacekeeping, but also a lot more — the NATO mission in Afghanistan.

The useful contribution made by peacekeeping towards the cause of international peace and security assures its continued and robust role in the future. In large part this is because peacekeeping has been shown to be a significant part of conflict management and resolution.[11] It stands out as an example of conflict management because it is so noticeable; military force rarely avoids attention. And in cases where conflict has escalated to hostility, peacekeeping is very effective.

More common than peacekeeping, negotiation involves bargaining and discussion to resolve a conflict. Much of foreign policy diplomacy falls within negotiation, as sides to a debate position themselves and their objectives, knowing that they will likely have to relent on at least some of their goals. There are times, of course, that negotiation does not result in a satisfactory conclusion, and so mediation is often employed. This is when parties outside the conflict get involved to bring the parties together to discuss ways to resolve it. Parties are not usually bound to the results, however, so the 'art' in mediation is essential: mediators must balance the various points of view and compose a scenario where all may be satisfied, even if none receive what they initially anticipated. Since parties will often be completely unsatisfied with a suggested conclusion to a dispute, mediation will sometimes fail. In these cases, arbitration takes mediation to a higher level, often requiring that parties adhere to the recommendation. However, these 'binding' arbitration results are very hard to enforce because comparable institutions, such as courts in international relations or international law, do not have the same level of enforceability. Rather, parties involved must agree to live up to the results, which they will often ignore if they feel their interests are not upheld.

Canada in Afghanistan

A month after the terrorist attacks of 9/11, Canada began its involvement in the international military engagement in Afghanistan. To be precise, Operation Apollo was a naval mission involving the HMCS *Charlottetown*, HMCS *Iroquois*, and HMCS *Preserver*, which were sent to the Arabian Gulf. Later, in November, members of Canada's elite military commando unit, the Joint Task Force 2 (JTF2), were part of international operations in Afghanistan against Taliban and al-Qaeda fighters. In February 2002, Canadian soldiers from the Princess Patricia's Canadian Light Infantry (PPCLI) landed in Afghanistan and subsequently set up a base on the outskirts of Kabul, the capital city. By 2004 the Canadian contingent stood at just over two thousand personnel, one of the largest national contingents in the country.

Canada's involvement in Afghanistan was part of the international alliance of states that responded to the terrorist threat that had materialized in the 9/11 attacks in the United States. Al-Qaeda, the terrorist organization responsible for the attacks, had its headquarters in Afghanistan, where the Taliban-controlled government gave it sanctuary. At that time, the Taliban was not recognized as a legitimate government; only three states gave it diplomatic recognition: Pakistan, Saudi Arabia, and the United Arab Emirates. In response to the 9/11 attacks, the United States and its allies invaded Afghanistan. Both the United Nations Security Council and the North Atlantic Treaty Organization (NATO) sanctioned the military action. The International Security Assistance Force (ISAF) was created by the UN in late 2001 to oversee military operations. ISAF first concentrated on establishing peace and security in Kabul while military forces from some countries, notably the US and the UK, continued a separate military operation called Operation Enduring Freedom (OEF) in other parts of the country. Later, in 2003, NATO took control of ISAF and slowly began to expand its geographical reach to include the rest of the country.

Until 2005, the Canadian mission was almost entirely in Kabul, the capital city, where the situation was much calmer than the rest of the country. Canada's mission in Kabul was part of the ISAF mandate there and as a member of the Kabul Multinational Brigade (KMNB). From 2003 to 2005 Canada's Operation Athena provided local peacekeeping, military patrols, as well as civilian assistance in the city and the region to aid the reconstruction effort.

Canada's role in Afghanistan began to change markedly in 2005. In August 2005 the Canadian government shut down its mission in Kabul and moved to the much more dangerous Kandahar region to take control of the Kandahar Provincial Reconstruction Team (KPRT) and the Multinational Brigade there. Building on the multi-faceted approach it had adopted in Kabul, Canada's role in Afghanistan included aid and assistance work, political relations, policing, training, and military operations. But it was the military operations that garnered most criticism.

Until Canada had moved to the southern part of Afghanistan, casualties and deaths had remained relatively low. In the mostly safer areas of Kabul, Canadian military deaths remained in the single digits. And while commentators, politicians, and the public in Canada scrutinized these deaths they were considered, for the most part, a tragic necessity for being in a war zone. However, in the unstable Kandahar region, where the Taliban had its centre of power during its rule and now where hundreds of fighters had fled due to the war in the rest of the country, the Canadians had a harder fight to wage. Operation Archer, the name given to Canada's Kandahar mission, involved far more conventional battle operations with Taliban insurgents. The death and casualty toll quickly rose, and with it new criticism and public outcry over the methods and objections of the mission. For many, Canada's image as a peacekeeping country (which has always been called into question by those familiar with Canada's actual war history), did not fit with this new and robust military role.

The Canadian mission in Afghanistan is complicated. Canada came to the aid of its military ally, the United States, but in a mission authorized by the UN and NATO; others were involved, as well, in a clearly identified multinational alliance. As part of a military alliance — NATO — Canada is required to assist when another member is attacked. Moreover, Canada's involvement in Afghanistan is not only military. In fact, much of the development and assistance work undertaken by Canadian agencies (including the Canadian International Development Agency, non-governmental organizations, the RCMP, Foreign Affairs, and the Canadian Forces) gets buried in media reports while the more sensationalistic stories about military deaths caused by roadside bombs and suicide bombers tend to receive more attention. It is natural, of course, to focus on the extreme, but the full role for Canada in Afghanistan has been comprehensive, and the real success or failure of the ISAF mission will only be known in the years to come.

The Afghan mission is an excellent example of the changing nature of international security today. A terrorist organization sheltered by a reclusive illegitimate regime in a far-flung country struck a devastating blow against the most powerful nation on earth, changing the course of history and the focus of international relations. But the ongoing response to that event is perhaps more significant: the success or failure of the mission in Afghanistan will speak volumes about the ability of rich nations to develop and facilitate change in the most underdeveloped and forgotten parts of the world. The mission is multi-faceted by design and by necessity; a military undertaking alone would not solve the problem and would certainly only usher in more instability after the battles were done. If it is successful, the development side of the mission could provide a template for other countries facing similar dire circumstances.

Conclusion

International security is a wide-ranging and important part of international relations and political studies. War and conflict have always been a part of human sociability, and the history of human relations shows the various ways that we inflict increasing levels of suffering and fear on one another. In an anarchical international system, arms races, weapons of mass destruction, and the use of force will continue to be used by nation-states as a means of attaining goals. Perhaps more optimistically, we might look to developments in peacekeeping and human security as more constructive ways to view and utilize armed force in international relations.

We have seen how international security often means that states will disagree or come into conflict with one another over a variety of reasons. But there is a co-operative aspect to security as well, rather than a simple 'all against all' view of the world. Conflict management requires co-operative behaviour, and modern conflict avoidance means greater attention than ever to work with others to achieve stability and peace. On this theme we now turn to the international political economy, an aspect of political studies that certainly requires co-operative action.

Self-Assessment Questions

1. How does the 'security dilemma' potentially make all states in the world less secure?
2. What is the connection between terrorism and Canada's involvement in Afghanistan?
3. How do geopolitics and international anarchy affect a country's relative security?
4. Can you have war without conflict? Conflict without war?
5. Humanitarian interventionism expands on the rights of states to include the responsibilities of states. How?
6. How is peacekeeping a form of conflict management?

Weblinks

CBC Information on Canadian Involvement in Afghanistan
www.cbc.ca/canada/story/2009/02/10/f-afghanistan.html

United Nations Department of Peacekeeping Operations
http://www.un.org/en/peacekeeping/

Human Security Network
www.humansecuritynetwork.org

BBC Information on Rwandan Genocide
news.bbc.co.uk/2/hi/africa/1288230.stm

Stockholm International Peace Research Institute
www.sipri.org

Canadian International Development Agency
www.acdi-cida.gc.ca/index.htm

International Security Assistance Force
www.nato.int/ISAF

Correlates of War
www.correlatesofwar.org

Further Reading

Betts, Richard K. *Conflict After Cold War: Arguments on Causes of War and Peace.* 3rd ed. New York: Longman, 2008.
Dannreuther, Roland. *International Security: The Contemporary Agenda.* Cambridge: Polity Press, 2007.

Nacos, Brigitte L. *Terrorism and Counterterrorism: Understanding Threats and Responses in the Post-9/11 World.* 2nd ed. Toronto: Prentice Hall, 2008.
Strachan, Hew, and Andreas Herberg-Rothe. *Clausewitz in the Twenty-First Century.* New York: Oxford University Press, 2007.

 CBC News Clips

Visit the companion website for *Politics: An Introduction* to listen to news clips from the CBC radio archives.

13 International Political Economy

LEARNING
OBJECTIVES

After reading this chapter, you will be able to:

✳ discuss the major tenets of the most important theories and perspectives of international political economy

✳ explain the link between wealth and power in the international system

✳ understand the development of international trade, production, and finance since the nineteenth century

✳ explain the growth of economic interdependence between states

✳ understand the importance of international economic organizations.

Introduction

In this chapter of the book, you will be introduced to an area of study that has grown remarkably in the past 40 years. International Political Economy became established as a sub-discipline of political science and international relations in the 1970s, and since then has produced many of the insights that have been most important in advancing our understanding of the international system, of the dynamic relationship between politics and economics, and indeed of politics itself. International Political Economy, or IPE as it is most commonly called, covers a vast area of political and economic activity and clearly demonstrates the intimate connection between national and international processes.

What Is IPE?

IPE studies the interaction between politics and economics, between states and markets. Of course, in IPE we are looking at this interaction at the level of the international system. This does not mean that other levels of analysis are ignored. On the contrary, IPE explicitly recognizes that domestic and international actors and processes continuously interact. The most obvious example of this is, of course, the making of foreign economic policy.[1]

IPE examines how the activities and distribution of power between states and other political authorities affect the international economic system; as well, it looks at the impact of the activities and power of states on international economic processes and actors. In this way, it studies the interaction between the distribution of power and of wealth, and the intimate connection between economic and political power.[2] Throughout history, states have depended upon their economic capabilities to develop power and influence in other forms. The Spanish Crown, for example, in the fourteenth and fifteenth centuries, depended upon the supply of gold and silver from its New World colonies to underwrite its military prowess. In the nineteenth century, Great Britain built its primacy on its industrial leadership and dominance of international trade. And, of course, the global predominance of the United States at the beginning of the twenty-first century was dependent on the continuing strength of its domestic economy.

The scope of IPE is broad: IPE scholars study trade, finance, environment, gender, and energy policy, to name just a few areas of focus. What's more, the study of the international political economy encompasses the activities of many different actors, both state and non-state. The work of the International Monetary Fund (IMF), the World Bank, and the World Health Organization fit equally well into the scope of IPE, as do the operations of Walmart, Exxon/Mobil, Toyota, and other major multinational firms. Of particular importance and interest is the study of the interaction between different kinds of actors, and studying the balance of economic power among them. In international financial affairs, for example, since 1945 there has been a fundamental shift in power and influence away from states and towards private financial actors, such as banks and securities firms. The changing relations among the actors that have an impact on the shape of the international economic system are a primary concern of IPE.

The Perspectives of IPE

The discipline of international political economy is dominated by three major perspectives: liberal, Marxist, and nationalist.[3] The liberal perspective on IPE is guided by the central concerns of liberal ideology, both political and economic. It is concerned with the free functioning of markets, increased individual freedom, and progress in the form of increased wealth. It is also concerned with the issue of international co-operation between states, particularly, but not exclusively, in the area of trade. It is through co-operation that states can reduce the distorting effects of tariffs and duties, as well as creating institutions that in turn create rules for international economic interaction and can rescue the international economic system in times of trouble, such as the role of the IMF during the Asian crisis of 1997–8. The focus of the liberal perspective, however, is mainly aimed at removing the state as much as possible from the economic sphere, in turn increasing the role that the market plays in issues of distribution, competition, and pricing.

Marxists, on the other hand, have a quite different outlook on the international system. They view the international capitalist economy as a tool of oppression whereby the controllers of capital exploit the labouring classes. This perspective is extended to states: for Marxists the international economic system is one in which the wealthy, powerful states exploit their poorer, weaker counterparts. As we saw in Chapter 10, the challenges of development are many for LDCs, but Marxists see the structure of the international system as one of the major hurdles standing in the way of true development. The major concern of Marxist international political economists, therefore, is to analyze the unequal conditions of the international economy, and to study the exploitation of certain groups by others. It is important to remember that for most Marxists analysis of the exploitative nature of the international system goes hand-in-hand with a commitment to change it.

Nationalists see the international economy as an arena in which states are involved in a constant battle for survival, at least, and supremacy, at best. International economic relations, therefore, are viewed in a competitive light, with states striving to surpass each other not only in their levels of productivity, growth, and power, but also in the benefits that each gains from economic intercourse. Nationalists call for an expanded role for the state so that it can manage its external economic relations to the best advantage. Mercantilism is the best example of a nationalistic approach to international political economy, for it sees the state directing its foreign trade according to the principle of maximization of state power. A good historical example of economic nationalism at work is Nazi Germany in the 1930s. Under Adolf Hitler and his finance minister, Hjalmar Schacht, the German government manipulated its trade and financial relations with other states so that German state power was increased.

These three perspectives on IPE allow us to view the international economic system from different points of view; each of the different perspectives should be seen as useful in its own way. As we will see, the history of IPE in this century alone is a mixture of growth, liberalization, state control, and exploitation of the weak by the powerful. The competing perspectives on IPE, therefore, should not be seen as mutually exclusive. Rather, we should use them to ask interesting and important questions about the international economic system, questions such as:

- Which are the most important actors in the international economic system?
- Who gains from an economic relationship, and how much?
- Who pays the costs of an economic process?
- How are bargains struck between important actors?
- What are the conditions under which co-operation takes place?
- Is the role of the state in the economy increasing or decreasing?

Economic Interdependence

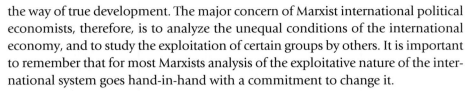

Interdependence
'mutual dependence';
a method of measuring dependent relationships among countries, based on the level of sensitivity and vulnerability one country has with respect to another

Much of the story of the development of the international economy contained in this chapter is the story of growing **interdependence** between states.[4] The term 'interdependence' refers to the mutual, but not necessarily equal, dependence between states. It can take an economic, political, environmental, or security form, but it always implies that actions and policies taken in one national political or economic system will have effects on other states in the international system.

An excellent example of interdependence can be found in the relationship between the United States and Canada. These two states have maintained peaceful relations since 1812, and their economies have become highly interconnected.

It is natural to think of Canada as being dependent upon the US, because it is clearly the less powerful partner in the relationship. But it would also be fair to say that the US is dependent upon the Canadian economy for a large part of its well-being. We must remember that the US–Canada trading relationship is the largest in the world, that many thousands of citizens of both countries work in the other country, that production processes extend North–South just as much as they do East–West, and that the environmental effects of economic activities in each state affects the other.

Interdependence, however, does not merely take the bilateral form that we see in the US–Canada relationship. It also applies to the interactions within and between regions, and between groups of states. As will be discussed later in this chapter, the international financial system, perhaps more than any other area of the global economy, has tied national economic systems together through flows of capital and currency trading.

International Economic Co-operation

The second half of the twentieth century saw unprecedented levels of economic co-operation between the great powers. The growth in international trade and finance, coupled with the emergence of new technologies and new markets in developing countries, pushed the industrialized states towards ever higher levels of interdependence. It would be easy to think that this happened spontaneously, that the growth in international markets was a natural phenomenon. Yet we must remember that states and other forms of political authority played a central role in increasing global economic interaction.[5]

Essential to the growth of interdependence were international organizations and institutions. To manage interdependence, and in many cases to propel it forward, the powerful states of the international economy created international institutions and international organizations (IOs) that facilitated the signing of multilateral agreements. Organizations such as the IMF and World Bank, the General Agreement on Tariffs and Trade (GATT), and the World Trade Organization (WTO) were all designed to increase levels of co-operation between states to maximize the beneficial effects of interdependence and to minimize the probability of conflict.[6]

But why are such institutions so important to international economic co-operation? Could states not just sign bilateral agreements and manage the international economy without the help of international organizations? The answer is that maybe they could, but history has shown that co-operation is more likely and more productive when IOs are used to promote it. International organizations perform many functions that contribute to the efficiency and probability of co-operation, such as providing a forum for negotiation and setting out definite rules and processes that make negotiation and the deals that emerge from it more predictable and reliable. International organizations also tie states into longer-term patterns of co-operation, which means that each individual state is less likely to cheat on a deal (which would mean missing out on the potential

13.1

International Economic Organizations and Their Functions

- International Monetary Fund (IMF) — international monetary co-operation, balance of payments stability, financial aid, technical aid;
- World Bank — lends money to developing countries for development projects, usually in the long term;
- Bank for International Settlements (BIS) — also known as the central bankers' bank, arranges loans for central banks and encourages central bank co-operation;
- International Labour Organization (ILO) — created in 1919 to improve working conditions around the world by setting minimum standards, providing technical assistance and promoting the development of labour unions; and
- World Trade Organization (WTO) — created in 1995 as a forum for promoting free trade between nations in goods and services.

benefits of such deals in the future). IOs can help to monitor and verify the implementation of international agreements, which helps to reassure negotiating parties that deals will be respected. All of these facets, of course, apply not only to the international economy but also to other areas of interstate interaction. But they have proven particularly important in the management of the international economy since 1945.

The World Trading System

Enter any grocery, department, or hardware store today and you will find the shelves stocked with goods from all over the world. The average consumer can now eat mangoes in any season, including midwinter (providing you are willing to pay the price), and choose from an array of home electronics made and assembled all over the world. International trade, by the beginning of the twenty-first century, has brought an unprecedented level of consumer choice to our society.[7] Trade, however, does not have merely economic effects. It can be a source of cultural contact between peoples, and is often responsible for the transmission of new ideas, concepts, and technologies. Indeed, throughout history trading routes have linked distant peoples together. The ancient Phoenicians brought goods from the eastern Mediterranean to the shores of the British Isles, thus linking the two peoples together through trade. African peoples who would never see each other's homelands were connected by trade routes that stretched for hundreds, even thousands of miles.

International trade is often credited with creating employment, increasing consumer choice, introducing new ideas and cultural ideals, and contributing to economic efficiency.[8] Indeed, there is a lot of evidence to support each of these claims. But international trade is not an issue on which everyone agrees, all accepting the great benefits to be gained from liberal trading policies. Just as trade creates employment, it has been known to destroy jobs in economies and industries that are not competitive by international standards, either in terms of their pricing or their quality. When such economies and industries are exposed to open international competition, they simply cannot maintain profitability, and may be forced to cut production and lay off workers if they are to survive. At times such as these, workers and producers alike call for **trade protection** from the government, seeking either **subsidies** to supplement their income, protective **tariffs** to reduce the price advantage of foreign goods, or other **non-tariff barriers** (**NTBs**) such as import licensing or quality controls.[9]

Equally controversial is the cultural aspect of international trade. As mentioned above, its proponents argue that trade introduces new ideas and norms to closed societies, thus contributing to mutual understanding between states and peoples.[10] However, trade can also be accused of contributing to the spread of dominant cultures at the expense of traditional values and norms. The spread of American products throughout the world, for example, has not been value-free. All one has to do is look at the packaging of a breakfast cereal box to realize that US culture is transmitted by the most unobtrusive means. And trade, of course, does not refer merely to manufactured goods or foodstuffs. Books, films, and music are also included within the sphere of international trade, as well as technology in the form of computers and software, for example. Faced with the overwhelming choice presented by goods from the industrialized states, it is very difficult for most traditional cultures to compete, particularly in the eyes of young people.

The Growth of Trade Since 1846

International trade as we know it today, with rapid transportation of goods from one side of the world to the other, with extremely low levels of government involvement and taxation, is a very recent development. High levels of growth in international trade have usually followed periods of rapid economic development and it was really only in the nineteenth century that the modern conception of international trade began to take shape. When it did, its development depended heavily on three factors: ideology, domestic political decisions, and the exercise of state power in the international system. The first factor, ideology, concerned the growing acceptance of Adam Smith's ideas concerning free trade, which had first been published in the eighteenth century. Smith's ideas were truly revolutionary, because prior to his work, *The Wealth of Nations*, mercantilism had been the dominant approach to international trade. Smith's argument was that free trade brought benefits in terms of efficiency, cost, and the division of labour.[11] The second factor, domestic politics, concerned the effects of industrialization. As Great Britain went through the Industrial Revolution and its economy became the most developed in the world, British producers needed to secure cheap supplies of food for their workers, so that they could keep wages low. Pressure from these British industrialists caused the government of that country to liberalize its food policy in 1846 by repealing the **Corn Laws**, a set of laws regulating the trade in corn, one of the most basic foodstuffs. This action led to the liberalization of

Trade protection
tendency of countries to safeguard their own economic sectors or industries using tariffs, quotas, or other forms of trade and investment legislation

Tariff
a duty placed on a particular categorization of imported or exported goods or services

Subsidies
payments made by government to businesses to compensate them for inefficiencies and lack of competitiveness

Non-tariff barriers (NTBs)
imposing national content requirements on certain products or applying quotas to their import

Corn Laws
set of laws regulating the trade in grains in Great Britain; the abolition of these laws in 1846 opened up British agricultural trade

Britain's agricultural trade, which in turn set the stage for that country opening its borders to all kinds of products from producers throughout the world.

When Great Britain did so, other nations reciprocated, though not to the same degree, and the overall result was a dramatic growth in the level of world trade, particularly among the European countries and their present and former colonies in Africa, India, and the Americas. Even when other states did not reciprocate fully in opening up their economies to trade, Britain still allowed its goods to enter with low tariffs. Britain was able to do so because its economy had become so much larger than other states', and thus the relative costs of such a policy were low. In order to maintain international trading routes, however, mere openness was not enough. The British navy, at the time by far the largest in the world, used its predominance to keep sea routes open and unmolested so that goods could travel unimpeded from one part of the world to the next. The transportation of goods was also greatly helped by British (and to a lesser degree German) investment in railway systems around the world.

The growth in international trade that went along with British economic and naval predominance continued until the early years of the twentieth century. With World War I, and the destruction that it wrought on European economies, trade would not regain its pre–World War I levels until long after World War II. One of the lessons of this period was that trade and peace were inextricably linked. Clearly, in a world where political and military relations between the Great Powers were unstable, it was very difficult for trade to flourish. However, some (liberal theorists) have also argued that high levels of trade between states help maintain peace.[12] The logic here is that if states depend on each other for their economic well-being, they would be unwilling to go to war because that would mean sacrificing the benefits of trade. Others have argued that the historical example of the First World War proves that even states who have high levels of trade between them (such as Britain and Germany at the end of the nineteenth century) will go to war with each other if they are rivals for military, economic, and cultural dominance.

The GATT

The end of the Second World War saw the emergence of the United States as an economic and military superpower. From this position of dominance, the US decided to shape the international economic system through the creation of institutions and organizations aimed at international economic management. In the area of trade the institution that emerged was the **General Agreement on Tariffs and Trade** (GATT).[13]

Though originally intended only as a temporary arrangement, the GATT became the world's permanent trade regime when the Havana Charter, a treaty aimed at creating an International Trade Organization (ITO), failed to be approved by the United States Congress. The GATT was designed to promote several values held to be central by the United States and its allies, values such as:

- **multilateralism**: that decisions would be taken in consultation with all members, and in their interests;

General Agreement on Tariffs and Trade (GATT)
originally intended only as a temporary arrangement when the International Trade Organization (ITO) failed; became the world's permanent trade regime and was later subsumed under the World Trade Organization (WTO)

Multilateralism
integration or coordination of policies or decision-making by three or more nation-states

- **reciprocity:** that the liberalization of trade would be beneficial for all parties concerned;
- **non-discrimination:** that no members of the GATT could be excluded from the benefits that one member state extended to another; and
- **free trade:** free trade was seen as promoting efficiency, prosperity, and peace.

The GATT came into operation in 1947 and until 1995 remained the world's trading regime. As an organization it proved incredibly successful in opening up international trade between the developed countries, and in particular in reducing tariffs between them.

However, the GATT system did not benefit all states in the international system equally. The communist bloc countries, of course, were excluded, but so were many developing countries whose industrial sectors were not sufficiently competitive to benefit from free trade, and most did not become members until the 1980s. A large number of LDCs chose to stay outside of the GATT rather than accept the principles outlined above, opting for policies of protectionism and state control of industries to aid rapid growth.

One of the major reasons why LDCs did not join the GATT system until the second half of the 1980s was that the achievements of the GATT in liberalizing trade were limited in one very important way. Until the late 1960s, the system focused on manufactured goods, leaving aside agricultural trade and commodities, traditionally two of the most difficult areas to liberalize. Agriculture and raw materials, of course, were two areas in which many LDCs had a comparative advantage, and thus it could be said that the GATT's operations were biased in favour of the developed states.

In response to these inadequacies of the GATT system, the developing states attempted to set up a rival organization for international trade in the 1960s. Under the auspices of the United Nations, the Conference on Trade and Development (UNCTAD) was created in 1964.[14] As its name suggests, the UNCTAD attempted to link the issues of trade and economic development directly, speaking to many of the developing states' concerns about agriculture and commodities. However, though the creation of the committee was a great achievement, the developed states refused to allow it to replace the GATT, opting instead to make small, conciliatory changes to that system to placate LDCs.

Despite the deep economic recessions that hit the industrialized states in the 1970s and early 1980s, international trade has continued to grow rapidly, slowing its rate of growth in the late 1990s only because of the financial and economic crises that hit Asia, Russia, and Brazil. Indeed, the growth in world trade has consistently outpaced the growth in the global economy as a whole, and continues to be a provider of employment in many parts of the world.

The WTO

The GATT was largely responsible for much of this growth from 1947 to 1995. In that year it was replaced as the world's trading regime by the **World Trade**

Reciprocity
complimentary or mutual behaviour among two or more actors; view that liberalization of trade would be beneficial for all parties concerned if co-operative policies were pursued

Non-discrimination
principle that no member of an organization be excluded from the benefits that one member state extends to another

Free trade
international trade among political systems unimpeded by restrictions or tariffs on imports or exports

UNCTAD
The United Nations Conference on Trade and Development

World Trade Organization (WTO)
created in 1995 as a forum for promoting free trade between nations in goods and services

Uruguay Round
longest round of GATT negotiations, eventually leading to establishment of the World Trade Organization

Dispute resolution
process by which trading disputes between member states can be resolved by an impartial tribunal, thus preventing such disputes from becoming too political or controversial

Regionalism
process of economic or political integration in a defined territorial area

European Union
the economic and political union of 27 European states

North American Free Trade Agreement (NAFTA)
agreement whereby Canada, the United States, and Mexico have opened their markets to each other

Organization (WTO).[15] The GATT was not discarded, but rather became part of a more formal international organization. During the **Uruguay Round** of GATT negotiations, which began in 1986, the world's most important trading nations agreed to overhaul the trading system and create a permanent international organization that is much more ambitious than the GATT was ever intended to be.[16] The WTO has a legal status matching that of the other major international economic organizations such as the IMF and World Bank, and places trade at the top of the international economic agenda alongside monetary and financial affairs.

Indeed, the WTO is one of the most important international organizations today, dealing with all aspects of trade, from manufactured goods to commodities, environmental aspects of trade to intellectual property, agriculture to trade and development. One of the key achievements of the WTO has been to institute a system of **dispute resolution**, by which trading disputes between member states can be resolved by an impartial tribunal, thus preventing such disputes from becoming too political or controversial, in theory at least.

Present and Future Challenges for Trade

Even so, trade has not become a controversy-free area of the IPE. Many LDC states continue to see the structure of the trading system as a reflection of the power and success of the developed states, and are pressing within the WTO for greater concessions that would spur growth in their economies. The link between trade and environmental issues remains a vital area for research and political action. But the biggest challenges for the future of the international trading system lie in the classic question of the struggle for power.

The first of these concerns the growing **regionalism** that has become a feature of the world economy since the 1980s. The emergence of regional free trade blocs, most importantly in Europe and North America, provides an alternative to international trade for the world's largest economies. Naturally this means that they have a fall-back option in the event that the WTO fails to maintain the current healthy state of global trade, which in turn provides a test of their commitment to maintaining that system. The countries of the **European Union** (EU) and **North American Free Trade Agreement** (NAFTA) have shown a distinct tendency over the last decade to trade more and more within their respective blocs, a trend which some see as threatening international trade. In fact these fears may be exaggerated, as the level of interregional trade continues to grow; it is just that intraregional trade is growing at a faster rate (see later in this chapter).

The second challenge for the future of the world trading system lies in conflict between these two regions. It is important to remember that the European and North American (and in particular US) conceptions of economic liberalism are far from identical. Europeans have traditionally seen a more expanded role for the state in the economy and are more comfortable with free trade taking a back seat to political and social concerns. The 1999 disputes between the US and EU over hormones in beef and the international trade in bananas are but two examples where the interests and ideals of these two economic giants have begun to clash.

The third issue is the rise of China and other LDCs as major trading powers and economies. Beginning in 2003, at a WTO ministerial conference in Cancun, Mexico,

13.2

The US–EU Banana Dispute

Though the United States and European Union are highly interdependent, this does not mean that their relations are trouble-free. In 1999 the United States accused the EU of distorting the international trade in bananas by giving preferential access to the European market to banana producers from select developing countries. This, the US argued, went contrary to the rules and principles of free trade protected by the World Trade Organization (WTO), which enforce the principle of non-discrimination between WTO members.

The accusation was based on fact. In 1975 the EU (then known as the EC or European Community) set up the Lomé Convention, an agreement with certain African, Caribbean, and Pacific (ACP) states, giving them access to the European marketplace at preferential tariff levels. The stated goal of the Lome Convention was to aid LDCs in their economic development. Bananas were one commodity included under the convention.

The United States brought the issue before the Dispute Settlement Mechanism of the WTO, which judged against the EU. This meant that the European Union was forced to dismantle its system of preferential access and grant the same privileges to all outside banana producers, or to none at all.

Why did the United States force this issue? The stated goal of the US was to promote and protect the principle of free trade in the world economy. A closer examination of the issue, however, suggests that the United States government was promoting the interests of US corporations that produced bananas in countries outside of the Lomé Convention, countries such as Mexico and Brazil. These corporations wanted the same access to European markets as those producers based in the ACP states, producers of largely European origin. This series of events showed once again that the link between states and markets, public and private actors remains a major force in shaping international trade.

a new group called the G20 emerged that would further complicate international trade negotiations. Led by five important LDCs (China, India, Brazil, Mexico, and South Africa), the G20 has successfully operated as a bloc in WTO negotiations to prevent any agreement in the organization that goes against their interests.

The International System of Money and Finance

Just as the international trade system is responsible for moving goods and services around the global economy, the **international financial and monetary system** is responsible for making sure that money flows to those areas of the global economy where it is needed.[17] It can be compared to the root system of a plant: just as the roots invisibly provide minerals, nutrition, and moisture to a plant, so the financial system provides currency and credit to the international economy.

International financial and monetary system
the set of rules, institutions, and agreements governing the flow of money in the international system; the relative values of currencies and the settling of accounts

13.3

The BRICs and BRICSAM

In 2001, the investment firm Goldman Sachs published a report, *Dreaming with BRICs: The Path to 2050*, that identified four rapidly growing developing country economies — Brazil, Russia, India, and China — as holding enormous potential for economic growth in the future and for changing the distribution of power in the international economy. Between them, the four countries currently account for over 40 per cent of world population, and promise much higher growth rates than the developed country economies. By 2050, Goldman Sachs predicted that these four economies combined would be larger than the world's leading economies today, with China being the world's largest economy and India, Brazil, and Russia in third, fourth, and sixth places respectively.

Political scientists and IPE scholars have begun to refer to the BRICSAM countries (comprising the BRICs, South Africa, the ASEAN countries, and Mexico) because of their growing political and economic weight in the system. Already, the G5 countries (Brazil, China, India, South Africa, and Mexico) have been included in a number of G8 (USA, Japan, Germany, Britain, France, Canada, Italy, and Russia) summits as important representatives of the developing world, and we should expect their influence to grow in the near future. These three challenges have meant that international trade negotiations are currently stalled and in great danger of being permanently damaged. The Doha round of trade negotiations that began in 2001 have yet to be completed, and analysts fear that the round in unsalvageable. If this is indeed true, it would be the first time since the creation of the GATT in 1947 that a round of trade negotiations has failed completely, raising further questions about the resilience of the international trading system.

Without a reliable and steady supply of loans and investment, the international economy would soon wither and die.

International finance is nothing new. In the fifteenth and sixteenth centuries, Italian banks lent huge sums of money to the monarchs of Europe for the purposes of exploration, personal enrichment, and war. The City of London emerged as the dominant financial centre of the nineteenth century, channelling funds to traders, investors, and governments throughout the world. Money and finance has always been central to the development of the international economy, and the health and stability of the two systems have always been intertwined.

What Is the International Monetary System?

For international economic interaction to be feasible and efficient, it is necessary to have either a global currency, that is, one form of money acceptable in every national economic system, or to have internationally agreed-upon rules dictating the relative values of national currencies. In former times gold performed the function of a global medium of exchange, being acceptable to individuals and governments all over the world. In modern times two alternative systems have emerged, one in which states agree upon set values for their currencies in terms of other national currencies, and a second in which the market has been left to decide the relative values of national monies. The first of these systems is known as a **fixed exchange rate system**, the second as a **floating exchange rate system**. Debates continue to the present day over which of these two systems provides more stability and efficiency to the international economy.

What Is the International Financial System?

Very closely connected to the monetary system is the international financial system, the means by which capital and funds are moved from one national economy to another. The financial system is made up of the financial transactions that take place between states, international financial institutions such as the IMF and World Bank, banks, and other private financial institutions and corporations and individuals. Throughout history the level of political control over the international financial system has varied, from almost complete control in the

Fixed exchange rate system
system in which states agree upon set values for their currencies in terms of other national currencies

Floating exchange rate system
system in which the market decides the relative values of national monies

Mary Evans Picture Library

The Great Crash of 1929

The great stock market crash of 1929 left millions in financial ruin, and pushed the United States and the world into the Great Depression.

The global financial crisis that began in the United States and quickly spread across the developed world surprised many who had come to believe that financial

13.4 Continued...

crises were things that happened in developing countries such as Mexico, Brazil, or Turkey. The recent history of crises, up to 2008, had indeed been of problems emerging in those parts of the world. However, financial crisis has in fact been much more common in the developed world and has a long history going back at least to the nineteenth century.

The most famous crisis of them all occurred in 1929, in the United States. New York had by then replaced London as the world's most important financial centre, and was closely linked to the international economy through a system of loans and credits. The financial markets in New York, however, were prone to what analysts have variously called 'manias', 'euphoria', or 'irrational exuberance', meaning that money would pour into the market periodically, according to what the latest trend in investment might be. Similarly, when attitudes and perceptions changed, money would be rapidly withdrawn from the markets, causing 'panics' and 'crashes'.

This turbulence was seen repeatedly throughout the 1920s, famously with the case of Florida real estate in the mid-1920s. But the biggest crash was to come in 1929, when an inflated stock market began to slip, setting off a panic that ruined thousands of stockbrokers and bankrupted hundreds of thousands of investors. The stories of this period are now classic — brokers and investors leaping from the upper floors of office blocks rather than face bankruptcy, individuals selling assets worth thousands of dollars (such as cars) for only a hundred dollars, just to try to get hold of cash to settle their debts.

But the effects of the 1929 crash were not just felt by individuals involved in the market. It caused a massive contraction of credit, as banks called in loans, shrinking the economy and forcing many firms to either lay off workers or close down completely. Internationally, it interrupted the flow of capital from New York to debtor countries, causing economic and financial crises there. What followed was the Great Depression in the United States, and the world economy began a slippery slide towards economic conflict and then war.

1940s and 1950s, to dominance by private financial actors at the beginning of the twenty-first century. The international financial system is fundamental to the international economy because without it surplus capital in one part of the globe could not be assigned to those parts of the world where it can be put to good and profitable use. A badly functioning financial system does not merely compromise economic efficiency, it also restrains economic development.

The Bretton Woods System

In July 1944, with the end of the Second World War close at hand, the governments of the Allied powers met at a resort in **Bretton Woods**, New Hampshire, in the United States to discuss the future of the international economy. The economic planners who met there, particularly those from the United States and Great Britain, were determined to avoid the mistakes of the interwar years, which had seen high levels of economic nationalism and competition between states, a situation that had eventually led to war. Foremost in their minds was

Bretton Woods agreement

postwar system of fixed exchange rates and heavy controls on private banks and other financial institutions so that their role in international finance would be limited

the determination to promote free trade and to avoid the kind of financial crisis which had been seen in 1929.

For the Bretton Woods planners, the solution lay in creating a system of fixed exchange rates and putting heavy controls on private banks and other financial institutions so that their role in international finance would be limited. In the place of private banks, the American and British representatives created the International Monetary Fund and the International Bank for Reconstruction and Development (World Bank). The IMF was designed to oversee the international monetary system, enforce a regime of fixed exchange rates, and lend money to states experiencing balance of payments difficulties. The World Bank was created to provide funding for the reconstruction of Europe after the destruction of the Second World War and for programs of economic development in the Third World.

This left very little space for private institutions to play a role in international finance. In the years following 1945 private finance remained largely national, international finance being dominated by the IMF and World Bank, by the **Marshall Plan** — a massive US government loan program to help the devastated countries of Western Europe — and later, by government-to-government loans in the form of **bilateral aid**.[18] This system of fixed exchange rates and public international finance lasted for a period of 25 years, bringing both stability and unprecedented levels of global economic growth. During this period the flow of finance obeyed distinctly political purposes, with inter-state loans being used to strengthen friendly regimes and to buy the support of governments in the Cold War struggle.

In August 1971, however, this situation changed. The US government of Richard Nixon made a unilateral decision that the Bretton Woods system no longer served the interests of the United States, and the US abandoned the system of fixed exchange rates. Despite months of negotiations, a rules-based alternative could not be found, and from 1973 onwards the world's major currencies have been floating, that is, their values have been decided by the activities of global currency markets. This new arrangement is sometimes referred to as a **non-system** because of the absence of clearly defined rules determining relative currency values.[19] The transition represented an abdication of power by political authorities over one of the most important areas of economic management, and can be seen as a part of a wider trend towards less state control over the economy.

Even before the system of fixed exchange rates had broken, private finance was beginning to break free from the controls instituted at Bretton Woods in 1944. First, European banks succeeded in evading national regulatory control by lending money denominated in currencies other than those used in the national economy. Such practices gave private banks the freedom to engage in international lending without the interference of national governments (see Box 8.4). Second, private banks, in particular those of the US, had gradually expanded their operations outside of national markets in response to the growth of MNCs and their need for capital. These two developments propelled the growth of private international finance, and helped to create the system we have today.

Another factor in the globalization of finance was the role played by technological advances, in particular in the area of communications. The development of satellite communications and computer technology allowed the transmission

Marshall Plan
US government loan program to help the devastated countries of Western Europe after World War II

Bilateral aid
military or development assistance given by one country to another

Non-system
the system of international money and finance that replaced the Bretton Woods system, so called because it lacked explicit rules

of information and funds from one side of the world to another at the touch of a button. This made the transfer of capital instantaneous, and gave banks and investors the ability to seize upon opportunities whenever, and wherever, they occured.

It was not only technology and the drive for profits that caused the internationalization of finance. States too played a central role. Particularly in the 1980s and 1990s, Western governments began to remove regulations restricting foreign competition in national financial markets, as well as those regulations restricting the activities of banks and other financial actors. This **deregulation** of finance was undertaken because it matched both the liberal ideology and the economic goals of leading states such as Britain and the US. By the late twentieth century national financial centres such as London, New York, and Tokyo were actively competing among themselves for the business of finance, and one advantage that could be offered by a financial centre was that its level of restrictions and controls was lower than that of its competitors.[20]

Deregulation
removal of government controls in an economic sector

13.5

The Euromarkets

In the 1950s, the government of the Soviet Union faced a problem. It needed to maintain US dollar reserves in banks outside the Soviet Union for use in buying exports, and commodities in particular. However, to place the money in United States banks would risk the US government freezing the money and thus cutting the Soviet state off from its deposits. Instead of risking this eventuality, the Soviet government persuaded a French bank to provide a bank account for it denominated in US dollars. The bank's cable address was EUROBANK, and thus were born Eurodollars and the Euromarkets.

A Eurodollar is simply a dollar held in a bank account outside of the US. The process can be copied with other national currencies, to produce Euro-pounds, Euro-francs, Euro-yen, etc. The bank does not have to be in Europe for the currency to become a Euro-currency.

The advantage for banks in providing such accounts was that they were able to evade the regulations of national authorities that chose to regulate only transactions conducted in the national currency of that country. This meant that huge amounts of capital were released from the control and supervision of national regulators, and this money was free to flow around the world as the bankers saw fit.

Today the Euromarkets continue, but have become much more complex. It is not only possible to set up a bank account in a currency other than that of the country where the bank operates, it is possible to borrow money, and conduct bond releases, swaps, and options in Euro-currencies. This growth in the complexity and size of international finance contributed greatly to the process of deregulation that took place in the 1980s and 1990s, and also, some claim, to the growing instability of global finance. However, by deregulating and speeding up international finance in this way, the stability of the international financial system has increasingly come under threat. It is now possible for billions of dollars to be moved from one national economy to another very rapidly, and this has contributed to a number of the deep financial crises witnessed at the end of the twentieth and beginning of the twenty-first centuries (see later in this chapter).

The Latin American Debt Crisis

In the 1970s, after the end of the Bretton Woods system and the relaxation of many national restrictions on foreign lending, banks in the advanced industrialized economies, in particular in the US, began looking to developing economies as an outlet for the capital that had been deposited with them. Developing countries offered potentially very high profits for the banks, as they were rapidly industrializing and were willing to pay higher interest rates than borrowers in developed markets.

However, the area of the globe that benefited most from this trend in the 1970s was Latin America, a region that was rapidly developing and showed immense potential. Those countries that exported oil in particular, such as Mexico, were prime candidates for loans as the price of oil was soaring due to the OPEC crisis. The flow of loans to Latin America in the 1970s and early 1980s was truly immense, reaching between 150 and 200 billion US dollars by 1983. This would not necessarily have become a problem if the money received through these loans had been invested wisely by the recipient governments and corporations. Instead, much of the inflow of capital was wasted in the form of economically non-viable projects and corruption. In addition, Latin American states' economic growth slowed at the end of the 1970s because of a number of factors, including declining commodity prices, and thus their ability to meet debt interest payments was reduced. The only way by which these economies were able to continue making debt payments was by accepting more money from the financial institutions to which they were already heavily indebted.

The combination of these factors brought about a situation in which several Latin American states found themselves unable to make their debt payments. In 1982 the Mexican government announced that it would not be able to make the interest payments on its debt, and the **Debt Crisis** had begun. This led to a crisis of confidence on the part of the banks, which then refused to lend any further money to economies in the region. This abrupt cut-off of new finance to Latin

Debt crisis
a situation in which a country is unable to meet its international debt obligations; sometimes used to refer to the Latin American Debt Crisis of the 1980s

13.6

Foreign Aid and Tied Aid

In the post-World War II period the advanced industrialized states began a system of bilateral aid, lending money to developing states in the form of economic or military assistance. This system replaced the private flows of capital that had been a feature of the nineteenth century and interwar years. Foreign aid became a crucial source of income for many states, and throughout the 1960s, 1970s, and 1980s there were calls for aid to be increased.

But foreign aid is not simply the transfer of money from one national government to another. It can take various forms, such as material (food, grain, emergency supplies, or military equipment), loans at preferential rates, or sometimes grants. Often, aid comes with a commitment on the part of the recipient to fulfill some responsibility to the donor state. During the Cold War this commitment was most commonly to support the foreign policy goals of either the Soviet Union or United States, thus involving the LDC in the ideological conflict.

13.6 Continued...

At others times, aid has been 'tied' in other ways. Frequently, loans given to LDCs by a developed state can only be used to purchase goods from producers in that state. Therefore, the developed country government is providing an economic stimulus to its own economy by lending money to the LDC, while at the same time making interest on its loan. Another example is the donation of some form of high-technology machinery to a developing country. Though the machinery is given free of charge, to maintain the equipment will require both expertise and parts from the donor state. In these ways, and others, aid can actually become a drain on the economic resources of the recipient state.

American countries meant that they could not meet their own debt obligations, thus deepening the crisis.[21]

A solution to this crisis took many years to find. The International Monetary Fund acted as a coordinating agency, bringing together both creditors and debtors, but was unable to come up with anything more than stop-gap measures between 1982 and 1989. It was only in that year, through a debt reduction plan proposed by US Treasury Secretary Nicholas Brady, that a lasting solution was discovered. In the meantime many years of economic growth were lost, and investor confidence in the region was put on hold.

The New International Finance and the Crises of the Late 1990s

With the ending of the Latin American debt crisis at the end of the 1980s, a new era in international finance began. This was to be a period in which banks faced stiff competition from other kinds of financial institutions (such as mutual fund companies, in which thousands of individuals pool their investments and the company invests the total amount), and international capital became much more mobile. The increased size and mobility of international capital proved to be both a blessing and a curse for the system. On the positive side it enabled huge sums of capital to move rapidly around the globe to take advantage of investment opportunities. On the negative side of things, however, this increased mobility meant that billions of dollars could be withdrawn from a national economy in a matter of hours.

Such was the case in Mexico in December 1994. Following a political crisis and rapidly worsening economic situation, the Mexican government devalued the national currency, the peso, causing both Mexican and foreign investors to pull their money out of the country. This precipitated a deep economic crisis in the country, one which took several years to resolve. The managing director of the IMF, Michel Camdessus, called the Mexican crisis the 'first financial crisis of the twenty-first century' because it involved millions of investors and enormous and immediate capital flight, unlike the Latin American debt crisis of the 1980s.[22]

The Mexican crisis was followed, three years later, by similar crises in a number of Asian economies. Beginning in Thailand in July 1997, the crisis spread throughout the region, a phenomenon that had deep effects not only on the region, but on the world economy as a whole. In addition to Thailand, countries such as Indonesia and South Korea, long considered economic powerhouses, were reduced to petitioning the IMF for loans to allow them to restructure their economies. In 1998, economic and financial crises followed in Russia, Brazil, and Argentina. It was not until 2003 that these crises stopped appearing in the developing world.

The Global Financial Crisis 2008–9

In 2008 a financial crisis that began simultaneously in the real estate markets of the US, Britain, and other developed countries began to spread throughout the world as banks found themselves unable to absorb the wave of loan defaults from individual customers who had borrowed more than they were capable of repaying.[23] The crisis spread rapidly across the world's financial systems and brought about a deep economic recession that came close to the levels of the Great Crash of 1929.

Solving the crisis required a massive injection of money (**liquidity**) from the world's leading central banks, emergency loans to the banks themselves, and international coordination of economic and financial policy among the world's leading powers. Even so, the recession caused the loss of hundreds of thousands of jobs in countries such as the US, and meant that 2008 was the first year since 1945 when there would be negative global economic growth.

The crisis caused analysts and policy-makers to think again about their commitment to liberal, free market policies and ideas, and governments increasingly turned to regulation of financial markets and of capitalism in general.

Liquidity
rate at which assets may be converted to cash

13.7

The G8 and Multilateral Leadership

We often hear talk of 'leaders' and the exercise of 'leadership' in the international economy, but few of us question what that leadership is, or why it is necessary. By leadership in the international economy we are generally referring to actions by one or a group of states that provide some good to the system that would not otherwise be provided. In recent years we have come to think of leadership as providing effective responses to problems or crises facing the international economy, such as the financial crises that struck Asia and Brazil in the late 1990s. Such responses may take the form of providing financial assistance to economies in crisis, formulating new rules for international finance, or opening up a domestic market to absorb exports from distressed economies.

For most of the post-World War II period we have become accustomed to thinking of the United States as the only leader of the capitalist world. Indeed, from 1945 to the 1960s the US was able to manage and guide the Western system with little help from its allies. However, beginning in the mid-1960s, the United States was forced to seek the help of Europe and Japan in providing stability to the system through the coordination of economic policies. This necessity became even more pressing in the aftermath of the end of Bretton Woods and the oil crises of the 1970s, and the ensuing turbulence in the world economy. In November 1975, the US and five other major economic powers (France, Britain, Germany, Japan,

13.7 Continued...

and Italy) came together in Rambouillet, France, to discuss the major political and economic challenges facing their countries. In 1976, in San Juan, Puerto Rico, these six states were joined by Canada to form the Group of Seven (G7).

Since 1976 the G7 has become one of the most important organs of world economic management, coordinating macroeconomic policies and national positions in fora such as the IMF. In the mid-1980s the G7 played a central role in attempting to restore stability to international currency markets through coordinated central bank interventions, but the importance of the grouping would grow in the 1990s. The G7's response to the financial crises that struck Mexico, Asia, Russia, and Brazil determined the longevity of these crises and the future shape of the international financial system. Though the reform of that system is far from complete, all important decisions concerning its future must first be approved by the G7.

In 1998 the seven members were joined by Russia to form the G8, and by 2006 an active debate began over whether the membership of this elite group needed to be expanded again to include the rising developing countries of the G5 (China, India, Brazil, Mexico, and South Africa).

Economic Regionalism

Much of this chapter has described the factors leading to the internationalization, or as some would put it, the globalization of the world economy. There can be little doubt that, since 1945, national economies have become more and more interdependent, and that trade, production, and investment have moved far from their predominantly national basis at that time. But the globalizing trend has been matched in recent years by another tendency, towards economic development based on geographic regions, or **economic regionalism**. This chapter has already discussed the concerns over the regionalization of trade, but the same trend can be observed in both finance and production, too.

In Europe, Asia, and North America, investment flows and production patterns have become based more and more on the region. This development has taken place for several reasons. First, in Europe and North America the logic has been to take advantage of the free trade arrangements in place, and to produce goods within these regional markets. Another rationale has been to take advantage of lower wages in other economies in the region. This has been a driving force behind the regionalization of investment and production in Asia and North America.

This process, liberal economists predict, will lead to the economic enrichment of these regions, but in particular of the poorer countries within them. Within NAFTA, Mexico has benefited from very high levels of foreign direct investment, a phenomenon that stems from the combination of its access to the US market and its comparatively low wage levels. This should lead, in the long term, to a more highly developed Mexican economy and, it is hoped, a higher standard of living for Mexicans. Less orthodox analysts of the situations, however, claim that the trend towards economic regionalism is resulting in the exploitation of the cheap labour and natural resources of poorer nations, something that will keep them in an inferior position to the economies of the advanced industrialized states.

Economic regionalism
the tendency of countries in the same geographic region to intensify economic interactions; both NAFTA and the European Union are examples

13.8

Gender and the *Maquilas*

Mexico's assembly plants are famous for their hiring of women and the bad conditions under which they have to work.

In the last quarter of the twentieth century a number of LDC states allowed the creation of what came to be known as *maquiladora* (meaning 'assembly') zones, or *maquilas*, in their countries. These zones hold a special status because they allow foreign corporations to come in, produce goods, and then export them back to their home country duty-free. *Maquilas* became an important source of employment and income to these economies, and further increased the level of interdependence between developed and developing economies.

However, these zones, though they provide employment and wages that are generally higher than those available locally, are a mixed blessing. Many companies operating in *maquilas* tend to hire women to the assembly plants, on the justification that female labour is better suited to the work involved and also that it is generally cheaper than its male equivalent. This in itself is problematical, but women in the *maquilas* face a range of other challenges.

Sexual harassment is one. Local governments tend to leave foreign producers alone when they operate in these zones, and so regulation and enforcement is often weak. Men, some of whom are foreign, generally dominate management positions. There have been many documented cases of managers sexually harassing or even raping female employees. A second area of rights abuse has been compulsory pregnancy testing. Despite the fact that such testing is illegal according to Mexican law, before a woman is hired, and periodically during her employment, she must face pregnancy tests. If she is discovered to be pregnant, she will not be hired, or if already employed, will be fired. The *maquilas* pose a challenge for state policy-makers, women's rights action groups, and gender analysts, and they raise the issue of gender relations within the new international production structure.

Oil and Oil Prices

One area of international production that remains central to the world economy is the production of oil.[24] Because so many of our means of production, transportation, and energy generation depend directly or indirectly on petroleum products, oil continues to affect the health of the international economy as a whole. For many years the international oil industry was dominated by what came to be known as the 'Seven Sisters', that is, the seven largest oil companies in the world (Standard Oil, Royal Dutch Shell, British Petroleum, Mobil, Chevron, Gulf, and Texaco). Since the early twentieth century they had controlled oil supplies and prices, manipulating the market to their advantage. However, in 1960 five of the world's most important oil-producing states — Iran, Iraq, Kuwait, Saudi Arabia, and Venezuela – came together and formed the Organization of the Petroleum Exporting Countries (OPEC). OPEC was designed to strengthen the hand of the oil producers and to bolster the international price of oil and thus their revenues.

A dramatic change occurred in 1973. During that year, OPEC and the major oil companies failed to come to a lasting agreement on the price of oil and the fourth Arab–Israeli war began, driving up the market price of oil. The oil-producing states soon realized that they possessed the power to control the supply and thus the price of oil in the world marketplace, a power that had once belonged exclusively to the Seven Sisters. The price of oil rose from US $2.48/barrel at the end of 1972 to US $11.65/barrel a year later. For the next five years, OPEC would manipulate the supply and the price of oil, consistently raising the price and bringing these states enormous revenues. The net result was a massive transfer of capital from the oil-importing states to the OPEC countries.

A second major price rise took place in 1979 and 1980. With the joint developments of the Iranian revolution and the onset of the Iran–Iraq war, the supply of oil was threatened because between them these two states were responsible for 10 per cent of global oil supplies. This second shock to the international oil market forced prices as high as $41/barrel, bringing still further transfers of wealth from the industrialized states to OPEC.

The effects of these oil price rises on the international political economy should not be underestimated. First, states that previously had played only a secondary role in global politics acquired a significance that made them major players. Saudi Arabia, in particular, became a state of primary importance because it was the central country in OPEC. Second, the dramatically higher oil prices contributed to the growing problem of inflation in the advanced industrialized states as prices for almost all goods were pushed higher. Third, the transfer of capital from the advanced industrialized states to OPEC members resulted in an enormous inflow of funds into the international financial system. This took place because many OPEC states were earning more from oil than they could possibly spend on economic development and infrastructure, so they deposited the surplus into international banks. Much of this money was funnelled to other developing states and contributed to the debt crisis in the 1980s.

Although oil prices dropped and remained very low between the early 1980s and the late 1990s, dropping as low as $10 a barrel in 1998, by 2007 high prices

Seven Sisters
the major oil companies in the mid-twentieth century: Esso, Shell, British Petroleum, Mobil, Chevron, Gulf, and Texaco

OPEC
Organization of the Petroleum Exporting Countries

13.9

Brazil and Renewable Energy

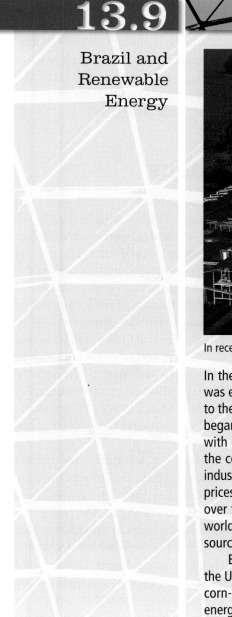

In recent years Brazil has become a global leader in renewable energy sources.

In the 1970s Brazil faced a serious challenge to its economic development, as it was entirely dependent on oil imports at a time when oil prices were soaring due to the OPEC oil price hike. In order to reduce oil imports, the country's government began to subsidize the production of sugar cane–based ethanol, to be blended with gasoline for use in automobiles and trucks. This program greatly benefited the country's sugar farmers and helped to develop the world's leading ethanol industry. Although this seemed to be of only national concern at the time, when oil prices again reached record levels in 2007 and 2008, and with growing concerns over the climate-change consequences of oil-based economic development, the world looked to the Brazilian experience in ethanol and other renewable energy sources as a model to follow.

Brazil now exports ethanol, although the world's largest ethanol consumer, the United States, restricts imports of Brazilian ethanol in order to protect its own corn-based ethanol industry. In the years to come, ethanol and the renewable energy sector in general promises to be a major source of growth and income, and is one of the multiple reasons why Brazil promises such high levels of economic development in the near future.

returned as rising demand outpaced supply. This high demand was driven largely by economic growth in China and other developing countries, forcing the price of oil up to $150 a barrel in 2008. There then followed a collapse in prices when the global recession slashed demand for energy. Nonetheless, we should expect high oil prices to return in the future as economic growth recovers and demand picks up again.

One of the effects of high oil prices has been a new enthusiasm for renewable energy sources, such as wind, solar, and biofuels (ethanol, biodiesel, etc). With high oil prices these alternative sources of energy became economically viable. Given the fact that oil supplies will eventually run out, and given the very real impact of the use of oil on climate change, renewable and clean energy sources are vital if sustainable development is to become possible on a global scale. The advances that take place in this area over the next few years will be pivotal in determining the fate of the global economy and of the planet itself.

Multinational Corporations

Throughout most of human history, production has been organized on a local basis, with small cottage industries predominating. This began to change in the seventeenth and eighteenth centuries, when the Industrial Revolution created large firms producing for national (and to a lesser extent international) markets. At the same time, improvements in communications and transportation created the right conditions for the integration of production processes on a national basis.[25]

The nineteenth century saw the internationalization of trade, but not of production. Although raw materials were transported across great distances to be used in national production processes, production itself remained rooted at the level of the nation-state. It was only in the second half of the twentieth century that production took on an international dimension. With the expansion of US firms into Europe and then Asia, national production processes began to be integrated, in turn drawing together national economies. Indeed, it was the spread of US **multinational corporations** (MNCs) that began a process that has led to the globalized production we see today.[26]

In 1945 one country dominated world production, namely, the United States. With the economies of Europe and Japan in ruins, the US was the only large economic system producing the goods necessary for postwar rebuilding and economic recovery. This meant that US producers found themselves in the enviable position of facing minimal competition from firms in other states. Not only did this allow them to make huge profits in the early postwar years, it also encouraged a process by which US corporations invested directly in European and Asian economies, setting up productive capacities there rather than merely exporting from their US base. Helping this internationalization of US producers was the strength of the dollar, which was also in great demand from European and Asian nations. Because there was such a strong demand for the dollar, US firms were able to invest in foreign economies very cheaply, as the governments of those countries tried to gather dollars from every source possible.

As US firms set up production facilities in various countries around the world, their production became 'multinational', and the era of the Multinational Corporation (MNC) was born. MNCs are simply firms whose productive and management activities take place in several different countries. The main advantage of multinational production is, of course, economies of scale, whereby mass production can be organized for huge numbers of consumers spread across many different nations. The post-World War II period saw a dramatic rise in this kind of production, and by the 1960s, US MNCs had been joined by European and Japanese competitors, and later by MNCs from developing states (such as CEMEX, a Mexican cement producer).

By the 1970s, some academics and policy-makers had begun to ask serious questions about the power and influence of MNCs, particularly with reference to their relations with LDC governments. Raymond Vernon even wrote of states facing a situation which could best be described as 'sovereignty at bay', where governments were increasingly challenged by large MNCs.[27] The reasoning behind this claim was simple: throughout the postwar period MNCs had grown in size to the extent where their economic and technical resources matched or even dwarfed those available to many LDC governments. What's more, with developing states desperate for foreign investment, MNCs found themselves in a strong bargaining position in their negotiations with LDCs. To make matters worse, even if a state secured investment from a foreign MNC, the corporation could always withdraw or divest from that country if the level of rewards did not remain satisfactory.

Such negotiating power enabled MNCs to negotiate preferential conditions for their investments, securing tax breaks and cheap access to labour and raw materials. More sinister, however, was the suggestion that MNCs were engaging in political activities within their host states, designed to manipulate the democratic process so that the political and economic preferences of the firm were promoted. A famous example of such interference in domestic affairs concerned a US telecommunications corporation, ITT, in Chile in the 1970s, when the firm conspired to bring down a Marxist government that threatened its interests.[28]

Other concerns about the influence of MNCs related to their close relationship with their home country (that is, their nation of origin) governments. Though there is little evidence to support it, the accusation has been made that MNCs sometimes act as agents of their home country government in foreign countries. Either through espionage, political activities, or economic dependence, MNCs have the potential to advance the interests of their home country at the expense of the host.

The Integration of Production

The internationalization of production has not only seen firms producing goods in many different geographical locations. The actual process of production has become internationalized. This means that automobiles, televisions, computers, and a host of other products are not made in a single country, but assembled from parts manufactured in many different countries. Honda, for example, has integrated its vehicle production process not only on a regional basis, but worldwide. The significance of integrated production processes is immense; it means the transmission of corporate management strategies and technologies, and links workers and consumers across the globe.

Conclusion

The international political economy that surrounds us today at the beginning of the twenty-first century is one that is almost unrecognizable from the system that was created at the end of the Second World War. The role of private actors has increased dramatically, and the level of interaction between states has reached levels unseen since before the First World War. Trade and financial flows continue to grow, both within and between regions, and advances in the fields of communications and transportation have made the world seem much smaller than once it did.

Yet many of the fundamentals of IPE remain the same. State power still matters and the powerful continue to write the rules of the game and thus shape the international economic system. Efficiency and competitiveness remain primary goals of states, as they seek to retain an edge over their rivals (and friends). Many of the question marks that haunted the beginning of the postwar international economy have returned today. How much freedom should states grant to private finance? What should be done to assist the poorer nations of the world? What is the role of the state in economic management?

The international economy remains highly dynamic, and in a state of constant flux. Our study of it tells us much about the nature of political economy, about the interaction among politics and economics, states, and markets. The development of the international economy in the early years of this century will bring new forces to the fore and substantial transformations, many unforeseen. We can hope to understand the political economy of our own nation only if we take into account the system of which it is a part.

Self-Assessment Questions

1. What have been the major forces behind the growth in international trade since 1945?
2. What is the balance between political authorities and market actors in the world economy today?
3. What is the role of negotiation and co-operation in the international economy?
4. Why does the international financial system tend towards crisis?

Weblinks

Bank for International Settlements
www.bis.org

Canadian International Development Agency
www.acdi-cida.gc.ca/index.htm

Multinational Monitor
www.multinationalmonitor.org

International Monetary Fund
www.imf.org

World Trade Organization
www.wto.org

Further Reading

Balaam, David N., and Michael Veseth. *Introduction to International Political Economy*. Upper Saddle River, NJ: Prentice Hall, 2001.

Cohn, Theodore H. *Global Political Economy: Theory and Practice*. 4th ed. New York, NY: Pearson Longman, 2008.

Ikenberry, John, et al. *The State and American Foreign Economic Policy*. Ithaca, NY: Cornell University Press, 1993.

Keohane, Robert O., and Joseph Nye. *Power and Interdependence: World Politics in Transition*. 2nd ed. Cambridge: HarperCollins, 1989.

Lichbach, Mark I., and Alan S. Zuckerman. *Comparative Politics, Rationality, Culture and Structure*. New York: Cambridge University Press, 1997.

Mingst, Karen A. *Essentials of International Relations*. 3rd ed. New York: W.W. Norton, 2004.

Spero, Joan E., and Jeffrey A. Hart. *The Politics of International Economic Relations*. 6th ed. Belmont, CA: Wadsworth Thomson, 2003.

Yergin, Daniel, and Joseph Stainslaw. *The Commanding Heights: The Battle for the World Economy*. New York: Simon & Schuster, 2002.

CBC News Clips

Visit the companion website for *Politics: An Introduction* to listen to news clips from the CBC radio archives.

14 Conclusion

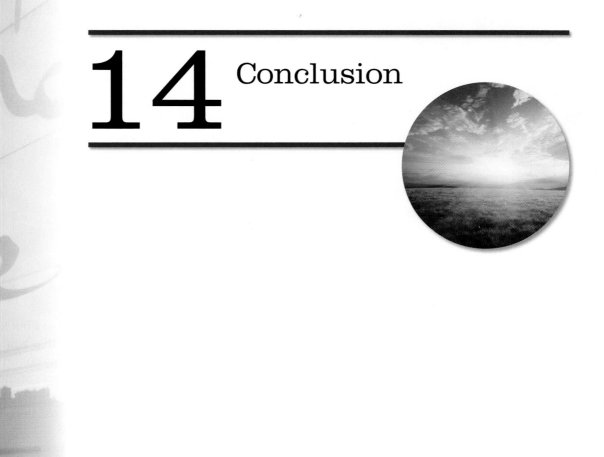

LEARNING
OBJECTIVES

After reading this chapter, you will be able to:

✳ review the major themes of the text

✳ relate significant concepts and theories to contemporary political activity

✳ demonstrate how we've introduced the major sub-fields of political studies

✳ provide a 'road map' for future studies in politics.

Introduction

Unless you are one of those people who likes to read the end of a book first (and spoil the development of the plot line!), we can presume that you've read at least most of this book. Indeed, you've likely read it all during your introductory course, and now you're probably quite comfortable with most of the material you've covered in your class, and in this text. Most introductory texts don't include a conclusion; rather, they simply end with the final chapter, usually one dealing with politics on a global scale. So, why have a conclusion in this book?

There are reasonable arguments for not having a conclusion — devotees of art films sometimes might make the case for a 'non-resolution' to the plot, thereby allowing the viewer to construct his or her own ending, and leaving the future for characters and plots 'open-ended' or up for personal interpretation. We aren't suggesting that others see the end of a text as interpretative; instead, we feel it's necessary to take the time to consider what we've dealt with, how we can use this information, and where we can go from here. After all, your involvement with politics doesn't end with this text or this course. While you could try to avoid politics by not taking further courses, the 'political' in your life is permanent. And now that you understand the nature of politics, it's not likely that you'll want to just leave that part of your life to the sidelines. This final chapter will give us that opportunity to take stock, and look ahead.

What Have We Learned?

At the very beginning of this text we discussed our tendency to become cynical about politics. It's an understandable reaction to politics, really. Even the most fleeting read of a daily newspaper shows ample reason to be suspicious of any good that might come from politics. It isn't surprising, then, that even the word 'political' becomes a disparaging reference: 'that committee has become so *political*'; 'I don't want to get involved because the others are *playing politics*.'

In this sense, 'political' gets reduced to a very basic, and simplistic, meaning. Politics becomes a 'power grab', or a contest of rigid views, rather than a process of deciding how our communities and systems can be made better, or how we can make a positive difference in the lives of others.

On the other hand, it's as easy to be as overly optimistic about politics as it is to be pessimistic. Some undergraduate students feel that they will 'change the world' (or at least 'their world') with a little political science under their belts. And certainly there have been many who have had an enormous effect.

I JUST CAN'T DO IT.... THE SCRIPT SAYS ENTER STAGE LEFT AND I'M A CONSERVATIVE

Some people deal with their politics intensely.

© Lindsay Foyle/CartoonStock.com

14.1

Craig Kielburger

Any time you hear that one person can't make a difference, or that children have no effect on the world around them, think of Craig Kielburger. Now an adult, Kielburger established Free the Children, a children's charity, when he was only 12. Free the Children was created to draw attention to the plight of child workers the world over by putting financial resources into education for children and young adults. Growing up in Toronto in 1995, Kielburger read a newspaper report about a child his age who was murdered for standing up for the rights of child workers in Pakistan. Shocked to hear that people his age were being persecuted for demanding their basic rights rather than going to school and enjoying childhood, Kielburger, his brother Marc, and friends began fundraising and raising awareness about child labour. He managed to get the attention of then Prime Minister Jean Chrétien, who was travelling to Asia to bolster Canadian trade with that region. Using money primarily raised among and by children, Free the Children took on development projects across Asia and Africa to improve education and social conditions for children in those countries. Kielburger hasn't stopped his work since. He is still involved with Free the Children, started the national 'Me to We' events to raise Free the Children's profile, authored books and produced television specials, and continues to speak with media and political leaders to aid the cause he championed that day in 1995.

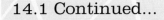

14.1 Continued...

He's been honoured many times over the years, receiving honorary degrees from universities, and the Order of Canada, among many other prestigious awards. More often than not, however, that isn't a reasonable objective in life. Not all of us, of course, can dedicate our lives to changing the world. However, we are all capable of change even if it won't be global. Our impact can and should be felt beyond our own lives, but it doesn't have to be worldwide.

One of the biggest problems in our world is apathy. We mean not simply doing nothing, but rather not caring about doing anything at all. It's a common reflex in modern life, to simply give up in the face of what appears to be insurmountable, rather than trying to understand how problems might be resolved. We hope, though, that after reading this text, you are now of the mind that even the smallest contribution can make a positive effect. Aside from acting malevolently, which few actually do, the worst thing we can do in our lives is to be indifferent. That is tantamount to ignoring our real responsibility as citizens, which is to be engaged in our communities. After all, if we don't act, who will act for us?

We've spent a great deal of time in this book considering what ought to be a natural conclusion: we are inextricably connected with our social environment. This connection includes the smallest details, like the seemingly insignificant decision to rezone a neighbourhood in the other part of town, far from where we live. But while this may seem to have no effect on us, it could indeed. What if that rezoning created a precedent that permitted a commercial development in the park across your street? What if your quiet street became a four-lane boulevard? Would it be too late to be involved then? To take this a few steps farther, more serious issues like poverty in sub-Saharan Africa or the razing of the Brazilian rainforest may also seem disconnected from our lives.

14.2

Cows or Climate?

The Amazon rainforest, which is mostly in Brazil but also includes eight other countries such as Peru, Venezuela, and Colombia, is a massive ecosystem, the largest rainforest in the world, with over 5.5 million square kilometres of rainforest in its full 7-million-square-kilometre area. A delicate system, it is home to millions of species of insects, and thousands of different plants and animals. Some of the rainforest, it is felt, may never have been explored by humans. But it is a bio-network under siege. Over a half million square kilometres have been forested, mostly for the growing demand for Brazilian beef worldwide. Now, it may be tempting to reduce complex problems to a simple explanation, but it's usually incorrect. To say that the core reason for the clearing of the Amazon rainforest is beef would not be entirely right. But, as the *New Scientist* magazine reported in 2004, it's a big contributor to the deforestation of this natural ecosystem.[1] In fact, deforestation in Brazil's rainforest is due more to the need

14.2 Continued...

for grazing land for beef cattle than the logging industry. Exports of Brazilian beef have increased massively in recent years, and the number of cattle in that country doubled in the 1990s alone.

© g01xm/iStockphoto.com

Beef production in the Amazon region has added pressure to the natural ecosystem there.

Add to that the sensitive nature of the rainforest's soil, which is used for soybean cultivation. Unlike other parts of the world, the rainforest cannot be constantly reused for agriculture. After a short time, the soil is rendered useless for further planting. Logging and agriculture have led to more roads built, towns erected, and more human interference. At the current rate of development, it's expected that by 2020, the rainforest will have been reduced by about half. Brazil, and other countries in the region, claims it needs to develop. Knowing what we do about that issue, along with national sovereignty issues, and the transnational threats of environmental degradation, we can see that there are no easy answers to this problem. Finding a way to allow for sustainable development of the Amazon rainforest is one of the most serious environmental and economic issues we face today.

Yet, the rainforests and poverty may be more like a municipal rezoning than we first think. Poverty leads to chronic underdevelopment, civil conflict, mass migration, disease, and animosities that extend far beyond borders. The rainforests provide the largest amount of oxygen in the Western hemisphere. These are not peripheral matters. Just as we may someday feel the effect of a decision in another city neighbourhood, poverty in Africa and environmental degradation of the rainforests could ultimately affect us in Canada.

We are indeed members of a global community. Although that statement may seem meaningless because of its overuse, and even commercialization (think of the numerous advertisements you've seen that use our 'global identity' to sell a product; it's easy to be cynical!), it's still the truth. We are political citizens of a country — Canada — and live in specific provinces, cities, or towns. While it may be true that our primary allegiances and actions will likely affect our own local and national communities first, our actions will have an impact, intended or not, on the global scene.

It was not a goal of this book to settle on the nature of humans. Aside from being an undertaking quite separate from what we set out to do with this book, no one would likely agree with our conclusions on human nature, anyhow. Yet, we did settle on one point: humans are both co-operative and competitive in their efforts to govern themselves. The very nature of politics is to strike a balance between these tendencies, as good can come from both. Balance is not always possible, so conflict emerges over the best options.

The common good, however, is often overlooked. Competitiveness is sometimes used as an excuse for why some do better or have more than others. The 'good' in this sense is not shared: the few with tremendous wealth or the countries that enjoy peace are not necessarily seeking ways to apportion their gains with others. And that is precisely where governance, or government to be more precise, comes in: governments distribute benefits. Co-operative behaviour may or may not be the core of our nature as humans, but it can become a routine part of our lives when we see the benefits.

We considered this in the context of public goods in society — those things that are provided for us, usually by government, and are supposed to be available for all. In reality, public goods aren't so universally obtainable. The simple fact is some will always have more than others, whether it is money, power, security, freedom, rights, or influence, as examples. A common theme that has appeared in this book, then, is the fundamental inequity of modern life. To be sure, life has never been equal for all — far from it — but it is nevertheless troubling that we continue to exist in a global system where a lot of attention is paid to the imbalance of public goods; however, there's never enough done to rectify the situation. It leaves one considering whether we, as a collective, are truly interested in making the necessary changes to provide for global equality.

Cast your memory back to the earliest parts of your course. Do you recall that exhaustive list of concepts (some new, some familiar) that, for some reason, we dealt with before just about anything else? Now it should seem obvious why we did that: we need to understand the terminology before we can really get into any topic. It's a bit like getting to know characters before settling into a book or a movie. Concepts aren't exactly the characters of this book, but we can agree that like any character, there are multiple angles we can use to describe them, or use them.

It's unlikely that the person who sits next to you in class has exactly the same view of, say, 'power' than you do. You may agree on certain aspects, such as the use of power, or the resources needed to carry out power, but no doubt you'll have diverging opinions on its utility or importance for politics. That's a good thing: we don't expect students to read this textbook and have the exact same views on just about anything. Rather, our goal has been to introduce and explain concepts for you to consider.

Some of these concepts are very broad, and you were probably familiar with them at the outset: power and order, for instance, are concepts that even non-political studies majors should be able to describe or talk about. Others, such as the state or the nation, may elicit more confusion. Most people see these concepts as interchangeable. You now know they aren't, even if you accept that they'll still be used as synonyms quite regularly. Still others, such as legitimacy or anarchy, would cause most individuals to stop and think about them before responding. They are more specific concepts, used in a special way by political scientists.

Then there are the concepts that move us from the 'hard ground' of definitions and argued positions (like those above) to 'softer ground' of interpretation and analysis. Values and justice, for instance, would give any of us pause were we asked to describe them in short form. They require more thought, more elucidation, and greater context. They aren't necessarily more important, but interpretation is always more difficult than description.

All of these concepts, and the many others that we covered in Chapter 2, were used repeatedly in this text. Your course instructor also used them widely in lectures and seminars. Like any field, political studies uses a specialized language that must first be understood (or, at the very least, recognized) before moving ahead. You are now conversant in this language.

Most readers of this text will be in Canada and will have some confidence in their knowledge about basic Canadian politics. We've used Canada as a foundation for this text, as we believe that it's essential to know your own system before studying others. To that end, we've tried to make reference to the Canadian context as much as possible. Of course, we've also looked in detail at other countries, including the United States, countries in the European Union, Japan, Brazil, India, China, and Mexico. Some, like the United Kingdom, the United States, and Mexico have appeared more than others. Again, given the concentration we have on Canada, it's logical to look closely at those countries with which Canada has an especially close relationship. In so doing, we've considered politics in a broadly comparative context, but also provided some perspective on Canadian interests both at home and abroad.

Regardless of the countries in question, some topics are essential. Our overviews of governments, participation, and political systems, for instance, showed the similarity and differences among various countries. Some concepts like sovereignty, for example, may apply to all states globally, but forms of political systems or modes of citizen participation vary widely. These sections provided some context for concepts in action, but were also necessary for the following chapters dealing with comparative country studies.

One enduring issue for all realms of political studies has been the various 'levels' of political action that take place at the same time. Individuals, non-state actors, states, international organizations and corporations, and global players may compete with or assist each other. Importantly, as we've learned, these actors perform their duties at the same time. We assume that these diverse levels of interaction are concurrent. For instance, an international financial transaction may involve an individual trader, a banking institution, government policy, international financial institutions, and global trading regulations. Another example might be a political leader who is deciding whether to intervene militarily in another country. That leader must take into account opinions of global institutions like the UN, other nation-states' actions, as well as the viewpoints of domestic actors such as individuals, pressure groups, and political parties.

We can't possibly ascertain what's happening at all levels at the same time — there's just not the time or the capacity to do so — so we make crucial decisions about what and whom to study. This involves the levels of analysis (to be distinguished from the levels of interaction), where evaluations are made about the most significant actors to scrutinize and why. In short, we can't know it all, so we must perfect our ability to settle on what is most important to know. This is an important skill that all political scientists must master: how to measure and choose the most significant factors in a political event. Knowing what to study, and what to leave aside, makes our job easier, and more relevant.

Earlier we noted the importance of knowing one's own system. Canadians, for instance, ought to have a basic understanding of their political structures, and Canadian political scientists should begin by analyzing their governments and politics. But the external environment is important, too. The broader world is affecting politics here in Canada all the time, and our introduction to politics must include the world beyond our borders. Hence our chapters on other countries, as well as international relations, foreign policy, international security, and international political economy. Countries like Canada operate in a global environment all the time. Our mission in Afghanistan, our free trade in North America, our part in international culture, even our notion of citizenship in Canada, are all affected by the essential role we play in global affairs, and the immediate impact felt by events beyond our borders. A citizen of Canada is also a member of a much larger community of nations. This text has explored that relationship in detail.

As a course textbook, there hasn't been an overarching theoretical or methodological approach used, at least in a conscious way. You will recall the various approaches — analytical, behavioural, post-behavioural, political economy, realist, liberal, socialist, feminist, conservative, etc. — that were described in detail earlier in the book. It's safe to say that at times this textbook has employed some of these approaches. For instance, in the chapters on politics and economics, the political economy approach was used, and the empirical examples such as country studies certainly employed some degree of the analytic approach. But we've tried to avoid the potential pitfalls of using a dominant approach at the expense of others. Rather, we've tried to introduce the discipline of political studies in a comprehensive manner. There will be plenty of opportunities for you in future courses to consider the pros and cons of using a particular methodological or theoretical framework.

Despite the fact that this course is an introductory one, teaching this material can be challenging for many instructors. None of us are experts in all these different fields, and all of us have specific areas of specialty. It's tempting, then, to concentrate on what one knows best. Both of the authors of this book, for instance, are international relations specialists. But we have other areas of interest (domestic politics, theory, comparative studies) that reflect our primary concentration in international relations. You too have likely developed particular attention to some of the areas covered in this text and course, and may have little interest in others. That's natural, and expected. Regardless of where we are in our studies, from an introductory student to a senior professor, our interests will bend and change over time, but we'll find those fields that intrigue us most. To that end, we've tried to introduce all the major areas in political studies in a balanced way. Canadian politics, comparative studies, theory, international relations; all of these overlap in many ways and each has its own sub-fields, too. If you choose to continue studying politics, you'll likely have to make choices about courses and fields that are most intriguing for you. We hope this book has helped you reach those decisions. With this in mind, let us turn our attention to your future as a politics student: what courses should you take? What occupations or careers might you prepare for?

Where Do We Go from Here?

Now that you've completed one course in political studies, what should you take next? This introductory class has prepared you for any of the major sub-fields — Canadian politics, comparative politics, international relations, political theory, or public administration. Some of these will be more interesting to you than others, but keep in mind that a broad base in politics will help you down the road if you continue to study in this discipline. You may discover, for instance, that you really need that political theory background when you're asked by a professor to assist in classroom instruction or research years later in your undergraduate, or maybe graduate, degree.

If you decide that you want to major in political studies, then the rules and guidelines for courses you have to take at your university would be the logical place to start. However, it's fairly common that most departments require students to take a series of courses that introduce you to the sub-disciplines in your second year. Keeping in mind that your decisions will be led by the requirements of your program, here is the chance for you to concentrate on those areas that really piqued your interest in this course.

A common question posed by students to their professor, particularly in the early stages of their studies, is 'What kind of job will I get with this degree?' You've no doubt thought about it, too. It would be odd, in fact, for anyone to enter a degree program at a university and not think about their future prospects. This thinking is further complicated by the pressures of family members who want to know what you'll 'do with your life' and the common wisdom that suggests a Bachelor of Arts degree will not properly prepare you for any career.

Let's begin, then, with the matter of the BA. Rather like politics, it's easy to succumb to cynical thinking about undergraduate degrees, especially when the economy slumps. It's a big decision to pursue a university degree: four years or so of your life, thousands of dollars, and choices that will affect your future. Before we get ahead of ourselves, let's consider where we are right now. You've already made some decisions that have led you here. You've chosen a degree program at a university, or a college program, or you may be taking courses on a selective basis for the time being. Importantly, you've chosen this course for one reason or another. We can presume that your reason for this course has something to do with your interest in politics. That means something: you know what you want to study, and where your interests and abilities lie. Therefore, whatever choices you've already made cannot be wrong, since you're pursuing your interests. You may discover, however, that politics is not your passion. But that's not a failure. Rather, it's part of your exploration of your post-secondary studies.

It's certainly true that politics is not a trade like plumbing or drywall installation. And it's not even exactly the same as other intellectual pursuits like medicine or commerce. Like medicine and commerce, however (and even plumbing and drywall installation at least to some degree), politics involves specialized knowledge. Politics is part of the social sciences, one of the two major wings of most Arts faculties (the other is the humanities). Studying politics hones the analytical mind. It trains us to utilize frameworks like theories and methodologies, and to explore new directions. Politics does not always 'fit' an existing framework, so we become expert problem-solvers, and our critical capacity is always in use in our analysis. We know that events don't always meet an existing category or outline. Part of our ability is to find the dissimilar, to identify the new, and to frame the innovative in a way that gives other researchers an ability to use our findings in their research. This is part of what we call the **heuristic method**, which is the process of laying out experience as a way to assist future research. We have called on past research in our study of introductory politics; someday down the road you may find a new direction that will assist others in their analysis.

Heuristic method
process of laying out experience as a way to assist future research

Your first step should be to ignore the cynical opinions. Those that tell you you'll never get a job with a BA are wrong. Those that tell you you'll never make a decent living are wrong. But remember that politics is not a trade, and you are not training for a job in your political studies courses. There are no designated fields for political science majors, like there are for plumbers. Think back to our discussion of Greek political thought. You might recall that Socrates thought the 'philosopher kings' should be trained in politics. Why shouldn't those that govern be expected to understand political science? Socrates envisions professional political masters, a 'politician' (rather like a statistician studies statistics). But politicians today certainly do not need a political science background (though they would benefit from one!), so that term is already in use.

But the emphasis on 'jobs' distorts the real issue. Bachelor of Arts graduates haven't trained for jobs, they've prepared for careers. Political studies graduates often go on to study at the master's level, or to pursue law, commerce, the public service, or journalism, for instance. You may think that the BA is only a stepping stone towards these careers, but turn that thinking around: the BA on its own may not be what earns you the career of your choice, but it's hard to imagine obtaining that career without one. It is possible, of course, to enter law school or journalism with no undergraduate degree. But these are exceptions, rather than the rule, and most lawyers or journalists, for example, will tell you that their choice of undergraduate specialty made them a far better professional. The BA gives you a field of emphasis, a speciality based on knowledge and study. And on that score, a degree in politics can be far more adaptable than many others. For example, if the foreign service interests you, your background in politics will serve you in a greater fashion than a degree in another social science or humanities field.

Just to give you pause for thought, here is a brief list of the jobs that some of our former undergraduate students have gone on to do:

- Senator
- Diplomat
- Government analyst
- Financial analyst
- Stock trader
- International textile importer
- Oil trader
- Sustainable development expert
- Consultant
- Industrial espionage specialist
- Professor of international relations
- Migrant worker rights advocate
- Public service worker
- United Nations worker
- Business owner
- Journalist

For those of you still unconvinced, or looking for hard evidence that a BA is a good idea, consider this. In 1999 the *Globe and Mail* newspaper published a story about a report that followed the career direction of hundreds of arts, science, and applied science (engineering) graduates in Ontario. The study showed that arts graduates earned as much as pure science colleagues when they were hired. And, as time went on, those arts graduates rose higher in their institutions, and had higher incomes than pure science and applied science graduates.[2]

Talk to your family about your choices. Get information from friends and peers who have taken similar programs, whether they've graduated yet or not. And most importantly, discuss your future with your professors. You'll find those instructors who are more open to your ideas, or those who you just 'click' with better. Use them as a resource. Talk about your aspirations, ask questions about your courses and your program, and compare what they all have to say. No one will tell you exactly what you ought to do; that's up to you. But you'll get to that point much more quickly with the help and advice of others.

Conclusion

At the outset of Chapter 1 we welcomed you to the study of politics. That chapter promised that this text would introduce you to the widest array of topics and issues that we could accommodate in a comprehensive first-year volume. If this book has been a success, then you likely aren't satisfied with this introduction to politics. This isn't to say that our design should be a failure, but rather that it should stimulate in you a deeper fascination with the material you've dealt with. An introductory text like this one cannot fully account for all perspectives or topics. But it got you thinking about issues that you hadn't before, challenged your opinions on things you thought you knew and understood, and no doubt left you in complete disagreement at other times!

Satisfying those interests will take time, much more time than your course could provide. Both of us still feel moved in different directions by our research and teaching, and we hope that continues as long as we remain political scientists. The dynamism of politics is what brought us in and keeps us here. We hope that you feel the same way. Welcome.

Self-Assessment Questions

1. What is the difference between an explanation of an idea and an interpretation of one?
2. What are the main sub-disciplines in political studies? How do they overlap?
3. What are some of the main concepts that have reappeared throughout this book?
4. What is the difference between 'theory' and 'methodology'?

Weblinks

Careers in the Social Sciences
deansoffice.ssc.uwo.ca/outreach

Canadian Political Science Association: Careers
www.cpsa-acsp.ca/guides.shtml

Careers in Political Science
www.sfu.ca/politics/department/careers.html

Political Science Majors: Careers
info.wlu.ca/~wwwarts/careers/programs/polsci. shtml

Further Reading

Brooks, Stephen. *Canadian Democracy: An Introduction*, 6th ed. Toronto: Oxford University Press, 2009.
Inwood, Gregory J. *Understanding Canadian Public Administration*, 3rd ed. Toronto: Pearson Education Canada, 2009.
Jackson, Robert, and Georg Sørensen. *Introduction to International Relations: Theories*

and Approaches, 4th ed. Toronto: Oxford University Press, 2009.
Kesselman, Mark, et al. *Introduction to Comparative Politics*. Toronto: Nelson Canada, 2010.
Veltman, Andrea, ed. *Social and Political Philosophy: Classic and Contemporary Readings*. Toronto: Oxford University Press, 2008.

CBC News Clips

Visit the companion website for *Politics: An Introduction* to listen to news clips from the CBC radio archives.

Notes

Chapter 1

1. Thomas Hobbes, *Leviathan, Or, the Matter, Forme and Power of a Commonwealth Ecclesiasticall and Civil*, ed. Michael Oakeshott (New York: Collier Books, 1962) (first pub. 1651).
2. Harold Lasswell, *Politics: Who Gets What, When, How* (New York: Meridian Books, 1958).
3. Aristotle, *Politics*, trans. T.A. Sinclair (Harmondsworth, UK: Penguin Books, 1986), 7.
4. Laozi, *Tao Te Ching* (Harmondsworth, UK: Penguin Books, 1963, 1976).
5. Kenneth McRoberts, 'The Future of the Nation-State and Quebec-Canada Relations,' in Michel Seymour, ed., *The Fate of the Nation-State* (Montreal and Kingston: McGill-Queen's University Press, 2004), 390.

Chapter 2

1. Andrew Heywood, *Political Ideas and Concepts: An Introduction* (New York: St. Martin's Press, 1994), 4.
2. Ibid., 56-7.
3. Richard Gunther et al., eds., *Political Parties: Old Concepts and New Challenges* (Oxford: Oxford University Press, 2002), 43.
4. Michael E. Morrell, 'Deliberation, Democratic Decision-Making and Internal Political Efficacy,' *Political Behavior*, 27/1 (2005): 51 (available at www.jstor.org/stable/4500184).
5. Michael Kenny, *The Politics of Identity: Liberal Political Theory and the Dilemmas of Difference* (Cambridge: Polity Press, 2004), 1-7.
6. Heywood, *Political Ideas and Concepts*, 116-17.
7. Robert Putnam, *Bowling Alone: The Collapse and Revival of American Community* (New York: Simon and Schuster, 2000), 67-8.
8. Samuel P. Huntington, *Political Order in Changing Societies* (New Haven, CT: Yale University Press, 1968), 3-4.
9. Joel S. Migdal, *State in Society: Studying How States and Societies Transform and Constitute One Another* (Cambridge: Cambridge University Press, 2001), 6.
10. Karen A. Mingst, *Essentials of International Relations*, 3rd ed. (New York: W.W. Norton, 2004), 83-4.
11. Robert O. Keohane and Joseph S. Nye, *Power and Interdependence: World Politics in Transition*, 2nd ed. (Cambridge: HarperCollins, 1989), 11-19.
12. Steven Lukes, *Power: A Radical View* (Houndmills, UK: Palgrave Macmillan, in association with British Sociological Association, 2005), 9-10.
13. William J. Lahneman, 'Changing Power Cycles and Foreign Policy Role-Power Realignments: Asia, Europe, and North America,' *International Political Science Review* 24/1 (2003): 106-8 (available at www.jstor.org/stable/1601332).
14. Jason A. MacDonald, 'Agency Design and Postlegislative Influence over the Bureaucracy,' *Political Research Quarterly*, 60/4 (2007): 683 (available at www.jstor.org/stable/4623866).
15. Huntington, *Political Order*, 74-5.
16. Heywood, *Political Ideas and Concepts*, 89-90.
17. Stanley A. Renshon, 'Political Leadership as Social Capital: Governing in a Divided National Culture,' *Political Psychology*, 21/1 (2000): 200 (available at www.jstor.org/stable/3792071).
18. Anthony Oberschall, 'Opportunities and Framing in the Eastern European Revolts of 1989,' in *Comparative Perspectives on Social Movements: Political Opportunities, Mobilizing Structures, and Cultural Framings*, ed. Doug McAdam et al., 3rd ed. (Cambridge: Cambridge University Press, 1996), 97-9.
19. Ronald Inglehart, *Human Values and Social Change: Findings from the Values Surveys* (Leiden and Boston: Brill, 2003), 5-7.
20. Heywood, *Political Ideas and Concepts*, 266-90.
21. Daniel Horowitz, 'Rethinking Betty Friedan and *The Feminine Mystique*: Labor Union Radicalism and Feminism in Cold War America,' *American Quarterly*, 48/1 (1996): 2 (available at www.jstor.org/stable/30041520).
22. Claus Offe, 'Fifty Years after the 'Great Transformation': Reflections on Social Order and Political Agency,' in *The Changing Nature of Democracy*, ed. Takashi Inoguchi et al. (Tokyo: United Nations University Press, 1998), 39-46.
23. Dennis R. Hoover et al., 'Evangelicalism Meets the Continental Divide: Moral and Economic Conservatism in the United States and Canada,' *Political Research Quarterly*, 55/2 (2002): 356 (available at www.jstor.org/stable/3088056).
24. David Miller, *Liberty* (New York: Oxford University Press, 1991), 6.
25. Judith N. Shklar, *Political Thought and Political Thinkers*, ed. Stanley Hoffmann (Chicago: University of Chicago Press, 1998), 95.
26. Eric Nelson, 'Liberty: One Concept Too Many?' *Political Theory*, 33/1 (2005): 60 (available at www.jstor.org/stable/30038395).
27. Heywood, *Political Ideas and Concepts*, 198.
28. Ibid., 152.
29. Ibid., 138.
30. Jean Blondel, 'Democracy and Constitutionalism,' in *The Changing Nature of Democracy*, ed. Takashi Inoguchi et al. (Tokyo: United Nations University Press, 1998), 82.

Chapter 3

1. Judith N. Shklar, *Political Thought and Political Thinkers*, ed. Stanley Hoffmann (Chicago: University of Chicago Press, 1998), 161-73.
2. Theodore H. Cohn, *Global Political Economy: Theory and Practice*. 4th ed. (New York: Pearson Longman, 2008), 108.
3. Karen A. Mingst, *Essentials of International Relations*. 3rd ed. (New York: W.W. Norton, 2004), 320.

4. Stephen C. McCaffrey, *Understanding International Law* (Newark: LexisNexis Group, 2006), 155.
5. Shklar, *Political Thought*, 10.
6. Pablo Beramendi and Christopher J. Anderson, *Democracy, Inequality, and Representation: A Comparative Perspective* (New York: Russell Sage Foundation, 2008), 39.
7. Mingst, *Essentials of International Relations*, 40.
8. David N. Balaam and Michael Veseth, *Introduction to International Political Economy* (Upper Saddle River, NJ: Prentice Hall, 2001), 14.
9. Andrew Heywood, *Political Ideas and Concepts: An Introduction* (New York: St. Martin's Press, 1994), 9–10.
10. These movements are named after the philosophers and theorists Robert Owen, Henri de Saint-Simon, and Charles Fourier.
11. Anthony Giddens, The Global Third Way Debate (Cambridge: Polity Press, 2001), 23.
12. Christopher M. Federico and Jim Sidanius, 'Sophistication and the Antecedents of Whites' Racial Policy Attitudes: Racism, Ideology, and Affirmative Action in America,' *Public Opinion Quarterly*, 66/2 (2002): 152 (available at www.jstor.org/stable/3078678).
13. Joel S. Migdal, *State in Society: Studying How States and Societies Transform and Constitute One Another* (Cambridge: Cambridge University Press, 2001), 30.
14. Cohn, *Global Political Economy*, 99–100.
15. Joan E. Spero and Jeffrey A. Hart, *The Politics of International Economic Relations*, 6th ed. (Belmont, CA: Wadsworth Thomson, 2003), 2.
16. Heywood, *Political Ideas and Concepts*, 57–60.
17. Henk Dekker et al., 'Nationalism and Its Explanations,' *Political Psychology*, 24/2 (2003): 347 (available at www.jstor.org/stable/3792354).
18. Sanford Lakoff, 'Tocqueville, Burke, and the Origins of Liberal Conservatism,' *Review of Politics*, 60/3 (1998): 447 (available at www.jstor.org/stable/1407984).
19. Sonia E. Alvarez, 'Latin American Feminisms "Go Global": Trends of the 1990s and Challenges for the New Millennium,' in *Cultures of Politics/Politics of Cultures: Re-visioning Latin American Social Movements*, ed. Sonia E. Alvarez, Evelina Dagnino, and Arturo Escobar (Boulder, CO: Westview Press, 1998), 295.
20. Hanspeter Kriesi, 'The Organizational Structure of New Social Movements in a Political Context,' in *Comparative Perspectives on Social Movements: Political Opportunities, Mobilizing Structures, and Cultural Framings*, ed. Doug McAdam et al. (Cambridge: Cambridge University Press, 1996), 168.
21. Rajeev Patel and Philip McMichael, 'Third Worldism and the Lineages of Global Facism: The Regrouping of the Global South in the Neoliberal Era,' *Third World Quarterly*, 25/1 (2004): 233 (available at www.jstor.org/stable/3993786).
22. Alan Carter, 'Analytical Anarchism: Some Conceptual Foundations,' *Political Theory*, 28/2 (2000): 231 (available at www.jstor.org/stable/192235).
23. Pippa Norris, *Electoral Engineering: Voting Rules and Political Behavior* (Cambridge: Cambridge University Press, 2004), 62.
24. Cohn, *Global Political Economy*, 99–100.

Chapter 4

1. For more information about the Canadian budget, see www.budget.gc.ca.
2. United States budget information is available at www.gpoaccess.gov/usbudget.
3. Carl Bernstein, *A Woman in Charge: The Life of Hillary Rodham Clinton* (New York: Knopf, 2007).
4. Adam Smith, *An Inquiry into the Nature and Causes of the Wealth of Nations*, 5th ed., ed. Edwin Cannan (London: Methuen, 1904).
5. Plato, *The Republic*, trans. G.M.A. Grube, rev. C.D.C. Reeve. (Indianapolis: Hackett, 1992).
6. Aristotle, *The Politics*, trans. Benjamin Jowett (North Chelmsford, MA: Courier Dover Publications, 2000).

Chapter 5

1. An excellent source for the mechanism of United States government is Susan Welch, John Gruhl, Michael Steinman, John Comer, and Susan Rigdon, *American Government*, 10th ed., (Florence, KY: Wadsworth, 2005).
2. David Beetham presents an excellent study of this in *The Legitimation of Power* (New York: Palgrave Macmillan, 1991).
3. Supreme Court of Canada, *Reference re Manitoba Language Rights*, [1985] 1 S.C.R. 721.
4. Canada, Constitution Acts, 1867 to 1982. For a good overview of peace, order, and good government, see Peter J.T. O'Hearn, *Peace, Order and Good Government: A New Constitution for Canada* (Toronto: Macmillan, 1964).
5. R. MacGregor Dawson and W.F. Dawson, *Democratic Government in Canada*, 5th ed., rev. Norman Ward (Toronto: University of Toronto Press, 1997), 90.
6. Philip Sworden has authored a good introduction to law in Canada: *An Introduction to Canadian Law*, 2nd ed. (Toronto: Emond Montgomery, 2006).

Chapter 6

1. Jonathan Rodden, 'Comparative Federalism and Decentralization: On Meaning and Measurement,' *Comparative Politics*, 36/4 (2004): 482 (available at www.jstor.org/stable/4150172).
2. Joseph S. Nye, Jr., *Understanding International Conflicts: An Introduction to Theory and History*, 6th 3d. (New York: Pearson Longman, 2007), 90.
3. David Cameron and Richard Simeon, 'Intergovernmental Relations in Canada: The Emergence of Collaborative Federalism,' *Publius: The Journal of Federalism*, 32/2 (2002): 60 (available at www.jstor.org/stable/3330945).
4. James J. Guy, *People, Politics and Government: Political Science: A Canadian Perspective* (Toronto: Prentice-Hall Canada, 1995), 142.
5. Arthur Benz, 'From Unitary to Asymmetric Federalism in Germany: Taking Stock after 50 Years,' *Publius: The Journal of Federalism*, 29/4 (1999): 67 (available at www.jstor.org/stable/3330908).

6. Ian Robinson and Richard Simeon, 'The Dynamics of Canadian Federalism,' in *Canadian Politics*, ed. James P. Bickerton and Alain-G. Gagnon, 3rd ed. (Toronto: Broadview Press, 1999), 239–42.

7. Cameron and Simeon, 'Intergovernmental Relations,' 55.

8. Jonathan Potter, *Devolution and Globalisation: Implications for Local Decision-Makers* (Paris: OECD, 2001), 16.

9. United Kingdom, Office of Public Sector Information, 'The Town and Country Planning (General Development Procedure) (Amendment) (Wales) Order 2008,' Welsh Statutory Instruments (available at www.opsi.gov.uk/legislation/wales/wsi2008/pdf/wsi_20082336_mi.pdf).

10. United Kingdom, Office of Public Sector Information, 'Explanatory Social Security Contributions (Transfer Of Functions, etc.) Act 1999' (available at www.opsi.gov.uk/acts/acts1999/en/ukpgaen_19990002_en_1).

11. Mikhail Filippov et al., *Designing Federalism: A Theory of Self-Sustainable Federal Institutions* (Cambridge: Cambridge University Press, 2004), 232.

12. Hamish Telford, 'The Federal Spending Power in Canada: Nation-Building or Nation-Destroying?' *Publius: The Journal of Federalism*, 33/1 (2003): 28 (available at www.jstor.org/stable/3331175).

13. Kenneth McRoberts, 'Canada and the Multinational State,' *Canadian Journal of Political Science*, 34/4 (2001): 702 (available at www.jstor.org/stable/3232879).

14. Paul Romney, 'Provincial Equality, Special Status and the Compact Theory of Canadian Confederation,' *Canadian Journal of Political Science*, 32/1 (1999): 31 (available at www.jstor.org/stable/3232771).

15. Michael Howlett, 'Federalism and Public Policy,' in *Canadian Politics*, ed. James P. Bickerton and Alain-G. Gagnon, 3rd ed. (Toronto: Broadview Press, 1999), 532.

16. Robinson and Simeon, 'Dynamics of Canadian Federalism,' 250–1.

17. Joseph F. Zimmerman, 'National-State Relations: Cooperative Federalism in the Twentieth Century,' *Publius: The Journal of Federalism*, 31/2 (2001): 18–20 (available at www.jstor.org/stable/3330955).

18. Cameron and Simeon, 'Intergovernmental Relations,' 49.

19. Telford, 'Federal Spending Power in Canada,' 24–5.

20. James Bickerton, 'Regionalism in Canada,' in *Canadian Politics*, ed. James P. Bickerton and Alain-G. Gagnon, 3rd ed. (Toronto: Broadview Press, 1999), 223.

Chapter 7

1. Michael Zürn and Jeffrey T. Checkel, 'Getting Socialized to Build Bridges: Constructivism and Rationalism, Europe and the Nation-State,' *International Organization*, 59/4 (2005): 1045 (available at www.jstor.org/stable/3877836).

2. Donald P. Haider-Markel et al., 'Lose, Win, or Draw?: A Reexamination of Direct Democracy and Minority Rights,' *Political Research Quarterly*, 60/2 (2007): 304 (available at www.jstor.org/stable/4623831).

3. Pippa Norris, *Electoral Engineering: Voting Rules and Political Behavior* (Cambridge: Cambridge University Press, 2004), 4.

4. Stephen C. Craig et al., 'Winners, Losers, and Election Context: Voter Responses to the 2000 Presidential Election,' *Political Research Quarterly*, 59/4 (2006): 579 (available at www.jstor.org/stable/4148060).

5. Gerry Stoker, *Why Politics Matters: Making Democracy Work* (Houndmills, UK: Palgrave Macmillan, 2006), 20.

6. Robert G. Moser, 'Independents and Party Formation: Elite Partisanship as an Intervening Variable in Russian Politics,' *Comparative Politics*, 31/2 (1999): 154 (available at www.jstor.org/stable/422142).

7. Joseph A. Aistrup, 'Constituency Diversity and Party Competition: A County and State Level Analysis,' *Political Research Quarterly*, 57/2 (2004): 267 (available at www.jstor.org/stable/3219870).

8. I. MacAllister et al., 'Class Dealignment and the Neighbourhood Effect: Miller Revisited,' *British Journal of Political Science*, 31/1 (2001): 45 (available at www.jstor.org/stable/3593275).

9. Gary W. Cox and Scott Morgenstern, 'Latin America's Reactive Assemblies and Proactive Presidents,' *Comparative Politics*, 31/2 (2001): 186 (available at www.jstor.org/stable/422377).

10. Richard Gunther et al., eds., *Political Parties: Old Concepts and New Challenges* (Oxford: Oxford University Press, 2002), 116.

11. Frederic Charles Schaffer, *The Hidden Costs of Clean Election Reform* (Ithaca, NY: Cornell University Press, 2008), 152.

12. Yves Schemeil, 'Democracy before Democracy?' *International Political Science Review*, 21/2 (2000): 111 (available at www.jstor.org/stable/1601156).

13. David M. Farrell, *Electoral Systems: A Comparative Introduction* (Houndmills, UK: Palgrave, 2001), 201–4.

14. Norris, *Electoral Engineering*, 168.

15. Farrell, *Electoral Systems*, 170.

16. Ben Reilly and Andrew Reynolds, *Electoral Systems and Conflict in Divided Societies* (Washington, DC: National Academy Press, 1999), 19.

17. Norris, *Electoral Engineering*, 224.

18. Reilly and Reynolds, *Electoral Systems and Conflict*, 19.

19. Ibid., 21.

20. Ibid., 22.

21. Ibid.

22. Rein Taagepera and Matthew Soberg Shugart, *Seats and Votes: The Effects and Determinants of Electoral Systems* (New Haven, CT: Yale University Press, 1989), 26.

23. Adam Przeworski et al., eds., *Democracy, Accountability, and Representation* (Cambridge: Cambridge University Press, 1999), 151.

24. Stoker, *Why Politics Matters*, 66–7.

25. Herbert Kitschelt and Steven I. Wilkinson, eds., *Patrons, Clients, and Policies: Patterns of Democratic Accountability and Political Competition* (Cambridge: Cambridge University Press, 2007), 28–30.

26. Gunther et al., *Political Parties*, 293.

27. Ibid.

28. Ibid., 140–5.

29. Ibid., 116–20.

30. Ibid., 120–2.

31. Lee Sigelman and Mark Kugler, 'Why Is Research on the Effects of Negative Campaigning So Inconclusive? Understanding Citizens' Perceptions of Negativity,' *Journal of Politics*, 65/1 (2003): 144 (available at www.jstor.org/stable/3449859).

32. Kim Fridkin Kahn and Patrick J. Kenney, 'Do Negative Campaigns Mobilize or Suppress Turnout? Clarifying the Relationship between Negativity and Participation,' *American Political Science Review*, 93/4 (1999): 879 (available at www.jstor.org/stable/2586118).

33. John G. Geer and James H. Geer, 'Remembering Attack Ads: An Experimental Investigation of Radio,' *Political Behavior*, 25/1 (2003): 70 (available at www.jstor.org/stable/3657315).

34. Stoker, *Why Politics Matters*, 189–90.

35. R. Kent Weaver, 'Electoral Rules and Electoral Reform in Canada,' in *Mixed Member Electoral Systems: The Best of Both Worlds?*, ed. Matthew Soberg Shugart and Martin P. Wattenberg (New York: Oxford University Press, 2001), 551–4.

Chapter 8

1. Gabriel Almond and Sidney Verba, *The Civic Culture: Political Attitudes and Democracy in Five Nations* (Newbury Park, CA: Sage Publications, 1989), 7.

2. Juan J. Linz, 'Totalitarian and Authoritarian Regimes,' in *Handbook of Political Science*, ed. Fred I. Greenstein and Nelson W. Polsby (New York: Addison Wesley, 1975), 270.

3. Jennifer Glass et al., 'Attitude Similarity in Three-Generation Families: Socialization, Status Inheritance, or Reciprocal Influence?' *American Sociological Review*, 51/5 (1986): 685–98 (available at www.jstor.org/stable/2095493).

4. William Gamson and David Meyer, 'Framing Political Opportunity,' in *Comparative Perspectives on Social Movements: Political Opportunities, Mobilizing Structures, and Cultural Framings*, ed. Doug McAdam et al., 3rd ed. (Cambridge: Cambridge University Press, 1996), 287–8.

5. Scott L. Althaus, *Collective Preferences in Democratic Politics: Opinion Surveys and the Will of the People* (Cambridge: Cambridge University Press, 2003), 289–96.

6. Ibid., 4–10.

7. Herbert B. Asher, *Polling and the Public: What Every Citizen Should Know*, 2nd ed. (Washington, DC: Congressional Quarterly Press, 1992), 152.

8. Ibid., 96.

9. Chappell Lawson, 'Building the Fourth Estate: Media Opening and Democratization in Mexico,' in *Dilemmas of Political Change in Mexico*, ed. Kevin J. Middlebrook (San Diego: Center for U.S.–Mexican Studies, UCSD, 2004), 57.

10. Gamson and Meyer, 'Framing Political Opportunity,' 287.

11. Karen A. Mingst, *Essentials of International Relations*, 3rd ed. (New York: W.W. Norton, 2004), 40.

12. Juan J. Linz and Alfred Stepan, 'Toward Consolidated Democracies,' in *The Changing Nature of Democracy*, ed. Takashi Inoguchi et al. (Tokyo: United Nations University Press, 1998), 64.

13. Robert Dahl, *Polyarchy: Participation and Opposition* (New Haven, CT: Yale University Press, 1971), 200.

14. Helen V. Milner, *Interests, Institutions, and Information: Domestic Politics and International Relations* (Princeton, NJ: Princeton University Press, 1997), 247–8.

15. Pippa Norris, *Electoral Engineering: Voting Rules and Political Behavior* (Cambridge: Cambridge University Press, 2004), 143.

16. Suzanne Berger, ed., *Organizing Interests in Western Europe: Pluralism, Corporatism, and the Transformation of Politics* (Cambridge: Cambridge University Press, 1981), 312.

17. Mancur Olson, *The Logic of Collective Action: Public Goods and the Theory of Groups* (Cambridge, MA: Harvard University Press, 1971), 12.

18. Dahl, *Polyarchy: Participation and Opposition*, 191–2.

19. Éric Montpetit and William D. Coleman, 'Policy Communities and Policy Divergence in Canada: Agro-Environmental Policy Development in Quebec and Ontario,' *Canadian Journal of Political Science*, 32/4 (1999): 695 (available at www.jstor.org/stable/3232509).

20. Philippe C. Schmitter, 'Still the Century of Corporatism?' in *Review of Politics*, 36/1 (1974), 4 (available at www.jstor.org/stable/1406080).

Chapter 9

1. Geir Lundestad, *East, West, North, South: Major Developments in International Politics Since 1945*, 5th ed. (London: Sage, 2004), 1.

2. Earlier in this book we examined the distinctive nature of Canada's 'federal' character, what many refer to as 'quasi-federalism'. See K.C. Wheare, *Federal Government*, 4th ed. (London: Oxford University Press, 1967).

3. For more on the Canadian Constitution, see David Milne, *The Canadian Constitution: From Patriation to Meech Lake* (Toronto: J. Lorimer, 1989).

4. David Mitrany, *The Functional Theory of Politics* (New York: St. Martin's Press, 1975).

Chapter 10

1. David N. Balaam and Michael Veseth, *Introduction to International Political Economy* (Upper Saddle River, NJ: Prentice Hall, 2001), 321.

2. Dietrich Rueschemeyer et al., *Capitalist Development and Democracy* (Chicago: University of Chicago Press, 1992), 10.

3. Brian C. Smith, *Good Governance and Development* (Houndmills, UK: Palgrave Macmillan, 2007), 1–3.

4. Seymour M. Lipset and Stein Rokkan, 'Cleavage Structures, Party Systems, and Voter Alignments', in *The West European Party System*, ed. Peter Miar (Oxford: Oxford University Press, 1990), 120.

5. Brian C. Smith, *Understanding Third World Politics: Theories of Political Change and Development*, 2nd ed. (Bloomington: Indiana University Press, 2003), 164–7.

6. Mark W. Zacher, 'The Territorial Integrity Norm: International Boundaries and the Use of Force', *International Organization*, 55/2 (2001): 229 (available at www.jstor.org/stable/3078631).

7. Thomas W. Croghan et al., 'Routes to Better Health for Children in Four Developing Countries', *The Milbank Quarterly*, 84/2 (2006): 345 (available at www.jstor.org/stable/25098120).

8. Theodore H. Cohn, *Global Political Economy: Theory and Practice*, 4th ed. (New York: Pearson Longman, 2008), 325–6.

9. Rueschemeyer et al., *Capitalist Development*, 60.

10. David Shambaugh, *China's Communist Party: Atrophy and Adaptation* (Berkeley: University of California Press, 2008), 7.
11. Ibid., 40.
12. Smith, *Understanding Third World Politics*, 12.
13. Daniel Yergin, in *The Commanding Heights: The Battle for the World Economy*, by Daniel Yergin and Joseph Stanislaw, rev. and updated ed. (New York: Simon & Schuster, 2002), 185–7.
14. Shambaugh, *China's Communist Party*, 42–5.
15. Susan L. Shirk, *How China Opened Its Door: The Political Success of the PRC's Foreign Trade and Investment Reforms* (Washington, DC: The Brookings Institution, 1994).
16. Takatoshi Ito and Anne O. Krueger, *Growth Theories in Light of the East Asian Experience* (Chicago: University of Chicago Press, 1995), 73–94.
17. For more about China's Open Door economic policy, see ibid. And about the SPE, see Mary E. Gallagher, '"Reform and Openess": Why China's Economic Reforms Have Delayed Democracy', *World Politics*, 54/3 (2002): 345 (available at www.jstor.org/stable/25054191).
18. Judith Adler Hellman, 'Continuity and Change in the Mexican Political System: New Ways of Knowing a New Reality', *European Review of Latin American and Caribbean Studies*, 63 (1997): 32.
19. Alberto Díaz Cayeros, 'Decentralization, Democratization and Federalism in Mexico', in *Dilemmas of Political Change in Mexico*, ed. Kevin J. Middlebrook (San Diego: Center for U.S.–Mexican Studies, UCSD, 2004), 57.
20. Pippa Norris, *Electoral Engineering: Voting Rules and Political Behavior* (Cambridge: Cambridge University Press, 2004), 188.
21. David R. Jones, 'Party Polarization and Legislative Gridlock', *Political Research Quarterly*, 54/1 (2001) (available at www.jstor.org/stable/449211).
22. Denise Dresser, 'From PRI Predominance to Divided Democracy', in *Constructing Democratic Governance in Latin America*, ed. Jorge Domínguez and Michael Shifter (Baltimore, MD: John Hopkins University Press, 2003), 67.
23. Nora Lustig, *Mexico: The Remaking of an Economy* (Washington, DC: The Brookings Institution, 1992), 79.
24. 'Obama, Calderón: Assault-Gun Ban Could Curb Border Violence', CNN, 16 April 2009 (available at edition.cnn.com/2009/POLITICS/04/16/obama.latin.america/index.html).

Chapter 11

1. Charles de Secondat, baron de Montesquieu, *The Spirit of Laws* (Amherst, NY: Prometheus Books, 2002).
2. Hans-Henrik Holm and Georg Sørenson, *Whose World Order: Uneven Globalization and the End of the Cold War* (Boulder, CO: Westview Press, 1995).
3. Jayantanuja Bandyopadhyaya and Rikhi Jaipal, *A General Theory of International Relations: Origins, Growth and Potential for World Peace* (Mumbai: Allied Publishers, 1993), 138.
4. Hans Morgenthau, *Politics Among Nations: The Struggle for Power and Peace* (New York: Alfred A. Knopf, 1948).
5. Plato, *The Republic Of Plato*, trans. F. M. Cornford (New York: Oxford University Press, 1945), 14.
6. Kenneth N. Waltz, *Theory of International Politics* (New York: McGraw-Hill, 1979).
7. Stephen D. Krasner, ed., *International Regimes* (Ithaca, NY: Cornell University Press, 1983).
8. Karl Marx and Friedrich Engels, *Manifesto of the Communist Party* (New York: Cosimo, 2006).
9. Vladimir Ilyich Lenin, *Imperialism, the Highest Stage of Capitalism* (Moscow: Progress Publishers, 1963).
10. 'Canada Information and History' (Washington, DC: National Geographic Society, 2008); see travel.nationalgeographic.com/places/countries/country_canada.html.
11. Data taken from CIA World Factbook, 2009, and Statistics Canada 2008.
12. 'By the numbers: The Canada/U.S. border' (CBC News, 30 July 2004).
13. See Alvin Finkel, *Our Lives: Canada After 1945* (Toronto: J. Lorimer, 1997), 120; John Herd Thompson and Stephen J. Randall, *Canada and the United States: Ambivalent Allies*, 3rd ed. (Athens: University of Georgia Press, 2002), 248; 'The Helpful Fixer: International Relations of Canada,' *Canada and the World Backgrounder* (September 1999).
14. Tom Keating, *Canada and World Order: The Multilateralist Tradition in Canadian Foreign Policy*, 2nd ed. (Don Mills, ON: Oxford University Press, 2002), 16.
15. Peyton V. Lyon and Brian W. Tomlin, *Canada as an International Actor* (Toronto: Macmillan, 1979).

Chapter 12

1. Winston S. Churchill, *Amid These Storms: Thoughts and Adventures* (New York: Charles Scribner's Sons, 1932), 245.
2. Gwynne Dyer, *War: The New Edition* (Toronto: Random House, 2004), 11.
3. Stephanie Lawson has a good discussion of security and insecurity in her book *International Relations* (Hoboken, NJ: Wiley-Blackwell, 2003).
4. For an excellent discussion of what conflict is, see Sandra Cheldelin, Daniel Druckman, and Larissa A. Fast, eds., *Conflict: From Analysis To Intervention* (New York: Continuum International Publishing Group, 2003), especially Part I.
5. One source for more ideas about the concept of war is Edward N. Zalta , ed., *Stanford Encyclopedia of Philosophy* (Stanford, CA: Center for the Study of Language and Information; first published 2000; substantive revision 2005).
6. There are many translations of this famous line. Though this is the common version, there are others: e.g., 'war is merely the continuation of policy by other means,' found in Carl von Clausewitz, *On War*, trans. Michael Howard and Peter Paret (Oxford: Oxford University Press, 2007), 28.
7. George C. Kohn, *Dictionary of Wars*, 3rd ed. (New York: Facts On File, 2006).
8. Mia Consalvo, 'It's No Videogame: Global News Media Commentary and the Second Gulf War,' paper delivered at the Digital Games Research Association Conference, Utrecht, the Netherlands, November 2003.
9. There are many definitions of terrorism. This one is a combination of two separate interpretations made by Walter Reich and Brian Jenkins. Their definitions, and others, are found in Gus Martin, *Understanding Terrorism: Challenges, Perspectives, and Issues* (Thousand Oaks, CA: Sage Publications, 2006).

10. John Stuart Mill, 'A Few Words On Non-Intervention,' first published in *Fraser's Magazine* (1859); reprinted in *Foreign Policy Perspectives*, 8 (1987).

11. Michael J. Butler explores peacekeeping as one of five major approaches to conflict management. The others are: peace enforcement and support operations; negotiation and bargaining; mediation; and adjudication. See *International Conflict Management* (New York: Routledge, 2009).

Chapter 13

1. David N. Balaam and Michael Veseth, *Introduction to International Political Economy* (Upper Saddle River, NJ: Prentice Hall, 2001), 3.

2. Peter Hall, 'The Role of Interests, Institutions, and Ideas in the Comparative Political Economy of the Industrialized Nations,' in *Comparative Politics: Rationality, Culture and Structure*, ed. Mark I. Lichbach and Alan S. Zuckerman (New York: Cambridge University Press, 1997), 185.

3. Theodore H. Cohn, *Global Political Economy: Theory and Practice*, 4th ed. (New York: Pearson Longman, 2008), 11.

4. Robert O. Keohane and Joseph S. Nye, *Power and Interdependence: World Politics in Transition*, 2nd ed. (Cambridge: HarperCollins, 1989), 8–11.

5. Milan Svolik, 'Lies, Defection, and the Pattern of International Cooperation,' *American Journal of Political Science*, 50/4 (2006): 911 (available at www.jstor.org/stable/4122923).

6. Karen A. Mingst, *Essentials of International Relations*, 3rd ed. (New York: W.W. Norton, 2004), 256–62.

7. Cohn, *Global Political Economy*, 208.

8. Joan E. Spero and Jeffrey A. Hart, *The Politics of International Economic Relations*, 6th ed. (Belmont, CA: Wadsworth Thomson, 2003), 113.

9. Ibid., 6.

10. Judith Goldstein, 'Ideas, Institutions, and American Trade Policy,' in *The State and American Foreign Economic Policy*, ed. G. John Ikenberry et al. (Ithaca, NY: Cornell University Press, 1993), 187, 197.

11. Patrick J. McDonald, 'Peace Through Trade or Free Trade?' *Journal of Conflict Resolution*, 48/4 (2004): 549 (available at www.jstor.org/stable/4149808).

12. Adam Przeworski and Fernando Limongi, 'Political Regimes and Economic Growth,' *Journal of Economic Perspectives*, 7/3 (1993), 62 (available at www.jstor.org/stable/2138442).

13. Mingst, *Essentials of International Relations*, 262–4.

14. Spero and Hart, *Politics of International Economic Relations*, 140.

15. Mingst, *Essentials of International Relations*, 262–4.

16. Spero and Hart, *Politics of International Economic Relations*, 6.

17. Cohn, *Global Political Economy*, 208.

18. Ibid., 22.

19. Spero and Hart, *Politics of International Economic Relations*, 20–4.

20. Balaam and Veseth, *Introduction to International Political Economy*, 62–3.

21. Kenneth M. Roberts, 'Neoliberalism and the Transformation of Populism in Latin America: The Peruvian Case,' *World Politics*, 48/1 (1995): 82–116.

22. Joan M. Nelson, 'The Politics of Economic Adjustment in Developing Nations,' in *Economic Crisis and Policy Choice: The Politics of Adjustment in the Third World* (Princeton, NJ: Princeton University Press, 1990), 32.

23. BIS Annual Report 2008/9, 'The Global Financial Crisis,' Bank for International Settlements (available at www.bis.org/publ/arpdf/ar2009e2.htm).

24. Roger Stern, 'Oil Market Power and United States National Security,' *Proceedings of the National Academy of Sciences of the United States of America*, 103/5 (2006): 1650 (available at www.jstor.org/stable/30048427).

25. Balaam and Veseth, *Introduction to International Political Economy*, 211.

26. Daniel Yergin in *The Commanding Heights: The Battle for the World Economy*, by Daniel Yergin and Joseph Stainslaw, rev. and updated ed. (New York: Simon & Schuster, 2002), 406–8.

27. Raymond Vernon, 'Big Business and National Governments: Reshaping the Compact in a Globalizing Economy,' *Journal of International Business Studies*, 32/3 (2001): 516 (available at www. jstor.org/stable/3069494).

28. Cohn, *Global Political Economy*, 307–8.

Chapter 14

1. Fred Pearce, 'Brazil's Beef Trade Wrecks Rainforest', *New Scientist*, vol. 2442, 10 April 2004.

2. See George Fallis, 'More Than a Pretty Degree: Never Underestimate the Practical Value of the Liberal Arts', *Globe and Mail*, 10 February 1999; also Jennifer Lewington, 'Arts Background No Handicap in Quest for Jobs', *Globe and Mail*, 26 October 1998.

Glossary

Additional member: mix of simple plurality and proportional representation voting; voters elect a representative and also cast a vote for a political party

African Union: international organization founded to promote co-operation among the independant nations of Africa

Analytical approach: perspective that views politics as an empirical discipline (one that can be observed), rather than a science; politics cannot be broken down into parts, but must be seen comprehensively

Anomic interest group: ad hoc interest group that does not have a standard organized composition; formed to deal with short-term issues

Arbitration: authoritative resolution to dispute made by impartial person agreed upon by all parties

Aristocracy: political system ruled by a hierarchical elite

Asia–Pacific Economic Cooperation (APEC): group for promoting open trade and economic cooperation among Asia–Pacific economies

Associational interest group: interest group closely related to particular political objectives

Attack ads: negative and aggressive television and media advertising by one political party or organization against another

Autarky: condition of complete self-sufficiency and isolation from the rest of the system

Authoritarian: form of political rule based on absolute obedience to a constituted authority

Authoritarianism: political system requiring absolute obedience to a constituted authority

Authority: the power or right to force obedience

Balance of power: situation in international politics where states strive to achieve equilibrium of power in the world in order to prevent any other country or coalition of countries from dominating the system

Ballot: card used to cast a vote

Behaviouralism: perspective that concentrates on the 'tangible' aspects of political life, rather than values; objective was to establish a discipline that was 'scientific' and objective

Bicameral: legislative or parliamentary body with two assemblies

Bilateral aid: military or development assistance given by one country to another

Bourgeois: according to socialists such as Marx, the property-owning class that exploits the working class (proletariat)

Boycott: refusal to deal with another political community often involving banning of political, economic, or cultural relations

Bretton Woods agreement: postwar system of fixed exchange rates and heavy controls on private banks and other financial institutions so that their role in international finance would be limited

Bureaucracy: division of government responsible for carrying out public policy, and staffed by public employees

Bureaucrats: those responsible for carrying out public policy; public employees

Cabinet: members of the executive level of government responsible for decision-making and administration of the bureaucracy

Cadre party: party created and directed by a small elite group; tends to control much power within legislatures

Caliphate: government inspired by Islam that rules over its subjects using Islamic law

Capitalism: economic system where production and distribution of goods relies on private capital and investment

Caucus: group of elected representatives, usually based on party membership, but which may also be grouped by race, gender, geographic representation, etc.

Centralization: concentration of power in a single body, usually the principal government

Centralized federalism: process whereby federal government increases its power relative to the provinces

Checks and balances: system of inspection and evaluation of different levels and branches of governments by others

Chinese Communist Party (CCP): governing political party in China, founded in 1921 as part of revolutionary movement

Citizenship: status granted to citizens that comes with responsibilities and duties as well as rights

Civil law: legal system where legislative bodies enact laws through statutes, ordinances, and regulations

Cold War: a period of rhetorical hostility not marked by violence; most often referenced to the period of 1945–91 that existed between the alliance systems centred on the United States and the Union of Soviet Socialist Republics (USSR)

Colonialism: exploitation of weaker country(ies) by stronger one(s), for political, strategic, or resource interests

Common Agricultural Policy (CAP): European Union program that provides economic benefits to agriculture in all countries in order to permit stable pricing and profits for agricultural producers

Common law: legal system where decisions are made on the basis of precedent, case law, or previous decisions

Common market: an economic arrangement among states intended to eliminate barriers that inhibit the movement of factors of production — labour, capital, and technology — among its members

Communism: political theory, based on writings of Marx and Engels, that espouses class conflict to form a system where all property is publicly owned and each citizen works to his or her own best ability and is compensated equitably

Community: social, political, cultural, and economic ties that bind individuals to one another

Comparative approach: method of political analysis that compares different systems of political authority, based on system type, time period, or form of leadership

Competitive party system: electoral system found in liberal democracies in which political parties are permitted to compete with one another for support from the electorate

Compulsory voting: system in which citizens have a legal obligation to vote in elections

Concept: general idea emerging from events or instances

Concurrent powers: when control is shared between provincial and federal levels of governments

Conditional grants: funds given to provincial authorities but with controls and conditions on how the monies may be spent

Confederalism: political system of divided powers where added power is given to the non-central governments, and limited authority and power is conferred to the central government

Conflict: a state of actual or perceived incompatible interests

Conflict resolution: process in domestic or international affairs where antagonism (either existing or potential) is sought to be reconciled through the use of mediation and negotiation

Congress: legislative chamber of government in the United States

Constituencies: territorial or geographical localities (ridings) represented by a politician chosen through the electoral process

Constitutionality: being in accordance with a constitution

Co-operative federalism: co-operation and coordination of policy between the federal and provincial levels of government

Corn Laws: set of laws regulating the trade in grains in Great Britain; the abolition of these laws in 1846 opened up British agricultural trade

Corporatism: approach to governance that entails close cooperation and coordination among government, business, and labour in the expectation that such activity will bring more stability to politics

Council of the European Union: main decision-making institution of the EU, made up of ministers from the EU national governments

Court of Justice: European Union court

Cronyism: in politics, the practice of choosing or preferring friends or associates

DC: developed country

Debt crisis: a situation in which a country is unable to meet its international debt obligations; sometimes used to refer to the Latin American Debt Crisis of the 1980s

Decentralization: process whereby power and authority is taken from the central government and conferred to non-central (for example, state, regional, or provincial) governments

Decision-making: mechanism or pattern of relations involving different levels of government where determinations and judgments regarding the governance of political system are made (sometimes referred to as the 'black box')

Declaratory power: federal government power to take control of any local project if it decides that this would be for the greater national good

Delegated authority: situation where some powers may be given to sub-national authorities by the national government in a unitary system

Democracy: political system based on the principle that governance requires the assent of all citizens through participation in the electoral process, articulation of views, and direct or indirect representation in governing institutions

Deregulation: removal of government controls in an economic sector

Despot: political leader who rules with absolute power and authority

Détente: warming of relations

Developed world: industrialized nations, including Western Europe, North America, Japan, Australia, and New Zealand, that are part of a structurally integrated system of global capitalism

Developing world: less developed nations that are not part of a structurally integrated system of global capitalism

Devolution: political system where some authority is given to regional governments, but the power to oversee, dismiss, or entrench these authorities is still held by the central government

Dialectical materialism: Marxist notion that material forces affect politics through social and economic change

Dialectics: in Marxism, where ideas and processes throughout history come up against each other, and from the clash of ideas, or of economic processes, a new reality is born

Diet: Japanese Parliament

Diplomacy: international negotiation and discussions that take place on an official — and sometimes unofficial — level between and among states

Direct democracy: political system in which citizens are directly involved in the decision-making process

Disallowance: when provincial legislation is rejected or vetoed by the federal cabinet

Dispute resolution: process by which trading disputes between member states can be resolved by an impartial tribunal, thus preventing such disputes from becoming too political or controversial

Duties: related to rights — responsibilities to protect rights

Economic justice: the redistribution of economic resources from certain groups in society to others

Economic regionalism: the tendency of countries in the same geographic region to intensify economic interactions; both NAFTA and the European Union are examples

Editorial line: particular perspective on world events offered by news outlets

Election: a form of choosing governors whereby individual citizens cast their vote for candidates running for office

Election platforms: positions of political parties or individuals regarding issues and political intentions

Electoral college: in United States, officials chosen from each state based on population who then directly elect the president and vice-president

Electorate: people in a political system with the right to vote in elections; enfranchised citizens

Emerging markets: poorer economies with potential for future growth

Empirical: analysis based not on concepts and theory, but rather what can be observed or experimented on

Enumeration: the process of determining the number of individuals eligible to vote in a constituency

Equality: 'parity' in a political system

Equalization payments: compensation given to more needy regions in a political system in order to create a general state of parity

Ethnic and religious conflict: war or opposition among different racial, linguistic or religious groups

European Atomic Energy Community (EURATOM) : community created to govern atomic energy in Europe, entered into force 1958

European Coal and Steel Community (ECSC): first institutional version of European integration (1951) involving Belgium, the Netherlands, Luxembourg, France, West Germany, and Italy

European Commission: responsible for implementing activities mandated by the European Parliament and Council

European Economic Community (EEC): second institutional version of European integration (1958) involving Belgium, the Netherlands, Luxembourg, France, West Germany, and Italy

European Parliament: parliamentary assembly for the European Union

European Union: the economic and political union of 27 European states

Excepted matters: powers not given to the Northern Ireland Assembly, and that will remain permanently under the control of the central government in Westminster

Executive: usually the top level of government, or the leader; maintains leadership of the entire political system, and often reflects the leadership and preoccupations of the dominant political party

Executive federalism: a generally conflictive relationship between the provinces and the federal government when provinces attempt (often successfully) to achieve greater autonomy from the federal government, which resists such attempts

Federalism: form of governance that divides powers between the central government and regional governments; often, particular roles and capacities are given to the regional governments

First-past-the-post: electoral system (simple plurality) where the winner receives the most (but not necessarily a majority of) votes

First World: industrialized nations including Western Europe, North America, Japan, Australia, and New Zealand that are part of a structurally integrated system of global capitalism

Fixed exchange rate system: system in which states agree upon set values for their currencies in terms of other national currencies

Floating exchange rate system: system in which the market decides the relative values of national monies

Foreign direct investment: investment in real foreign assets, such as domestic structures, equipment, and organizations

Foreign Policy: foreign diplomatic relations and policies of a country beyond its borders

Fourth estate: media; other estates: clergy, nobles, commoners

Francophonie: international linguistic organization based on shared French language and humanist values

Freedom: ability to act without constraint

Free trade: international trade among political systems unimpeded by restrictions or tariffs on imports or exports

Functionalism: collective approach by countries to provide full range of social and welfare services through functionally specific international organizations

Fusion of powers: political system where legislature and executive powers are combined, though specific powers may be granted to each level

G8: Group of Eight (formerly G7 — Group of Seven) major economic actors: United States; United Kingdom; France; Germany; Canada; Italy; Japan; Russia

General Agreement on Tariffs and Trade (GATT): originally intended only as a temporary arrangement when the International Trade Organization (ITO) failed; became the world's permanent trade regime and was later subsumed under the World Trade Organization (WTO)

General will: the will of the community as a whole

Genocide: deliberate and systematic killing of a group based on their ethnicity, nationality, culture, or race

Geopolitics: relationship of political relationships to the geographical location of a state

Gerrymandering: controversial method of grouping together, or dividing, groups of voters in order to maximize or reduce their power

Globalization: the intensification of economic, political, social, and cultural relations across borders

Global village: term used to describe the 'shrinking' of the world, largely due to modern communications, into a more interconnected place where all people have a closer relationship and more frequent contact

Government: the institutions and people responsible for carrying out the affairs and administration of a political system

Great Leap Forward: Chinese program of economic policies designed to revolutionize rural production by replacing private ownership of land with communes, in which all agricultural production was to be sold to the state

Gross domestic product (GDP): total value of goods and services produced in a country in one year

Gross national product: total value of goods and services produced in a country in one year, plus total of net income earned abroad

Hegemon: one country with inordinate capability to uphold and protect the system

Heuristic method: process of laying out experience as a way to assist future research

Human rights: rights granted to people on the basis of being human, not to be denied by governments; includes rights to life, liberty, religion, information, as well as economic, social, political, legal, and constitutional rights

Human rights abuses: maltreatment of human rights

Ideology: set or system of ideas that form the basis of a political or economic system and provide guidance and direction for political leadership

Imperialism: extending one country's authority over another through conquest or political and/or economic control

Independents: Candidates for public office belonging to no political party

Indirect democracy: political system of representation in which citizens elect a delegate to act on their behalf

Industrialized world: nations including Western Europe, North America, Japan, Australia, and New Zealand that are part of a structurally integrated system of global capitalism

Influence: the ability to change behaviour in others without exerting direct power over them

Insecurity: threat of danger or injury

Institutionalism: belief in utility of institutions to provide collective goods

Institutions: organizations developed and mandated to attend to particular needs for society

Interdependence: 'mutual dependence'; a method of measuring dependent relationships among countries, based on the level of sensitivity and vulnerability one country has with respect to another

Interest groups: groups in a political system that seek to either alter or maintain the approach of government without taking a formal role in elections or seeking an official capacity in government

International anarchy: condition where there is no 'world government'; the sovereign nation-state is the highest authority in the international system

International financial and monetary system: the set of rules, institutions, and agreements governing the flow of money in the international system; the relative values of currencies and the settling of accounts

International governmental organizations: institutions formed by three or more countries that have grouped together for a common purpose, including economic, social, cultural, or political

International Monetary Fund (IMF): postwar institution designed to help stabilize currency exchange rates by loaning countries money to meet international currency demands, thereby keeping the supply and demand stable

International organizations: an international grouping, governmental or non-governmental, with activities in several states

International politics: also called international relations; the study of foreign policy and relations among states and other actors at the international level

International relations: see International politics above

International system: a system of two or more actors that interact regularly using established processes in given issue areas in the global arena

Interwar period: the years 1919 to 1939 between World Wars I and II

Invisible hand: Adam Smith's notion that economic forces left on their own would lead to maximize efficiency and economic growth over time as they engage in competition against each other; benefits to society as a whole exist without political interference

Islamic fundamentalism: religious movements advocating a return to the 'fundamentals' of Islamic religious texts

Jihad: two meanings: first, a moral struggle or struggle for righteousness; second, a form of holy war

Judicial review: power of the courts to interpret the constitution, varying from the ability to resolve disputes between levels of government in federal systems to the ability to annul legislative and executive actions outright

Judiciary: judicial (courts) level of governance

Junta: military government, usually a dictatorship

Justice: state of affairs involving the maintenance of what is morally right and fair

Keiretsu: a business group or set of companies found in Japan that work together in decision-making and production to provide increased benefits for all

Kuznets Effect: economic formula that demonstrates that as a country develops economically, income distribution will become more unequal before it becomes more equal; named after Simon Kuznets, the Russian-American economist who formulated this concept

Laissez-faire: 'to let be' — economic theory that suggests that a reduction in political control will benefit the economic system

Länder: 'states' in German

Laws: rules imposed on society by governing authority

Leadership: group of individuals that lead society

Legislation: laws enacted by governing authority

Legislative: referring to the body of a political system with the responsibility to make laws and known as the legislature

Legitimacy: what is lawful, appropriate, proper, and conforms to the standards of a political system

Legitimation: providing legitimacy, or legal force or status to political decisions; in accordance with established or accepted patterns and standards

Less Developed Countries (LDCs): countries that may be characterized by the following: low levels of per-capita income, high inflation and debt, large trade deficits, low levels of socioeconomic development, a lack of industrialization, or undeveloped financial or legal systems

Levels of analysis: approach to political studies that suggests that accurate analysis must be inclusive of international, domestic, and individual arenas of interaction

Liberal democracy: political system based on freedom and individual liberty, and on the principle that governance requires the assent of all citizens through participation in the electoral process, articulation of views, and direct or indirect representation in governing institutions

Liberalism: view of politics that favours liberty, free trade, and moderate social and political change

Liberal institutionalism: international relations theory that suggests that international institutions make co-operation more likely and advantageous

Libertarianism: ideology based on freedom of speech, action, and thought; the role of government should be limited

Liberty: freedom from despotic control

Licence: unlimited freedom to do as one pleases

Liquidity: rate at which assets may be converted to cash

Lobbying: method by which business/interest groups apply direct pressure to the executive, legislative, and bureaucratic branches of government

Los Estados Unidos de Mexico: United States of Mexico

Marshall Plan: US government loan program to help the devastated countries of Western Europe after World War II

Mass party: party organized in society at large, rather than within government, and having public influence through power of membership, rather than in the hands of a small minority elite

Materialist: in Marxism, understanding the physical and economic basis for society

Mediation: voluntary process using impartial party to bring about resolution of dispute

Member of Parliament: representative of voters in a parliamentary system

Middle power: country that does not have great power or superpower status but has significant influence in international relations

Militia party: party system with a centralized leadership system; often having martial leadership, and frequently found in one-party system

Ministerial responsibility: principle in parliamentary systems that requires members of the political executive, both individually and as a group, to remain accountable to the legislature

Minority government: government by party that received the most, but not a majority of, votes in an election

Monarchy: form of government with monarch as head of state

Multiculturalism: where several racial, cultural, or ethnic identities coexist peacefully in one nation

Multilateralism: integration or coordination of policies or decision-making by three or more nation-states

Multinational corporations: corporate bodies that operate in more than one country

Multi-party system: competitive party system with more than two parties

NAFTA: the North American Free Trade Agreement, whereby Canada, the United States, and Mexico have opened their markets to each other

Nation: a group of persons who share an identity that is based on, but not limited to, shared ethnic, religious, cultural, or linguistic qualities

Nation-state: autonomous political unit of people who share a predominant common culture, language, ethnicity, or history

NATO: North Atlantic Treaty Organization

Negative liberty: areas of activity in which governments *do not interfere*, where an individual is free to choose

Negotiation: bargaining process among parties to seek commonly agreed upon resolution of dispute

Neoconservative: advocate or in favour of return to conservative values or policies

Neorealism: also called structural realism; 'new' realism approach that views international relations from a systemic approach where states are constrained by the international structure

Nepotism: in politics, the practice of choosing or preferring relatives

Newly Industrializing Countries (NICs): countries benefiting from external trade relationships, growing export markets, and burgeoning industrial development

Non-associational interest group: interest group not closely related to, or not connected with, particular political objectives

Non-discrimination: principle that no member of an organization be excluded from the benefits that one member state extends to another

Non-governmental organization (NGO): non-profit group organized on a local, national, or international level

Non-system: the system of international money and finance that replaced the Bretton Woods system, so called because it lacked explicit rules

Non-tariff barriers (NTB): imposing national content requirements on certain products or applying quotas to their import

North: industrialized nations including Western Europe, North America, Japan, Australia, and New Zealand that are part of a structurally integrated system of global capitalism

North American Free Trade Agreement (NAFTA): agreement whereby Canada, the United States, and Mexico have opened their markets to each other

North Atlantic triangle: geographic region of Canada, the United States, and the European Union; most significant and strategic modes of interaction for each other ; historically, refers to the relationship between Canada, the U.S., and Great Britain

One-party system: political system in which only one political party is allowed to form the government, or compete in elections

OPEC: Organization of the Petroleum Exporting Countries

Open Door policy: approach taken by Chinese government starting in the late 1970s to introduce the Chinese economy (and by extension political system) to the Western world

Opinion poll: investigation of public opinion conducted by interviewing a sample of citizens

Opposition: one or more parties that are not part of government but form a check on the ruling power of the elected party

Order: condition in which both units and interaction within a political system are marked by regularity and stability with the imposition of accepted and enforced rules, structures, and practices

Organisation for Economic Co-operation and Development (OECD): international organization co-ordinating governments' approach to economic, social and governance challenges of a globalized economy

Organizations: structured relations existing within a political community that are established to distribute both the responsibilities and the privileges that arise from formal association with others

Parliament: legislature in Westminster form of government

Particular will: the will of the individual, as expressed by Rousseau

Partido Revolucionario Institucional (PRI): Institutional Revolutionary Party of Mexico

Party list: voting system in which voters in multi-member constituencies choose from a list of candidates; parties are rewarded with a percentage of the seats available in each constituency

Patriation/Repatriation: process of transferring power from one government to another

Patronage: awarding of key government positions to favoured and loyal supporters

Peace, Order, and Good Government (POGG): clause in the Canadian constitution that specifies that powers not specifically given to the provinces are reserved for the federal government

Peacekeeping: military and civilian personnel in a conflict area used to stop or contain hostilities or supervise the carrying out of a peace agreement

PEMEX: Petróleos Mexicanos — Mexico's national oil company

Perception: awareness or understanding through use of human senses

Philosophy: study of questions about existence and knowledge, ethics, justice, and morality based on logical reasoning rather than empirical methods

Plebiscite: when citizens vote to express their opinions on a particular policy the results of which will determine whether or not that policy is adopted by the government; also known as a referendum

Pluralism: society in which several disparate groups (minority and majority) maintain their interests, and a number of concerns and traditions persist

Pocket boroughs: in Britain, areas where very small electorates were controlled by (or in the pocket of) the major local landowner

Policy: laws or principle of performance adopted by a government

Policy community: collection of actors who have a direct or indirect interest in an issue

Political action committees: conglomerations of several interest groups to more effectively influence the decision-making process

Political cohabitation: political cooperation among parties without forming a coalition

Political culture: set of attitudes, beliefs, and values that underpin any political system

Political economy: approach that views political and economic spheres as harmonious and mutually dependent perceptions of the world; relationship between people, government, and the economy

Political globalization: political processes that span across national borders, and frequently circumvent them entirely

Political gridlock: lack of political progress because of entrenched differing of opinions

Political party: organization that seeks to gain and maintain political power

Political realism: an approach to politics that emphasizes power and interests over ideas or social constructions

Political studies: formal study of politics within and among nations

Portfolio investment: acquisition of shares (stocks) in a corporate actor for the purpose of profit; does not imply ownership

Positive liberty: freedom to achieve one's full potential

Positive sum: relationship between two or more entities where results, as a sum, are better as a result of that relationship

Post-behaviouralism: approach that attempted to reconcile the problems encountered by behaviouralism by allowing for values and ideology in its analysis

Post-colonialism: following a period of colonial rule

Post-industrial: developed economies that maintain a high-technology, or high-value, economy

Postwar era: period after World War II; since 1945

Power: ability to achieve goals in a political system, and to have others do as you wish them to

Pressure group: group in a political system that seeks to either alter or maintain the approach of government without taking a formal role in elections or seeking an official capacity in government

PRI: Partido Revolucionario Institucional (Institutional Revolutionary Party) of Mexico

Progress: advancement in society towards a better and improved state of affairs; an integral element of liberal political theory

Propaganda: spreading of information, true or otherwise, for the purpose of aiding a cause or to make an audience react in a certain way

Proportional representation: electoral system in which seats are designated according to the parties' popular vote; used in countries as a whole in order to institute proportions between votes allotted for all the parties

Protectionism: tendency of countries to safeguard their own economic sectors or industries using tariffs, quotas, or other forms of trade and investment legislation

Public goods: resources that are present in a political system where use by one individual should not affect use by others

Question Period: time allotted in House of Commons for members of the house to ask questions of the prime minister or cabinet ministers

Rapprochement: reconciliation

Realpolitik: pragmatic approach to world politics; countries should practice balance-of-power politics and strive to achieve an equilibrium of power in the world in order to prevent any other country or coalition of countries from dominating the system

Recession: decline in economic productivity or affluence; specifically, a decline in GDP for two or more consecutive quarters

Reciprocity: complimentary or mutual behaviour among two or more actors; view that liberalization of trade would be beneficial for all parties concerned if cooperative policies were pursued

Recruitment function: role played by political parties to help bring new voters into the political process

Referendum: when citizens vote to express their opinions on a particular policy the results of which will determine whether or not that policy is adopted by the government; also known as a plebiscite

Regimes: rules and decision-making procedures

Regional integration: economic or political integration in a defined territorial area

Regionalism: process of economic or political integration in a defined territorial area

Relative power: method of distinguishing the comparable strength of a political unit by contrasting it with another

Repatriation: to restore or bring back to a native land

Representation: the act of standing for the views of others; election of a representative to symbolize the collective view of all constituents

Representative democracy: political system in which voters elect others to act on their behalf

Republic: political unit in which supreme power is held by the people or elected representatives of the people

Reservation: when provincial legislation is put up for consideration by the federal cabinet

Reserved matters: powers not given to the Northern Ireland Assembly, but that may be transferred to the region at a later date

Rights: socially acceptable, morally correct, just and fair privileges granted to members of a political community

Rotten boroughs: in Britain, areas with very small populations and electorates that were given equal standing with normal-sized constituencies

Run-off system: a form of electoral system in which a first round of voting takes place and the two (or three) candidates receiving the most votes pass to a second round of voting to determine an outright winner

Security: freedom from danger or injury

Security dilemma: conception in world politics that states are both protected by the existence of states, and threatened by them

Self-determination: ability to act in free choice without external compulsion

Separation of powers: division of powers among several institutions in government (e.g., legislature, executive) to avoid concentration of authority

Seven Sisters: the major oil companies in the mid-twentieth century, formed by Esso, Shell, British Petroleum, Mobil, Chevron, Gulf, and Texaco

Sexenio: six-year term for the Mexican presidency

Sharia law: sacred law of Islam

Simple plurality: electoral system (first-past-the-post) where the winner receives the most (but not necessarily a majority of) votes

Single European Act: European removal of 'non-tariff barriers' to the free movement of goods, services, capital, and labour

Single Transferable Vote (STV): voting system in which voters cast their ballot in multi-member constituencies, expressing their first and second choice for candidates; second choices may be transferred and counted if all seats are not filled in first count

Social constructivism: a sociological and political meta-theory that explains the interactions between individual agents, their social groupings, and their environment

Socialization: process whereby individuals act in a social manner; creation of social and political authority and rules to regulate behaviour so as to permit operation of social units

Social justice: an equitable distribution of goods and values in society

Social order: recognized structure of power, responsibility, and liberty

Social sciences: scientific study of human society and social relationships

South: categorization of less developed nations that are not part of a structurally integrated system of global capitalism

Sovereignty: recognition by other political authorities that a government is legitimate and rightful for a political community

Special Economic Zones: regions in China with different economic regulatory controls and more independence meant to spur economic growth

State: a recognized political unit, considered to be sovereign, with a defined territory and people and a central government responsible for administration

Structural anarchy: in international relations, the assumption that no higher authority exists above the nation-state

Structural-functionalism: approach that focuses on the role of political structures and their functions in society

Structural realism: also called neorealism; 'new' realism approach that views international relations from a systemtic approach where states are constrained by the international structure

Subsidies: payments made by government to businesses to compensate them for inefficiencies and lack of competitiveness

Sub-systemic: international groupings or relations among states that do not include all actors

Suffrage: granting of the right to vote

Suffragette: female advocate of women's right to vote

Superstructure: political, legal, cultural, and religious justifications, structures, and practices

Supranational: international organization or union where decision-making is shared by all members

Sustainable development: model of economic growth that seeks to use renewable resources so as not to destroy the environment in which human beings have to live

System: a group of individual entities or actors that interact with each other to form an integrated whole

Systems theory: approach that views politics as a system of interaction, binding political structures, such as government to individual action; argues that politics is a dynamic process of information flows and responses that encompasses political institutions, groups, and individuals

Tariff: a duty placed on a particular categorization of imported or exported goods or services

Terrorism: strategy of violence designed to bring about political change by instilling fear in the public at large

Theocracy: political system ruled by religious leaders

Third World: largely Cold War categorization of less developed nations that are not part of a structurally integrated system of global capitalism

Toleration: the acceptance or protection of individuals, groups, and types of behaviour that may be disapproved of by the majority in society

Totalitarianism: authoritarian political system that not only controls most social interaction, but is also marked by a desire by the government to force its objectives and values on citizens in an unlimited manner

Trade protection: tendency of countries to safeguard their own economic sectors or industries using tariffs, quotas, or other forms of trade and investment legislation

Traditional approach: method in politics drawing heavily on fields of law, philosophy, and history that relies on subjective evaluation of the observer; also called the analytical approach

Transatlantic Bargain: postwar arrangement whereby former great powers of Europe conceded to American leadership in exchange for United States support of economic and military stability of Europe

Transfer payments: funds given by the federal government to provincial governments on a conditional or unconditional basis

Transitional government: political system in which the move from authoritarianism to liberal democracy results in elements of both, with a gradual change to democracy

Treaties of Rome: European treaty of 1958 that created the European Economic Community and the European Atomic Energy Community

Treaty of Paris: European treaty of April 1951 that created the European Coal and Steel Community (ECSC)

Two-party system: competitive party system marked by two competing parties

Two-round system: see Run-off system above

Umbrella parties: political parties that cover a wide range of ideologies and beliefs in society, with the idea of incorporating as many different groups in society as possible

Unconditional grants: payments from the federal government that may be spent by the provinces in any way they see fit

UNCTAD: the United Nations Conference on Trade and Development

Unicameral: legislative or parliamentary body with one assembly

Unitary systems: political systems that concentrate political authority and powers within one central government, which is singularly responsible for the activities of the political unit, both domestic and foreign

Uruguay Round: longest round of GATT negotiations, eventually leading to establishment of the World Trade Organization

Utilitarianism: a branch of political thought that states that the worth of a particular action is determined by its contribution to overall utility, meaning the balance of happiness and unhappiness in society

Units of analysis: entities being studied in politics; the 'what' or 'whom' as the basis of analysis

Utopian: idealized place or system, an ideally perfect society; individual or approach aspiring to impractical perfection

Values: principles, standards; what an individual or community esteems as meaningful

Veto: refusal to endorse, or blocking of, a decision

Voter apathy: condition in which individuals do not vote, or do not follow the election process, because they believe elections do not affect or influence them, or that they have little influence over outcomes

Voter turnout: number of voters who show up to the polls on election day

War: use of armed forces in conflict with enemy

Welfare state: political system that creates the means for individual protection and quality of life, such as health care, employment insurance, pensions, social programs for the elderly, children, and unemployed

Westminster system: British model of parliamentary representative government

World Trade Organization (WTO): created in 1995 as a forum for promoting free trade between nations in goods and services

Yoshida Doctrine: postwar Japanese political and economic policy to establish a more non-interventionist role in international affairs, support the United States as hegemon in the global system, deepen links with the Americans; and focus on the domestic economy of Japan as a means of reassembling power and influence; named after Japan's postwar prime minister, Shigeru Yoshida

Zero-sum game: political or economic situation where whatever is gained by one side is lost by the other so the net change is always zero

Index